# a history of
# MODERN EUROPE
# 1789–1978

sixth edition

by
# HERBERT L. PEACOCK m.a.

HEB

HEINEMANN EDUCATIONAL BOOKS
LONDON

Heinemann Educational Books Ltd
22 Bedford Square, London WC1B 3HH

London   Edinburgh   Melbourne   Auckland
Hong Kong   Singapore   Kuala Lumpur   New Delhi
Ibadan   Nairobi   Johannesburg
Exeter (NH)   Kingston   Port of Spain

ISBN 0 435 31717 2

First Published 1958
Second Edition 1961
Third Edition 1969
Fourth Edition 1971
Fifth Edition 1977
Sixth Edition 1980

Printed Offset Litho and bound in Great Britain by
Fakenham Press Limited, Fakenham, Norfolk

# contents

# CONTENTS

# maps

# illustrations

# preface

This book is designed to give the history student a comprehensive picture of the period under consideration and at the same time to provide the detail necessary for examination work. At Ordinary Level the work meets the needs of those pupils capable of a full treatment of the period. For those who omit History at Ordinary Level and proceed straight to the Sixth Form course the book should meet the needs of the rather sharp transition. I hope the Advanced Level student will not only find the book helpful but will be adequately guided to further reading.

The book-list at the end is a selection from the older standard works and some of more recent date. The questions are directly related to the text of each chapter.

I received much help and encouragement in the preparation of the original edition of this book, and I must especially record my appreciation of very helpful criticism by the following: Mr. T. S. Turner of the Commonwealth Grammar School, Swindon, Mr. F. Modral of Loughborough Grammar School, Mr. R. C. Smith, Headmaster, Ebbw Vale Grammar School, Mr. Charles Blount of King Edward's School, Birmingham, and Dr. E. J. Fisher of Harrogate Grammar School. I am particularly indebted to Mr. L. W. White, Headmaster of Beckenham Grammar School, for his careful reading of the proofs of the original edition and for his invaluable help in the preparation of this revised and up-dated edition.

H.L.P.

*Note to Sixth Edition*

With the sixth edition the book now extends to the end of 1978 and even includes one or two outstanding events of 1979, such as the Rhodesia Conference and the Pope's visit to Poland. Other important subjects on which new material has been added to this edition include President Sadat's peace initiatives in the Middle East, Vietnam after the Americans, the situation in China, and the EEC.

October 1979.

# introduction

# A GENERAL SURVEY OF THE YEARS 1789–1978

During the eighteenth century Europe had seen the rise of strong despotic monarchies in some of the European states. In Prussia, notably, Frederick the Great had developed that administrative and military machine which was to become the dominant system of Germany in the following century. Russia, from the time of Peter the Great, had likewise become a formidable military power and had humbled the power of Sweden. Prussia, Russia and Austria had all benefited territorially from the ruthless partitions of Poland. Yet just at this peak of their influence and power all these monarchies were to find themselves humbled, first by the armies of the French Revolution and then by Napoleon.

France alone of the great despotic monarchies had seriously declined during the eighteenth century. Not only was the internal administration increasingly corrupt and inefficient, but external defeat at the hands of Britain in India and Canada had lowered seriously her international prestige. Her support of the American colonists against Britain was the last effort of the "ancien régime" to regain some of its lost prestige, but this effort, as we shall see, added enormously to the difficulties of France.

The French Revolution of 1789 struck not only at the foundations of the "ancien régime" but also of the other states of Europe, great and small. In 1792 we see the beginning of French efforts to spread the Revolution abroad by military means and likewise the efforts of the Great Powers to crush the Revolution almost at its birth. From that time the fate of Europe was to be decided by the outcome of this great struggle which, after the fall of the Directory in 1799, came to be dominated from the French side by the aims and personality of Napoleon. The French control of Europe which resulted from the victories of Napoleon gave rise in part to new forces of great importance for the nineteenth and twentieth centuries. The victories of the French led to radical changes in the map of Europe. Moreover, the Revolutionary element in the practice of Napoleon led to the emergence in Europe of new classes who were to constitute a challenge to the privileged position of the old aristocracy of Europe. However, the Napoleonic Empire overreached itself against Russia, was unable to contend with the naval and economic power of Britain, and in Spain met a new type of national resistance which was to make that country of key importance in the struggle against Napoleon. These factors alone were not, however, sufficient to defeat Napoleon, and new sources of national energy had to be found in all the states of Europe. The most reactionary rulers were forced to call upon all classes to unite in the common struggle. This sense of national unity and common nationality which was above class barriers was to remain a permanent factor in the history of Europe, despite the efforts of reactionary rulers and statesmen to turn back the tide as soon as Napoleon had been defeated.

The settlement by the Congress of Vienna in 1815 showed that the statesmen who met there were more concerned with the principle of the Balance of Power between groups of states or with the principle of royal rights known as Legitimacy than with either middle-class Liberalism or Nationalism. For the next thirty years the Congress decisions were mostly maintained, and the dominating figure in the European situation was the Austrian Chancellor Prince Metternich. His overriding influence led to the vigorous suppression of Liberalism and Nationalism in the German States and in Italy.

During the years 1815–1848 the forces of Liberalism and Nationalism were weak, and the risings in Italy in 1820 and in Italy and Germany in 1830–1832 were easily suppressed. Yet underneath there were strong currents of discontent and a new idealism based on the growing influence of the European middle class. The favourable opportunity for the expression of this discontent arose with the revolution of 1848 against Louis Philippe. Once again, as in 1789, France was the inspiration of progressive movements elsewhere—in Vienna, Budapest, Berlin, Naples—and even in Britain the Chartists once again took heart. However, all these movements were crushed by the end of 1849. The reasons for their failure are numerous—military, social and political. The Austrian Imperial forces had remained almost intact and won the day in Italy and the Empire, Nicholas I sent Russian troops into Hungary, while in Paris, Vienna and Berlin the middle class found the new alliance with the "proletariat" decidedly uncomfortable. It was above all the "spectre" of Socialism and Communism which threw the middle class and peasantry of France into the authoritarian arms of Louis Napoleon Bonaparte. However, the appearance of the revolutionary proletariat on the scene was hailed by Karl Marx and his collaborator Friedrich Engels as the really significant development, and from 1848, when the Communist Manifesto appeared, European Communism began to take on a more and more organised form—until in the twentieth century we have seen its world-shaking results.

The revolutions of 1848 were not entire failures, for they led to modifications of some importance—serfdom was ended in Hungary, and even in Austria and Prussia the franchise was somewhat extended in the next twenty years. But in the main the conception of nationalism with a liberal foundation had received a heavy blow. Louis Napoleon established the Second Empire, which was authoritarian and non-liberal in spirit, while Bismarck, by a process of war and diplomacy of consummate skill, achieved the unification of Germany on Prussia's terms. Only in Italy did a liberal monarchy unify the country.

The defeat of France by Prussia in 1870 led also to the outbreak of the Paris Commune, when, together with new forces, some of the old revolutionaries of 1848 again emerged. The Commune was finally crushed amid scenes of revenge and bloodshed such as Paris had never before witnessed. This episode left a permanent mark on the political history of France, for a considerable section of the town proletariat distrusted and hated the new republican constitution and its authors from the beginning and was to constitute the basis for the later growth in France of revolutionary Socialism and Communism.

Thus in many senses the year 1870 was one of the most significant in the history of modern Europe.

The years 1870–1914 witness new and distinctive trends in national and international affairs. In Germany Bismarck completed the task of internal unification and at the same time fought a ruthless but only partially effective battle against Socialism and the Catholic Church. Towards the end of his time the circumstances of the new world imperialism forced him to modify his purely European view of Germany's future. Germany entered decisively into the general scramble for territory both in Africa and the Far East. With the advent of the Kaiser William II and Bismarck's dismissal in 1890, German foreign policy took on an even more "forward" character, supported by an ever-increasing emphasis on the need for naval power. This policy led to the famous rapprochement of Britain, France and Russia, who by 1907 formed something in the nature of a "united front" against Germany. These developments were in part related to the complicated struggle for power in the Balkan Peninsula, where the weakness of Turkey and the struggle of Serbian nationalism against Austria-Hungary led on to the Austrian ultimatum to Serbia in July, 1914. The war of 1914–1918 really began in the Balkan Peninsula, though its deeper causes were world-wide.

The division of Africa among the Great Powers and the extension of trading and colonial interests to the Far East is one of the most important developments of this period. It was stimulated by important changes in Europe in the field of science and economic organisation. The old-style family business had in all great states given way during the nineteenth century to larger industrial units based upon widely-spread shareholding capital. From this developed even greater concentrations of capital and economic power in the form of monopolies and international cartels. These concerns were compelled by their very nature to seek wider and wider markets for their products and more and more sources of essential raw materials. It is almost impossible to distinguish between the competition among these concerns and the actual political competition between the states of their origin—indeed, in many cases they had direct state support. This economic competition between the great states had intensified greatly by 1914, and the struggle for economic privilege was undoubtedly a factor contributing to the outbreak of the Great War.

Over against this development of a new type of capitalism there grew up powerful movements of the working class designed to protect the workers from ruthless exploitation by the seekers of profit. In the case of Socialism and Communism especially these movements aimed at the replacement of a society based on private capitalism by one in which the state would be the sole owner of the means of production and exchange. The influence of these doctrines in the European trade union movement was very great.

After the Great War of 1914-1918 and the defeat of Germany, the makers of the Treaty of Versailles attempted to settle the political and economic problems which arose from the collapse of the Austro-Hungarian and German Empires. It left many problems unsolved and made a number of arrangements which held great dangers of future complication. On the other hand, many of its decisions were good—the most important was the establishment of the League of Nations in an effort to maintain permanent peace between the nations. However, the period 1919-1939 was one of constant economic world crisis—unemployment and poverty on a devastating scale afflicted all the major states. From the resulting unrest the extreme movements of Communism and Fascism were able to make considerable headway against the groups and parties of the middle or parliamentary way. However, the greatest extension of power went to Fascism, for by 1939 the Fascist states of Germany and Italy had succeeded in their aggressive aims, as had the Japanese against China in the Far East. In Spain also a form of Fascism had triumphed.

A new and critical factor in the world situation after 1917 was the existence of the first Communist state in Russia, from which the main inspiration of international Communism since the First World War has been derived. The Revolution of 1917 has had its sequel in the vast extension of Communist power in the states of Eastern Europe and in the new Communist China.

The whole period with which we are concerned (1789–1978) is characterised by a constant examination in philosophy of the ideas of "freedom", "liberty", "free will" and determinism, etc., etc. These ideas haunt the literature of the arts and of science. The political struggle between authoritarianism of various brands and the anti-authoritarians produces its great thinkers and writers. Christian doctrines especially are enlisted in the cause of social and political reform and the struggle against tyranny. On the other hand, attempts are made to separate Christianity and the State altogether— religion is to be one thing, the State another.

Again, the whole period shows how difficult it has been both to establish and maintain the forms of government which we term "liberal" and "constitutional," in which governments and monarchies are controlled by sovereign and popularly-elected assemblies. This was a great problem in France after 1875, and likewise in Italy and Germany. In Russia, the belated attempts of the early years of this century to establish a liberal parliamentary system were pathetic failures. Among the great European states, Britain alone during the nineteenth and twentieth centuries had a steady development along the "liberal-democratic" path.

The years 1939–1945 witnessed the challenge of the Nazi tyranny to nearly every human value laboriously built up since the Renaissance. The defeat of this tyranny was followed by the creation of the United Nations Organisation, whose valuable work took on ever wider and wider scope in the years 1945 to 1978. But over against the progressive and constructive work of UNO there developed the dangerous intricacies of the Cold War—the political struggle between Communism and its opponents which had its ramifications from Berlin to Korea. With the appalling shadow of the nuclear bomb as its backcloth, this struggle produced numerous points of tension between the great powers. It is symptomatic of human desire to lessen this conflict that great interest has been shown in the possibility of Soviet–United States co-operation in the exploration of outer space, which could well throw the situation on earth into a new and better perspective.

This work cannot attempt final judgments on the great questions to which this introductory chapter has briefly referred, but it is hoped that the student, while being given basic factual information, will be encouraged to delve deeper.

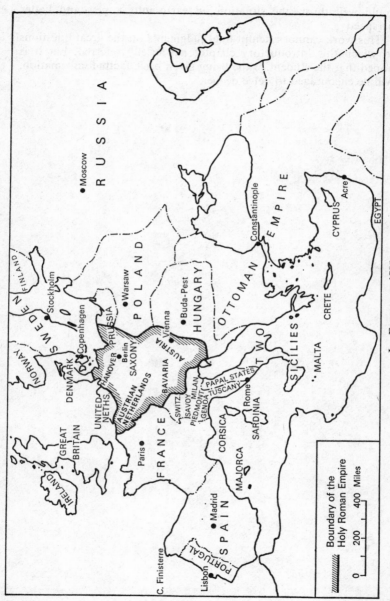

I.—EUROPE IN 1789.

chapter one

# THE FRENCH REVOLUTION, 1789

## I. CAUSES

**Introductory.** The French Revolution of 1789 is one of the great events of human history. It deeply affected men's ideas and conduct for many generations. Within the space of six years, 1789-1795, the monarchy and the old privileged aristocracy were swept aside and a new state was created. New men arose to power from classes who had enjoyed little or no political influence under the monarchy. Merchants and lawyers became leading politicians, the French Army was completely reorganised with promotion from the ranks, the peasants took over the land of the nobility and the Catholic Church, and Louis XVI and his Queen Marie Antoinette went to the guillotine.

Naturally, this upheaval in one of the great states of Europe had profound effects on other countries. To the serfs and poorer classes of Europe the Revolution of 1789 came in time to represent their hope of better things, while, naturally, to the privileged classes themselves and the kings and princes who supported them it represented the horrifying spectre of their own future destruction. In every country of Europe and America the impact of the Revolution created hope, enthusiasm, hatred or fear according to men's position in society and their intellectual convictions.

Why the Revolution took the course it did after it had broken out is an extremely difficult question, and historians are by no means agreed on this. On the other hand, there is fairly general agreement on the causes of discontent in France which led to the actual outbreak in 1789. One thing is certain—conditions in a society have to be very bad indeed before men in any large numbers will undertake its overthrow by violence. Men will not risk everything for nothing.

If we consider French society in the eighteenth century, beginning with the peasants and moving up through the middle class, the nobility and clergy, and finally to the King and his officials, we shall see that conditions were very unhealthy.

FIG. 1.—VOLTAIRE.
(*From a contemporary engraving*)

## CONDITION OF FRENCH SOCIETY BEFORE THE REVOLUTION

**The Peasantry.** At the time of the Revolution the peasantry numbered about 23,000,000 in a total population of 25,000,000. In some districts of France the peasants were still serfs in the strict sense of the word, being bought and sold with the land when it changed hands. These serfs numbered about 1,000,000. Another section of the peasantry were the "métayer" tenants who shared both the profits and losses of cultivation with their landlords. Others owned small patches of land from which they scraped a very bare living indeed. But the great majority of the peasants held land from the nobility and paid various forms of rent for it.

**Burdens of the Peasantry.** (a) *Direct taxation.* It was above all the weight of taxation which prevented the existence of a contented and prosperous countryside. Firstly, there were the taxes paid directly to the State treasury and collected by government officials. The "taille" was a tax imposed in some districts on land, but in most cases was imposed on the estimated income of the individual and his wealth in any form of property. Many sections of the wealthier classes obtained exemption from this tax, but there was no escape for the peasant. Indeed, this tax hindered the development of agriculture in France, for as soon as a peasant appeared to be more prosperous his "taille" was immediately raised. There was no incentive whatever to improve cultivation. Then there was the capitation or poll-tax upon the head of each household. The peasantry were strictly assessed by the tax officials, but the nobles obtained so many exemptions that while the peasantry were paying eight times their fair share the nobility were paying only one-eighth. The same situation applied to the "vingtième", a tax on all property. Here again both the nobility and the clergy gained wide exemptions while the peasant had to pay. The "vingtième" tax was more than the twentieth which its name implies—it was, in fact, about one-sixth of income. The unfairness of the burden which all this meant for the peasantry will be understood when it is realised that these three State taxes alone deprived the peasant of more than half his yearly income.

In many parts of France these direct taxes were collected by certain peasants themselves in each parish, and they were answerable to the government officials. Under the system then existing, they were chosen by their own neighbours, and, such was the reluctance of anyone to undertake the task, they had to be forced to do it.

*De la Chicane Delivrez nous Seigneur*

*Des Capitaineries et Gardes de Chasses
Delivrez nous Seigneur*

From Fraudulent Lawyers . . . from Wardens and Gamekeepers . . .

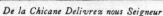

FIG. 2.—THE GRIEVANCES OF THE PEASANTS.

These peasant collectors had the greatest difficulty in obtaining the sums demanded, for their neighbours constantly protested poverty and inability to pay. If they failed to obtain the required sum they either had to make up the deficiency themselves or go to prison. Immediately before 1789 there were many hundreds of these peasant collectors in gaol.

(b) *Indirect taxation.* But this was not the end of the taxation story. There were the indirect taxes, of which the most notorious was the "gabelle" or salt tax. Every individual over eight years old was legally compelled to purchase at least seven pounds of salt a year and could be fined for not doing so. The individual was then taxed on the actual amount purchased. This State monopoly in the sale of salt led to the employment of 50,000 troops and officials to enforce it. It was forbidden to use sea-water for cooking, nor could a peasant feed his cattle in salt marshes or allow them to drink from salt springs. No wonder there was widespread hatred of this tax and desperate efforts to evade it. Punishments for evasion were savage. In the year 1783, out of 11,000 arrests made, 6,600 were of children, and some authorities have estimated that for many years before the Revolution the annual imprisonments averaged

*De la Milice Delivrez nous Seigneur*      *Des Barrières Delivrez nous Seigneur*

... from the Militia ... and Toll keepers, Good Lord Deliver us.

FIG. 2.—*(continued)*

30,000, and 500 persons were hanged or sent to the galleys. Another reason for the harshness of these punishments was the method by which the tax was commonly collected. The government gave this task to individuals who paid the government for the privilege and took a proportion of the proceeds of the tax. These were known as tax-farmers and there were many cases of revolting cruelty by the agents they employed who were entitled to enter the houses of the peasants at any time of day or night, and often ransacked them from top to bottom. One French writer (the father of one of the great figures of the Revolution, Mirabeau) described how he had seen a tax official cut off the hand of a woman who clung to her cooking utensils which he was trying to seize because of her evasion of taxes. No wonder that many victims of the revolutionary guillotine were tax-farmers

The peasant had to pay feudal dues to the "seigneur" for the use of the latter's mill, oven or wine-press. He was also liable to forced labour for the upkeep of roads—the "corvée". Besides these impositions, the landowners also demanded other feudal dues, such as the hearth tax, tolls to be paid for the use of local roads and bridges, for the right of a peasant to take his herd of cattle through the lord's estate, and a tax to be paid when the peasant inherited property. The lord alone could possess flour-mills, pigeon-cotes and bake-houses. He also had the right to appoint the judges and lawyers in case of any dispute between himself and the peasantry. Justice to the peasant was almost impossible in these feudal law-courts. In the Middle Ages, when the feudal courts were set up, the lord had at least lived on his estates and was expected to show concern for his tenants, but in the eighteenth century he was very frequently an "absentee landlord" who lived in luxury in town or city and was not seen by his tenants from one year's end to the other. The Church also claimed from the peasant the tithe—not quite a tenth of his produce as the name implies, but more frequently a fifteenth. In addition to all this, the peasantry was the only class in France which could gain no exemption from military service in the militia. This was a six-year period of service and was detested. It is not surprising that many peasants gave up their land in despair and took to brigandage, smuggling and poaching. In these activities they were often given shelter and protection by sympathetic villagers. Tax-collectors and gamekeepers were murdered, and soldiers had constantly to be used to suppress food riots.

All this adds up in our imagination to a miserable picture, and yet the French peasant was probably better off than his counter-part in most other European states. In Austria, Russia and Prussia he was an outright serf—the chattel of his lord. But serfdom affected only a remnant in France, and Louis XVI himself reduced it further by freeing the serfs on the royal domains. The French peasant had certain definite legal rights and often gained support from the lawyers of the countryside who had their own grievances against the nobility and the government. It was this element of legal right and independence which accounts in part for the peasant's desire for *more* independence, which only freedom from the unfair and crushing burden of taxation could give him. The peasants were neither sufficiently united nor sufficiently educated to produce a revolution themselves, but the importance of their grievances was that they were ready to become the allies of other discontented classes.

**The Bourgeoisie.** Nearly all the leaders of the Revolution were drawn from the numerically small class of the " bourgeoisie", which included merchants, traders, industrialists, lawyers, doctors and other professional groups.

The merchants and industrialists lived mainly in the towns, for the feudal conditions of the countryside and the heavy taxation of land had prevented them from purchasing country estates. In the reign of Louis XVI (1774–1792) they were reasonably prosperous. They enjoyed many exemptions from taxation, though (to their great annoyance) these exemptions were far greater for the nobility and clergy. They usually enjoyed exemption from service in the militia. They owned most of the non-agricultural wealth of the country, being also bankers, moneylenders and the controllers of the rich governing corporations of the towns. With their wealth they endowed town schools, where their sons received a good education.

But the bourgeoisie had serious causes for discontent. In the first place, they were almost completely excluded from the government of France. In other words, they had very little *political* power, despite the fact that they were both wealthy and educated. Real political power was concentrated in the hands of the King, the Royal Council, a small section of the privileged nobility at Versailles and, in the provinces, the Intendants or royal officials (see page 12). There was also no prospect of promotion for the bourgeois class in the French Army, where the commissioned ranks were the preserves of the nobility. It is no wonder, therefore, that the writings of those great thinkers of the eighteenth century who challenged the existing order, such as Rousseau and Voltaire, found considerable favour with this class.

Besides political grievances, the merchants and industrialists had economic grievances. The finances of the government went from bad to worse in the reign of Louis XVI. The cost of France's assistance to the Americans in the War of Independence (1775–1783), the blatant extravagance and luxury of the Court at Versailles and bad financial management led to a situation in which the expenses of the government far exceeded its income. The government tried to meet the situation by raising huge loans from the nobility, the bourgeoisie and even from the Church. This meant a vast increase in the National Debt and, as things became worse, a growing uncertainty among the bourgeoisie as to whether they would ever recover their money. Above all, they needed a government whose credit was sound, yet, long before 1789, France was bankrupt. And amidst all this financial chaos the nobility clung obstinately to their exemptions from taxation! If France had possessed an expanding Empire, perhaps the bourgeoisie would have been less discontented; but India and Canada had been lost to Great Britain in the Seven Years War (1756–1763).

**The Nobility.** A striking feature of French society before the Revolution was the absence of any real unity among the wealthy and privileged. The bourgeoisie envied and detested the nobility, which in its turn was seriously divided against itself. There were three main divisions of the nobility: the Great Nobility, the Lesser Nobility and the Nobility of the Robe.

The Great Nobility comprised about 1,000 families who owned the largest and wealthiest landed estates in France. They had been accorded privileges which placed them above all other classes in the State. The highest commands in the Army and Navy were reserved for them and they alone could represent France abroad as ambassadors. The most influential amongst them were the Court Nobles at Versailles who strongly resisted all attempts to end their exemptions from taxation and were implacably determined to maintain their privileges. From these were drawn the absentee landlords—that is, the nobles who left their landed estates in the hands of bailiffs and went to live at Versailles, Paris or other town centres.

The Lesser Nobility comprised about 99,000 families. Their country estates were only just sufficient to maintain them and they could not have afforded the luxuries of absenteeism and the life of Versailles even if the Great Nobility had been willing to receive them into their select society. Like the bourgeoisie, the Lesser Nobility had very little political power in the provinces, where the King's officers, the Intendants, were all-powerful. Moreover, all their sons inherited noble titles, and this led to the existence of more nobles than could possibly live up to their grandiose pretensions. It is not surprising, therefore, that we find a number of supporters of the Revolution in this class, for they envied the Greater Nobility's privileges and were frustrated by their own exclusion from the higher social and political life of the times.

The Nobility of the Robe were those who had been given titles as a reward for their services to the State. This was the only section of the nobility who could claim that they held their titles on merit alone. Yet they were unable to enjoy the privileges of the Great Nobility, while at the same time they despised the rather ramshackle and pretentious Lesser Nobility.

The nobility was thus divided against itself long before the Revolution began. Moreover, it was much more concerned with its own sectional interests than with the badly-needed reform of the whole country. Real and effective pressure for change could therefore only come from other classes—namely, the bourgeoisie and its peasant allies.

**The Church.** The Catholic Church was the established church of France. Various forms of the Protestant faith existed in France, but were not recognised by the law. The only public worship allowed was that of the Catholic Church, while education was largely in the hands of the clergy or under their supervision. This monopoly of religious power was the subject of violent attacks by many great French writers, among whom the most outstanding was Voltaire, who demanded complete religious toleration. Within the Church itself there were great inequalities of income—so great, indeed, that it completely separated the poor parish priest from the higher clergy. During the Revolution the parish priests were, in the main, supporters of the peasantry, for they were often poorer than some of the peasants themselves and had a strong fellow-feeling for them. The majority of the 60,000 parish priests in France received a salary somewhere between £30 and £70 a year, while the 134 Archbishops and Bishops received an average of about £2,500 (60,000 livres), and often had additions to this income from abbeys and other church institutions in their dioceses. There were, of course, some well-paid priests and some higher clergy who worked conscientiously, but the general picture of the Church before the Revolution is decidedly unflattering. The higher clergy frequently took well-paid political posts under the Crown, and many of these posts were sinecures. In the palaces of the bishops life was lived in a luxury very similar to that of the royal court and nobility. Many of the bishops did not live in their dioceses and spent much of their time in the pleasures of hunting. There was widespread cynicism and irreligion among the higher clergy, typified by a remark of the famous Cardinal de Rohan that "it is impossible to sin in good company". It was the parish priest who did the really hard, day-to-day work of ministration in the countryside, but he was not even allowed to retain the local tithe for his own upkeep.

It must also be remembered that the wealth of the Church was enormous, and on that account excited envy from both peasantry and bourgeoisie. It owned one-fifth of the land of France and received a yearly income of 500,000,000 francs of which only some 30,000,000 were used to maintain hospitals, schools and other institutions. No wonder, then, that the freethinkers of the eighteenth century attacked it, and no wonder the parish priest had little love for his superiors in the Church.

**The Army.** A vital support of any despotic monarchy must be its armed forces, but the French Army in 1789 was far from being the reliable instrument of the monarchy which it had been at the time of the great victories of Louis XIV. There were serious causes of discontent which encouraged the spread of democratic and revolutionary ideas in the army. The most important grievance was the law of 1781 by which commissioned rank was restricted to those born into the nobility. Non-commissioned rank was therefore the highest to which the well-educated sons of the bourgeoisie could rise. It is not surprising that secret societies of various kinds existed in the army and tended to undermine its discipline. Some important regiments were quite unreliable when the Revolution began. This was the case with one of the most important regiments of France, the Gardes Françaises, stationed in 1789 at Paris, and many of its officers were ready to throw in their lot with the Revolution. Another grievance of the unprivileged bourgeoisie and common soldier was the excessive number of officers. This policy had been designed to please the nobility and give them some outlet for their pretensions. In 1789 there was one general for every 157 private soldiers and one staff officer for every 79. Many of these entered the army very early in life and with few qualifications. A noble's son could become a colonel at the age of sixteen. Thus the class divisions and privileges which marked French society in 1789 were to be seen in the French Army itself.

Another influence affecting the army was the American War of Independence (1775–1783). During the war between England and her colonies Louis XVI's government had made an alliance with the colonists, and French forces under General Lafayette had served in America. After the war many French soldiers returned with democratic ideas. They had defeated what appeared to them the despotic aims of George III. They had fought in the cause of "no taxation without representation". They had absorbed many democratic ideas of justice, not only from the famous Declaration of Independence (July 4, 1776), but from the writings of the Englishman Thomas Paine, who had been the great propagandist for Washington during the war. And they returned to a country where the people had no control whatever over taxation, had no representative parliament, and where a recent Royal Decree had given the officers of the army the right to strike the ordinary soldier with the flats of their swords, as was the practice in the serf army of Frederick the Great of Prussia.

**The Government of France.** The real government of France in the eighteenth century rested with the King, the Royal Council and the Intendants. All power, in the last resort, emanated from the King. "L'état, c'est moi," the famous dictum ascribed to Louis XIV, expressed the despotic power of the King over his subjects. The King was *above* the law, not controlled by it. The strongest expression of this power was the "lettre de cachet" signed by a Minister and ordering the imprisonment "during the King's pleasure" and without trial of any individual who sufficiently displeased the government, or had been denounced by a private enemy. Louis XVI was a mild and liberal-minded monarch compared with his predecessors, but even during his reign "lettres de cachet" were issued at the rate of 70 to 80 a year.

But this despotic government was becoming more and more inefficient. Any intelligent citizen of France in the reign of Louis XVI scarcely needed the philosophers to point out the waste, corruption and injustice of the government. It was everywhere around him. There was, indeed, chaos and delay in every department. There existed two different systems of taxation, one for the thirteen central provinces, another for the remoter districts. There existed two systems of law, the Roman Law in the southern half of the country and the Common Law in the north. There was complete freedom of trade between the central provinces, but customs duties on all manner of goods and foodstuffs at the frontiers of the remainder. It can well be imagined how irritated were the bourgeoisie by this state of things, for it made the processes of law uncertain and difficult (and the criminal law applied far harsher penalties to the peasantry and the bourgeoisie than to the nobility), and it seriously hindered their trade. The economic system of France compared most unfavourably with that of her great rival England, where the last remnants of old feudal restrictions on trade and industry were being swept away. It must be remembered that the free-trade writings of the great British economist Adam Smith were widely known among the educated bourgeoisie in France, and a group of French economists known as the Physiocrats denounced the absurd and wasteful economic system of their own country.

Since the seventeenth century the Kings of France had developed the system of provincial Intendants to supervise every detail of government and taxation. These officials were the direct servants of the Crown and were answerable only to the Crown. Their powers had been deliberately increased by successive monarchs with the aim of reducing the political power of the great nobles. It is true, of course, that the ancient offices of Governors of the Provinces were still mainly in the hands of the nobility, but the districts supervised by the Intendants cut across old provincial boundaries and thus interfered with, and reduced, the Governors' powers.

The old Estates General of France, representing the Three Estates of Nobility, Clergy and Commons, had not met since the year 1614. There was nothing approaching a parliamentary or representative system for the whole country. Provincial Estates did exist, however, in some regions of France. These were "parliaments" of the three estates entitled to discuss affairs relating to their own districts and had arisen during the Middle Ages. At one time they had exercised great powers almost independently of the early kings of France, but by the reign of Louis XVI their smallest action had to receive the approval of the Intendants who had first to consult the Royal Council. Thus in France before the Revolution there were neither national nor provincial assemblies to which one could, with the wildest stretch of imagination, apply the terms "parliamentary", "constitutional" or "democratic". There were, in fact, no regular and recognised means by which grievances could be expressed.

The only type of local government in France which could be termed popular in our sense of the word today was the commune, or parish. All classes were entitled to attend parish meetings, but even in these smallest subdivisions of France the hand of the Royal Council and the Intendant was seen. The smallest detail of proposed expenditure had to be approved by the Royal Council through the Intendant. One case is recorded where the expenditure of £1 by a commune had to receive the consent of the Royal Council. It is not surprising that the business of the parishes was often years behind. Efficient and popular local government, which might have eased many dangerous social strains, was unknown in France before the Revolution.

Even in the towns, where the bourgeoisie were socially important, the Intendants and their agents kept a tight control over administration.

Thus the *State*, and not the people, was in control. The State did not mean the people. Everything that was wrong in France was attributed to the State, which consisted of the King and his officials.

## INFLUENCE OF THE GREAT FRENCH THINKERS

**Voltaire (1694–1778).** The great French writer Voltaire did more than any other man in the eighteenth century to undermine the old society of France. As a young man he showed a remarkable capacity for writing satiric verse, and this was always one of his most effective weapons against those aspects of French society which he hated. Voltaire, in his numerous plays, novels, histories and lampoons, was essentially a destroyer. His influence with the educated bourgeoisie was immense and he was courted by kings and nobles—until he said too much for them. There were curious contradictions in his character, as is so often the case with the brilliant thinker. He had no faith in, nor love for, the common man, and yet he went to immense pains to take up the cases of individuals who had been treated unjustly by the harsh laws of France.

Voltaire reserved his most bitter attacks for the Catholic Church and Christianity in general, both of which he regarded as the essence of superstition and ignorance. Yet, when some of his atheistic followers went to extremes in their attacks on all religion, he himself asserted the need of belief in some Supreme Being. Such a belief he regarded as a common-sense necessity, but most other aspects of religion he considered quite opposed to common sense. He particularly attacked religious intolerance and denounced the laws which allowed only public worship of the Catholic kind. He attacked all the faults in French society which we have already described, and was so effective that long before the Revolution he had caused many a noble to laugh at his own class. Voltaire undermined the faith of the privileged classes in themselves.

Voltaire was much influenced by what he saw when he visited England, and in 1734 he published his famous *Letters on the English*, from which most of his later ideas developed. He praised the high degree of religious toleration in England and the absence of a privileged nobility of the French type. Later, in 1763, he enlarged further on these ideas in another work in which he praised English freedom of the press and trial by jury. In fact, he considerably exaggerated English liberties in order more forcibly to attack the state of things in France.

Voltaire, however, was not a Republican, and he considered that all necessary reforms could be brought about under the French monarchy if only the enlightened and educated few in France would exert their influence—and follow Voltaire. To his disciples he was known as "Le Roi Voltaire".

**Montesquieu (1689–1755).** The influence of Montesquieu was great in a more strictly political sense than that of Voltaire. Montesquieu's main concern was to limit the powers of the Monarch, and anything, even privileges of the nobility, which hindered the absolute power of the King, was good. He wished for a method of government in which all kinds of interests would have the right to debate and amend the laws before they came into force. In this system, with such numerous checks, the power of the King could never become despotic. It is not surprising, therefore, that Montesquieu found the English system of government more satisfactory than most. At the time of the Revolution his ideas influenced strongly those who wanted to maintain the monarchy in France with the kind of checks on its power that existed in England. Montesquieu had expressed his most important ideas on this subject in his work *The Spirit of the Laws* (1748).

**Jean-Jacques Rousseau (1712–1778).** The basic idea of Rousseau as he expressed it in his famous work *Du Contrat Social* (*The Social Contract*) was that the General Will of the people should be the ruling force in any society. His theory of the "social contract" was, briefly, that when originally the people had given their assent to the existence of kings and governments there had come into being a

Fig. 3.—Rousseau.

definite contract between king and people by which the former only ruled by the latter's consent. This contract the people were entitled to break if the kings and governments did not keep their side of the bargain, which was to protect and promote the interests of the people. Rousseau loved the people, believed that the finest aspects of their character would be brought out by their being liberated from oppression, and, following on from this, he wanted government by the people for the people. In this way he differed from most of the other thinkers of France at that time. He was the only "complete democrat" among them. Voltaire, Montesquieu and the Encyclopedists had no real faith in the natural goodness of the people, for they wanted enlightened rule by a small number rather than rule by "the masses". But Rousseau meant by "the people" the poorest and the least "cultured". In the peasant and workman Rousseau saw his ideal. Men are born free and equal, but "everywhere they are in chains".

Yet even Rousseau, when seeking a practical solution for France herself, was far more cautious than when he was denouncing kings, priests and governments and describing the virtues of primitive man. He regarded the best form of government for France as the representative system. By this system, not everyone would have the vote for such a privilege should not be given to the "abject and brutish populace, easily swayed by agitators". In fact, he favoured political power being in the hands of the educated and responsible middle class. It was even unwise to do away with the monarchy of France, for, says Rousseau, "who, once it had started, could keep such a convulsion within bounds or see its effects?" It was better to reform such a system rather than abolish it. Thus Rousseau spoke with two voices—one theoretical, idealistic, believing in the "natural goodness" of man—the other practical, cautious, afraid of too sudden a change in society. His followers of the Revolution (especially Robespierre) listened with fanatical devotion to the first voice, but ignored the second.

**The Encyclopedists.** Among the great intellectual influences of the eighteenth century we must certainly number the famous *Encyclopédie*. The two great moving spirits behind this were Diderot and D'Alembert. Their aim was to produce a work which would summarise all existing knowledge, and the finest thinkers of the age contributed to the instalments of the *Encyclopédie* which appeared at irregular intervals for over twenty years (1751–1772). It had an extremely stormy history. Its editors were imprisoned and it was twice banned by the government. The reason for this attitude of the government was simple: the *Encyclopédie* was far more than a mere statement of historical and scientific knowledge. Its articles often consisted of attacks on everything in France that was hated by the great philosophers we have mentioned. Its contributors included Voltaire, Montesquieu and Rousseau. (The latter contributed an article on music, for he had much to say on education and the arts.) Yet so fascinating was this great work, that even some of the Court Nobility at Versailles pleaded with the King for the lifting of the ban upon it, and parts of it were even circulated secretly among them. At one time the printers, alarmed for their own safety by some of the attacks on Church and State, deliberately altered whole sections of manuscript and printed the amended version before Diderot detected it. These parts had to be destroyed and the work begun again.

**Influence of England.** It is important to observe how much of the thought of the great writers was derived from their impressions of England. Naturally, they tended to see English institutions and life through rose-coloured spectacles just because life in England was undoubtedly very different from France, and in many respects was better. As we have seen, Voltaire and Montesquieu were greatly influenced by England, and even though Rousseau was less influenced, many of his ideas are to be found in the writings of the great English philosopher John Locke (1632–1704). Even the great *Encyclopédie* was the development and expansion of an English encyclopedia which had been translated into French. Again, during the eighteenth century there was an increasing imitation by the French bourgeoisie of English dress and manners, while noblemen also wore English fashions which made them indistinguishable from commoners—a levelling influence of some importance in an age when dress had more class significance than it has now. English newspapers circulated among educated Frenchmen, and the English "club" also had a vogue in France. One of the very first political clubs in Paris, set up on English lines, was suppressed as early as 1731 because of the "dangerous" political topics being discussed there. Then there followed after 1782 a rage for everything American, with some of the results we have already seen.

All these intellectual influences were causing the spread of discontent and free thought in France, and many historians regard them as the very first causes of the Revolution. At least it can be said that they contributed fundamentally to the collapse of the old system.

### Events Leading up to the Revolution of 1789

It is possible that a more adequate King than Louis XVI (1774–1793) would have been able to exercise decisive control over the course of events. But Louis XVI inherited from his predecessor the position of a despot without having the character of a despot. He was amiable and well-intentioned, with a sincere concern for his subjects—tears would come to his eyes when, in meetings of the Royal Council, he referred to his desire for the happiness of his people. But such sentiments were not enough. On many critical occasions, when he should have been attending to the business of state, he was indulging either in his passion for making locks or hunting on the royal estates. He lacked the will to persist with reforms when he met with the opposition of the privileged nobility. His Queen Marie Antoinette also exercised a reactionary influence over him and did much to bring the monarchy into disrepute. She was the daughter of Maria Theresa, Empress of Austria. She was unpopular in France with the bourgeoisie and nobility, for she represented the alliance of Austria and France which had led to the complete defeat of France by England and Prussia in the Seven Years War (1756–1763) and the loss of Canada and India. Her education had been narrow. Her mother the Empress confessed that she had never learnt to write a good letter, had no taste for reading and possessed none of the accomplishments which the Court of France expected. At critical points in the reign her narrowness, bigotry and lack of judgment led her to support the most selfish demands of the Court nobles. The name by which she was known in France, "L'Autrichienne", the Austrian woman, was a sign of popular contempt.

**Turgot and Necker.** Louis XVI began his reign well with the very best intentions. He dismissed the unpopular ministers of Louis XV and replaced them by better men of whom the most important was the Controller General of Finances, Turgot. The latter was a man of great administrative ability and honesty and had occupied the post of Intendant for the province of Limousin. Turgot's first reform was to abolish several thousand sinecures—positions which had been bought by their holders. He also abolished the "corvée" and replaced it by a tax on all landowners. He allowed free trade in corn between the provinces (one purpose of this being to reduce the dangers of famine), and permitted labourers to move freely from one province to another in search of work. Voltaire himself thought that these reforms were the beginning of a new life for France and that further reforms would follow, but he was wrong. When Turgot proposed a system of local councils to govern France it was the signal for his bitterest enemies at Court to take action. There followed a conspiracy against Turgot by Marie Antoinette, the King's brothers and the nobility. Louis XVI was prevailed upon to dismiss Turgot (1776), and the reforms he had introduced were swept aside. The King weakly exclaimed to one of the ministers who resigned at the same time: "How happy you are! Why cannot I also quit my place!"

To Voltaire the dismissal of Turgot was a disaster, as indeed it eventually proved for the monarchy. "I see nothing before me now", he wrote, "but death. I am struck to the heart by this blow, and shall never be consoled for having seen the beginning and end of the golden age that Turgot was preparing for us."

A similar situation arose when Louis appointed Necker, a Swiss banker, as his minister of finance. Necker began by drastically reducing the expenses of the Court at Versailles, which were at this time one-twelfth of all government expenses. He persuaded the King to reduce the grants of favours and pensions, to cut down the number of tax-farmers, free the serfs on the Royal domains and create a number of provincial assemblies. These reforms, which only touched the fringe of the real problems of France, were, however, violently resisted by the Queen and the nobility. For a time, however, Louis XVI persisted in his support of Necker. But then a fatal complication occurred. France, in order to revive her fortunes by a blow at the old enemy, England, entered the War of American Independence on the side of the colonists. Necker had to raise huge public loans to meet the expenses, and the National Debt of France increased enormously. There were demands for the publication of the government's accounts, which had always been secret up to now—in fact, the very discussion of such a question had at times led to the imprisonment of the critics. But in 1781 Necker persuaded the King to allow the publication of the accounts, and the "Compte Rendu au Roi" appeared. Necker's famous document aroused immense interest and 100,000 copies were sold in a few weeks. He tried to show the state of things as much better than it really was. His aim was to maintain some confidence in the government. But certain curious facts appeared in the statement. The public learnt, for instance, the astounding fact that pensions given to Court favourites cost the country as much as the navy and the French colonies together; or such disturbing items as a yearly payment still given to the hairdresser of the Princess d'Artois, although the princess had died years before at the age of three.

Then the picture of Louis XVI's weakness repeats itself. The Queen and the Court naturally disliked Necker's disclosures. Necker was removed and replaced by a Court favourite, Calonne, under whose administration the financial state of the government deteriorated rapidly. Eventually Necker was recalled in August, 1788, but he himself admitted that it was too late to retrieve the situation of bankruptcy into which the government had fallen.

A widespread popular clamour now arose against the government. A very bad harvest in 1788 added to disorder and distress in town and countryside. The industrialists were also suffering from the effects of competition from English imports under a commercial treaty of 1786, and there was increasing unemployment amongst workmen in the town. The government's reply to riots and disorder was to throw thousands into prison. This was a policy of desperation which in no way improved the state of the country.

On all hands demands arose for the meeting of the States-General, and eventually it was the pressure from a section of the privileged classes themselves which decided Louis to agree to the demand. The Church Assembly also made this demand, for Necker had raised considerable loans from the Church and it naturally had an interest in the serious financial position. Likewise, a special assembly of Notables added their voices to the demand for the meeting of the States-General. Louis XVI, as unaware as the nobility of all the vast forces which his action would unleash, issued his instructions for the compiling of "cahiers", or lists of grievances, in the provinces, and fixed the meeting of the States-General for May, 1789.

chapter two

# THE FRENCH REVOLUTION

## II. EVENTS, 1789–1795

**Introductory.** There are three reasonably clear phases in the movement of the Revolution from 1789 to 1795. The first phase sees the abolition of feudalism and the attempts to create a constitutional monarchy. The second phase is ushered in by the deposition and execution of the King and Queen, the death of Mirabeau and the growing power of the Jacobins in Paris. In this second period the Revolution comes to be dominated by the powerful figures of Marat, Robespierre, Danton and their followers. War breaks out against the Great Powers, and Belgium and Holland are overrun by the Revolutionary armies. The fluctuating fortunes of the Revolutionary War radically affect the fate of parties and individuals. Danton loses power to Robespierre, under whose direction the Reign of Terror reaches its height. The third phase is entered with the fall of Robespierre and the events leading up to the creation of the Directory Government.

**The Elections to the States-General.** The States-General which met at Versailles on May 5, 1789, comprised representatives of the clergy (First Estate), the nobility (Second Estate) and of the bourgeoisie and peasantry (Third Estate). The method of electing the members of the States-General was that employed in the year 1614, when it had last met. The regulations allowed the vote to the great majority of the clergy, nobility and peasants, each voting for the representatives of his own Estate. So closely did the government keep to the ancient forms of election that the old districts known as the "bailliages" were to be the electoral divisions, although they were no longer of much importance in the general government of France. There was a system of a general assembly of the voters in each "bailliage", in which they elected their representatives for the States-General. The latter was not a "parliament" in the English sense of the word. The elected deputies were not given freedom to speak for their constituents on every question, but were expected to keep strictly to a discussion of the lists of grievances which the local

FIG. 4.—RELEASE OF THE PRISONERS AFTER THE CAPTURE OF
THE BASTILLE, JULY 14TH, 1789.

A contemporary print, which reveals the popular opinion of the nature of this event.

assemblies had entrusted to them and which they were commanded to present to the government.

**The "Cahiers".** These lists of grievances were known as the "cahiers", and had been asked for by the government. The "cahiers" of the Third Estate contained much the same demands throughout France, namely, the abolition of all feudal dues (see pages 3-6), the ending of privileged exemption of the nobles and clergy from taxation, the abolition of the special feudal law courts of the nobility, the establishment of a system of law which was equal for all classes, and the abolition of the oppressive direct and indirect taxes (see pages 3-6). The militia service came in for special denunciation, some "cahiers" declaring that men had been known to mutilate themselves rather than accept service. They asked that all citizens should be able to gain promotion in the armed forces, the Church and the government without regard to their social station, and that there should be an elected assembly with the members responsible to this assembly in the first place, and not to the King.

On the other hand, the "cahiers" of the nobility and clergy showed no such uniformity. In general, the clergy wished to reduce the nobles' privileges, while the nobles wished to reduce those of the clergy. The Lesser Nobility made attacks on the privileges of the Greater Nobility, but wished to maintain their own. The parish priests attacked the privileges of their wealthy superiors in the Church. From the beginning, therefore, the First and Second Estates were in conflict among themselves, whereas the Third Estate was united. This unity was to give the Third Estate a decisive political advantage in the near future.

The "cahiers" contained no demand whatever for the abolition of the monarchy, but they did demand an end to its despotic powers. The demand was frequently made that the States-General should meet regularly, have control over taxation, and not be dissolved without its own consent. Above all the "lettre de cachet" was denounced as the very essence of despotism (see page 11). The Church was frequently the object of attack, and many demands for the confiscation of its property were made.

The way in which Louis XVI and his ministers dealt with these demands, and their attitude to the States-General, was to decide the fate of France and the monarchy.

**The States-General.** The newly-elected States-General met at Versailles at the beginning of May, 1789. It comprised 308 clergy, 285 nobles and 621 members of the Third Estate. This arrangement, by which the Third Estate had double the representation of each of the other estates, had been agreed to by Louis on the advice of Necker. This was a recognition of the great importance of the Third Estate, and yet the government's handling of the Third Estate at Versailles was clumsy from the very first. All the ancient ceremonials were rigidly maintained, which emphasised the social superiority of the First and Second Estates. The Third Estate were even kept waiting a considerable time in the draughty corridors of the meeting-place at Versailles while the nobles and clergy were given immediate entry. This, irritating as it was, proved of minor importance compared with Louis's handling of the first important question of procedure: Should the three estates deliberate apart in their own assemblies or should they all sit together in the same assembly? If the first procedure was followed, then the ancient rule would be carried out that each estate, after considering any important question, should cast one vote for or against. In that case, the two privileged orders would always be able to outvote the Third Estate by two votes to one. If, on the other hand, they sat as one assembly and voted by individuals and not by estates, the Third Estate would be able to outvote the other two.

The Third Estate immediately put forward the demand for a single assembly voting by heads. Louis's reply was to insist on the ancient procedure of voting by separate estates. The next action of the Third Estate constituted their first defiance of the King, for they now invited the clergy and nobles to send representatives to discuss this matter with them. Several such conferences were held between May 23 and June 9, but a majority of the nobles and clergy refused to accept the arrangements proposed by the Third Estate. On June 12 the Third Estate declared themselves the National Assembly, and invited the other estates to join them.

**The National Assembly.** The self-conversion of the Third Estate into the National Assembly was the real beginning of the French Revolution. This decision ended six weeks of wrangling and time-wasting over the question of procedure. It meant a complete break with the old law of the constitution. The defiance of the King by the Third Estate created a tense situation, for the Third Estate had literally swept aside the assemblies of nobles and clergy.

**The Tennis-Court Oath.** Louis was alarmed by the stubborn determination of the Third Estate, and, under pressure from his advisers of the Court, decided to hold a "Royal Session" of all three estates together at which he would give them his direct personal instructions. For this purpose it was necessary to prepare the hall in which the National Assembly was meeting and, without any previous notice to the deputies of the Third Estate, workmen were sent into the hall while it was unoccupied, and the doors were locked. When the deputies arrived under the leadership of their President, they were alarmed and angered at finding the building shut against them in this high-handed manner. Rumours at once flew round that Louis intended some military move against the Assembly. The members of the Assembly, not to be beaten, moved to a tennis-court building in the vicinity, and took an oath never to dissolve "until the constitution of the kingdom shall be established".

**The Royal Session, June 23.** The royal session of all the estates occurred on June 23. This was one of the most dramatic events of the early days of the Revolution. Louis's coach moved to the hall through the ominously silent crowds of the people of Versailles. In his speech to the assembled deputies he announced a series of reforms for the consideration of the estates. His proposals went a long way to meet the demands expressed in the "cahiers", but he made one fatal mistake. Against the urgent advice of Necker, he ordered the three estates to separate, and he declared illegal the recent action of the Third Estate in naming itself the National Assembly. Having ordered the three estates to meet separately to consider the proposals he had put before them, he then left the hall. The nobility and clergy withdrew promptly, but the whole mass of the Third Estate remained defiantly in their seats. The King's Master of Ceremonies repeated the command to withdraw. It was now that one of the great figures of the early days of the Revolution came to the fore. Count Mirabeau strode towards the Master of Ceremonies and exclaimed: "Go tell your master we are here by the will of the people and that we shall not leave except at the point of the bayonet!"

Against this resistance of the National Assembly Louis did nothing. The clergy and nobility began to join the Third Estate. On June 27 Louis himself accepted the situation and ordered the clergy and nobles to join the Third Estate.

Thus, within less than a week, Louis had proposed reforms which he should have put forward at the very first meeting of the States-General in May, had given orders which he was either unwilling or unable to carry out, and then, in an effort to put the seal of his own faded authority on the action, had accepted the demand of the

National Assembly for the union of the estates. No French King had ever been in a more humiliating position.

**Preparations for Counter-Revolution. Increase of Violence.** The Court nobles and members of the Royal Family were not prepared to accept the situation as resignedly as Louis himself. All their efforts were now concentrated on the defeat of the National Assembly by force or the threat of force. A large body of troops under Marshal de Broglie, mostly composed of the foreign regiments, was now concentrated at Paris and Versailles. The members of the National Assembly, fearing that some attempt was about to be made to suppress them, spread the alarm to their constituents throughout France. Demonstrations and riots occurred in many places. The unrest was greatly aggravated by the high price of bread caused by the extremely bad harvest of the previous year. Bread-riots became widespread and the discontent flared up among the regular troops and the militia. Paris itself was crowded with paupers who had been attracted there by the relief schemes set on foot by the city corporation. Numerous political pamphlets appeared, for the censorship of the press was no longer effective. Every open space in the city had its political orator, and political clubs were formed or emerged from the secrecy into which the old system had forced them. Everyone became a politician overnight. To maintain order in Paris there were only 1,000 police, the Swiss Guards and the Gardes Francaises. Of these, only the Swiss Guards were reliable defenders of the monarchy. The Gardes Françaises were almost completely in favour of the National Assembly and had been increasingly insubordinate since some soldiers of the regiment had been imprisoned when a secret society had been discovered amongst them. On June 30 a mob of Parisians attacked the Abbaye prison and released the imprisoned soldiers. In this action the attackers were aided by a number of regular soldiers who had deserted.

In an effort to prevent indiscriminate pillage and disorder, the electors of Paris who had voted for their representatives in the States-General formed their own committee, established themselves at the Hôtel de Ville, and began to take measures for the establishment of a new force, the National Guard.

It was in these conditions that the forces of Marshal de Broglie arrived in Paris and Versailles. Almost at once events took a more violent turn. It was above all the dismissal of the popular Necker by the King on the demand of the Court party that was the signal for action.

**The Capture of the Bastille, July 14, 1789.** Necker was dismissed by Louis on July 11 and the news became generally known in Paris on the following day. For some weeks the gardens of the Palais Royal had been the scene of popular oratory, and now the crowds, under the impassioned influence of the young journalist Camille Desmoulins, burst into the Hôtel de Ville and the Invalides, seizing all the arms they could find. They were supported in this action by many deserters from the Gardes Françaises. The soldiers brought into Paris by Marshal de Broglie were already fraternising with the crowds, for revolutionary propaganda had been sedulously spread in their encampments in the Champs Élysées and the Champs de Mars. Possibly for this reason, or because of the unwillingness of Louis himself to shed blood, no action was taken against the rioters, not even when the cry "To the Bastille!" was raised amongst them.

On the morning of July 14 the attack on the Bastille began. After some hours of fighting and several parleys between the Governor, de Launay, and the attackers, a surrender was agreed upon, the assailants promising de Launay and his garrison their safety. Some attempt was made to conduct de Launay and his guard to the Hôtel de Ville, but his escort was overwhelmed and the Governor and some of his attendants were murdered by the mob.

Only seven prisoners—common criminals—were found inside the Bastille, but the capture of the grim eight-towered fortress in the first fighting of the Revolution assumed a meaning out of all proportion to the actual event itself. It was the symbol of the downfall of tyranny. Many political prisoners arrested under the odious system of "lettre de cachet" had in the past been imprisoned there, and it had had such distinguished inmates as the great Encyclopedists Diderot and Voltaire. Its capture was hailed both in France and elsewhere as the greatest and most significant event of the century. "Whatever act or day may be taken as the beginning of the French Revolution," writes one French historian, "with the fall of the Bastille, flames of revolt went leaping skyward." Everywhere the people elected new local councils in town and countryside. The old courts of justice, both provincial and manorial, were swept away. Widespread attacks were made by the peasants on the mansions of the nobility, the manorial records were destroyed and property pillaged. In the national army, the officers were no longer able to control their troops. In a word, the old social and political fabric of France was being torn to shreds by an enraged people.

The electors' committee at the Hôtel de Ville now established the National Guard, declared July 14 a national holiday and adopted the new tricolour of the red, white and blue in place of the old white royalist flag. The Assembly at Versailles sent a special deputation to Paris and their President, Bailly, was now chosen Mayor of the City. Thus Paris and the Assembly threw in their lot together, for the Assembly realised that any plot by de Broglie for a counter-revolution had been defeated by the armed action of the people of Paris.

The Assembly now asked Louis to order the withdrawal of the troops which had been sent by de Broglie to Versailles. Louis agreed to this demand, and the troops were withdrawn. He also consented to go to the Hôtel de Ville to address the new council, but when he arrived there, he was too overcome by humiliation to give his speech, and the mayor Bailly spoke on his behalf. Placing the new tricolour emblem in his hat, Louis returned to Versailles amidst cries from the onlookers of "Long live the King!" But he returned to Versailles defeated and almost alone, for the King's brothers and others of the Court party who had been the instigators of the military moves made by Marshal de Broglie had already left the country at the King's request to join other "émigrés" across the Rhine.

**The Session of August 4, 1789.** The events of August 4 in the Assembly were the direct outcome of the spread of unrest and the attacks on the nobility in the countryside. The Assembly was faced with the problem of maintaining some semblance of order in France and yet at the same time satisfying the just demands of the peasants. In the middle of a debate on this question, two members of the nobility suddenly rose in their places and proposed equality of taxation for all and the ending of a number of feudal burdens. This self-abnegation electrified the Assembly and other members of the privileged classes were soon vying with one another to outdo these proposals. A bishop proposed the abolition of the game laws, another even proposed that the Assembly should have the right to dispose of the property of the Church, and an archbishop proposed the abolition of the "gabelle" salt tax. And so it went on. The Assembly at last embodied these various proposals in thirty decrees which swept away the whole system of feudal dues and declared the old system of taxation illegal.

The decrees of August 4 were destructive of the old order. However, the Assembly had created another grave problem for itself: the payment even of the State taxes, which the Assembly had authorised to continue, now fell away drastically. The government was suddenly deprived of a large part of its income, and soon would have to take desperate measures to gain revenue in other ways.

**Declaration of the Rights of Man.** The Assembly had already begun the task of setting up a new form of government for France and, after July 14, had taken the title of Constituent Assembly. After prolonged debate it was decided to issue a Declaration of the Rights of Man as an introduction to the new constitution. This decision was the result of the excitement of the times and a general feeling of the vast importance of the Revolution for the whole of mankind. Above all, the Declaration showed the influence upon the deputies of American ideas and of the teachings of Rousseau. It asserted the right of the people to rule and that men were by nature equal, that there should be freedom of speaking, writing and printing, that every citizen should have the right through his representatives to make laws and impose taxation, and that nobody was to be imprisoned except by forms of law decided by the people.

It was when the Assembly came to the question of the King's position in the new constitution that serious trouble began. Some of the nobility demanded that the King have the right to veto any laws, other members of the Assembly wanted this to be a six-year veto only—that is, that the King would have the power of delaying the passing of a law for six years but no longer. The popular orators outside the Assembly, and a number of deputies within (but not a majority), denounced the right of the King to have any power of veto whatever. On the matter coming to the vote, the Assembly decided by 673 votes to 325 that the six-year suspensive veto be adopted.

**The March of the Women.** The decision of the Assembly on the question of the King's veto led to intensified action by the popular orators. Robespierre and the Jacobins in the Assembly had opposed the right of veto because it would give to the King powers which he would use in defence of the aristocracy. The Jacobins already had a considerable influence in Paris. Their campaign of opposition to the Assembly's decision was made easier by the state of things in the city. The price of bread was high, there was much unemployment because of the crowds who had flocked into Paris and also through the desertion of the city by many wealthy employers. The agitation was roused to a new height of fury by the King's refusal to accept the decrees of August 4 abolishing feudalism. He had also refused to sign the Declaration of the Rights of Man.

The Jacobin orators in Paris had for some time been demanding that the King be brought to Paris out of reach of the aristocrats at Versailles who were influencing him against the Assembly. The

Centre and Right Parties in the Assembly, alarmed for the King's safety, now proposed secretly to Necker (who had been reinstated) that the King and the Assembly should both move to the provinces—to Compiègne or Soissons. Louis himself, however, opposed the idea on the grounds that it was undignified and that the disturbances in Paris would soon die down. But even during the debate on this crucial question in the Council of Ministers, Louis had been asleep most of the time—he was tired after hunting.

FIG. 5.—"A VERSAILLES!" OCTOBER 5TH, 1789.

Then the news reached Paris that, at a military banquet at Versailles, the officers of the King's bodyguard had insulted the Constituent Assembly and persuaded members of the newly-formed National Guard whom they were entertaining to throw aside the tricolour in their hats for the white cockade of the royalists. At once the rumour flew round of a military plot against the Assembly instigated by those who were still attempting to influence the King. It was out of this situation that the famous march of the women to Versailles took place. On the morning of October 5 a huge crowd of women forced their way into the Hôtel de Ville, seized arms and, dragging cannon along with them, began a march on Versailles. Their declared aim was to get the King to order a reduction in the price of bread and to ensure the punishment of the officers who had insulted the tricolour. On the way they were joined by a crowd of men, some dressed as women.

Lafayette, the popular hero of the American War of Independence, had been elected Commandant of the National Guard. His position was one of great difficulty. If he prevented the marchers from reaching Versailles, he would be identifying himself with the opponents of the Assembly. In any case, it was by no means certain that the Guard itself would obey his instructions. After much hesitation, he followed with the National Guard to Versailles, arriving only to find that the marchers had already invaded the Assembly and demanded a decree lowering the price of bread. They had also sent a deputation to the King. Lafayette now took charge of the arrangements for protecting the Royal Palace, but during the early morning of the next day, October 6, the marchers found an unguarded door, rushed into the Palace and attacked the Queen's apartment. She managed to make her escape just before the crowd burst in and thrust their pikes into her bed.

Lafayette now succeeded in restoring order by persuading Louis and the Queen to appear on a balcony before the crowd. Lafayette himself announced the King's acceptance of the declaration of the Rights of Man and his willingness to go to Paris. Louis made a promise of bread to the people.

In the early afternoon the royal family set out in a coach for Paris surrounded by the marchers, some of them carrying on pikes the heads of the guards killed during the assault on the Palace. On reaching Paris the Royal Family was lodged in the Tuileries Palace. Ten days later the Assembly also moved from Versailles to Paris.

From this moment in October, 1789, Paris dominated the Revolution. The Royal Family were little more than prisoners. The clubs, the orators, the pamphleteers took increasing control of the situation. This control was greatly assisted by the fact that the public were admitted to the gallery seats of the Assembly, whose members were thus under constant pressure from the mob.

**The Assembly and the Church. The Assignats.** The complete breakdown of the old system of taxation after the decrees of August 4 had left the government without funds to meet the expenses of the State. This was one of the first problems which the Assembly had to face after the removal to Paris. Already the great wealth of the Catholic Church had been discussed in the Assembly, and now it was made to come to the rescue of the government. A new paper currency was printed, and the guarantee or security for this paper money was to be the lands of the Church, which were decreed State property. The paper "assignats" were sold by the government to gain a necessary revenue, and could be redeemed by their holders in the new State land. For a time this helped to ease the revenue problem, but as the Revolution progressed these "assignats" were issued with little reference to the actual value of the Church lands. The result was that they rapidly lost value. An "assignat" worth 100 francs in 1789 was only worth one franc by 1796. However, the issue of the

FIG. 6.—ASSIGNAT DE DIX SOUS.

(*Actual size*)

"assignats" was one of the cleverest moves made by the National Assembly, and it cannot be overestimated in the history of the Revolution. If ever the clergy and nobles returned to their former land and power the "assignats" would be destroyed. It was therefore to the interest of every holder of the "assignats" to see that this power was never regained. In other words, every holder of the "assignats" became a supporter of the Revolution from economic self-interest.

**Civil Constitution of the Clergy, July, 1790.** The Assembly now went further in its determination to alter the position of the Church in France. The law known as the "Civil Constitution of the Clergy" had the effect of making all ecclesiastics servants of the State. Bishops and priests were now to be elected by the same people who appointed civil servants. The salaries of the clergy were to be paid by the government. The Pope of Rome was to have no power of altering elections or other matters decreed by the State. The law reduced the salaries of the bishops considerably, but increased those of the parish priests. Finally, all priests were to take an oath of loyalty to the Civil Constitution of the Clergy.

Many bishops and clergymen supported these changes, because they sincerely thought that they would improve the life of the Church, do away with its scandals and inequalities and bring it nearer to true Christianity. Most members of the Assembly took this view, and it was therefore not a measure merely dictated by violent hatred of the Church or of Christianity, although, of course, some members of the Assembly supported the change from these motives.

However, these considerations do not alter the fact that many priests and bishops refused to accept the control of the State over the Church in any way. This, of course, was the attitude adopted by the Pope, and he secretly urged Louis XVI not to accept the Civil Constitution.

The oath was resisted by about two-thirds of the parish priests and by 130 of the 134 bishops. Those accepting were known as the juring priests, those refusing as the non-jurors. Thus the result of the change was to alienate from the Revolution a considerable number of priests who had so far supported it. The non-juring priests had considerable support in the countryside and continued to carry out their functions in defiance of the Assembly's decrees. This was particularly the case in the western region of La Vendée, where royalist sympathies were strong and where shortly a counter-revolution was to be attempted. This situation, of course, encouraged "émigrés" to continue their intrigues against the Revolution and gave them a number of allies among the priesthood in France.

**The Flight to Varennes, June, 1791.**   Louis XVI signed the law for the Civil Constitution much against his will. A devout Catholic, it was a humiliation to him to have to oppose the Pope and what he considered to be the best interests of religion. It was this situation which determined him to make an effort to escape from France. He placed his last hopes on being able to join the "émigré" forces over the frontier and especially his brother-in-law, the Emperor Leopold of Austria. With the aid of these forces he hoped to return to France and impose his terms on the people. This was a last desperate gamble for independence, but it failed. Louis, Marie Antoinette and their children were recognised at the little eastern frontier village of Varennes. Their coach was escorted back to Paris, amidst hostile demonstrations all along their route. The final humiliation was the hostile silence of the watching crowds in Paris itself.

The effects of the attempt of Louis XVI to escape from France were decisive for the future of the Revolution. He lost what personal regard the people still had for him. By attempting to fall back on foreign help he had wounded the French people in their tenderest spot, their love of the motherland. A second result of Varennes was the emergence of an openly republican party which came more and more to dominate the course of the Revolution.

FIG. 7.—LOUIS XVI FORCED TO
PUT ON THE "PHRYGIAN CAP".

**The New Constitution Decided, September, 1791.** We have already noted the Declaration of the Rights of Man which prefaced the new constitution (see page 28), and the granting of the six-year veto to the King. The Assembly now completed the constitution. The new assembly was to consist of 745 members. It was decided to adopt a system of indirect election. All men over twenty-five years of age paying State taxes equivalent to three days' labour and enrolled in the National Guard were to be styled "active citizens". These "active citizens" were to vote for electors who in their turn elected the members of the Assembly. This was a moderate form of representative government and shows that in 1791 the Constituent Assembly was still prepared to accept a form of constitutional monarchy, even after the flight of Louis to Varennes. Again, the new voters were mostly people of property, for, while the "active

citizens" numbered about 4,000,000, the electors for whom they
voted in the first stage had to pay in direct taxes the equivalent
of ten days' wages. The electors who finally chose the assembly
numbered not more than 43,000. It must also be noted that the
"passive citizens" who did not qualify to vote at all numbered
about 3,000,000. No wonder that the strict followers of Rousseau's
doctrine, such as Marat, Robespierre and Camille Desmoulins,
loudly protested, and carried on a violent campaign against the proposals. Desmoulins declared that the Constitution "hands France
over to the aristocratic government". He pointed out that under
its provisions Rousseau himself would not have had a vote. "Active
citizens", he declared, "are those who have taken the Bastille, they
are those who till the fields, while the idlers of Church and Court
are parasitic plants that should be thrown to the flames like the
barren tree in the Bible."

At the same time the Constituent Assembly remodelled the entire
local government of France. The old provinces were abolished and
France was divided into eighty-three Departments about equal in
size. These were subdivided into districts or "arrondissements",
into "cantons" and (smallest division of all) "communes".

Finally the Constituent (or National) Assembly which had first
met on May 5, 1789, dissolved itself in September, 1791, in preparation for the new elections. Many people were glad when these pro-
tracted labours of the old Assembly were complete, and the belief
was widely held that the Revolution was at an end.

**Summary of the General Position in France in September, 1791.**
France was by this time radically changed. Feudalism had been
swept away on August 4, 1789, the Intendants had gone and new
local elected councils had been set up. A new constitution had been
established and the monarchy had been retained, but it was shorn
of its despotic powers. Moreover, the position of Louis XVI in the
eyes of the French people had been heavily compromised by his
attempted flight. Hatred of the Queen, who was regarded as the
main opponent of the Revolution in the royal circle, was intense
and bitter.

**Count Mirabeau.** Louis XVI had already lost one leading member
of the Assembly who had been well disposed towards him, Count
Mirabeau, who died in April, 1791. Mirabeau, although a member
of the nobility, had early thrown in his lot with the Third Estate.
He belonged to no faction or party, but played a great part in the
affairs of the National Assembly. His life had been thoroughly

disreputable. He had been disowned by his father on account of his debts and dissolute life. He was a powerful pamphleteer against the abuses of the times, his pamphlets being in the main written for him, or partly plagiarised from the writings of others. He had also at one time served as a secret agent of France in Berlin. His part in the States-General had been a prominent one, for he had strongly supported the declaration of the Third Estate as the National Assembly and, as we have seen, had taken a strong lead against the King on the occasion of the Tennis Court Oath (see page 23). He was one of the most violent opponents of the Church and had been the main instigator of the sale of Church lands, the issue of the "assignats", and the Civil Constitution of the Clergy. Besides his activity in the Assembly, he had been for a time President of the Jacobin Club (see page 36).

Where Mirabeau differed from many others was in his view of the monarchy. He foresaw only chaos if the King's powers were to be completely destroyed. Towards the end of his life he had entered into correspondence with the Court, which began to trust him. Louis even paid his personal debts for him. Mirabeau's influence is particularly seen in the Constitution of 1791, which had been pieced together since 1789 by numerous debates in the Assembly.

Mirabeau had constantly urged the King to remove himself from Paris and go to some provincial town where he could rally all his supporters unhindered by the extreme revolutionaries. But he urged the King to accept all that had so far been achieved by the Revolution for there was no going back to the past, and it was now only necessary to hold the Revolution in check. Yet Mirabeau had so many enemies, both in the Court and in the Assembly, that all his proposals were regarded with extreme jealousy and dislike. To many people it seemed that Mirabeau was only striving for personal power. They were afraid of him and distrusted him, and he died having accomplished nothing towards his aim of a constitutional monarchy which would have restrained the extremes of the Revolution. It certainly appears that he had played a double game. In public he had supported the most extreme of the Jacobins and became the idol of the people of Paris, but secretly he supported the King. At one time he even suggested to the King that the Assembly should be encouraged to pass further laws against the Catholic Church in order to make the Assembly so unpopular in the countryside that the King would be able to gain further supporters!

Had Mirabeau survived, it is still difficult to see how his influence could have continued. He would have counselled the King against flight from France, but would the advice have been taken? Mirabeau was a solitary adventurer whose isolation alone made him vulnerable to attack on all sides. One man could scarcely have controlled the course of the Revolution.

From May, 1789, to September, 1791, is the first stage of the Revolution. We shall see that entirely new forces now take charge of the situation. Far from being finished, the Revolution had only just begun.

## THE REVOLUTION FROM SEPTEMBER, 1791, TO THE DIRECTORY, 1795

The elections to the new Legislative Assembly resulted in the return of 136 Jacobins, 264 Feuillants (page 37) and a centre group of about 350 deputies. The old National or Constituent Assembly, with the idealistic motive of preventing itself gaining a monopoly of power, had barred its members from being elected to the Legislative Assembly. Thus the new Assembly was composed of men with energy and enthusiasm, but with little previous political experience. But let us consider first the parties or groups which composed the new Assembly.

**The Jacobins.** This group came eventually to dominate the Revolution and were members of the Jacobin Club. The original members of the club were some deputies of the National Assembly from Brittany, and they gained their name from the fact that they held their meetings in the old convent of the Jacobins in Paris. The public was admitted to the debates of the club, and it gradually became the rallying centre of all those popular elements which brought pressure to bear on the Assembly from outside. At first its membership had been wide, and even Mirabeau had been one of its presidents. But as time went on it became dominated by outright republicans, of whom the most prominent were Robespierre and Marat. The club had more than two thousand affiliated clubs in the towns, cities and villages of France and they acted as a concerted, disciplined force. They played a prominent part in the elections to the Legislative Assembly and carried on a violent campaign against all moderate elements and supporters of the constitutional monarchy.

Another important Paris club of this period was that of the Cordeliers, of which Danton was the most prominent member. Its activities were confined to Paris and its members were more distinctly working class or "proletarian" than the members of the Jacobin Club. It was strongly republican.

The Jacobins, despite their campaign, were outnumbered in the Legislative Assembly by the Feuillants, and the Centre. The Feuillants were numerically strong, but lamentably weak in organisation and unity compared with the Jacobins. They wished to preserve a constitutional monarchy, but wanted to improve the new constitution. There were serious divisions in their ranks as to the way in which the constitution should be changed. From the position the Feuillants occupied in the Assembly they are usually referred to as the Right.

The Centre group wished to be independent of both Right and Left. But in the prevailing temper of Paris, and under pressure from the Jacobins and their supporters in the galleries, the Centre became confused, divided and brow-beaten. One of the first measures which the Jacobins secured in the Legislative Assembly was the "appel nominal" by which each deputy had to declare aloud his vote on any question. This procedure resulted in the gallery being able to bring the weight of insult and terror to bear on individuals.

**Declaration of War, April, 1792.** The history of the Revolution is from now on closely related to events abroad and the activities of the "émigrés". Louis himself had disapproved of their violent threats against the Revolution, for such threats only increased his own danger and played into the hands of the extreme revolutionaries. Despite his written requests to his brothers, the threats continued, and an army of about 20,000 men was concentrated on the frontier of France in the territory of the German Elector of Trier. Then in August, 1791, the "émigrés" persuaded the King of Prussia and the Emperor of Austria to issue the Declaration of Pillnitz. The two rulers asserted that the cause of Louis XVI was the cause of every monarch of Europe. The main result of this declaration was to strengthen republicanism in France and unite with it the forces of patriotism, a consequence which its authors had certainly not foreseen. Another serious development was the outbreak of civil war in western France, in the region of La Vendée. Here the peasants had risen in revolt to support the non-juring priests and had expelled the constitutional priests from their parishes. When the National Guard was sent to restore order the revolt took on an armed and counter-revolutionary character under the leadership of the Comte de Rochejacquelin. Thus the "émigrés" had a considerable body of armed supporters within France itself.

The Assembly replied vigorously to the "émigrés". By decree it fixed January 1, 1792, as the day on which the "émigrés" must return to France or come under sentence of death. This decree was aimed also at the King's brothers, and was a manœuvre on the part of the Jacobins especially to discredit Louis himself, for they knew that he could not possibly sign such a decree. In this they were quite correct, for Louis used his veto against the decree the day after it was passed by the Assembly. Likewise, the Assembly passed a decree in November, 1791, by which all priests who had not taken the Civil Oath within one week were to be deprived of their livings. As his opponents expected, Louis also vetoed this decree. By these two actions Louis had appeared to identify himself with the enemies of France and the Revolution.

**The Girondins.** A section of the Jacobins under Brissot now demanded that Louis should order the Elector of Trier to disband the "émigré" army. They knew well that this would lead to war, which they wished to bring about in order to overthrow the King. This section of the Jacobins were known as the "Girondins", taking their name from the Gironde district of south-western France from which a number of them came. If they could bring about war, then Louis, having vetoed the decrees against the "émigrés", could easily be shown as unfitted to lead the nation. The war policy was demanded by the principal leaders of the Girondins, including Vergniaud, Madame Roland and Brissot.

From this point a rift appears between the Girondins and the remainder of the Jacobins, for Robespierre, Marat, Danton and those supporting them were opposed to a war policy on the grounds that it led, not to a democracy of the people, but to dictatorship in which the wealthiest classes would be supreme.

The Girondins were, however, aided in their policy by support from an unexpected quarter. The Feuillants had secured the appointment of one of their number, Narbonne, as Minister of War, and they demanded a war policy from exactly opposite motives to the Girondins. They considered that a successful war would restore the popularity and power of the King. Thus, from entirely opposite motives, two main groups of the Assembly looked to war in order to gain their ends. Lafayette, also, was a party to this plan, but both Louis and the Queen opposed it, mainly out of distrust of Lafayette, whom they now regarded as the part-author of all their misfortunes through his failure to use the National Guard on their behalf. Louis dismissed Narbonne, and the Girondins succeeded in securing the appointment of one of their members, Dumouriez, as Minister of War. War was thus made certain, for a large majority of the Legislative Assembly was now in favour of it. It was regarded as the means of spreading abroad the spirit of the Revolution against kings and to the lasting benefit of peoples. "Peace to the peoples, war against the tyrants" became the ideal held before the French soldier. An ultimatum was sent to the Emperor of Austria demanding that he cease to support the "émigrés". His reply was to make some unacceptable demands against the Revolution. The result was the declaration of war against Austria on April 20, 1792.

The declaration of war was a momentous change in the course of events. France was to be involved in war for more than twenty years, but the immediate results in France itself were to sharpen the conflict with the King and hasten the country towards a republican form of government.

The French armies first moved against the Austrians in Belgium, and at once suffered severe defeats. Louis immediately dismissed the Girondist ministry and installed another composed mainly of the followers of Lafayette. He also vetoed further decrees against the non-juring priests and for the formation of an army to protect Paris.

These actions by Louis led to the organisation of a popular demonstration against the King on June 20, 1792. It was under Jacobin leadership that the crowd of demonstrators assembled in the Tuileries gardens and eventually broke into the Palace. Louis himself was surrounded for some hours by a group of demonstrators and was forced to don the red cap of the Revolution and to drink to the health of the nation. There were loud demands that he should withdraw his vetoes on the subjects of the "émigrés" and the non-juring priests, but Louis remained firm. Marie Antoinette had been similarly insulted. Some of his opponents probably hoped that Louis would be assassinated, but eventually the crowd was persuaded by some of the deputies from the Legislative Assembly to withdraw.

**Effects of June 20. Last Moves of Lafayette.** An effort was now made by the opponents of the Jacobins to suppress them, and the lead was taken in this by Lafayette. The humiliations suffered by the King on June 20 had led to a strong reaction in his favour among large sections of the public, and Lafayette determined to take advantage of this situation to restore the credit of the monarchy and put an end to the Jacobins. Louis himself had been greeted in the Assembly by cries of "Vive le Roi!"

Lafayette had been given the command of the army on the eastern frontier, and he now left it in order to appear before the Assembly. The Jacobin organisation now showed itself at its most effective. As soon as Lafayette appeared he was accused of having deserted the army in the moment of France's greatest peril, and they were able to sway the Assembly against him, while, of course, their gallery supporters took up the hue and cry. Marie Antoinette herself, harbouring an intense dislike of Lafayette, had actually warned the Jacobins herself that he intended to make a direct appeal to the National Guard!

Lafayette's plan was entirely foiled by the Jacobins and Marie Antoinette—a tragically ironic combination! Lafayette returned to the army, soon afterwards fled over the frontier and was imprisoned by the Austrians till 1797.

**The Rise of Danton.** It was now that a new figure began his rise to power in Paris—Danton. Besides being the guiding spirit of the Cordeliers Club, he had also gained important office in the citizens' council of Paris at the Hôtel de Ville. He now took a leading part in organising a new insurrection, for which purpose the Jacobins had set up a special committee known as the Directory of Insurrection. He supervised the military organisation of the Paris sections which were under Jacobin control, the guards at the Tuileries were changed, and the National Guard itself was reorganised in order to remove any possibility of its supporting the King. At the same time a number of special volunteer regiments were introduced into Paris known as the "fédérés", of whom the most strongly pro-Jacobin were the Marseillais. At this very moment the plans of the Jacobins were aided by the stupidity of the "émigrés" and the commander of the Prussian forces which had now joined the Austrians. The Manifesto of the Duke of Brunswick declared that if the Tuileries Palace were again invaded as on June 20 then he would subject the city of Paris to "military execution and total subversion and the guilty rebels to the death they deserved", and he spoke of "exemplary and never-to-be-forgotten vengeance". The main result of this Manifesto, the actual work of an émigré, was to enable the Jacobins to rouse the patriotic feelings of the French people to furious heights. The Manifesto was a threat to the motherland and to the city of Paris, and was to be resisted by every patriotic Frenchman. The Manifesto had welded together in unity Jacobinism and Patriotism—a formidable combination.

**The Insurrection of August 10, 1792. The Commune Established.** It was Danton who gave the signal for insurrection. The forces of the sections and the "fédérés" were summoned by the tocsin bell of the Cordeliers Club in the early morning of August 10. The commandant of the National Guard, despite the changes made in its composition, still hoped to be able to oppose the insurrectionists and he made preparations for this. At the Hôtel de Ville a committee of Danton's supporters drawn from the city sections suddenly seized power, suspended the old council and established the revolutionary Commune. Meanwhile at the Tuileries the King reviewed the National Guard, but received a very mixed reception. His advisers urged him to take refuge in the Legislative Assembly, and after some hesitation he agreed to this course, and the Royal Family were temporarily lodged in a reporters' box in the gallery. At the Tuileries a general attack by the insurgents now began and they broke into the Palace. The National Guard had now joined them, and the only resistance came from the King's Swiss Guards. At a critical moment a written message was received from Louis ordering them to retire, and in the course of doing so they were forced to surrender. The following day the prisoners were massacred.

Thus the real power in Paris passed into the hands of Danton and the revolutionary Commune. The Assembly was reduced to a position of subservience, and it was at this point that Lafayette on the frontier decided to leave the sinking ship of the monarchy.

The Commune now forced the Assembly to suspend the King, and to make arrangements for the calling of a Convention to alter the constitution. The elections to the Convention were to be by universal manhood suffrage and not on property qualification.

**Maximilien Robespierre.** It was immediately after the successful insurrection of August 10 that Maximilien Robespierre (1758–1794) became a member of the Paris Commune. From the time of his election to the States-General in 1789 he had been a member of the Jacobin Club. A fanatical follower of the ideas of Rousseau (see page 14), he preached virtue and incorruptibility. A provincial lawyer by profession, he had also dabbled in literature, and assumed an air of superiority and cultured refinement which came in time to exercise a fascination over his audience. Yet Robespierre, who was to bear much responsibility for both the September Massacres and the Reign of Terror, had abandoned his lawyer's practice rather than be a party to the passing of a death-sentence in the courts! Of his complete incorruptibility in all money matters and his unselfish devotion to the Revolution there is no doubt whatever.

The closest ally of Robespierre at this time was Marat, a member of the Cordeliers Club and editor of the revolutionary paper *L'Ami du Peuple*. This paper was renowned for the sharpness and scurrility of its attacks on the aristocracy, the Church and the monarchy. Marat was one of the decisive, controlling influences behind the actions of the Paris mob at critical points of the Revolution, and was the main instigator of the September Massacres.

Robespierre and his supporters in the Commune now began a furious campaign against all those, and especially the Girondins, who had in any way given support to the monarchy. The Commune established a censorship of the press and also removed from the voters' lists large numbers of people considered unfit to vote. The barriers of the city of Paris were closed, and an examination of letters entering and leaving the capital began. Robespierre demanded from the Assembly the custody of the Royal Family, who were now taken to the Temple prison. The Commune also gained the right to take action against all those who were suspected of acting against the security of the State.

Thus the Commune became the decisive ruling force in Paris, and the advance of the Austrians and Prussians towards the capital made the measures taken increasingly severe. A ruthless discipline was enforced.

**The September Massacres.** Further measures were now planned against all those suspected of royalist sympathies. The police activities of the Commune had filled the prisons of Paris to overflowing, and plans were now made by Marat to dispose of the inmates. The Commune and Assembly were both making great efforts to raise troops to stop the enemy advance, and the extreme Jacobins considered that the possible traitors in the prisons were a grave danger to the rear of the French armies. On September 2, orders were issued to bands of assassins, who went from prison to prison, dragged the inmates before hastily-formed tribunals and then massacred them. About 1,200 persons in Paris were killed between September 2 and September 6. The policy of terror was also extended to the provinces. The September Massacres were mainly prepared by Marat, supported by Robespierre and, at least, connived at by Danton, who was at this time Minister of Justice.

**The Convention, September, 1792–October, 1795.** The first months of the new assembly, the Convention, were marked by increasing conflict between the Jacobins and the Girondins. In the first place the Girondins were deputies of the provinces and were not prepared to accept the supremacy of Paris. The Jacobins, however, relied for their strength on Paris. Secondly, there was intense personal enmity between the leaders of the Girondins, such as Madame Roland and Vergniaud, and the Jacobin leaders, Marat, Robespierre and Danton. Thirdly, there was a marked difference between the two parties in their attitude to the King.

**The Execution of Louis XVI.** The King was now brought to trial on a charge of having conspired against the nation by supporting the "émigrés" and the foreign sovereigns who were then attacking France. His vetoes (see page 38) had made the case against him a very strong one, and the Jacobins were especially determined to secure his conviction. Evidence of the King's correspondence with the enemies of France had been found among his papers seized in the Tuileries. After the trial the Convention voted unanimously that Louis was guilty.

At this point the Girondins attempted to secure a vote of the people as a final court of appeal, but they were overborne by Robespierre, and the Convention rejected the idea. By a majority of 53 the Convention next voted for death, and Louis was guillotined on Sunday, January 21, 1793. He had become a tragic figure incapable of controlling the course of events. He was honest within narrow limits, he was sincerely religious, but was hampered by self-seeking advisers and a bigoted Queen, and, above all, he was too weak for the exercise of despotism.

**The War.** Already on September 20 the French armies had begun to recover from their first defeats by their victory over the Prussians at Valmy. Their armies had then swept everything before them in the Austrian Netherlands. England entered the war against France in February, 1793. The policy of the British Prime Minister, William Pitt, the Younger, had been very cautious up to 1793. He had no wish to entangle England in a war against France, but became alarmed when the Revolution began to spread beyond the frontiers of France. The Girondist policy of war against other countries brought about a gradual change in British policy, especially when the French denounced certain European treaties which affected the position of Britain. The French denounced the right of Holland to control the navigation and commerce of the River Scheldt—an arrangement dating back to the Peace of Westphalia, 1648. At this time (1792) Holland was an ally of Britain, and Pitt was greatly concerned for the possible effects on Britain's trade and naval power if Holland came permanently under French control, which was an obvious aim of the French government. Again, in November, 1792, the National Convention issued the Edict of Fraternity, in which they promised help to all peoples who rose against their rulers— "all governments", it declared, "are our enemies, all people our friends". Lastly, the execution of Louis XVI appeared to many people in England as a barbarous and unwarrantable act which made the revolution the enemy of all kings. Pitt protested to the French Ambassador in London, and the French reply was a declaration of war against England on February 1, 1793. Spain, Holland, the German and Italian states also entered the war against France. The execution of Louis had undoubtedly filled the rulers of Europe with horror and alarm and they now hoped that a concerted attack would destroy the new Republic. Besides this, they all had territorial aims against France, for they were not fighting out of pure idealism by any means. The result of these developments was the defeat of the French forces and the beginning of another retreat in the Netherlands.

The Convention now decided on the creation of a new system to meet the serious situation which had again developed. It set up three important organs of government which came to control the life of Paris and the country—the Committee of Public Safety, the Committee of General Security and the Revolutionary Tribunal.

**The Committee of Public Safety.** At first the Committee was given control of the army and foreign affairs, but soon came to be the guiding force of the Revolution, controlling the Convention which had created it. It consisted of twelve members whose duties extended to every department of State. These duties entailed the issuing of decrees, the appointment and dismissal of officials, the sending of its special agents to the departments and to the army, the consignment of suspects to the guillotine. Under its direction the Committee of General Security took charge of the actual police arrangements in Paris and the provinces. The Revolutionary Tribunal was a specially created court for the trial of those ordered before it by the Committee of Public Safety, and no appeal was possible from its verdicts. From day to day it fed the guillotine with victims.

While these measures were being adopted, the Girondins made a last vain effort to defeat the Jacobins. They wished to punish those who had been responsible for the September Massacres, and actually succeeded in having Marat brought before the Revolutionary Tribunal. But the Tribunal acquitted him, and he at once organised an attack on the Convention by the forces of the Commune. The

Convention hall was surrounded by an armed force of 80,000 and the members were made to expel the Girondins. Thus the Commune had once again taken control of the Assembly. The reply of the Girondins was to rouse their supporters in the provinces to revolt.

The situation in the summer of 1793 was briefly this: a Royalist revolt in La Vendée (see page 37); a revolt by the Girondins; and further defeats for French arms on the frontier.

**The Reign of Terror.** The Convention and the Committee of Public Safety now made ruthless and gigantic efforts to retrieve the situation. They raised 700,000 fresh troops in a few weeks, and, under the direction of their organising genius, Carnot (a member of the Committee), these armies thrust back the foreign invaders. Success was the ruthless demand of the Committee, and its agents with the armies sent unsuccessful generals to the guillotine and promoted new men from the ranks. During these late months of 1793, a new French Army emerged, powerful, well-disciplined and successful. This was the result of the combination of terror and Herculean effort which marked the work of the Committee of Public Safety, mainly directed by Danton. On August 23, 1793, the famous "levée-en-masse" was decreed by the Convention. Under this decree the whole population of France was brought into "permanent requisition" for the defence of the country and the prosecution of the war against the enemy. Unmarried citizens or widowers between the ages of eighteen and twenty-five were the first to be called for military service, while married men, women and children were all assigned tasks directly related to the war effort.

The Terror extended all over France. The Committee secured the passing of a "Law of Suspects" which was so loosely worded that even those only "guilty" of a lack of enthusiasm for the Revolution could be brought before the Revolutionary Tribunal. In these months, many thousands were guillotined in Paris and the provinces. In the City of Lyons, which had supported the Girondins, about 1,500 persons were executed. In La Vendée the rebel forces were defeated and prisoners were shot indiscriminately by the victorious armies. And, as was to be expected, the Girondist leaders were now executed, among them Madame Roland. The ferocity of the Terror was only increased by the despairing action of the young Girondin, Charlotte Corday, a Norman girl, who went to Paris and stabbed Marat to death in his bath. Marie Antoinette was also executed on October 16, 1793.

**The Worship of Reason, November 10, 1793.** There were now really two main bodies attempting to direct the Revolution, the Commune and the Committee of Public Safety. In the Commune the control was now gained by the group which wished to carry the Terror to even more ruthless extremes. They also attempted to destroy Christianity in France altogether. Under the influence of their leader, Hébert, they forced the Convention to introduce a new non-Christian calendar, which did away with saints' days, Sundays and religious festivals of various kinds. The months were named after nature (e.g. April became Germinal or budding time), the day was divided into ten hours and general dating of events was to be, not from the birth of Christ, but from the Year One of Liberty—September 22, 1792. This was followed by a campaign against Christianity itself and on November 10 the Cathedral of Notre Dame became a Temple of Reason, and a special ceremony took place in which a dancer from the Opera sat in the Cathedral as the Goddess of Reason in the place formerly occupied by the statue of the Virgin Mary. Many churches in France became at this time Temples of Reason.

Robespierre was opposed to this policy for two reasons: he held that some form of religion and belief in a Supreme Being was necessary (here again he followed Rousseau strictly), and, secondly, he wished to destroy the power of the Commune as the rival to the Committee of Public Safety which he dominated. Danton was also opposed to Hébert and the Commune for an entirely different reason—he wished to bring the policy of terror to an end, whereas the followers of Hébert wished to continue it. Robespierre skilfully formed an alliance with Danton to destroy the Commune and, after elaborate intrigues, the Convention ordered the arrest of the Hébertists. They were guillotined in March, 1794.

Having defeated the Hébertists, Robespierre now turned against Danton. He had skilfully used him as an ally, but was violently opposed to Danton's attempts to end the policy of terror. In the view of Danton, the successes of the French armies made the Terror no longer necessary and would only further divide and weaken the nation. He wished also to secure peace with foreign powers as soon as possible and not to carry the Revolution by force into other territories. This policy, openly and courageously expressed, led to furious attacks upon him by Robespierre and his followers in the Committee of Public Safety, which eventually ordered Danton's arrest. Shortly afterwards Danton was tried before the Revolutionary Tribunal which he himself had helped to establish, was condemned and guillotined on April 5, 1794.

Robespierre had gained supreme power in both the Commune and the Committee of Public Safety. He now secured the recognition by the Convention of the existence of the Supreme Being and a great festival was held on June 8 in the Tuileries Gardens at which Robespierre made an oration before the crowds and the members of the Convention.

At the same time Robespierre intensified the Terror. The Revolutionary Tribunal's procedure was made even more severe. The jury was packed with Robespierre's supporters and no counsel was allowed to the accused. In the seven weeks of Robespierre's rule more victims went to the guillotine than in the whole period of the Terror up to that time.

This policy led to a sudden hardening of opposition to Robespierre. He had carried his policy to the point at which the moderate elements who feared for their heads were prepared to risk them in outright opposition. On July 27, 1794, the opposition to Robespierre broke out in the Convention where he was shouted down with cries of "Down with the tyrant!" The Convention ordered his arrest, but his followers released him and he joined the Commune at the Hôtel de Ville, where preparations were made to bring about a rising against the Convention. But the Convention moved first with the troops under its command, the Hôtel de Ville was attacked and Robespierre (who was shot in the jaw by a soldier) and his supporters were arrested. On July 28 Robespierre was guillotined together with twenty of his followers, and others were executed during the next two days.

Whatever the judgments historians pass on the character and career of Robespierre, there is no doubt that he carried his policy of "revolutionary virtue" beyond the point at which he could rally effective support. Not all the conspirators against him were high-minded idealists, however. By his attempts to control the price of foodstuffs (the "Law of the Maximum") and by the severity of the laws passed against those speculators in food who were attempting to grow rich from the sufferings of the people, Robespierre had roused the opposition of important sections of the merchant class. France was not ready to follow Robespierre along the strait and blood-stained path of "virtue" and "incorruptibility" as he understood them.

# chapter three

# THE REVOLUTIONARY AND NAPOLEONIC WARS, 1795–1815

**Introductory.** The French military recovery of the years 1793–1795 had thrown the allied powers into confusion and uncertainty. The years 1795–1815 see the extension of French power over the whole of Europe. The internal difficulties of the Directory and the very uneven military achievements of 1796–1799 open the way to the seizure of power by Bonaparte who, by 1807, consolidates French power in Europe by the defeat of Austria, Russia and Prussia and the parcelling out among the talented members of his own family of a number of important territories. The economic war reaches new intensity after 1806 through the efforts of Napoleon to strangle British trade by the Continental System. Napoleon also carries out important internal reforms in France itself which have left a permanent mark on French law and institutions. The year 1808 sees the opening of the British campaign in Portugal and Spain under the command of Wellesley, but the full effect of this is not seen till Russia begins to break away from the Napoleonic system. In 1812 comes the disaster of Napoleon's Moscow campaign and the re-entry of Prussia and Austria into the war. The new force of nationalism, supported by the monetary, naval and military power of Britain, brings about the downfall of Napoleon.

**The Directory.** After the death of Robespierre the policy of the Terror was abandoned. The Commune and other organisations created by the Jacobins were abolished. The Jacobins made attempts to regain control, but, after a period of confusion, the Convention succeeded in closing down the Jacobin Club itself.

The Convention now produced another constitution for France. It determined to uphold a republican form of government, but one which was less under the influence of the populace of Paris. To promote this object the idea of universal suffrage was abandoned and the vote in elections was confined to tax-payers. France was to be governed by two bodies, the Council of Elders, consisting of 250 members over forty-five years of age, and the Council of Five Hundred, consisting of men of thirty years of age or over. The Council of Five Hundred could alone propose laws, but it was necessary for these proposals to be accepted by the Council of Elders. The actual day-to-day government was to be carried on by a Directory of five persons, one retiring each year, his successor being appointed by the Legislature. This system was an attempt to apply the lessons of recent experience, to have a check upon the power of the Council of Five Hundred and, by the system of yearly retirement, to prevent the possibility of a dictatorship being established by the Directory. The restriction of the vote to tax-payers was to insure against mob rule and to place elective power squarely in the hands of those possessing property.

However, the Convention was distrustful of certain groups in Paris and elsewhere who favoured a restoration of the monarchy. The defeat of Robespierre and the relaxation of the censorship and Terror had encouraged these groups of royalists to come into the open. To avoid the possibility of the royalists gaining substantial support in the elections, the Convention declared that two-thirds of the Council of Elders and Five Hundred should be chosen from members of the Convention itself. In opposition to this the royalists and Jacobins

FIG. 8.—"THE WHIFF OF GRAPESHOT".

organised an insurrection against the Convention. On October 5 (13th Vendémiaire, Revolutionary Calendar) the insurrectionists began to march on the Tuileries Palace in which the Convention was sitting. When they arrived before the building they found it surrounded by cannon. An order to fire upon the demonstrators was given and the crowd was dispersed. The episode became famous as "the Whiff of Grapeshot", and the man who had given the order to fire was a young artillery officer, Napoleon Bonaparte.

**Babeuf's Conspiracy.** The next most serious internal opposition which the Directory had to face was that organised by François Babeuf. He was the leading member of one of the numerous societies to which the Revolution had given rise, the "Society of Equals". Babeuf's doctrines were the first organised expression of socialist or communist thought in these years. He aimed at the abolition of private property and the nationalisation of all land. Naturally, his ideas were not to the liking of the merchant class and the new propertied class created by the sale of church lands, but he had a considerable following among the poorest classes of Paris and other towns. The conspirators decided to attempt the seizure of power, and the preliminary to a rising of the masses was to be the murder of the Directors. However, the plot was betrayed and Babeuf and several of his leading supporters went to the guillotine. Despite this fiasco, the ideas of Babeuf were to be revived and developed in the nineteenth century in the doctrines and activities of socialism and communism.

**The Directory and the War.** In the two years 1793–1795 victory had gone everywhere to the French armies. The heroic work of Carnot, "the organiser of victory", had turned the scales against the invading armies. Carnot had raised great armies, newly equipped and trained. The efforts of the French people had been prodigious. In Paris itself hundreds of forges had been set up in the open spaces of the city to produce the weapons of war. New generals had been promoted from the ranks as the unsuccessful were guillotined. New military tactics were developed which were effective against the standardised methods of the leaders of the old European armies. Another factor which had greatly assisted the French was the disunity among the allies of the First Coalition. Austria and Prussia were more concerned with their own territorial aims than with the restoration of the monarchy in France, while Catherine II's known ambitions against Poland also caused them to fear that she would take advantage of their involvement in the war against France. When the Directory was formed in 1795 Prussia, Spain and Holland had all been forced to make peace with France, but Austria, the German states, England and the north Italian state of Piedmont still remained in the war against her.

The Directory decided to launch its main campaign against the Austrian Empire and to force the Austrians to accept the French conquest of the Austrian Netherlands (Belgium). Two great thrusts were planned by Carnot, one north of the Alps into southern Germany and the other into northern Italy. After that, England would be dealt with. The command of the armies of Germany was given to Generals Jourdan and Moreau, that of Italy to General Bonaparte.

**Napoleon Bonaparte.** The rise of Bonaparte to fame and power is one of the most astonishing in history. He was born at Ajaccio in the island of Corsica in 1769, one of a family of thirteen of whom eight survived childhood. The island had recently been acquired from the republic of Genoa by France. Napoleon was sent to the military academies of Brienne and Paris. Placed among cadets from wealthy families, he had felt his social inferiority keenly, especially as he considered his own abilities to be far greater than those of his comrades. In these circumstances, he was intensely unhappy. He was studious, aloof, and scornful of those around him—attitudes which only served to increase his unpopularity. Above all, he remained a Corsican and dreamt of a Corsican rising against France. Returning to Paris in 1792 from Corsica he had been dismissed the service for having overstayed his leave. His aim became now to secure reinstatement. He dabbled in the Revolution, read revolutionary literature and was sufficiently close to Robespierre to be imprisoned for a time after the latter's downfall. Owing to the extreme scarcity of good artillery officers, he at last regained his place in the army, and in 1793 had played the leading part in the defeat of a royalist rising at the port of Toulon, which was being aided by the English fleet. Then in 1795 he had saved the Convention from another royalist insurrection (see page 50). Soon after this, he forwarded to the Directors detailed plans of campaign against Austria. Carnot recognised the force of Bonaparte's ideas and secured him the command of the army of Italy. The young Corsican had also at this time married the beautiful Josephine de Beauharnais, a mistress of the principal Director, Barras.

**The Italian Campaign.** The army of which Bonaparte assumed the command in March, 1796, had been carrying on minor and ineffective campaigns on the Italian frontier but was now idle and

H.M.E.—E

demoralised. Even the officers were without sufficient clothing and the soldiers were in rags. Bonaparte, only twenty-seven years of age, was in command of old campaigners—generals far senior to himself who received him at his headquarters at Nice with open hostility. All these difficulties his organising genius quickly overcame, while his communiqués to his troops promised "honour, glory and wealth" to an army which had been almost idle for three years.

In April, 1796, the army of Italy began its campaign. Bonaparte's forces numbered about half those at the command of the Austrians and Piedmontese. Bonaparte by skilful manœuvre turned his attack chiefly upon the Piedmontese who quickly sued for an armistice at Cherasco (April, 1796). Bonaparte now carried forward the campaign against Austria. At the battle of Lodi, May, 1796, when Bonaparte himself rushed at the head of his troops across a bridge raked by Austrian fire, he gained another decisive victory and entered Milan, the Austrian headquarters. A large part of the Italian population hailed the French as their deliverers from the Austrian tyranny, for Bonaparte had not failed to use the revolutionary propaganda of liberty which he really despised. The main Austrian armies now fell back upon the fortress city of Mantua, which they held for several months. But Bonaparte defeated the main force sent to relieve Mantua at the Battle of Rivoli, January, 1797, and the city surrendered. Bonaparte now marched his army towards Vienna, but at Leoben, one hundred miles from the Austrian capital, the Austrians sued for peace, April, 1797.

**Importance of the Italian Campaign.** The Italian campaign was typical of the military brilliance of Bonaparte. It was now that he displayed all the infectious enthusiasm, the organising ability, the personal courage and dash which were to rank him with the great conquerors of history. He had adopted the method of out-marching and out-manœuvring the enemy and then attacking him at his weakest spot. The Austrians, while by no means poor soldiers, were far too restricted by the traditional tactics and lack of imagination of their leaders to be able to meet this situation. Bonaparte had, above all, gained immense prestige with his troops and had done the work intended for Jourdan and Moreau in Germany. Single-handed, with an army which had been little more than a rabble when he took command of it, he had brought down in defeat the great Austrian Empire.

In other ways, too, the Italian campaign was the overture to his career. Under the instructions of Carnot and the Directory, he systematically looted works of art from the great Italian galleries and private houses. Numerous masterpieces of painting and sculpture were sent to adorn the museum of the Louvre. In 1797 he conquered Venice, and the famous bronze horses of the cathedral were removed to Paris where they remained until Napoleon's final defeat eighteen years later. He also adopted the principle of making the conquered states pay huge indemnities in order to cover the costs of his campaigns and to replenish the French exchequer. For example, the Duke of Modena was forced to pay 10,000,000 francs. It also became the practice of the French armies to live on the countries they invaded.

While negotiations were proceeding with the Austrians, Napoleon lived in regal state at the villa of Montebello near Milan. Here his relatives, ambassadors, artists, scientists, philosophers crowded to pay court to the brilliant young general who could talk about everything and who was already expressing his contempt for the "lawyers" of the Directory.

**The Treaty of Campo Formio, October, 1797.** By the final treaty signed at Campo Formio, Austria gave up all claims to Belgium. France also gained control of the left bank of the Rhine. Both agreements were valuable strategic and territorial gains for France. Austria gave up her claims to Lombardy and recognised the new Cisalpine Republic which Bonaparte created out of the northern Italian states. In this latter connection Bonaparte compensated the Austrians by a most unscrupulous arrangement, for he handed over to them the ancient and independent state of Venice. The Venetian deal completely ignored the instructions of the Directory. To Bonaparte the rights of small nations and the principles of liberty expressed by the Revolution meant nothing, although he regularly employed revolutionary-sounding propaganda. Bonaparte also seized the Venetian navy and added it to French naval forces in the Mediterranean.

**The Egyptian Campaign.** Bonaparte now returned to Paris, where he kept quietly in the background except on the occasion of a special ceremony for himself and his victorious generals of the Italian campaign. By order of the Department of Paris, the street in which Bonaparte was living was renamed Rue de la Victoire in celebration of the peace of Campo Formio. Nevertheless, Bonaparte held aloof from politics, for he realised the growing unpopularity of the Directory at home. Moreover, the Directors were anxious to rid themselves of two dangers: Great Britain, who now alone remained in the fight, and—Bonaparte himself. The popularity of the young general in Paris was causing the Directory daily alarm and misgiving.

So Bonaparte was offered the command of an army for the invasion of Egypt. This offer he accepted with alacrity, for everything connected with the East dazzled his imagination. He saw the possibility of a French dominion in the Middle East and the reconquest of India. Here was his opportunity to repeat the exploits of one of the outstanding heroes of history, Alexander the Great. Again, to cut England's trade routes with India was, to the Directory and to Bonaparte, a surer way of bringing England to her knees than the alternative plan for the invasion of England which had been considered.

In May, 1798, Bonaparte set sail from Toulon with an army of 38,000 men. He was accompanied by a group of young generals of whom the most distinguished was Murat. Also with him were a hundred scholars and scientists who were to make a detailed study of the land of the ancient Pharaohs. Bonaparte's adventure began well. On the way he captured the island of Malta from the Knights of St. John and succeeded in eluding Nelson's fleet. On landing in Egypt he seized Alexandria and then marched his army in appalling conditions of heat and thirst (the Arabs had filled the drinking wells with stones) towards Cairo where he defeated the ruling caste of Egypt, the Mamelukes, at the Battle of the Pyramids. But soon afterwards the news reached him that Nelson had attacked and destroyed the French Fleet in the bay of Aboukir off Alexandria on August 1, thus isolating Bonaparte's forces in Egypt.

Bonaparte now determined to strike out against the Sultan of Turkey and attempt to re-enter Europe by land. He marched his forces into Syria. At Acre, on the coast, he suffered his first serious reverse, for he was unable to capture the town which was constantly reprovisioned by the English fleet which had complete command of the eastern Mediterranean. He dared not continue his march and leave Acre untaken. He was forced to return to Egypt where he defeated a Turkish army which had landed there in his absence. But now news reached him of difficulties at home. The Second Coalition had been formed against France and the Italian gains of Campo Formio had been lost to Austrian and Russian Armies. The Directory's position was weak. Now was the time for him to move, for even his abortive Egyptian campaign was a success compared with the dismal failures of the Directory. Leaving General Kléber in command of the forces now marooned in Egypt, he left secretly in a frigate with a few companions, managed to elude Nelson's patrols, and landed at Fréjus in the south of France.

**The Coup d'État of 18 Brumaire (November 9, 1799).** Bonaparte found a state of disorder and discontent reigning in France. In half the departments brigandage was rife, and a new revolt had broken out in Brittany against the government. The finances of the government were falling into ruin through the depreciation of the currency. The financial position of the country was little better than it had been in 1789. The Second Coalition of Austria, Russia and England had succeeded in driving the French from Italy and Switzerland and from the German states back to the Rhine frontier. In these circumstances the position seemed propitious for the rise to power of the brilliant victor of the Italian campaign of three years previous. Bonaparte decided to intervene directly in politics.

Accordingly, he made contacts with those groups of politicians opposed to the Directory. His principal supporters were the Abbé Siéyès and his own brother Lucien Bonaparte. Siéyès, the great expert in constitutions, wished to use Bonaparte as the means of bringing about the "perfect constitution" for France. Lucien Bonaparte held the vitally important position of President of the Council of Five Hundred. A majority of the Council of Elders also supported the conspiracy. The rumour was now put about that a serious plot existed against the Republic, and the Council of Elders proposed that Bonaparte be given command of the troops in Paris in order to "protect" the Directory. But the Council of Five Hundred violently opposed Bonaparte when he appeared to address them. He was shouted down and physically attacked by some of the members and had to be carried half-fainting from the hall. At this juncture his whole future was at stake. He was saved from utter defeat by his brother Lucien who, seizing a sword and swearing to "pierce the heart of his own brother if ever he should attack the liberty of Frenchmen", persuaded the soldiers to invade the assembly and drive the members out.

This was the famous Coup d'État of Brumaire, ostensibly undertaken to protect the Republic. The members of the Council of Elders and Five Hundred who supported Bonaparte now abolished the Directory and set up a special committee to work out a new constitution for France.

**The Consulate.** Bonaparte dominated the constitutional committee from the first. He poured scorn on the elaborate and pretentious schemes proposed by Siéyès. The final scheme placed almost supreme power in his own hands. Three Consuls (a name harking back to the days of Republican Rome) were to be appointed, of whom the most important was the First Consul—Bonaparte himself. The First Consul appointed all the chief officials of the State, both military and civil, and he had the right to make war and peace. The First Consul alone was to propose laws, which were to be drafted by a special Council of State and then to be submitted to the Legislative Body which was to vote without discussion. The Tribunate was a special assembly which could discuss the proposed laws without voting. A vote by the people for members of the Legislative Body gave an appearance of democracy, but this was little more than a sham, for the voting was on lists of candidates already prepared by the government. The only real check on the First Consul was the limit of ten years placed upon his holding of the office.

Bonaparte now proceeded to change the system of local government set up by the Revolution. He himself appointed the local officials, who thus became completely the servants of the central government, of Bonaparte himself. He appointed prefects of the departments, sub-prefects of the arrondissements and mayors of the communes. Thus all government was centralised in Paris under the direct control of the First Consul.

**Defeat of the Second Coalition.** Bonaparte now turned his attention to the serious military situation. Of the three members of the Second Coalition—England, Russia and Austria—the last was, in the geographical sense, the easiest to attack. Above all, Bonaparte determined to retrieve the position in Germany and northern Italy. For this purpose he planned and accomplished one of the truly astonishing military feats of the age. With 40,000 men he crossed the Great St. Bernard Pass and thus placed his troops between the Austrian armies and Austria itself. At the Battle of Marengo, June 14, 1800, the French, after some early reverses, defeated the main Austrian army, and forced the Empire to sign an armistice. In Germany, General Moreau was equally successful and decisively defeated the Austrians at Hohenlinden, December 3, 1800. By the Treaty of Lunéville, 1801, France regained all the territories she had secured by the Treaty of Campo Formio. The Russians had retired from the Coalition—their great general Suvorov, who had defeated the French armies in northern Italy and Switzerland in 1799, blamed the defeats of 1800 on the lack of adequate support for his armies from the Austrians. The very jealousies and mutual suspicions of the two great powers had once again played their part in the defeat of the Coalition.

Britain now remained alone against France. The idea of invading England had been abandoned by the Directory just before the Egyptian campaign, and it was Bonaparte himself who had advised this abandonment. Since the Revolution the French navy had been much inferior in discipline and numbers to that of England. The revolutionary doctrines of liberty, fraternity and equality greatly reduced the rigid discipline on which victory at sea in these years depended. However, the Directory had attempted to use the fleets of other nations who were allied to France. In 1797 the Directory succeeded in bringing Spain into the war on their side, but in February 1797 the British fleet under Jervis and Nelson inflicted a severe defeat on the Spanish at the battle of Cape St. Vincent. Next, the Directory seized the Dutch fleet, but this also was defeated by Admiral Duncan at Camperdown, off the Texel River, in October, 1797—despite the fact that there had been severe mutinies in the English fleet at Spithead and the Nore. Another of the Directory's plans was to assist the rebellion of Wolfe Tone in Ireland, but, although a French army under General Hoche reached Bantry Bay, it was unable to land, and on the return journey was almost wiped out by storms and attacks by British vessels.

The naval superiority of Britain enabled her to capture important overseas territories such as Cape Town, Malacca, Ceylon and Amboyna from the Dutch in 1796, the French West Indian island of St. Lucia and the Spanish island of Trinidad in the same year.

After his defeat of the Second Coalition in northern Italy, Bonaparte decided on another approach to the problem of defeating Britain. His aim now became to hinder as much as possible the overseas trade of Britain on which a good deal of her power depended. For this purpose he was able to exploit the annoyance which other countries felt at the activities of the British navy. Britain was attempting to prevent all neutral vessels trading with France whether they were carrying contraband of war or not. Bonaparte now persuaded the Czar Paul I of Russia to form the League of Armed Neutrality with those commercial states who had been particularly offended by British policy, namely, Sweden, Denmark and Prussia. Denmark and Sweden succeeded in closing the entrance to the Baltic by their control of the narrow straits of the Kattegat. Britain thereupon sent a naval force against Denmark, and at the battle of Copenhagen (or the Baltic), April, 1801, the British fleet under Sir Hyde Parker, with Nelson second in

command, destroyed the Danish fleet. Soon afterwards the League
of Armed Neutrality collapsed after the murder of the Czar Paul I
(see page 236).

**The Peace of Amiens, 1802.** England once again remained the
only power fighting against Napoleon, but the war was causing great
distress due to trading difficulties. There was a considerable body of
opinion in favour of peace with France. Bonaparte also viewed the
possibility of a period of peace as favourable to him, for it would
enable him to consolidate his position in France itself. Addington
now replaced Pitt as Prime Minister and negotiations for peace
began. By the Treaty of Amiens, 1802, England restored the French
colonies she had captured, but retained Ceylon and Trinidad.
England promised to evacuate Malta (which she had captured from
the French) and Egypt, where the French army had been forced to
capitulate to an English army under General Abercrombie. England
recognised the boundaries of the French Republic as they existed
in 1802.

**Napoleon's Reorganisation of France.** There were two bases to
Bonaparte's system of government in France: firstly, his belief in his
destiny and in his right to rule absolutely and, secondly, the "career
open to talent". He promoted many men to high offices in the State
on ability alone, whatever their origins. By this means the new forces
liberated by the Revolution were now used for the promotion of
Bonaparte's ideas. Many of his generals were men of quite lowly
birth—Murat, for example, was the son of an innkeeper. The
principle of the "career open to talent" undoubtedly accounts for
much of the strength of France at this time.

**The Concordat.** Bonaparte's policy was now to put an end to the
party strife which had been the lot of France since 1789. All who
were willing to support him were welcomed, whatever their past, but
his opponents were ruthlessly suppressed. The laws against the
"émigrés" were slowly relaxed and all except unrepentant royalists
were allowed to return to France. He also determined to reach
agreement with the Church and thus heal the breach with the Pope
and priesthood caused by the Civil Constitution of the Clergy (see
page 31). Bonaparte saw the Church in a purely political light as a
valuable and essential support to his power. He fully realised that
behind the Church stood the vast majority of the peasantry of France,
without whose loyalty his own power could not be maintained.
Moreover, he had been alarmed by further risings of the peasantry
against the government in the western regions of France—outbreaks

encouraged by a discontented clergy. The Catholic Church was quite prepared to accept his advances, and in 1801 he made his famous agreement, or Concordat, with the Pope. The Catholic religion was recognised as that of "the great majority of the French people". The Church was allowed to conduct its own affairs as it pleased. In return the Pope recognised the sale of the Church lands, and this was a part of the agreement which naturally pleased the peasantry who had purchased their land after the Revolution. Bishops were to be appointed by the First Consul, but their investiture was to be carried out by the Pope. The bishops were to appoint the parish clergy with the approval of the government. Bishops and priests were to be paid by the state. The Concordat, by bringing together Church and State, greatly strengthened Bonaparte's position. Another very important consideration for Bonaparte related to his government of the conquered states in Europe and his own dream of establishing a great French Empire by which he would become the modern Charlemagne. With the friendship of the Pope of Rome he hoped to have the alliance of the Catholic Church wherever his power extended.

**The Code Napoleon.** The work of which Napoleon was afterwards most proud was the Code Napoleon. This was a clear and definite statement of the laws of France as they affected every citizen. Since 1789 the law had been in a constant state of confusion, but on the urgent demand and with the active assistance of Bonaparte himself, a specially appointed committee of lawyers completed the immense task of codifying the law. No French subject need now have any doubt as to his position before the law—the rules were uniform and equal for all. The Code aimed at strengthening the family as the foundation of the State. To do this, the authority of the father was greatly increased, sons being unable to marry under twenty-five years of age without the father's consent and daughters under twenty-one. The wife's position was also made inferior to that of the husband in the family. (Napoleon, in his private correspondence, indicated that he thought women's brain power far inferior to that of men and that they were fitted for little more education than that involved in needlework.) It will be noted that these changes were totally against the ideas of the Revolution which had raised women in all matters much nearer to equality with men. On the other hand, the Code preserved a number of important changes brought about by the Revolution—equality of all classes before the law, toleration of all religions, and trial in public by the jury system.

Other important changes brought about by Bonaparte at this time were connected with education, industry and commerce. In education he set up the "lycées", which were schools entirely controlled by the government. These schools, while aiming at improved scientific education, also aimed at producing citizens who were absolutely (and uncritically) loyal to the State and devoted to the military idea. The lessons began and ended with the roll of drums. He established many technical schools with the object of improving French industrial processes and discovering new ones. The University of France was also founded, with its branches in numerous districts. In industry he increased production by high tariffs on imports and by encouraging new inventions. Roads, canals and ports were greatly improved and aided the expansion of industry. He also pleased the business interests by stabilising the value of the French currency on a gold basis and by setting up the Bank of France to aid industrial development.

Finally, he instituted the decoration known as the Legion of Honour for distinguished services to the State, for he believed as strongly as the former kings of France in the power of ceremonies, forms and symbols. "Men", he said, "are led by toys."

All this centralised legislation helped to please many interests and strengthen Bonaparte's position. Despite this, however, there was a serious Jacobin plot against Bonaparte and he only narrowly escaped assassination in 1801, before he secured, in 1802, the position of First Consul for life and the right to name his successor. A royalist plot directed from London by the Comte d'Artois, brother of Louis XVI, was unearthed in 1804 and the conspirators executed. Bonaparte's reorganised police system succeeded in crushing the last opposition to him. Finally, in 1804, he was proclaimed Emperor, and the decision was overwhelmingly supported by a plebiscite. At the crowning ceremony in the Cathedral of Notre Dame Napoleon seized the crown from the Pope's hands and placed it on his own head and then crowned the Empress Josephine, the Pope anointing them with the holy oil. Thus, sanctified by the Pope and approved by the people, the Empire which was to produce eleven years of war and ultimate disaster for France was established. All the pomp and ceremony of Empire was now organised and Napoleon's Court became as much the centre of things as the royal court before 1789.

**Renewal of the War.** The Peace of Amiens proved only an uneasy breathing-space before the renewal of the war in all its old intensity. England had hoped to be able to trade with France more freely, but in fact Napoleon set up a severe tariff system. The French also continued to send spies and agents to Egypt. England, alarmed by these developments, refused to evacuate Malta. Moreover, England had never recognised the French occupation of the Austrian Netherlands. Her traditional policy was to keep the Belgian coastline clear of a potential enemy. Thus there was no lessening of mutual suspicions and intrigues, and, after various provocations on both sides, the war broke out again in May, 1803.

**Trafalgar.** Napoleon now made his first aim the defeat of England. He immediately seized control of Hanover in northern Germany, a state still belonging to the English crown. He declared the whole European coastline from the Baltic round to the Mediterranean closed to English trade. A great military camp of 180,000 men was set up near the coast at Boulogne and a huge fleet of flat-bottomed boats was prepared for the invasion of England. But before this scheme could be carried out it was essential to gain control of the Channel for a sufficient time to enable the troops to pass over unmolested by the British fleet. With this in view, Napoleon ordered the French fleet to break through the blockade which the British had established at the ports of Brest and Ferrol and to join the Spanish fleet (Spain having made an alliance with Napoleon). They were then to move across the Atlantic to the West Indies, draw the English fleet after them and slip back unobserved to gain control of the Channel for the invasion project. Villeneuve, the French admiral, did, in fact, succeed in drawing Nelson after him and then sailed back to Europe. But Nelson realised the manœuvre just in time and succeeded in warning the British Admiralty by means of a fast vessel sent ahead of the main English fleet. Villeneuve, knowing that he had not gained the time needed for the· project, put in at Cadiz. Napoleon finally ordered Villeneuve to come out with his fleet and, reluctantly, he emerged on October 21, 1805, with thirty-three ships against Nelson and Collingwood's twenty-seven. By the brilliant manœuvre of breaking the line, Nelson, although killed in the hour of victory, completely smashed the combined French and Spanish Fleets off Cape Trafalgar. England was thus saved from invasion and was henceforth in almost undisputed control of the seas.

**The Third Coalition.** On the renewal of the war Pitt had again become Prime Minister and he succeeded in forming the Third Coalition of England, Austria and Russia. The object of the alliance was to drive the French back to their original boundaries—out of Belgium, the German states and Italy. The Czar of Russia,

Alexander I, was alarmed by Napoleon's ambitions in the Middle East and against Turkey. Russia above all wanted to be free to deal alone with Turkey and the Balkan Peninsula. The Austrians wanted to regain their controlling position in Italy and wipe out the defeats of 1796 and 1800.

Even before Trafalgar, Napoleon, despairing of any real success by Villeneuve, broke up his camp at Boulogne and carried out another brilliant campaign against the Austrians and Russians. He marched across Europe, a distance of five hundred miles, in twenty-three days, got behind the Austrian armies and approached them from the east. The Austrian commander Mack was completely out-manœuvred and defeated at the Battle of Ulm, October, 1805. In this part of the campaign Napoleon took 33,000 prisoners, including 30 Generals. He himself had lost 1,500 men. He next moved along the Danube to Vienna, which he occupied unopposed. The Emperor had retired his forces in order to join with the Russians. At Auster-litz, December 2, 1805, the French defeated the combined Austrian and Russian armies.

At sea, the Coalition had the advantage with Trafalgar, but on land once again decisive victory had gone to Napoleon. The news of Austerlitz was really the final blow to Pitt, who was already ill. He died soon after receiving news of Napoleon's victory.

By the Treaty of Pressburg, December, 1805, Austria lost 3,000,000 of her foreign population, and Venetia was now incorporated in Napoleon's Kingdom of Italy. Austria also had to cede to France important territories along the Adriatic coast, Istria and Dalmatia.

**Napoleon's Dynastic Policy.** The results of the Battle of Aus-terlitz were greatly to increase Napoleon's power in Germany. Arrangements which he had already begun to make before the campaign were now hurried forward. The free cities and the purely church or ecclesiastical states along the Rhine were handed over to those princes prepared to support him. The rulers of the German states who thus gained territory as a reward from Napoleon now renounced their allegiance to the Holy Roman Emperor, Francis II of Austria, and formed themselves into a grouping of states known as the Confederation of the Rhine, pledged to support Napoleon with their armies. Napoleon then forced Francis II to abandon his title of Holy Roman Emperor.

Napoleon had the great problem to face of consolidating his power, for his dominions now extended over a wider area in Europe than ever before. For this purpose he made good use of his own family. His sisters were married into Italian princely families, Marshal Murat was given a German Dukedom, Napoleon's brother Joseph was made King of Naples and Louis Bonaparte King of Holland.

At this point the Prussians, who had been neutral between 1795 and 1806, entered the war against Napoleon. Frederick William III had been under pressure for some time from his own subjects to take up arms again, for the Prussian seizure of Hanover ordered by Napoleon had resulted in the closing of her ports to British trade and great losses to the commercial and trading classes of Prussia. However, Prussian entry into the war was too late and resulted in complete disaster for her arms. She was defeated by Napoleon at the Battle of Jena, October, 1806, and his decisive victory over the Russians was at Friedland, June, 1807.

**The Treaty of Tilsit, July, 1807.** The Czar Alexander decided to sue for peace, and the two emperors met at Tilsit on a raft in the middle of the River Niemen. During the interview Napoleon showed every desire to flatter and please the Czar. By the Treaty of Tilsit they reached agreement on their respective "spheres of influence". Alexander was told that Napoleon would not oppose his seizure of Finland from Sweden and he was free to pursue his own policy in the Balkan Peninsula. Above all, Alexander was attracted by Napoleon's promise that he would receive his due share in the Turkish Empire when that Empire came to be divided among the victors. Alexander recognised Napoleon's control of Europe and promised that if England refused to make peace he would enter Napoleon's Continental System against her.

**The Continental System.** The greatest problem now left to Napoleon was Great Britain. The war from now on between these two great powers becomes of more decisive importance than ever before. It intensifies and takes on new forms. The Battle of Trafalgar had made a French invasion of Britain impossible. England's wealth, due to the Industrial Revolution and an expanding world trade, was always sufficient to enable her to supply the members of the various coalitions with the necessary funds for the continuance of the war, and Napoleon realised that further efforts would certainly be made by Britain to form coalitions against him. It was the economic power of Britain which was the real source of danger to Napoleon, and he therefore decided to strike at it. He aimed at ruining Britain's overseas trade, and thus bringing about such unemployment, financial chaos and general suffering in England that the people would force the government to make peace. He therefore issued the Berlin Decrees, November, 1806. He declared a blockade of the British Isles and forbade any of France's allies to trade with Britain or her colonies and announced the immediate confiscation of all British goods on the continent. The British Government replied by the Orders in Council, 1807, which declared a blockade of all continental ports accepting Napoleon's decrees—in other words, England would prevent, by naval action, any other countries trading with those countries accepting the Berlin Decrees. In December, 1807, Napoleon added to his system by the Milan Decrees, while the British Government issued further Orders in Council. The economic war between Britain and France continued with increasing violence.

**Results of the Continental System.** During the years 1807–1810 Napoleon made strenuous efforts to make his decrees effective. He attempted to seal off the whole of the European coastline. For this purpose he had to take increasingly drastic action. In 1807 Denmark was forced into the system and in 1810 French troops occupied the ports of North Germany, such as Hamburg, Bremen, Danzig and Lubeck. When Louis Bonaparte refused to ruin the Dutch merchants by accepting the decrees, Napoleon deposed his brother and put Holland directly under French control. His policy also led to conflict with the Pope who wished to remain neutral, which would have meant that British trade could be carried on through the Papal States. To prevent this, Napoleon imprisoned the Pope and added the Papal States to the Kingdom of Italy.

The ultimate results of this policy were extremely bad for Europe. Trade declined and unemployment spread widely, especially in northern Germany. Napoleon's policy led to the hardening of opposition to him on the part of the merchant class of Europe, and it was this middle class which played a great part in the new nationalist movements which developed against Napoleon and helped to bring about his downfall. Again, France did not possess the naval power to reply effectively to Britain's counter-blockade. Napoleon had planned to use the Danish Fleet for this purpose, but in 1807 it was attacked and destroyed by the British fleet in the harbour of Copenhagen before Napoleon could carry out his project. The English traders also smuggled goods into Europe through unprotected spots in the immense coastline, such as Heligoland, Portugal, Sicily and Salonica.

**The Peninsular War.** One part of the European coastline over which Napoleon had no control was that of the Kingdom of

Portugal. Great Britian had a long-standing treaty of commerce with Portugal, which was therefore a clear challenge to Napoleon's Continental System. When Portugal refused to apply the Berlin Decrees, a French and Spanish army invaded the country in 1808 and the royal family fled to Brazil. Napoleon also decided to gain complete control of Spain. The King of Spain, Charles IV, and his Queen were both extremely unpopular and were openly opposed by their son and heir Ferdinand, who was as popular as his parents were unpopular. Napoleon persuaded them all to attend a conference at Bayonne where he bullied the King and Queen into abdicating and imprisoned Ferdinand and his brothers. Napoleon followed up this unscrupulous trick by creating his own brother Joseph King of Spain, while Marshal Murat took the place of Joseph as King of Naples.

Despite Napoleon's offer of better government to the Spaniards, the national opposition to him was intense. He was hated as a foreigner, a trickster, and, above all, as a persecutor of the Pope, whom he had imprisoned. He gravely miscalculated the whole business, as he himself later confessed. He even thought that he could conquer Spain with only 30,000 men, but in fact over 300,000 were permanently tied down there. A national guerrilla movement developed which harassed his supply lines, and this movement had the direct assistance of the priesthood. Then in 1808 a totally new phase of the war began, for Britain intervened in the Peninsula.

Britain's intervention was greatly encouraged by certain significant events of the year 1808. At Baylen a French force of 20,000 men was forced to surrender to the Spanish guerrillas. Such a surrender had not occurred in the whole fifteen years in which French forces had been in the field. King Joseph left Madrid in a great hurry and withdrew towards the French frontier. These events were followed by the landing of Arthur Wellesley (later Duke of Wellington) near Lisbon, the Portuguese capital, with an English army which defeated General Junot who, by the Convention of Cintra, August, 1808, evacuated Portugal.

These defeats stirred Napoleon to take command himself of the French forces in Spain. With an army of 200,000 men he swept everything before him and entered Madrid at the end of 1808. An English force under Sir John Moore attacked Napoleon's lines of communication from the north in order to prevent him from moving towards Portugal. This diversion drew aside a large part of Napoleon's forces. Eventually this English army retreated towards Corunna where Moore himself was killed, but the embarkation of the English force was successful. The aim of the diversion had been achieved—it enabled Wellesley to complete his own preparations in Portugal unmolested. These preparations took the form of a deep defensive system known as the Lines of Torres Vedras constructed in an arc around Lisbon. Ahead of the defensive works the country was laid waste for thirty miles. The French forces found it impossible to penetrate the fortifications in a countryside which gave them no supplies whatever. From behind this system, the English forces, carried to Lisbon by the fleet, emerged for their campaigns in Spain and Portugal during the next six years.

**Austria Re-enters the War.** Austria had taken advantage of Napoleon's preoccupation with Spain to re-enter the war, April, 1809. Her armies had been reorganised and a new national militia created. The Austrian militia was designed to arouse a nationalist feeling in the country and to give all classes a share in the defence of the fatherland—it was a patriotic and popular addition to the standing army. Yet the Austrian entry into the war was impetuous. Russia was still Napoleon's ally, and English forces were not yet a decisive factor in the land war. The moment was not well chosen. Nevertheless, the Austrian forces fought well and with a new understanding of Napoleon's tactics. The old element of surprise was no longer as effective as it had been, and, under the fresh leadership of the Archduke Charles, brother of the Emperor, the Austrians came near to defeating the French and forced Napoleon to call for many more troops during the campaign. But this spirit of resistance was of no avail. The Austrians were decisively defeated at the Battle of Wagram, 1809. By the Treaty of Vienna which followed, Austria lost a large part of her share of Poland to Russia and provinces on the Adriatic to France. She was also compelled to enter the Continental System. Napoleon now attempted to make sure of future Austrian friendship and the raising of his prestige in Europe by asking in marriage the hand of the Archduchess Marie Louise, daughter of the Emperor. Napoleon had already secured a dissolution of his marriage with Josephine by a decree of the French Senate supported by the Church. She had borne him no heir and he wished to perpetuate the line of Bonaparte. The Emperor of Austria agreed to the proposed alliance.

**The Situation in 1810.** The year 1810 had seen what appeared to be a repetition of the old pattern—the defeat of all his opponents by Napoleon with the exception of Great Britain. Yet it was not the

Fig. 9.—Napoleon at the Battle of Wagram. (*See page 66.*)

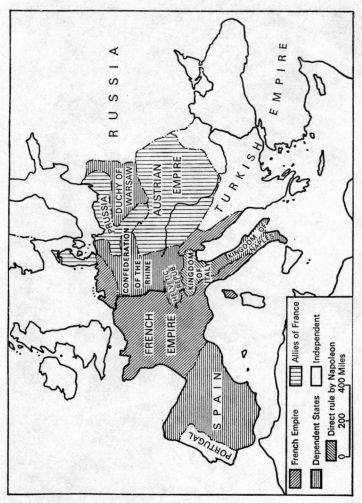

II.—NAPOLEONIC EUROPE, 1810.

French Empire

Dependent States

Allies of France

Independent

Direct rule by Napoleon

0    200    400 Miles

same situation as that of 1806 or 1800. We have noted the development of a new spirit of nationalism in Spain and in Austria. Moreover, England had succeeded in establishing a permanent military base in Portugal which could be supplied through her command of the sea. Then, again, the Continental System was arousing intense opposition to Napoleon from the merchant class of Europe, for everywhere French agents were busy confiscating illegal imports from Britain and punishing the offenders. In addition to this, Napoleon was drawing an increasing amount of his revenue from the taxation of the states under his control, a burden which fell heavily on the bourgeoisie of those states.

**Alexander and Napoleon.** Another factor now complicated the position for Napoleon. The Czar Alexander was no longer the eager ally he had been at Tilsit in 1807. He had gained Finland as well as territory in the Balkans and in Poland through his alliance with Napoleon. But the greatest prize, Constantinople, was still eluding him. It became increasingly obvious that Napoleon had no intention of breaking up the Turkish Empire for the benefit of Alexander. The Czar had certain personal grievances as well, for Napoleon had seized the north German state of Oldenburg, ruled by the Czar's brother-in-law, in order to enforce the Continental System. But even more decisive opposition was coming from the nobility of Russia, and particularly that section which had gained its wealth from the valuable trade with England in such products as timber and hemp. Their trade was being ruined, and the Czar's revenue was suffering. Between 1809 and 1811 the Russian evasions of the Continental System became more frequent and British products were being re-exported from Russia to many parts of Europe. Despite Napoleon's protests, this trade continued.

**Revival in Prussia.** The Prussians had many causes of grievance. The pride of a country which had boasted of the military prowess of Frederick the Great was humiliated by the limitation after Jena of her army to 40,000 men. French troops were in permanent occupation of the main Prussian ports and her traders were watched at every turn. This situation forced a change in the policy of the Prussian monarchy and government. They realised that a true national revival could only take place if all classes, and not merely the landed nobility and aristocracy, were roused to action. The two leading ministers of the government, Stein and Hardenberg, were responsible for important changes in Prussian society. Stein secured the abolition of serfdom and also introduced a system of elected councils for the towns by which the middle class as well as the land-owners had a voice in local government. Hardenberg was responsible for a new land distribution which greatly benefited the peasantry. The Minister of War, Scharnhorst, also introduced a trained militia which served one year with the colours and then passed into the reserve. In this way a trained reserve of over 120,000 men was in existence by 1811. All these changes were aided by the new propaganda for national independence, the centre of which became the newly-founded University of Berlin.

**The Moscow Campaign.** In 1811 the Czar of Russia broke away completely from the Continental System for the reasons we have already mentioned. Napoleon's reply was to organise one of the most gigantic military campaigns of history—and bring upon himself one of the greatest military disasters. With an army of 600,000 men, with contingents conscripted from the numerous European states under his control, he marched in the summer of 1812 into Russia. The Russian reply to his attack was a skilful use of the vast terrain and a gradual retreat before the Grand Army. With the object of bringing the war to a quick end Napoleon decided to take Moscow itself. Already his troops were suffering severely from disease and hunger, for the Russians had adopted a "scorched earth" policy on their retreat. Buildings, crops, livestock and whole villages were destroyed. The French moved through a country which was little more than a barren waste. The first great battle was fought at Borodino within thirty miles of Moscow, which the French won at the cost of enormous casualties. When Napoleon reached Moscow he found the city deserted by all but 15,000 of its 250,000 inhabitants. Soon afterwards fires broke out in the city and rapidly spread everywhere. Napoleon, from his headquarters in the Kremlin, which had been spared the fires, sent proposals of peace to Alexander, but no reply was received.

Napoleon was now isolated in the Russian capital seven hundred miles from the frontier of the River Niemen. He had entered Moscow on September 14 and remained there for a month hoping that Alexander would sue for peace. But at last he had to accept retreat. One of the most horrifying episodes in the history of warfare now ensued. All along the route of the retreating army the Russian attacks were continuous, both by the army under the command of General Kutusov and by guerrilla bands of the Cossacks. The French fought back with their usual discipline—especially the rear-guard under the command of Marshal Ney. But everything was against them. The preposterous over-optimism of Napoleon himself had led to many of the troops being only clothed for the summer in which the campaign had begun. Now the appalling rigours of the Russian winter descended upon them. Gradually despair and panic affected the French morale, and at the crossing of the River Beresina the most terrible scenes of all were witnessed. The bridges thrown across by the French engineers were raked with fire by the Russians, and thousands of Napoleon's troops died in the river. Even before the crossing of the Beresina the French cavalry, which at the beginning of the campaign had numbered 32,000, was then only 100 strong. When at last the River Niemen was reached not more than 20,000 men of the original 600,000 crossed the frontier. Napoleon himself had already left his army under the command of Murat and was travelling to Paris incognito. He had boasted that in the spring of 1813 he would be back at the Niemen with 300,000 men —a boast he was not destined to fulfil.

**The War of Liberation.** The disaster of the Moscow campaign was the signal for Prussia to take action. We have already seen how a new national spirit was developing in Prussia (see page 69) and many of the ideas of the French Revolution of 1789—liberty, brotherhood of all classes, national freedom—were now used even by the King of Prussia to arouse his people. Napoleon's own "ideological weapon" was at last turned against him! Prussia now made an alliance with Russia by the Treaty of Kalisch, February, 1813. England strengthened her alliance with Russia and called upon Austria to join with the other powers, but at this point Austria still held back.

**The Campaigns of 1813–1814.** By a colossal effort of organisation Napoleon raised another army of 300,000, although many of his troops were only partly trained and had to receive further training while on their march into Germany. For the first time soldiers as young as sixteen years of age were part of Napoleon's forces. Moreover, he had been unable to make good the losses of cavalry which he had suffered in Russia. Despite this, he succeeded in defeating the Prussians and Russians in the battles of Lutzen and Bautzen in May, 1813. But he was unable to follow up these victories. At this point the Emperor of Austria intervened with a proposal for an armistice—a proposal accepted by Napoleon as a means of gaining reinforcements and by the allies as a means of completing the coalition and fully preparing their forces. This armistice lasted six

III — Europe in 1815

## Map labels

RUSSIA

Moscow

Constantinople

OTTOMAN EMPIRE

CYPRUS

Acre

EGYPT

CRETE

NORWAY AND SWEDEN

Stockholm

DENMARK

Copenhagen

P R U S S I A

POLAND

Berlin

HANOVER

SAXONY

AUSTRIAN EMPIRE

BAVARIA

Vienna

AUSTRIA

Buda Pest

HUNGARY

SCOTLAND

IRELAND

WALES

ENGLAND

UNITED NETHER LANDS

SWITZ.

SAVOY

PIEDMONT

MILAN

GENOA

PAPAL STATES

TUSCANY

Rome

TWO SICILIES

MALTA

FRANCE

Paris

CORSICA

SARDINIA

MAJORCA

SPAIN

Madrid

PORTUGAL

Lisbon

Cape Finisterre

Boundary of the
German Confederation

0    200    400 Miles

weeks and was ultimately more to the advantage of the allies than to Napoleon.

During the armistice Austria joined England, Prussia and Russia, and the final stage of the war was now reached. At the battle of Dresden, August, 1813, Napoleon won his last great victory, defeating the Austrians. But his commanders in other parts of Germany had been defeated and once again he was unable to follow up his success. At Leipzig the "Battle of the Nations", involving 500,000 men, was fought on October 16–18, 1813. The allies included Austrians, Prussians, Russians and the Swedes under Bernadotte (who had deserted Napoleon for the allies). Napoleon was defeated and flung back over the Rhine. The Confederation of the Rhine which he had created in 1806 now turned against him. Wellington had entered Madrid, driven out King Joseph and was now crossing the Pyrenees into southern France. The allies followed up their victory and carried the war into France for the first time since 1793. Despite brilliant manœuvres by Napoleon in this phase of the struggle, the Czar Alexander and the King of Prussia entered Paris on March 31, 1814. Napoleon now capitulated, and was exiled by the allies to the island of Elba off the coast of Italy. He was allowed to retain his title of Emperor. France herself, by the First Treaty of Paris, 1814, lost all her conquests in Germany, Belgium and Italy, but even then had more favourable boundaries than she had had in 1790. Also the allies neither deprived her of the stolen works of art nor demanded money compensations for the destruction she had caused in Europe. This was, in the main, a generous treaty.

**Louis XVIII.** The brother of Louis XVI was now proclaimed by the French Senate King of France, taking the title of Louis XVIII. As one of the leading "émigrés" and a consistent opponent of Napoleon, he was acceptable to the allies. He granted a Constitutional Charter which established a parliamentary system of government and gave guarantees of liberty to the people, but surrounding him were many royalists who were determined to repudiate everything which the Revolution of 1789 had achieved. These advisers exercised a great influence with Louis XVIII and in a few months they succeeded in making him thoroughly unpopular. The King behaved unwisely in abolishing the tricolour flag, in putting Napoleon's officers on half-pay or retiring them altogether, in showering distinctions on returned nobles who had been fighting against France, and, above all, in permitting the nobles and clergy to demand the return of the lands which had gone to the peasantry. The offence given to the peasants was the most serious blunder of the opening months of the reign.

**The Hundred Days.** On the island of Elba, Napoleon had been granted considerable privileges and had been put under a very lax and ineffective supervision. He had received news of the state of France and also of the quarrels which had broken out among the allies at the Congress which was meeting at Vienna to decide the future of Europe. He succeeded in making his escape from the island and landing in the south of France. His journey to Paris was a triumphal procession. To all those who were dissatisfied with the government of Louis XVIII his return meant another great hope of revival. The forces sent by Louis XVIII to take him prisoner simply went over to him and Louis XVIII fled. Within three weeks of regaining power, Napoleon had a new army prepared to march into Belgium against the forces of Wellington and the Prussians. His object was to strike at them before they could be supported by the Austrians and Russians. The statesmen meeting at Vienna had already suspended their quarrels and intrigues and had once again banded together against Napoleon.

On June 18, 1815, was fought the battle which ended the career of Napoleon and brought to its conclusion the long period of war which had begun in 1793. At Waterloo the Napoleonic Empire finally crumbled. The battle, fought twelve miles south of Brussels, continued during the whole day, the French foot and cavalry making constant but unavailing attacks on the English lines. Wellington was relying for final victory on the arrival of the Prussians under General Blücher, and late in the afternoon they appeared on the battlefield at the moment when Napoleon had ordered the Imperial Guard to launch itself against the English positions. This attack was already being repelled when the Prussians entered the battle. From that moment it became a rout of the French forces, and Napoleon fled to Paris, where he found the parliament unwilling to give him further support. Finally, he surrendered to the captain of a British warship, H.M.S. *Bellerophon*, and was sent to his second exile on the island of St. Helena in the south Atlantic, where he busied himself with writing his memoirs and giving his own version of his triumphs and ultimate defeat. He died in the year 1821.

**Summary of the Main Reasons for the Fall of Napoleon.** It is not possible to deal with every factor leading to Napoleon's defeat but the main causes are reasonably clear. Firstly, Napoleon never possessed adequate naval power. After Trafalgar, the British navy, which had held the superiority for many years before, was almost unchallenged. The possibility of the invasion of Britain was thus removed. Secondly, without adequate naval power Napoleon's Continental System had many loopholes. Thirdly, the Continental System became a far greater burden to the countries under Napoleon's control than to Britain, whose natural resources enabled her wealth and power to increase by leaps and bounds during these years, despite her considerable losses to privateers, and the numerous bankruptcies this caused. Again, Britain's increased grain production was sufficient to ward off any threat of starvation. We must also remember that Napoleon's disastrous Moscow campaign of 1812 had its origins in the Czar Alexander's refusal to continue his support of the Continental System. Fourthly, in his attempt to control the whole coastline of Europe Napoleon attacked both Spain and Portugal. He underestimated the national resistance to him in both these countries. He also made a grave miscalculation after British forces had entered Portugal under Wellesley in 1808. "If I thought it would need 80,000 men to master the Peninsula I would not undertake it," declared Napoleon, "but 30,000 will suffice." In fact, by 1811 he had over 300,000 French troops in Spain and Wellington defeated some of Napoleon's outstanding generals. British sea power was once again of vital importance, for Wellington's forces were kept fully supplied through Lisbon. The Battle of Talavera (1809), was a victory for a combined British and Spanish army, followed by Fuentes D'Onoro, 1811, and Salamanca, 1812. The French never recovered from these blows. Finally, nationalism had its strongest support from the middle class of Europe which was adversely affected by Napoleon's taxation and Continental System. It might also be noted that after 1807 Napoleon's judgment declined —for example, his belief that Moscow was the heart of Russia and that to capture it would lead to Russian defeat, and the very poor opinion he had of Wellington as a soldier right up to the battle of Waterloo itself.

# chapter four

# THE CONGRESSES, 1815–1824

**Introductory.** To settle the main problems of Europe after twenty years of turmoil was the gigantic task facing the statesmen who first met for this purpose at Vienna in November, 1814. Their work was interrupted by the escape of Napoleon from Elba, but was resumed immediately after Waterloo. The presence of so many brilliant personalities was the occasion for lavish hospitality by the Emperor of Austria. Vienna became the gayest city of Europe. Dancing, feasting and brilliant conversation gave an air of buoyancy and optimism to the Congress. The most important personages attending the Congress were Alexander for Russia, Prince Metternich for Austria, Lord Castlereagh for England, the King of Prussia, and Talleyrand for France. The business of the Congress was so conducted that the deliberations of these few individuals decided the main settlements. Some smaller powers were consulted, but in fact the decisions were those of the Great Powers.

The main problems facing the Congress were these:

(1) How to insure against any further aggression from France.
(2) How to divide among the Great Powers certain disputed territories in a way acceptable to all.
(3) How to maintain the effective alliance of the four Great Powers.

**The Prevention of Aggression by France.** The territory of the former Austrian Netherlands (Belgium) and Holland were now united in the Kingdom of the Netherlands. In this way it was hoped to create a much stronger power on the north-eastern frontier of France. It was this direction that the Revolutionary Armies of 1793 had taken so successfully. Holland, having existed as a completely independent state since its heroic defeat of the Spaniards in the sixteenth century, was regarded as a reliable guarantee of the strength of this new combination. As we have seen, Holland had not been faithful to Napoleon even under the rule of his brother Louis, and this was an important consideration to the statesmen of the Congress.

On purely defensive lines there was much to be said for the union of Belgium and Holland. But there was also another motive in the minds of the Congress statesmen. In 1793 the French invasion had

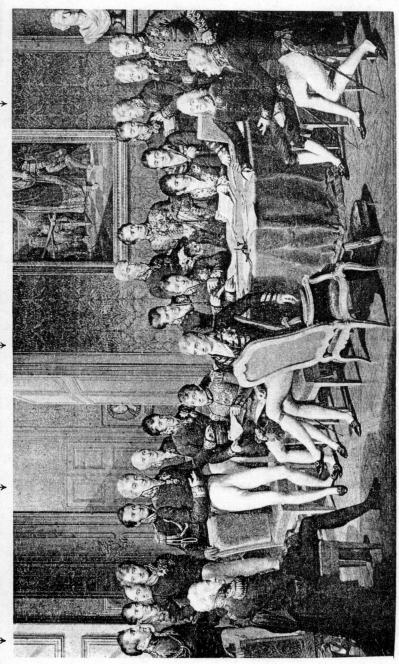

FIG. 10.—THE CONGRESS OF VIENNA.
(*From a contemporary painting by Isabev.*)

been greatly aided by the existence of a revolutionary, pro-French movement in Belgium, and it was hoped that the Dutch would be able to hold this in check in the future. This motive was, of course, anti-revolutionary as well as defensive.

The influence of the idea of a barrier against France is also seen in the settlement of Northern Italy. The King of Piedmont, who had taken refuge from Napoleon in the island of Sardinia, was restored

IV.—The Prussian Rhineland.

to his throne and, in order to strengthen his kingdom, the valuable port and formerly free republic of Genoa was added to it.

The Congress statesmen had similar defensive motives in agreeing to Prussia taking over the Rhine Provinces. This meant that Prussia now undertook the defence of the Rhine frontier, for Austria had entirely withdrawn from northern Europe when she gave up the Austrian Netherlands (Belgium).

**Division of Disputed Territories.** The two most important territories in dispute between the Powers were Poland and Saxony. It was the Czar Alexander of Russia who caused the dispute over Poland. He demanded that the whole of the Grand Duchy of Warsaw created by Napoleon should be handed over to Russia. He also demanded for Russia those parts of Poland which had been taken over by Prussia in the partitions of the country at the end of the previous century. To these proposals the Prussians were agreeable, provided that the whole of the Kingdom of Saxony should go to Prussia as compensation.

These demands of Russia and Prussia caused the first serious quarrel among the Great Powers at Vienna. It enabled Talleyrand to intervene and to form an alliance between Austria, England and France by which those three powers would go to war against Russia and Prussia if the last two powers persisted in their demands. Thus Talleyrand had suddenly brought France, the defeated power, right into the forefront of European politics once again—in fact, he had shown that, without France, there could be no real Balance of Power in Europe.

It was at this very grave point in the Congress that Napoleon escaped from Elba. He had, indeed, been greatly encouraged by the news of these quarrels among the allies. But the allies rallied their forces once again, and after Waterloo their attitude towards France greatly hardened, and this made them willing to compromise among themselves on important questions. The escape of Napoleon from Elba had thoroughly frightened them into unity.

The final settlement of the Polish question gave most of the Grand Duchy of Warsaw to Russia, while Prussia retained Danzig and Posen (2,000,000 Polish inhabitants) and gained about two-fifths of the Kingdom of Saxony. Prussia also obtained the important Baltic territory of Western Pomerania from Sweden and, as we have seen, considerable territory on the Rhine.

Other arrangements made by the Congress included the cession to Austria of Lombardy and Venetia in northern Italy, in place of her abandoned Netherlands, and territory along the Adriatic coast. Sweden gained Norway from Denmark partly as compensation for her loss of Finland to Russia and partly as a punishment of Denmark for her continued alliance with Napoleon. In Germany thirty-nine states were formed into the German Confederation. As for Britain, her gains were mainly in the colonial field. She took final possession of Cape Colony, Ceylon and some islands in the West Indies. She gained the valuable naval bases of Heligoland in the North Sea, Malta in the Mediterranean and a protectorate over the Ionian Islands which gave her command of the entrance to the Adriatic Sea. This was adding further to Britain's position as a World Power which the conquest of India and Canada in the eighteenth century had already made her.

**A Judgment on the Congress of Vienna.** Like all great treaty arrangements designed to settle the affairs of Europe, the Congress of Vienna settlement has been the subject of much controversy. The balance of judgment has, on the whole, been against it. It is possible to see certain principles at work in the settlement—some good, sensible and practical, others extremely bad, shortsighted and of little lasting value.

The main features of the settlement were:

(1) Defensive arrangements against France.
(2) The principle of the Balance of Power.
(3) The principle of Legitimacy.
(4) The almost complete ignoring of the principle of nationality.

We have already seen how certain arrangements were made to restrain France from aggression (see pages 76–79), but we must briefly consider the others.

**Balance of Power.** This was really a principle of eighteenth-century diplomacy designed to prevent any one State gaining a dominant position in Europe. When there was danger of the balance not being maintained, then new leagues and alliances had been formed to redress the balance. Sometimes this had led to war and sometimes it had prevented it.

At Vienna the idea was still very much alive. The first demands of Alexander for the Grand Duchy of Warsaw had produced the alliance of Austria, England and France against Russia and Prussia, and it had nearly led to conflict. Metternich was particularly anxious to limit Russian power, for already in the Balkans Russia had gained Bessarabia from Turkey during the Napoleonic wars. In gaining further provinces on the Adriatic for Austria, Metternich had sought to re-establish a balance of power in the Balkans. Towards Russia Castlereagh and Metternich were able to pursue a common policy, for, in view of Britain's Mediterranean interests, Castlereagh was equally anxious to keep Russia out of the Balkans and to prevent her breaking up the Turkish Empire. At last a compromise settlement was reached over Saxony and Poland which ensured that no single power could dominate eastern Europe. In this instance, therefore, the Balance of Power principle was obvious. Similarly, Austria's new provinces of Lombardy and Venetia were more than compensation for the loss of Belgium—they were rich territories, closer to Vienna, and their possession enabled Austria to dominate Italy for the next forty years. Thus we see that where Prussia gained in the north, Austria gained in the south, and where Russia gained in the north and in the Balkans, Austria gained in the west in Italy and (as we shall see later) in Germany, while England's power was growing in such a way that she could take a decisive part in world politics.

Thus, through the working of the principle of the Balance of Power, all the four Great Powers emerged from the Congress of Vienna stronger than before, without any one being able to exert complete dominance.

**The Principle of Legitimacy.** It was Talleyrand who had originally persuaded the other powers to accept this doctrine, though, in fact, they required very little persuasion. Briefly, the idea implied that those kings and princes of Europe who had held their thrones from long historic ancestry before Napoleon and the French Revolution removed them, were to be restored to their rightful inheritance. This principle led to the restoration to power of some of the worst rulers Europe has ever seen, such as the two Ferdinands, Ferdinand VII of Spain and Ferdinand I of Naples. Again, we see the principle at work in the allies' treatment of Marshal Murat whom Napoleon had made King of Naples. Murat had attempted to unite the whole of Italy, but had been forced to flee from Italy in 1814. He landed again in 1815, attempted to re-establish his power, but was defeated, captured and shot. This was followed by the restoration to power of the rulers of Parma, Modena and Tuscany, all of whom were connected by family ties with the Austrian Imperial family. The principle of legitimacy thus suited the aims of Metternich in Italy. Finally, we must remember that the principle of legitimacy was regarded as a safeguard against the doctrines of the French Revolution, for the restored monarchs, including Louis XVIII, could be relied upon to stamp out revolutionary movements of all kinds, irrespective of the wishes of their subjects.

**The Principle of Nationality ignored.** At the time of the final struggle against Napoleon the rulers of Europe had openly appealed to the new spirit of nationality. In order to rouse their peoples to the maximum effort they had made very high-sounding promises. For example, Alexander of Russia and Frederick William III of Prussia had declared in a manifesto: ". . . the object of the war, and of the peace, is to secure the rights, the freedom, and the independence of all nations". To what extent, if any, was this promise carried out in the Vienna settlement?

As to Belgium and Holland, it is obvious that the Congress was more concerned with defensive arrangements than with nationality. The two countries were almost totally different—in history, religion, economics, language and general culture. There had been a long history of antagonism between them. The actual arrangements made for the Kingdom of the United Netherlands were also defective, for the Belgians were not given equality of treatment with the Dutch and, as we shall see in a later chapter, the whole arrangement broke down in 1830.

Poland is another illustration of the tendency to ignore the force of nationality. Napoleon had created a large Polish State, the Grand Duchy of Warsaw. From this it would have been quite possible to create a natural Polish State independent of the Great Powers, but the actual policy pursued by the Powers was to look backwards to the eighteenth-century policy of partition. Poland, which had a partial revival as a state under Napoleon, was now formed into a Kingdom of Poland, comprising the parts annexed by Russia and most of the Grand Duchy. This Alexander ruled as King of Poland under a constitution.

Similar comments could be made on the handing of Lombardy and Venetia to Austria. Venice herself had been a free republic in the eighteenth century and had no affinity whatever with Austria. In the same way Genoa was incorporated in the Kingdom of Piedmont. There is no doubt that Murat's influence in Italy had encouraged the Italians to think of themselves at last as a nation which could act together as one natural political whole, but in 1815 nationality was entirely ignored by Austria, who was determined to maintain her influence in the peninsula by supporting above all the principle of legitimacy. Metternich had valuable allies in the rulers of Parma, Modena, Tuscany and Naples, and also in the Pope, who was now restored to the Papal States and supported the policies of the great Catholic state, Austria. As we shall see, the later movement of Italian unification was really the effort to destroy the settlement made in 1815. There were, indeed, revolts in various parts of Italy within five years after the Congress.

**The Quadruple Alliance.** By the Treaty of Chaumont, 1814, renewed in 1815, England, Prussia, Russia and Austria formed the Quadruple Alliance. They pledged themselves to meet in congresses in order to promote their common interests and discuss any important matters affecting Europe. Castlereagh was enthusiastic for this scheme, and even looked forward to the time when nations might be able to collaborate so closely as to form a single state. This scheme did, in fact, bring on the European scene something entirely new—the idea of the permanent co-operation of the great states of Europe. But, unfortunately, this system of European congresses had a rather brief life, for Castlereagh and his successor at the British Foreign Office, Canning, found themselves more and more out of sympathy with the purposes for which Metternich and the Czar Alexander wished to use the alliance.

**The Holy Alliance.** In 1815 Alexander I of Russia, partly inspired by strong religious emotion, was going through a kind of "liberal" phase. He had already made promises of freedom to the Poles under Russia's benevolent patronage, and now he urged upon his fellow monarchs the need to accept fully the principles of Christianity in their dealings with one another and with their subjects. His own somewhat unstable mind had been turned in this direction partly by the lavish praises bestowed on him as the "White Angel" who had defeated the "Black Angel", Napoleon. He now persuaded the Emperor of Austria (Francis I) and the King of Prussia (Frederick William III) to sign a document which, among other high-sounding phrases, declared that "the eternal religion of God . . . should influence the resolution of princes and guide their steps". The signatories pledged themselves to live in brotherhood, to protect "religion, peace and justice" and to treat their subjects in the light of the principles of the Christian religion. Every monarch in Europe signed this document, except the Sultan and the Prince Regent. The latter, whose father George III was insane, was sympathetic, but declared that his powers did not allow him to sign. Castlereagh regarded the Holy Alliance as "a piece of sublime mysticism and nonsense" and Metternich took a very similar view of its pious verbiage. The actual practical work of statesmanship was to be done within the framework of the Quadruple Alliance and the congresses which followed from it.

**The Congress of Aix-la-Chapelle.** The first important meeting of statesmen under the terms of the Quadruple Alliance occurred in 1818 at Aix-la-Chapelle. The Congress was attended by Francis I, Alexander I, Frederick William III, Castlereagh and, of course, Metternich. Richelieu represented France.

The immediate question before the Congress was the request of Richelieu for the removal of occupation forces from France. As France was now in a reasonably tranquil state and seemed to be

FIG. 11.—ALEXANDER I OF RUSSIA.

going on the even course of a constitutional monarchy under the guidance of Louis XVIII and his minister Richelieu, it was agreed to withdraw foreign forces from France. But at the same time the four powers of the Alliance secretly pledged themselves to unite to suppress any revolutionary movement in France which might spread to Europe.

This secret agreement was only signed after much conflict of opinion among the four powers. In the first place, it was well known to Castlereagh and Metternich that the Czar Alexander had been encouraging his agents to support liberal revolution in both Spain and Italy. To Castlereagh and Metternich this "liberal" activity of the Czar was only the preliminary to actual intervention by Russian forces in Europe. They suspected, in other words, that Alexander's "liberalism" was a mask for the spread of Russian power. They further feared that Alexander would act in European affairs without consulting them or perhaps in conjunction with some other power. The aim of Metternich and Castlereagh was to keep the Czar within the system of the Quadruple Alliance and not allow him to pursue his own policies.

Alexander was at last persuaded to sign a special declaration, to which France was invited to adhere, and by which France was admitted to what now became the Quintuple Alliance. This declaration, signed by the five powers, repeated their determination to uphold their close union and to maintain peace by enforcing respect for treaties. No separate group of the powers was to interfere in the concerns of any state without being expressly invited to do so.

Other disagreements were shown at Aix-la-Chapelle. A proposal was put forward by Frederick William of Prussia that an allied army under Wellington should be permanently stationed in Belgium in readiness to suppress revolution anywhere in Europe. This brought about serious disagreements between Castlereagh and the Prussians. He opposed the idea that every government in Europe, however bad, should be automatically supported by the Powers. Each case, he thought, must be judged on its merits by the Great Powers acting together. Castlereagh was no lover of revolution. His main concern was that Britain should not be dragged automatically into any war which the other three Powers might think necessary.

The Congress of Aix-la-Chapelle was really a success for Metternich and marks the further development of his influence in Europe. He had restrained Alexander to keep within the alliance system by the General Declaration and had also received the support of Castlereagh.

But besides those disputes which were settled, there were other disagreements among the Great Powers which showed how much suspicion and mistrust lay beneath the surface of agreement. This came out strongly in connection with the two problems of the Barbary pirates and the slave trade. In the Mediterranean the pirates were a constant menace to shipping, and the Czar Alexander proposed the formation of an international fleet to stamp them out. Castlereagh, however, opposed this suggestion mainly because of his opposition to the presence of Russian warships in the Mediterranean. In regard to the slave trade, Castlereagh proposed that a naval force formed by the Powers should have the right to search vessels for slaves, but the other Powers opposed this as giving the largest navy, that of Great Britain, too much power to interfere with the commerce of other states. Even on humanitarian and trade matters there was no complete agreement.

**The Congress of Troppau, October, 1820.** Between 1818 and 1821 there were revolutionary movements and disturbances in various parts of Europe. In Spain a revolution broke out against Ferdinand VII and he was forced to grant the liberal form of constitution which had been set up in 1812 before his restoration. In Naples there was a similar move against Ferdinand I in 1820. The opponents of despotism were beginning to stir. In Germany there were student demonstrations against the influence of Metternich and the rule of the princes. In 1819 the journalist and dramatist, Kotzebue, who was also a spy for Alexander I, was murdered. In the New World the colonies of Spain and Portugal revolted from the control of the mother countries and set up their own independent governments.

Whatever liberal principles the Czar Alexander possessed were now rapidly fading in the face of these events, especially as he had considerable trouble with his new Polish subjects and even a revolt in one of the most important regiments of the Russian army. The murder of Kotzebue enabled Metternich to gain a complete personal ascendancy over the Czar and to alarm him finally into abandoning his flirtations with liberal principles. "You have nothing to regret," the Czar remarked to Metternich, "but I have." In this state of contrition Alexander attended the Congress of Troppau in Austria—a congress which he had urged on Metternich as necessary owing to the disturbed state of Europe. The Congress was attended by representatives of Prussia, Russia and Austria with full powers to act, but Britain and France sent observers only.

It was now that Metternich, confident of the support of Alexander, came forward with a scheme for the suppression of liberal revolution in Europe. He proposed that the Quintuple Alliance should undertake this task wherever revolution occurred. He suggested that the allies should accept the idea of revolution from *above*—that is, a revolutionary change in government brought about or approved by a monarch or an upper class, but that they should pledge themselves to stamp out at once a revolution from *below* by the mass of the people. In this way he hoped to establish a counter-revolutionary police system for the whole of Europe such as he had already established in Germany and the Austrian Empire. Alexander accepted

Metternich's proposal at once, but both England and France opposed it.

Castlereagh's objection to the scheme did not arise from any tenderness on his part towards revolutions—in fact, he used the term "revolutionary pest" to show what he thought of them. But he pointed out that the revolutions in Spain and Naples were the concern of those states only. Furthermore, England would not tie herself to a policy of automatic intervention in any state on the decision of an international council such as Metternich wished to make of the alliance. In another important way England's self-interest decided Castlereagh's policy. Alexander proposed a joint expedition of the powers across the Atlantic to force the colonies of Spain and Portugal back to allegiance to the home governments. Here English interests were very much concerned, for it was now possible for England to trade perfectly freely with the South American states, which were valuable markets for England's growing industrial production. Castlereagh was therefore strongly opposed to the Czar's scheme, and instructed the English observer to make his views clear. In regard to Naples, Castlereagh suggested that if Austria considered the revolution there a matter of domestic concern to her, then she would be entitled to intervene in Naples on her own responsibility. In other words, England would not actively oppose Austria.

**The Troppau Protocol, October, 1820.** The agreement between Austria, Russia and Prussia known as the Troppau Protocol was signed in October, 1820. It stated the attitude of the three powers to "states which have undergone a change of government due to revolution". It declared: "If, owing to such alterations, immediate danger threatens other states, the Powers bind themselves by peaceful means or, if need be by arms, to bring back the guilty state into the bosom of the Great Alliance."

It is obvious that to Alexander, Metternich and the King of Prussia a popular revolution anywhere would threaten them, and the revolutionaries were sure to be "guilty".

The French government supported the Protocol with some reservations, but Castlereagh indicated his opposition to the whole scheme and declared that it could never apply to Great Britain.

Britain did not definitely break away from the Quintuple Alliance at Troppau, but the differences of opinion we have noted were beginning seriously to weaken the Congress System.

**The Congress of Laibach, January, 1821.** The next congress at Laibach in Austria was really the adjourned congress of Troppau.

Ferdinand of Naples was invited to attend the Congress, which he did after promising the Neapolitans that he would observe the new constitution which the revolution in Naples had established. No sooner had he got beyond the frontier of Naples than he denounced the new government and all its works. After meetings between Ferdinand and Metternich at Laibach, an Austrian army marched south, defeated the Neapolitans and restored Ferdinand with all his previous despotic powers, while the revolutionary leaders and many of their supporters were executed or thrown into the dungeons of Naples. Similarly, a liberal revolution in Piedmont was suppressed by an army of 80,000 Austrians with 100,000 Russians held in reserve. In this way Metternich carried out the aims of the Troppau Protocol.

These actions of the Protocol powers threatened to drive Great Britain right away from the European system. But this break-up was temporarily prevented by the commencement of the Greek War of Independence in 1821. At the same time there was the situation in Spain arising from the 1818 revolution to be considered.

**The Congress of Verona, October, 1822.** Before the next Congress met at Verona in northern Italy, Castlereagh and Metternich had once again come together against Alexander of Russia. This sudden outburst of harmony was due to their anxiety to prevent Alexander intervening alone to support the Greeks against their Turkish overlords. Once again the fears of Russian penetration in the Balkans and the Mediterranean were the dominant motives of the two statesmen. Castlereagh also insisted on no interference by the Powers in Spain.

When the Congress of Verona met, Castlereagh was no longer British Foreign Secretary, having committed suicide. He was succeeded by George Canning, who sent the Duke of Wellington to Verona as British representative. Canning's instructions to Wellington amounted to a continuation of Castlereagh's policy.

A serious difference arose at once between the Powers over Spain. The Czar Alexander declared his wish to send 150,000 Russian troops into Spain to suppress the revolution on behalf of the other Powers. This at once ranged against him Wellington, Metternich and the French representative, none of whom wished to see a huge Russian force marching through the heart of Europe.

But now complications arose which led to the break-up of the Congress system. The French government had become ultra-royalist and therefore violently opposed to liberal revolution. The French offered to send an army into Spain to do the work of suppression for the Great Powers. The signatories of the Troppau Protocol naturally wished to support the royalist cause in Spain and withdrew their ambassadors from that country. In 1823 a French army invaded Spain and restored Ferdinand to his previous position of control.

Under Canning's instructions, the Duke of Wellington had refused to support the idea of French intervention in Spain and he had completely withdrawn from the Congress. Canning saw the possibility of Ferdinand of Spain attempting, with the help of the other powers, to regain control of the South American states whose independence the previous government had recognised.

**Canning's Foreign Policy and the Final Break-up of the Congress System.** Canning accepted the earlier undertakings to intervene in France in case of revolution there, but otherwise he continued steadily to oppose the policies of Austria, Prussia and Russia. He supported the idea of nationality and the independence of small nations, and in this respect he went further than Castlereagh. "Every nation for itself and God for us all" was his way of describing his own policy. But, like Castlereagh, he was above all concerned with defending and extending British interests. This is particularly seen in his opposition to any attempts by the Powers to bring back the South American states under the control of Spain and Portugal. In fact, he warned France in 1824 that England would fight if such a policy were pursued—a warning which helped to prevent a proposed expedition of the other powers across the Atlantic. He was greatly aided in this policy by the famous declaration of President Monroe of the United States, December, 1823, that any interference by European powers in the affairs of the American continent would be regarded "as the manifestation of an unfriendly disposition to the United States". This became known as the Monroe Doctrine. Canning had already made treaties with the former Spanish colonies of Brazil, Mexico and Colombia, which had also been fully recognised by President Monroe. These moves prevented any attempt to reconquer these states for Spain. Britain's trade with them was now perfectly free to develop.

The final blow to the Congress System was given by Canning in connection with the Greek War of Independence which broke out against Turkey in 1821. Canning and Metternich succeeded in preventing the intervention of Alexander of Russia alone on behalf of the Greeks. So far the policy of Castlereagh was being followed, but then in 1825 Alexander died and was succeeded by the Czar Nicholas I who was much more determined to help the Greeks and to accelerate the break-up of the Turkish Empire. Canning's response to this situation was to form an alliance with Russia and France by the Treaty of London, 1827. His motive was both to support the Greek cause and to prevent Russia acting alone. Both Metternich and the Prussians opposed this policy as it amounted to the giving of assistance to rebels and was completely opposed to the terms of the Troppau Protocol of 1820. Moreover, it did mean a considerable increase of Russian influence in the Balkans. The independence of Greece was ensured by the destruction of the Turkish fleet by a combined Russian, British and French force at Navarino Bay, 1827.

By this time it was clear that the Great Powers could not remain permanently united on important European matters as had been hoped in 1815 under the terms of the Quadruple Alliance. The Congress System had come to an end. On the other hand, the Concert of Europe was by no means dead. The idea that the great states of Europe should attempt to settle international affairs by agreement led to many important and fruitful conferences during the nineteenth century. And we must remember that there was no major war for forty years after the Congress of Vienna.

# chapter five
# FRANCE, 1815–1848

**Introductory.** The years 1815–1848 witness the last attempts to wed the institution of monarchy to the French nation. The history of France in these years is marked by constant conflict between, on the one hand, the forces which the "ancien régime" had created and, on the other, those created by the Revolution of 1789. The constitution of 1815 is a half-way measure between the Republic of 1792–1795 and the despotism of the "ancien régime". The Republican conspirators are, however, still active and, over against them, the Ultra-Royalists are attempting to change the settlement of 1815 in the direction of more authority both for the Church and the Monarchy. The attempt of Charles X, 1824–1830, to carry out the Ultra-Royalist programme brings about the Revolution of 1830 and the election of Louis Philippe as King with more constitutional restraints on the King's power than had been imposed by the Charter of 1814. However, the narrow middle-class basis of his rule and his great difficulties in foreign policy lead to increasing friction in the state. Moreover, the rising influence of the Socialist and "proletarian" movement in general create further sources of trouble for the bourgeois monarchy, while the conspiracies of Bonapartists, Legitimists and Republicans all gradually undermine the King's position. The Revolution of 1848, which sets off the revolt of the whole of Europe, is the consequence of these complications. The Bourbon Monarchy ends in 1830 and the Orleanist in 1848, and neither is ever to be revived.

**Louis XVIII, 1814–1824.** The new king was the brother of Louis XVI who had been executed by the revolutionaries in 1793. Louis XVIII was now sixty years old, rather fat and unprepossessing in appearance, but cultured and well-meaning. He was without any desire for revenge against the supporters of the previous governments. He was quite prepared to keep the system of administration built up by Napoleon and many of the changes brought about by the Revolution, especially the distribution of land to the peasantry. He was not prepared to restore to the Catholic Church the land and power it had enjoyed before the Revolution. He had the political sense to see that there was danger of another revolution if he attempted to restore the pre-1789 position, and such an event as revolution would bring down upon France once again the might of the Great Powers. He also realised that the days of absolute monarchy were over and that his best course was to rule strictly in accordance with the constitutional Charter to which he had pledged himself on his restoration.

**Richelieu.** Louis XVIII's chief minister was the Duc de Richelieu, sprung from the same family as the Cardinal Richelieu of the seventeenth century. He was now forty-one years old and had had a colourful and adventurous career. Several years before the Revolution he had joined the army of Russia and in 1785 had taken part in an important campaign against the Turks. On the outbreak of the Revolution in 1789 he had joined the "émigrés" and fought in their armies till 1794, when he returned to Russia. When Alexander became Czar in 1801, he appointed Richelieu governor of the Crimea, which became under his administration a thriving province, and the port of Odessa became one of the greatest in Russia. In the Moscow Campaign of 1812 Richelieu had fought with the Russian Army against Napoleon. Naturally enough, Richelieu was strongly approved by Alexander as the first minister of France after the defeat of Napoleon. Moreover, Richelieu had the advantage of knowing personally all the important statesmen of Europe and was the minister most likely to bring back France to equality with the other powers. Above all, his ideas exactly coincided with those of Louis XVIII, namely, to maintain the liberties guaranteed by the Charter, to prevent indiscriminate revenge or revolution by either extremes of Right or Left in France.

**The Charter.** Louis XVIII had issued a constitutional Charter in 1814. It set up a parliamentary system consisting of a Chamber of Peers nominated by the King and a Chamber of Deputies elected by voters. The Charter guaranteed certain important personal freedoms which were partly the outcome of the Revolution of 1789 and the government of Napoleon. All Frenchmen were declared equal before the law, while people of every class were eligible for civil and military appointments. No one was to be arbitrarily imprisoned—the days of "lettres de cachet" were not to return. Religious toleration was decreed. The press was to be free from censorship and, finally, all those who had purchased the land and property of the Church or the nobility during the Revolution were guaranteed their possessions.

The new franchise was, however, a very narrow one. Only those who paid 300 francs in taxation were entitled to vote in elections—only 100,000 persons in a population of 29,000,000. Moreover, in order to be eligible for the Chamber of Deputies a man had to be over forty years old and pay 1,000 francs in taxes—which meant that only 12,000 persons in the whole of France were eligible to stand as candidates. Again, only the King or his ministers could propose laws, although the Chamber of Deputies could refuse to pass them or grant taxes.

Despite its limitations, the French Constitution of 1814 was the most liberal in Europe, with, perhaps, the exception of England.

**The Ultra-royalists.** Not all those who returned to France in 1814 and 1815 had the same moderate aims as the King and his chief minister. Surrounding Louis XVIII were those courtiers who thirsted for revenge against upholders of the Revolution and Napoleon. Chief amongst these was the King's brother, the Comte d'Artois. He had been the acknowledged leader of the "émigrés", and had fought both against the Revolution and Napoleon. He and his followers were known as the Ultra-royalists. They wished to restore the powers and the privileges of the nobility and the Catholic Church much as they had existed before 1789. They wished especially to put education under the control of the Church. They also believed in the necessity of a rigid control of the press so that the government could completely control public opinion. Some of their leaders, especially the influential writer Chateaubriand, wanted France to embark on a policy of warlike adventures abroad, to restore the tarnished military glory of France and thus make the loss of liberty at home acceptable to the people.

**The White Terror.** In the first elections held in 1815 after the defeat of Napoleon, the Ultra-royalists gained a majority in the Chamber of Deputies. This did not oblige the King under the Charter to appoint an Ultra-royalist government, and Richelieu continued in office. But the position of the King and Richelieu was now extremely difficult, and they were unable to control the activities of the Ultra-royalists in the country. The Ultras began a policy of outright revenge on their opponents. Marshal Brune, one of Napoleon's foremost generals, was murdered by Ultra-royalists while on his way to swear allegiance to Louis XVIII. Marshal Ney, the hero of the rearguard in the retreat from Moscow, was tried, condemned and shot, although the commander of the firing-squad could not bring himself to give the order to fire and his second-in-command had to do so. Marshal Ney had sworn allegiance to Louis XVIII in 1814, but then deserted to Napoleon on the latter's escape from Elba. This was treason against Louis XVIII, but when France capitulated, a pardon had been promised to all those who had taken part in the Hundred Days. The execution of Ney was really forced by the Ultra-royalists, but it was an act which was held by many against Louis XVIII and the Bourbon family in the future. At Marseilles Ultra-royalist mobs attacked the houses of known supporters of Napoleon and murdered them, and this example spread to other towns. The Ultra-royalists forced the popular Carnot (the organiser of victory for the Revolutionary armies and Napoleon) into exile. Numerous "treason trials" were also held.

**Defeat of the Ultra-royalists, 1816.** The King and Richelieu saw clearly the dangers of the policy of revenge and attempted to secure a general pardon for all those not already convicted in the treason trials. But the Ultra majority in the Chamber of Deputies defeated them. By this time alarm and fear had spread throughout France, especially among the peasantry, who expected the confiscation of the land they had gained from the Revolution. In May, 1816, a serious peasant revolt broke out at Grenoble, which the government suppressed with great severity, but nevertheless it was a warning to Louis XVIII and Richelieu that unless the Ultra-royalists were stopped they might have another revolution on their hands. In 1816 Louis dissolved the Chamber of Deputies and ordered new elections. His calculations proved correct. The electors were tired of, and alarmed by, the policy of revenge, and returned a majority in favour of the King's policy. The King was now able to put a stop to the Ultra-royalist persecutions.

**Importance of the Years 1815–1816.** The years 1815–1816 in the history of France show clearly the type of conflict which was to continue, in one form or another, till 1830 and the overthrow of Charles X. The important thread which runs through these fifteen years is the conflict between the idea of constitutional monarchy accepting many of the principles of the Revolution of 1789 and, in outright opposition, the Ultra-royalist idea of absolute monarchy supported by the Church.

Richelieu's moderate policy in France was generally acceptable to the Great Powers, for they were all afraid of the results of political strife leading to revolution. In 1818 Richelieu was able to persuade them to withdraw the army of occupation from France and to reduce the money reparations by one-third. This was a considerable achievement and partly a reward to France for her good conduct.

**The Growth of Reaction. The Ultras regain Influence, 1819–1824.** But the Ultra-royalist movement in France was by no means dead and certain events of the years 1819–1824 were exploited by them in order to reassert their policy. In the first place, the King himself was alarmed by the results of the elections of 1819. Not only were the moderate liberals returned in increased numbers, but twenty-one extreme republicans were also elected. Amongst these was a certain Abbé Grégoire, a churchman who had denounced kings as monsters and had taken an active part in destroying the power of the Church in the Revolution of 1789. Louis and his ministers took active measures to prevent Grégoire taking his place in the Chamber of Deputies. Irregularities in his election campaign were discovered and he was not permitted to take his seat. The government also proposed to alter the franchise in such a way as to give the larger landowners two votes instead of one. The Ultras were naturally delighted that the King had been alarmed into this policy, but he was still not going far enough for them. Then an event occurred which gave them the opportunity they were looking for.

**The Murder of the Duc de Berri, 1820.** In February, 1820, Louvel, a fanatical opponent of the Bourbons, assassinated the Duc de Berri, the second son of the Comte d'Artois. The Duke was in direct succession to the throne, the eldest son, the Duc d'Angoulême, being childless. The assassination seemed an attempt to extinguish the Bourbon line. The minister who had replaced Richelieu, Decazes, was forced to resign and Richelieu came back to power. He himself, while still attempting to restrain the Ultras, began to reduce the liberties guaranteed by the Charter of 1814. He imposed a censorship of newspapers and other publications, abolished the secret ballot in elections and gave a double vote to the great landowners. These measures were still not enough for the Ultras, who were able to achieve the dismissal of Richelieu and his replacement by a minister who would carry out completely their own policy. The day of the Ultras had at last arrived.

**Villèle, 1821–1827.** The new minister was Villèle, and his political method was to administer his medicine gradually so as to arouse as little opposition as possible with each dose. He relied for his support on two strong influences, the Catholic Church and the propertied class or "bourgeoisie".

The Catholic Church now began to assert strongly its influence with the royal court. A special Catholic society known as the Congregation carried on a continuous campaign in the country and formed a link with the banned Jesuit Society. A sign of this increasing influence was the appointment of an Archbishop as President of the University of Paris in 1822, the Church thus gaining an important control of education.

Villèle made strenuous efforts to win the support of the bourgeoisie —the manufacturers and traders especially. By promoting their prosperity he hoped to make them accept the limitations which were being imposed on liberty. In fact, money-making was to replace liberty. He therefore adopted a system of high import duties on manufactures and on agricultural produce so as to favour the home producers.

**Influence of Chateaubriand.** Another extremely important personality among the Ultra-royalists in these years was the writer Chateaubriand. He was minister for foreign affairs in Villèle's government, and he now attempted to put into practice his policy of adventures abroad in order to reconcile the people to the loss of political liberty at home. He advocated the intervention of a French army in Spain to suppress the revolution there and, as we have seen (page 88), a French army under the Duc d'Angoulême successfully restored King Ferdinand VII in 1823. Encouraged by this success, Chateaubriand wanted France to expand eastward to the Rhine frontier and regain territory which she had held in the eighteenth century. But this policy involved great dangers, for the Great Powers were likely to oppose it by force. Moreover, the British Foreign Secretary, Canning, had already threatened war against France if she attempted to regain control of the Spanish American colonies for Ferdinand VII. Villèle, anxious to avoid war, found this policy too dangerous and Chateaubriand was dismissed.

Villèle continued to strengthen the Ultra-royalists by other and less risky means. He had the French constitution altered in such a way that general elections were to be held every seven years, this method replacing the arrangements made by the Charter of 1814 by which fifty members retired each year and new elections were held for their places. Villèle's change of the electoral system meant the continuance for several more years of the Chamber of Deputies in which the Ultra-royalists had regained control. Thus by the time Louis XVIII died in 1824, the Ultra-royalist policy had already made great headway, despite the violent opposition of liberals and republicans.

**The Reign of Charles X, 1824-1830.** Louix XVIII was succeeded by his brother the Comte d'Artois who took the title of Charles X. Thus at last the leader of the "émigrés", the believer in the Divine Right of Kings, the plotter and intriguer against the moderate policies of Richelieu in the years 1814-1821, was now the head of the State. And within six years his policy was to lead to revolution against him and his flight from France. Even on his death-bed, Louis XVIII had warned his brother against the adoption of the complete Ultra-royalist policy.

**Compensation to the "Émigrés".** The elections of 1824 increased the Ultra-royalist majority in the Chamber of Deputies, and Villèle considered the time ripe to give compensation to the "émigrés" for what they had lost in the Revolution of 1789. They were now given a money payment amounting to £40,000,000. The money was raised by reducing the interest paid to the holders of State bonds on the National Debt. This simply meant that the holders of these bonds, who were mostly members of the bourgeoisie or middle class, were being penalised in order to support the claims of the old aristocracy whose political influence they detested.

**Religious Policy.** The government of Charles X now allowed the re-establishment of the Jesuit Society in France and also various monastic orders and nunneries. The King and Villèle were determined to base their power on the old alliance of Church and King which the Revolution of 1789 had overthrown. In addition to this, a mediaeval law against sacrilege—that is, burglaries of churches—was re-established, and in certain cases this crime carried the death penalty, which, however, was not actually enforced. In the Chamber of Peers, where the liberals had a majority, this harsh ecclesiastical law was strongly opposed, even by Chateaubriand himself. The middle and lower classes, among whom free thought and opposition to the Church was strong, were repelled by such religious fanaticism. The coronation ceremonies of 1825 also showed the people how much the political influence of the Church had revived. After being anointed with holy oil and crowned by an archbishop at Rheims, Charles X headed a procession through the streets of Paris clad in the violet robes of a church dignitary and carrying a lighted candle.

**Increasing Opposition to the Royal Policy.** The liberal and republican groups in France now began to rally their forces against the King, the aristocracy and the Church. A sign of this development was the election of the republican leader Lafayette to the Chamber of Deputies in 1827. He had for some time been organising both open and secret societies known as the "carbonari" or "charbonnerie" to oppose the Ultra-royalists. In 1821 he had attempted to raise a rebellion against Louis XVIII in the garrison at Belfort. Another significant event occurred in connection with the National Guard in 1827. As Charles X was holding a review of the Guard, cries were suddenly raised from its ranks against the government.

Charles X's reply to this demonstration was to disband the National
Guard, and thus the force which had been regarded as the protector
of the liberties guaranteed by the Charter no longer existed. Soon
afterwards, the censorship of newspapers and publications was again
imposed. These actions only served to increase the opposition to
Charles in the country and in the Chamber of Peers, where there was
a liberal majority. Instead of moderating his policy, Charles went
forward headlong with his own plans. Villèle could not stand the
pace, and resigned in 1827. His successor, Martignac, was dismissed
in 1829, and Charles appointed as his chief minister the Prince de
Polignac, his chief personal adviser.

**The Revolution of 1830.** Polignac bluntly stated his policy to be to
"reorganise society, to give back to the clergy their weight in state
affairs, to create a powerful aristocracy and to surround it with
privileges". To the middle class and the working people of Paris this
looked like a complete return to the days before 1789. Charles X and

FIG. 12.—DEFENDERS OF THE BARRICADES.

Polignac seemed quite unaware of the exact extent of the opposition to them. The King ordered fresh elections, confident that the voters would give his supporters an even greater majority in the Chamber of Deputies, but in fact they lost fifty seats. Charles then declared a state of emergency, set aside the election and reduced the numbers of those entitled to vote. The newspapers were also placed completely under government control. These were the Ordinances of Saint-Cloud.

These actions of the King were the signal for immediate revolt in Paris organised by the republicans and the journalists, who set up a government in the Hôtel de Ville headed by the veteran of 1789, Lafayette. The middle and working classes of Paris united in the erection of barricades and the royal troops sent against them merely fraternised with the rebels. Soon the whole of Paris was controlled by the revolutionaries.

These events took place in July, 1830, and, seeing the hopelessness of his position, Charles X abdicated on August 1, 1830, and fled to England. He had failed entirely to restore the monarchy of Divine Right and destroy the liberties guaranteed by the Charter of 1814, and his downfall had been sudden and dramatic.

## The Orleans Monarchy, 1830–1848

**The Middle Class.** The republicans under Lafayette had taken a leading part in the July Revolution, but a republic was not set up. The main reasons for this are reasonably clear—republicanism was not the most powerful influence throughout France, although it was strong in Paris. The commercial middle class feared that republicanism would lead to attacks on the rights of private property. One of the strongest reasons why a republic was not established was the general understanding that the Great Powers would not tolerate a republic in France, who would therefore be isolated and open to attack. The middle class wanted a peaceful policy and good relations with the other powers, especially England. Moreover, the middle class were satisfied that the old aristocracy and the Church had both been decisively defeated and that the days of the Ultra-royalists were over, and that now they themselves were at last to gain control of political affairs.

**Louis Philippe, 1830–1848.** The king whom the middle class trusted to promote their interests was elected by the Chamber of Deputies with the new and more democratic-sounding title of "King of the French". Louis Philippe was the son of Philippe

Égalité, Duc d'Orléans, who in the Revolution had voted for the death of his cousin, Louis XVI. In 1789 Louis Philippe had been sixteen years old, was a member of the Jacobin Club and fought in the revolutionary armies against the Austrians. Then in 1793 he had fallen out of favour with the revolutionaries, had fled first to Switzerland, then to England, where the government of the day gave him a pension. After Waterloo he returned to Paris, where he lived in the Palais Royal. Here he kept in contact with men of all classes, but especially the middle class. He adopted the manners and dress of the middle class rather than the finery of the aristocracy. His round hat, middle-class frock-coat and umbrella made him a familiar figure of the boulevards.

It will be seen that Louis Philippe's peculiar career made him something of an enigma to his contemporaries. The republicans were not quite certain about his real intentions in 1830, and nor was anyone else. Charles X died in the belief that Louis Philippe was merely holding the French throne in order later to ensure the succession of Charles's grandson, Comte de Chambord. We shall see that the reign of Louis Philippe is a record of increasing opposition to him on the part of all classes, for eventually even the middle class lost faith in him.

From the very commencement of his reign his position was insecure. He was the first *elected* monarch in French history, and this implied the right of those who had elected him to get rid of him if he did not live up to their expectations. Even his election itself was only by a bare majority of the Chamber of Deputies—219 votes out of 430. It is therefore some tribute to his political skill that he was able to hold his position for eighteen years.

**The New Charter, 1830.** Some important changes made in the Charter of 1815 were intended by the Chamber of Deputies to limit further the King's powers. Firstly, it was now expressly stated that the King could not issue special decrees in emergencies as Charles X had done under the old Charter in 1830. In other words, the King could no longer put forward the excuse of a national emergency in order to impose his own rule and get rid of the Chamber of Deputies if the elections went against him. Secondly, the Chamber of Peers and of Deputies could now introduce laws themselves and not merely debate those proposed to it by the King or his ministers. Thirdly, the number of voters in elections was increased from 100,000 to 200,000 by lowering the tax qualification for the franchise. This placed voting power firmly in the hands of the upper-middle class, but it was certainly not democratic in a population of 30,000,000.

But the first great test of the reign for Louis Philippe came in the field of foreign politics, and his ultimate fall in 1848 is as much related to foreign policy as to internal affairs with which we will deal later.

**Foreign Policy.** The problems facing Louis Philippe in foreign policy were very great. The previous governments since 1815 had to a certain extent revived the prestige of France as a military power. There had been the successful intervention in Spain in 1823 and, in the reign of Charles X, the success of a campaign to gain a French foothold in Algeria. Many people therefore expected Louis Philippe to go forward with this policy, especially the Bonapartists, the Legitimists, and the Liberals. The Republicans also wished to see France give active support to revolutions abroad. Thus numerous groups were pressing for military adventures of one kind or another, but Louis Philippe himself considered the best policy to be the maintenance of peace in order to promote the trade and industry of the middle class on whom he relied for his power. Then suddenly in 1830 he was confronted by an extremely dangerous situation.

**The Belgian Revolution.** The Belgian people had become more and more restive under the union with Holland made by the Congress of Vienna. There were many causes for this discontent which really sprang from the fact that the whole tradition and mode of life of the Belgians was different from that of the Dutch. Belgium was the first European country to follow Britain's example and undergo a full-scale industrial revolution. Belgium was a manufacturing country and Holland a trading and seafaring state. The government of the United Netherlands, being mainly controlled by the Dutch, favoured a policy of free trade while the Belgians wanted a policy of protective duties on imports in order to promote their manufactures. In religion Belgium was mainly Catholic and favoured the Catholic control of education, a policy to which the Calvinist Dutch were strongly opposed. Even the official language was Dutch, while Belgian newspapers were subjected to censorship. The Belgians also had the special grievance that King William favoured his own countrymen in all important posts—the army officers, the government itself and ambassadors abroad were mainly Dutch. Another great grievance of the Belgians was that they had to bear half the National Debt of Holland. In the Parliament at The Hague there was equal representation of Belgians and Dutch, but this was scarcely satisfactory to the Belgians who comprised two-thirds of the population.

**Louis Philippe and Belgium.** When the Belgians rose in revolt in 1830 and forced the Dutch troops to withdraw, the problem for Louis Philippe became a difficult and dangerous one. The Belgian Revolution was a challenge to the Vienna settlement of 1815 and the Great Powers who had made it. If Louis Philippe intervened on the side of the Belgians he might well have the Great Powers unitedly against him. Yet he could scarcely stand aside, for the July Revolution which had given him power in France was itself the encouraging signal for the Belgians to revolt. Moreover, he was being urged on by the various groups already mentioned, and he was anxious to placate them. Could he in any way revive the expansionist policy of 1793 in favour of revolution abroad?

Then came the offer of the throne by the Belgians to the Duc de Nemours, the second son of Louis Philippe. To this offer Palmerston, the British Foreign Secretary, was entirely opposed, and he soon acquainted Louis Philippe with his opinion. Certain leading French statesmen urged Louis Philippe to go forward even against Great Britain. This was the policy of the Liberals and their leader Adolph Thiers especially. But Louis Philippe, anxious for peace with Great Britain, at last agreed to withdraw the candidature of his son for the Belgian throne, and finally agreed to the offer of the throne by the Belgians to Leopold of Saxe-Coburg, the uncle of Queen Victoria. This was in reality a diplomatic triumph for Britain. Leopold had married Charlotte, the only daughter of George IV, had lived in England for many years, and had received a pension of £50,000 from the British Government after the death of the Princess Charlotte in 1817.

In 1831, a Dutch attack was launched against Belgium, but was defeated by the Belgians with the help of French forces and the British Navy. William for several years refused to accept the fact of Belgian independence, but eventually he had to recognise that the other Great Powers of the Vienna settlement were by no means likely to support him, for they had revolutions in their own territories to deal with, and they were not prepared to fight a war against Britain and France. Finally, in 1839 Palmerston persuaded Russia, Austria and Prussia to join with France and Britain to guarantee the future neutrality of Belgium in case of war in Europe—the treaty which the Germans were to violate in 1914.

Thus Louis Philippe had failed to please the various groups in France who had wanted Belgium to come under French control, and they accused him of weakness in not going forward even against Britain. On the other hand, he could claim that French troops had materially aided the revolution, and therefore France could take considerable credit, especially as his daughter Louise married Leopold I. But, of course, his opponents did not fail to point out as well that France had been forced to play second fiddle to Britain, and thus his policy increased the opposition of the Bonapartists, the Legitimists, the Liberals under Thiers, and the Republicans.

**Poland and Italy.** The year 1830 saw other stirrings of revolt encouraged by the fact of the July Revolution in France and the events in Belgium. In Poland there occurred one of many efforts in the nineteenth century to free the country from the control of Czarist Russia. After the death of Alexander I the Poles had become more and more rigidly controlled by Russia under the rule of Nicholas I and the earlier hopes of a liberal constitution had entirely faded. Many of the leaders of the revolt of 1830 hoped for assistance from Louis Philippe, but, as in the case of Belgium, he pursued a very cautious policy. He realised that official support by France alone would in all probability lead to a war against Russia, Austria and Prussia, who all had Polish subjects. Moreover, he could not count on the support of Palmerston. France would be isolated and in danger of defeat. But these considerations were swept aside by the King's opponents in France, and they once again demanded action. Many of these demands were quite irresponsible, for some of the King's opponents—especially the Legitimists—would have been glad of any failure on his part which would bring the Orleanist Monarchy crashing down.

The same situation arose when revolt against Austrian influence suddenly flared up in Italy, and once again the King gave no effective aid. He was attacked on every side, and especially by the Liberals under Thiers in the Chamber of Deputies. But Louis Philippe could rely on a majority support from his middle-class allies elected to the Chamber of Deputies under the narrow franchise of 1830. He kept a close personal control of foreign policy and skilfully avoided entangling France in actions which might have led to war in Europe. His chief opponents were temporarily defeated, but they continued to denounce his policy as one of weakness, or even worse.

**The Affair of Mehemet Ali.** In 1836 the Liberal leader Thiers became chief minister and attempted to force the King's hand by a more adventurous policy, but he soon afterwards resigned when Louis Philippe refused to intervene in Spain on the side of the liberals in a civil war then raging. Thiers was again chief minister when, in

1839, he considered that a great opportunity had occurred to increase the influence of France in Egypt and the Middle East.

Mehemet Ali, the ruler of Egypt for the Turkish Empire, had for some years been on very bad terms with his overlord the Sultan. Mehemet Ali's grievance was that he had not received the promised rewards of territory for the assistance he had given the Sultan against the Greeks during the Greek War of Independence, 1821-1829. In 1833, Mehemet Ali had seized Syria from the Turks. There, in 1839, the Turks launched a full-scale campaign against him.

Thiers wanted to give full support to Mehemet Ali in order to have a valuable ally in the Middle East against both England and Russia. Up to a point, Louis Philippe supported Thiers, and French representatives pledged aid to Mehemet. French arms actually reached Mehemet Ali, he defeated the Turks, and then moved his armies through Syria to attack the Turkish Empire.

Such a situation was one of great concern to the Powers, especially to Russia and England. It looked as though Mehemet Ali and his French allies were going to break up the Turkish Empire and settle the whole business for themselves. Palmerston adopted a line of action very similar to the one he had pursued at the time of the Belgian Revolution. He summoned a conference in London of all the parties concerned—except France. The Convention of London, 1840, was signed by Russia, Austria, Prussia and Britain. Mehemet Ali was offered the permanent rule of part of Syria on the understanding that he would call off his campaign against Turkey.

Thiers was furious—as were many other Frenchmen—that France had been ignored at the Conference of London. He wanted to wage war against the Powers and he was supported by a considerable amount of hysteria in France. But Louis Philippe, facing realistically the force of the Great Power alliance against France, refused to agree to Thiers' proposals, and the latter resigned office.

Meanwhile, Mehemet Ali had refused to accept the Convention of London, and his forces were defeated by those of the Powers— Russian forces being involved on land, and the British Navy in the Eastern Mediterranean. He was deprived of both Syria and the island of Crete. Louis Philippe, having withdrawn his support for Mehemet Ali, secured the participation of France in this final agreement. Thus he had avoided a clash with Britain, which pleased his conservative middle-class supporters, but angered those like Thiers who wanted an adventurous, expansionist policy and the revival of French power abroad.

During these years a consistent supporter of the King's peaceful policy had been Guizot, the historian and conservative, who represented above all the cautious policy desired by a majority of the middle class in France. After the resignation of Thiers he became chief minister, and remained in that position till the Revolution of 1848.

**The Spanish Marriages.** Guizot followed the King's policy of peace with other countries, especially with Britain. He accepted the British interpretation of the law relating to the search for contraband of war on the high seas, a concession to the superior naval power of Britain. He also repudiated the action of a French naval commander in the Far East who had succeeded in securing the expulsion of the British from the island of Tahiti and their replacement by the French. A strong protest from Palmerston on this matter had been sufficient to cause a French withdrawal.

But even Guizot and Louis Philippe could not resist the temptation of a master-stroke in foreign policy. This arose from the situation in Spain in 1846. The Queen, Isabella, and her sister were both unmarried, and in view of the great importance of Spain to both Britain and France as Mediterranean powers, there was considerable anxiety to ensure that they married the "right" persons. As in the case of Belgium, Palmerston put forward the claim of a German prince and Louis Philippe that of his youngest son, the Duc de Montpensier. Eventually England and France agreed that Isabella should be married to the Duke of Cadiz and that her sister should be married to the Duc de Montpensier. But the condition attached to the agreement was that the second marriage should take place only after the first, and after Isabella had had children to succeed her. Actually, Louis Philippe broke this agreement and the marriages were celebrated on the same day. It was therefore possible that the children of the second marriage would in the future succeed to the throne, thus bringing France and Spain together in a permanent dynastic alliance.

Behind all this seemingly petty detail of the Spanish marriages, there were certain important forces at work. British foreign policy for the last hundred and fifty years had strongly opposed any form of union between France and Spain. By the Treaty of Utrecht in 1713 we had gained permanent possession of Gibraltar as the guardian of the entrance to the Mediterranean for British warships and merchantmen. Indeed, the previous long war had been fought in part to prevent Louis XIV carrying out his own scheme for the union of France and Spain. Now again, in the nineteenth century,

France was attempting to do what the "Grand Monarque" had failed to achieve. Palmerston was furious at this breach of the agreement made by Louis Philippe and Guizot, and from this moment the official friendship between England and France broke down. This undoubtedly contributed to the weakening of Louis Philippe's position in France, especially when Palmerston scored a resounding diplomatic victory against Louis Philippe over the position which arose in Switzerland in the same year. In that country a civil war had broken out between the Catholic and liberal cantons over the form of government to be adopted. Palmerston, while pretending to be anxious to hold his usual European conference to help in the settlement of this question, secretly urged the liberal forces to finish the war against the Catholic league of the Sonderbund as soon as possible. The liberal forces defeated their opponents decisively before a conference could be called, and French policy suffered a severe defeat. Louis Philippe had at least hoped that a victory for the Catholic league would strengthen his support among Catholics in France, but his efforts proved a fiasco.

**General Conclusions on the Foreign Policy of Louis Philippe.** Whatever course Louis Philippe pursued in foreign affairs he was sure to arouse the opposition of a substantial part of French opinion at home. His reign began with a partial success in Belgium, but Palmerston had forced him radically to alter his policy and withdraw the candidature of his son for the throne. Over Poland and Italy he offended the liberals and republicans. Over Mehemet Ali he set out on a course from which he was once again forced to withdraw, for he failed completely to gain a foothold for France in the Middle East —a failure exploited by Thiers to discredit him. Over the Spanish Marriages he offended many of his middle-class supporters who wanted above all friendship with Britain. And, finally, over Switzerland he was defeated by Palmerston and failed to gain credit from the Catholic Church in France. It can well be imagined how these partial successes or outright failures were fully exploited by all his opponents—especially by the Bonapartists, Legitimists, Liberals and Republicans. And it must be remembered that Louis Philippe, having kept the conduct of foreign affairs almost entirely in his own hands, had to bear personally the full blame for the results.

**Internal Affairs of France, 1830-1848.** As we have seen, the main support of Louis Philippe was the middle class which comprised the main body of voters in the elections. The mainstay of the King and of the Charter of 1830 was the revived National Guard. This was middle class in composition—the uniforms alone were in any case too expensive for the working class, while there were definite property qualifications needed for enrolment. This reliance of Louis Philippe on the moneyed middle class meant that he ignored the condition of the wage-earners and became more and more isolated from the mass of the people as his reign progressed. Similarly, the Chamber of Deputies became more and more out of touch with general opinion and appeared to the workers as an assembly where various scheming politicians were jostling for power and for the bribes which ministers like Guizot lavished upon them.

**Guizot, Chief Minister, 1840-1848.** Guizot represented as no other minister in Louis Philippe's reign the cautious, conservative middle-class policy of peace and satisfaction with the Charter of 1830 with its limited franchise of 200,000 voters. Guizot resisted all demands for an extension of the vote, the tenor of his argument being that people who wanted the vote in elections must work hard, make money and thus qualify as taxpayers for the vote. "Enrichissez-vous!" was his answer to a deputation. While refusing to make France more democratic, Guizot maintained his hold on the Chamber of Deputies by a deliberate policy of bribery and corruption—nearly half the members were either in receipt of government pensions or had their business enterprises directly assisted by the government. No wonder that such an assembly was very little concerned for the welfare of the poorer classes. This narrow selfishness was the greatest weakness of the Orleanist monarchy.

**Opponents of Louis Philippe.** There were many movements and groups opposed to Louis Philippe throughout his reign. This opposition came mainly from the Socialists, Republicans, Liberals, Legitimists and Bonapartists. The Socialists supported the rights of trade unions, demanded a working-class vote and the setting up of a state in which the working class had control. The Republicans, driven underground by laws against them, also demanded the extension of the vote and the setting up of a republic. The Liberals demanded that the King's ministers should be approved by the Chamber of Deputies and should be directly responsible to it for their actions. The Legitimists supported the claims of the descendants of Charles X to rule, and thoroughly despised the middle-class monarchy and the popular, handshaking manners of Louis Philippe. The Bonapartists staged two efforts during the reign to replace Louis Philippe by Louis Napoleon Bonaparte, nephew of Napoleon I.

The Catholic Church was also a force very much opposed to Louis Philippe, for its leaders could not forget that Charles X had aimed to increase its power in France. The prizes almost within the grasp of the Church had been wrested from it by the Revolution of 1830. Above all, Louis Philippe had greatly reduced the influence of the Church in education.

It is not surprising that many of the intellectuals of France—journalists, writers, pamphleteers—were critical of Louis Philippe. Most of them, despite their intelligence and education, were denied the vote in elections by the narrow franchise of 1830. The cartoonists of the Paris newspapers were especially unflattering towards the King, and a law was passed controlling and censoring their activities.

Many of these groups took every possible opportunity of weakening the position of the King. Even the Legitimists, who had little sympathy for the working classes, encouraged working-class demonstrations against the King in order to undermine his authority.

**Economic Growth of France. The "Proletariat".**    France was the second European country (after Belgium) to undergo the industrial revolution which had begun in Britain. The transformation of France into a modern industrial state was going on rapidly in the reign of Louis Philippe. Production of all important materials—such as coal, iron, cotton and woollen cloth, silk—rose steeply. The wealthy investors thrived. Money-making was a safe business under the peaceful and cautious government of Louis Philippe.

But there was another side to this economic development. By 1846 the town workers in France numbered about 9,000,000 in a total population of 35,000,000. The workers in the factories and mines were becoming an increasingly large proportion of the population. The wealth earned by the middle class was very much the result of the efforts of the working population, but the conditions of the workers were appalling. Young children aged five years worked for sixteen hours a day, accidents in the mines due to bad ventilation became increasingly common, and the workers were housed in filthy garrets and cellars. It was common, in such large cities as Marseilles and Lyons, for a whole family to live in one room. No wonder, then, that half the children of the working classes died before they were fifteen months old. In France at that time it was a commonplace to compare favourably the conditions of negroes in the West Indies with those of the French workers, who were referred to as the "white negroes". It is true that when entirely new factories were built and new settlements were established the employers made some efforts to provide new houses at moderate rents, but in general the factory system was adopted in crowded towns where the old domestic system of production already existed, and old, unsatisfactory buildings were used for new (and dangerous) machinery, as well as to provide dwellings for the workers. These conditions were particularly bad in the ancient cities of Lyons, Marseilles, Paris, Lille, Rouen and Mulhausen.

**Rise of Socialism.** It was amidst these conditions that the new doctrines of Socialism gained ground rapidly after 1830. Before that date Socialist ideas had been expounded by St. Simon (1760–1825) and Fourier (1772–1837). The first of these wanted society to be organised by selected intellectuals or experts who would have the good of everyone at heart and would ensure the fair and proper distribution of wealth to all the people. The second, Fourier, proposed the setting up of communities of 1600 individuals in each, where property was owned in common and no private capitalists existed. These settlements were to be linked together throughout France in a loose federation, with no strong central government. (His ideas were similar to those of Robert Owen in England, but they never had the same practical influence with the working class as did Owen's.) These two writers were idealistic or "utopian" Socialists and they had little direct effect upon the workers. But it was a different story with other reformers whose main activities occur after 1830. There was the socialist Blanqui, who attempted to stir up working-class insurrection, and timed his activities so badly that they failed dismally, with the consequence that he himself spent a great part of his life in prison. P. J. Proudhon (1809–1865) advocated the redistribution of property which was unfairly concentrated in a few hands. His famous assertion that "property is theft" was an exaggerated denunciation of this unfair distribution. But the most important Socialist thinker and active agitator in Louis Philippe's reign was Louis Blanc. In 1840 he published his famous work *L'Organisation du Travail*. In this book he argued that every man had the right to be given productive work and it was the duty of the State to see that he got it. He demanded that the State establish its own workshops which were to be run co-operatively by the workers employed in them. The profits of their labour were to be shared amongst them. He wanted to see the whole State organised on this basis, and he expounded plans for the ownership of all retail trade and of agricultural land by the State. His programme might with reasonable accuracy be described as full-scale nationalisation, with "workers' control" substituted for that of the private owner or capitalist. Blanc particularly stressed the importance of his workshops as a means of preventing unemployment. His influence became widespread among the workers and, as we shall see, he played a considerable part in the revolution of 1848.

**Early Opposition to Louis Philippe.** From the very commencement of his reign the King was the object of hatred by many political groups, and this hatred took violently active forms. Between 1830 and 1835 there were six outbreaks of serious revolt. In La Vendée, the western district of France where the old royalists had resisted for many years the Revolution of 1789, the Legitimists attempted a rising which was suppressed by troops. Then came the attempt in Paris of the conspirator Fieschi to assassinate Louis Philippe by firing at a royal procession with a twenty-four barrelled gun concealed in a house along the route. This was the first of many conspiracies to assassinate the King. There were two risings of the workers of Lyons: in 1831, over their demands for increased wages, and again in 1834, when they controlled the town for three days before giving in to government troops sent against them. In Paris itself there occurred a Republican rising in 1832 which resulted in two days of desperate fighting between the National Guard and the insurrectionists. It was at this time also that Blanqui attempted a socialist rising against the government. To end a somewhat violent catalogue, we must mention that Louis Napoleon Bonaparte also attempted unsuccessful conspiracies against Louis Philippe in 1836 and again in 1840.

**Louis Philippe's Internal Policy.** Louis Philippe's reply to these activities was to introduce the Law of Associations, by which heavy penalties were imposed for forming societies aimed at the overthrow of the government. This law was used not only against Republicans, Legitimists and Bonapartists, but also against the socialist societies and trade unions. (The Lyons rising of 1834 was in the main a protest against this law.) Newspapers were subjected to censorship. Finally, in 1835, the government passed a law which forbade even the discussion of any other form of government than the existing one, and prohibiting anyone from declaring himself a supporter of a former ruling family in France. This last regulation was aimed, of course, at the Legitimists and Bonapartists.

These laws therefore drove opposition to a great extent underground, where an increasing number of conspiracies dangerous to Louis Philippe were hatched. Only the mild representatives of the 200,000 middle-class voters who dominated the Chamber of Deputies were accorded anything like freedom of discussion.

Perhaps we should mention at this point one action of Louis Philippe's in 1841 which increased rather than (as he had hoped would be the case) decreased his difficulties. The body of the Emperor Napoleon was brought back from St. Helena and re-interred with much pomp and ceremony in the Invalides. Although great play was made in the newspapers about the friendliness of the British government in agreeing to this, the incident only served to emphasise for many Frenchmen the relative "tameness" of the foreign policy of Louis Philippe. It increased that peculiar "Napoleonic" nostalgia which was already beginning to influence sections of public opinion.

**The Demand for Parliamentary Reform.** There was one point on which many of the groups opposed to Louis Philippe were agreed, namely, the need to extend the vote in elections in order to make the Chamber of Deputies more representative of the nation. But Guizot was as much opposed to this change as was the middle-class Parliament in England to the demands of the Chartists. As we have seen, Guizot's attitude to all such demands was contained in his celebrated reply to a deputation which visited him: "Enrichissez-vous!"—which simply meant that the poorer classes should work hard, save money, gain a middle-class income, and then they would qualify for the vote!

**Guizot's Stagnant Social Policy.** In matters affecting the lives of the mass of the people Guizot was equally obdurate against change. One Factory Act affecting young workers was passed in 1841, but otherwise nothing was done to improve the condition of the workers. But at the same time Guizot did everything possible to promote business enterprise and the interests of the wealthy. In wider social matters the government was complacent and self-satisfied, relying for its support upon the corrupted Chamber of Deputies (see page 107). It was from this selfish policy of "laissez-faire" pursued by Guizot that the increasing opposition of the socialist workmen under Louis Blanc arose, especially as low wages and unemployment were becoming great problems for the workers.

**The Reform Banquets.** In 1843 the Socialists and Republicans united in their demand for Parliamentary Reform. They published an influential newspaper, *Réforme*, in which they demanded the lowering of the tax qualification for the vote to 100 francs, which would have enfranchised skilled workers and the lower middle-class, professional people and shopkeepers especially. They also demanded the abolition of the property qualification for becoming a member of the Chamber of Deputies. Guizot refused even to agree to a debate on these demands in the Chamber of Deputies, although they were put forward year after year.

In reply to Guizot's attitude the organisers of the reform movement began to hold what were known as "Reform Banquets" in Paris and other centres. Throughout France these banquets, at which the demand for parliamentary reform was toasted, became increasingly popular. Louis Philippe's reaction was an attempt to suppress them. On February 22, 1848, a Reform Banquet was planned in Paris at which 87 sympathisers from the Chamber of Deputies were to be the principal guests. The government prohibited the banquet and the organisers actually cancelled it. Nevertheless, a huge crowd assembled for the march to the banqueting hall. There was some disorder but nothing serious occurred.

It was at this point that the Socialists and their Republican allies forced the pace of events. During the night of February 22–23 barricades were thrown up in the working-class quarters of the city. Louis Philippe called out the National Guard, which, far from being willing to attack the barricades, fraternised with the demonstrators. At this point Guizot resigned his post, but a demonstration was organised against him in front of his apartments at the Foreign Office. Fighting broke out between the guards and the demonstrators in which twenty people were killed. Some of the corpses were paraded on a cart through the streets and everywhere the cry was raised "Long live the Republic!" The National Guard being completely unreliable, Louis Philippe abdicated on February 24 and fled to England.

The sudden and dramatic fall of the July Monarchy showed how great was the discontent with Louis Philippe's government—a discontent the widespread nature of which he had failed to appreciate and with which he attempted to deal by means of suppression. In February, 1848, the underground political clubs suddenly appeared in the open and others which had disguised themselves as non-political workmen's clubs or literary societies showed their true political colours. The circumstance that above all shook the confidence of the King was the realisation that the middle-class National Guard itself could no longer be relied upon to support him as had been the case in the stormy years of 1830–1835. Discontent had spread even into the ranks of his middle-class supporters.

The Republicans and Socialists had taken the main part in the dethronement of Louis Philippe, and they now formed a Provisional Government at the head of which was the Republican poet, Lamartine, and in which the Socialist Louis Blanc also had a place.

# chapter six

# THE SECOND REPUBLIC AND THE SECOND EMPIRE, 1848–1870

**Introductory.** The Revolution of 1848 was brought about essentially by the alliance of the middle and working classes. This alliance was uneasy, especially in Paris and the great provincial towns, for the working class programme took on socialist forms which were directly contrary to the propertied interests of the middle class. These differences led to serious conflict in Paris between the socialist movement and the government, resulting in four days of violent fighting in June, 1848. Out of this conflict of interests Louis Napoleon Bonaparte was able to gain support for the revival of the Empire based on order and the protection of property rights. The first stage towards his Imperial goal is his election as President in December, 1848, and from then on he builds up his power to the point of the proclamation of the Empire in 1852. As Napoleon III he attempts to consolidate and increase the power of France by a dynamic foreign policy, but his efforts are hampered and divided by the conflicts of opinion and interest among his advisers and in the nation itself. The results of his foreign policy are half-accomplishments or, as in the case of Mexico, downright failures. He is outmatched in guile and diplomatic skill by Bismarck, and the defeat of 1870 sees the end of the second Napoleonic era.

**Socialist Aims and Influence.** No sooner had the Second Republic been established than wide differences of opinion appeared among those who had united to overthrow Louis Philippe. The Socialists under Louis Blanc wished to press forward to great schemes of social reform as advocated in *L'Organisation du Travail* and thus convert France into a Socialist Republic. At this stage of the Republic's history the Socialists were in a seemingly strong position, for they held the chief posts in the Provisional Government. This advantageous position of the Socialists was primarily due to their strength in Paris and the leading part they had taken in the revolution. Lamartine, the head of the Provisional Government, refused to substitute the red flag for the tricolour as the emblem of the Republic, for this would have meant his acceptance of the idea of a Socialist Republic.

Fig. 13.—Tree of Liberty on the Boulevard St. Martin, Paris. (*See* page 119.)

On the other hand, he agreed to the demands for the National Workshops and some other Socialist proposals.

**The Luxembourg Committee.** The Socialists demanded, and obtained, the establishment of a department of government especially concerned with the condition of the workers. This department was known as the Ministry of Labour and Progress. Besides this, a special committee was set up under the chairmanship of Louis Blanc. This was the Luxembourg Committee, named after the palace in which it met. The committee sat separately from the main government, however, and thus became isolated from the work of the other ministers. The Luxembourg Committee at once proceeded to draft a number of decrees lessening the hours of work in factories, establishing minimum wages and strengthening the position of the trade unions. But the employers were so firmly united against these reforms, and the Luxembourg Committee was so isolated from the remainder of the government, that these decrees were never put into force.

**Suppression of the Demonstration of April 16, 1848.** In April, 1848, a huge demonstration under Socialist leadership occurred at the Hôtel de Ville, where the Provisional Government had its headquarters. The demonstrators demanded the abolition of the capitalist system and the organisation of all work on a co-operative basis as advocated by Louis Blanc.

This was a critical moment for the Provisional Government. If they had accepted the Socialist demands the Republic would have taken on an entirely different nature, for the demands of the Socialists were a challenge to the rights of private property. The Provisional Government decided to use force against the demonstrators. The newly-formed "garde mobile" was summoned and dispersed the crowd. This was the commencement of that sharp conflict between the Socialists and their opponents which played a leading part in the events of 1848.

**The Elections of May, 1848.** Elections were held in May to the Constituent Assembly whose main task was to work out a new form of government for France. These elections were very significant, for they showed that the influence of the middle class was still dominant in France. Every Frenchman over twenty-one years of age had the vote, giving an electorate of 9,000,000. In Paris itself only three out of twenty-four Socialist candidates were elected. At the other extreme 130 Legitimists (supporters of the descendants of Charles X) were elected. The majority of the 900 members of the Assembly were middle-class Republicans strongly opposed to Socialism.

**The National Workshops.** The next violent clash between the Socialists and their opponents occurred over the National Workshops. These had been set up towards the end of February and continued till the end of May. The scheme consisted of giving the unemployed of Paris work of a "navvying" type at the rate of two francs a day. The number employed rose from 6,000 in March to over 100,000 in May, for the unemployed flocked in from the countryside and other centres. This vast horde was given work of an almost useless character—for example, digging out the foundations for a railway station and then filling them in again. These purposeless "diggings and refillings", as they were described, brought the whole scheme into disrepute. At last, through lack of sufficient work, the unemployed were put on "inactivity pay" of one franc a day.

The expense of the scheme led to an increase of taxation which was strongly resisted by the wealthier classes, who regarded the scheme as a direct challenge to their own interests. They were also alarmed to see such a vast horde under the influence of Socialist organisers. It looked as though a Socialist "army" was being created.

It is important to realise that the National Workshops were nothing like the co-operative workshops and factories proposed by Louis Blanc. Moreover, the government of Lamartine had never been enthusiastic for the scheme, and they had entrusted it to a minister, Marie, who had no faith in it whatever. Thus the actual schemes of Louis Blanc were never given a fair trial.

On June 21, 1848, the government brought the National Workshops to an end, and in doing so brought on one of the worst conflicts the turbulent city of Paris had ever witnessed.

**The Four Days: June 23–26, 1848.** No sooner had the news of the government's decision spread throughout the city, than workmen of the eastern districts of Paris threw barricades across the streets. The Assembly replied to these moves by appointing General Cavaignac military dictator, having under his command a force composed of the regular soldiers, the National Guard and the newly-formed "garde mobile". These forces were launched against the barricades and fierce fighting raged for three days. The casualties on both sides were enormous. More than 10,000 of the insurgents were killed and wounded and, after the victory of Cavaignac, many thousands were imprisoned or sent to Algeria. Thus the final conflict between the Socialists and their opponents had ended in a hard-won victory for the latter.

The effects of the "four days" were, on the one hand, to make the

Socialists even more bitter opponents of the Republic, and, on the other, to make the propertied classes, and especially the French peasantry, eager for order and discipline in the state as a protection against the spectre of socialism and communism. They looked for the strong hand. They were to find it in the person of Louis Napoleon Bonaparte.

**The Constitution.** The Assembly set up a constitution for France composed of a single Chamber of Deputies of 750 members elected for four years by universal male suffrage. The Chamber of Deputies could not be suspended or dissolved without its own consent—an arrangement designed to prevent the President acting on his sole authority against the Chamber. The President was to be elected also by universal suffrage for a term of four years only and was not then re-eligible as a candidate for another four years. The President appointed his own ministers, was head of the armed forces and, being elected by the people directly, did not regard himself as answerable for his actions to the Chamber of Deputies.

What was the important fact about this peculiar form of government? Obviously, the President, in case of a clash between himself and the Chamber of Deputies, could summon to his aid the armed forces. Being elected by the people, he could claim that he was answerable to them only. This was the situation exploited by Louis Napoleon Bonaparte for his own ends.

**Louis Napoleon Bonaparte elected President, December, 1848.** Louis Napoleon was the son of Louis, King of Holland, and thus a nephew of Napoleon I. He regarded himself as the direct heir to the great Napoleonic tradition and his whole life had so far consisted in the cultivation of the "Napoleonic Legend". In 1836 he made a ludicrous failure of his attempt to raise the garrison of Strasbourg to revolt in his favour. At Boulogne in 1840 he made a further attempt to oust Louis Philippe. He landed with a number of supporters, failed to gain effective support in the town and saw his party driven back to their boats with a number of casualties. He himself was wounded, captured and imprisoned in the fortress of Ham, whence he escaped in 1846 disguised as a workman. In 1848 he enrolled as a special constable in London to help police the city against the Chartists. In all these adventures there is no consistent vein of principle whatever. He is apparently a good liberal or democrat in 1831, a mere egoistic plotter and conspirator in 1836 and 1840, and a thoroughgoing supporter of "law and order" in England in 1848.

The inconsistency and "adventurism" which characterise his later career were already well marked before 1848.

**Writings of Louis Napoleon Bonaparte.** During his imprisonment he had passed the time in writing treatises on various important questions of the day. For example, in his pamphlet *The Extinction of Pauperism* he evolved schemes for the abolition of unemployment and for the planned development by the State of all unused land. In other works he appealed to the military side of the French nature by demanding the reform of the French Army and its revival as in the days of Napoleon I. He even elaborated a scheme for a Panama Canal. But most important of all was his work entitled *Napoleonic Ideas* (*Des Idées Napoléoniennes*). In this work he was at pains to explain the real aims of his famous uncle. This work was a further attempt to justify the ideas which Napoleon I himself had elaborated while a prisoner on St. Helena. According to Louis Napoleon Bonaparte, the one great aim of his uncle had been to bring to Europe an era of peace and liberty, but he had been frustrated in these aims by the other Powers of Europe. He had not wished to "shed a sea of blood", but others had forced the necessity upon him.

To the great majority of Frenchmen these ideas seemed to hold a promise of order and progress and national dignity after the disorder and strife of 1848. In December, 1848, Louis Napoleon Bonaparte, who had already been elected to the Chamber of Deputies by five constituencies, was also elected President by 5,400,000 votes, against 1,400,000 for Cavaignac and 17,000 for the poet-republican Lamartine.

**Reasons for the Election of Louis Bonaparte.** We have seen how attractive to many Frenchmen were the ideas of Louis Napoleon, but his rise was aided by many factors which were not of his own making. The return of Napoleon I's body from St. Helena in 1841 had encouraged that nostalgic looking to the Napoleonic past which was a reaction against the cautious and unadventurous policy of Louis Philippe. Again, a number of French historians had done their best to "glamorise" the name of Napoleon I. Among these writers was Adolphe Thiers, whose work *A History of the Consulate and the Empire* showed the first Napoleon in a decidedly heroic light. Then, again, there were many divisions in the Republican ranks in 1848—some wished to conciliate the Catholic Church, others wished to oppose its attempts to gain control of education, others supported Cavaignac, but other Republicans were afraid that he intended to assume personal powers. Even more important, many Liberals and even Socialists, voted for

Louis Bonaparte in the hope that he would genuinely live up to his professions of concern for the workers. For entirely different motives, the French peasantry voted solidly for Louis Bonaparte. They saw in him the guarantee of the private ownership of their land which the Revolution of 1789 had brought about and which Napoleon I himself had recognised. To the peasantry the name of Bonaparte meant security of possession against the nationalisation of land which communism and socialism implied. Finally, before his election, Louis Bonaparte had indicated that he would favour the Catholic Church.

Thus Bonapartism in 1848 seemed to have something to offer to everybody, while Louis Bonaparte himself showed great skill in exploiting the situation. He refused to ally himself with any particular group or party and thus he appeared to be "above party".

**Louis Bonaparte strengthens his Position.** The first government appointed by Bonaparte was composed of representatives of those groups he was most anxious to conciliate and then win over to his complete support. These were the Orleanists, Catholics and Legitimists. But the key post of head of the police was given to—a Bonapartist!

A definite attempt was now made by the Minister of Education, Falloux, to give more control over education to the Catholic Church. But the only immediate effect of this was merely to show that Bonaparte was at least attempting to keep his promises, for the proposals were defeated in the Assembly where the Republicans had a majority. Then another attempt—and this time more successful—was made by Louis Napoleon to gain Catholic support. General Oudinot was dispatched to Rome to suppress the Roman Republic which had been set up by Garibaldi and Mazzini. After some reverses to the French force, Oudinot succeeded, with the help of the Austrians, in restoring the Pope to Rome.

The Roman expedition was authorised by the President himself, but he was acting against the constitution in interfering between the Pope and his subjects. He was heavily criticised by the Republican majority in the Assembly. The problem that really faced him was how exactly to get rid of the Republican majority and then suppress altogether the Republican movement. The attitude of the Republicans to the education question and to the Roman expedition enabled the President to win over Catholic support for his ultimate object.

Louis Bonaparte now ordered his chief of police to take every possible action to stamp out Republican ideas. Even the trees of liberty which, on the model of 1789, had been planted in many towns after the overthrow of Louis Philippe, were now destroyed. And action began to be taken against various Republican societies.

**The Party of Order.** To strengthen their position against republicanism and socialism, the Legitimists, Bonapartists and Catholics formed an alliance just before the elections of 1849 under the new constitution. This alliance, aided by the measures of suppression of the Republicans already taken by the Bonapartist chief of police, succeeded in gaining 500 representatives in the Chamber of Deputies out of 750.

Two important measures followed—firstly, Falloux now succeeded in passing his law by which the local priest was made the official inspector of the elementary school. One purpose of this was to prevent the employment of teachers of Republican sympathies, who were generally regarded as atheists, freethinkers or, at least, anti-clericals. Secondly, the Assembly decided to reduce the Republican vote by disfranchising about 3,000,000 of the 9,000,000 voters.

**Louis Bonaparte and the Assembly.** At this point Louis Bonaparte played his master card. Instead of accepting the disfranchisement of the 3,000,000 voters, he demanded that the Assembly should withdraw the new regulation. His aim in adopting this unexpected attitude was to pose as the protector of the Republic and of the people against the Assembly and then to change the government to a purely Bonapartist one with the support of the people. Thus, under the guise of protecting the nation and "democracy", he would be able to take another decisive step in the direction of his own form of dictatorship. His plan was further strengthened when the Assembly stupidly refused to repeal the disfranchisement law. He now went on various official tours throughout France, and his supporters made the most of them. The cry of "Long Live the Empire" was heard on many occasions. Nearly every local council in France also supported his own demand that the constitution should be revised to enable him to be President for another ten years. The only opposition to this proposal came from the Assembly in Paris. Thus he once again was able to show that the people supported him against the Assembly. At this time he was increasing his popularity with the army by holding parades and organising demonstrations in his own favour.

**The Establishment of the Second Empire.** Louis Bonaparte now calculated that the time was ripe for stronger action still against his opponents of all groups. He appointed mainly his own supporters to the government. His half-brother Morny was responsible for the various stages of the plot, and, as Minister of the Interior, he appointed a Bonapartist to command the National Guard. He also persuaded the commander of the regular troops in Paris to join in the preparations. Suddenly, on December 2, 1851, the anniversary of Napoleon I's coronation, the police arrested the leading men of all parties who opposed the revision of the constitution as demanded by Bonaparte. The troops seized the Palais Bourbon where the Assembly met and over 200 Monarchist deputies who opposed Bonaparte were arrested. On December 3 and 4 the Republicans attempted a rising against him in Paris, but were defeated by troops under the command of the Bonapartist General St. Arnaud. Louis Bonaparte now seized the opportunity to set up special tribunals to try his opponents, and over 20,000 were imprisoned or exiled. In this way he cowed his opponents and destroyed the Republican Party.

He claimed that he had carried out these ruthless measures to protect the nation, and he therefore appealed to the nation to accept what he had done. The resulting plebiscite gave him a vote of 7,500,000 in favour and only 640,000 against. Known Republicans were not allowed to vote and Morny "manipulated" the elections to a certain extent, but even if these allowances are made, the vote showed decisive support for Louis Bonaparte.

The new constitution was only a preliminary to the revival of the Empire. The President was to hold office for ten years, a Senate chosen by him was to propose laws and the Legislative Assembly had to pass them. This was little more than a dictatorship, for even elections were only to be made for the Assembly from lists of candidates approved by the President. All these measures further consolidated his hold on the country. He flattered the army by restoring the eagle standards of Napoleon I, he went on further tours to enhance his popularity, and then persuaded the Senate to vote for the restoration of the Empire. This proposal was then put to a plebiscite in which he received 7,800,000 votes and only 253,000 against.

Thus by ruthlessness, subtlety and appeal to the people as the true guardian of their interests and those of the Republic, he destroyed the Republic—with popular approval! The Second Empire was established on December 2, 1852.

**Internal Government of Napoleon III.** The Emperor had promised order first and liberty at a later time. We have already seen that "order" meant the suppression of his main political opponents as the first step. His next step was to reorganise the government in such a way as to consolidate his power still further. The real basis of his power was the army, and in 1855 he introduced a Conscription Law by which men were able to buy exemption from conscription. With the money thus obtained Napoleon III paid specially-selected men and officers and thus built up a strong professional army entirely devoted to himself.

Before the army reforms, however, he had consolidated his hold more firmly on the civil government. Only lists of candidates approved by the Emperor were allowed in elections, the ministers of the government were all compelled to swear an oath of allegiance to him and were only answerable for their actions to himself and not to the Assembly. The most important local officials, the Prefects of the Departments, were carefully selected supporters of the Emperor and were answerable to him for all actions. They were "little emperors" and had very great powers—for example, they appointed all teachers in the State schools and could dissolve at will any local council which opposed the Emperor's wishes.

Strong measures were taken to control the press. Newspapers were compelled to deposit with the government 50,000 francs as surety for their "good behaviour". The Minister of the Interior could suppress newspapers at pleasure, but a system of warnings was also used. On

FIG. 14.—CENSORSHIP IN PARIS: The Office of the "Newspaper Police".

a third warning a newspaper would inevitably be suppressed. More-over, cases affecting newspapers and journals were tried without the jury system.

The University of Paris was subject to a close government sur-veillance. Professors had to take an oath of allegiance to the Em-peror, and certain "dangerous" subjects (such as History and Philo-sophy) were no longer taught. All this control was reinforced by the employment of spies in every department of life—they haunted the cafés and theatres of Paris especially, and persons making the mildest criticisms of the government were liable to immediate arrest.

**Reasons for the Lack of Opposition.** For the first ten years of the Second Empire there was very little opposition to Napoleon III's system. The reasons for this are not far to seek. The propertied classes had been saved from the "spectre" of socialism and com-munism and were willing to accept a dictatorship which guaranteed their safety. Not only were they safe, but they prospered through the economic policy of the government. In numerous directions there were profitable avenues of investment, especially in the basic indus-tries and in railways. Napoleon III established special banks to assist manufacturers and farmers to borrow capital, and France now took her place among the great industrial nations of Europe. In 1855 a great exhibition of her industrial products and arts was held in Paris, only four years after the Great Exhibition in the Crystal Palace in London. The interests of the working class were not completely neglected as they had been in the reign of Louis Philippe. Napoleon had learnt the lesson that the "masses" were beginning to count in the order of things. He therefore redeemed some of his pledges as expressed in his pamphlet *The Extinction of Pauperism* by promoting public works with government money (shadow of the National Work-shops!), by preventing profiteering in foodstuffs, and by extensive slum clearance in the big towns, especially Paris. Under the super-vision of Baron Haussman, the central part of the city was rebuilt with the beautiful setting of the boulevards which it has today. This rebuilding served another purpose. It cleared away many of the narrow streets which had been ideal for the erection of the revolu-tionary barricades.

Added to all this were the new splendours of a Court dominated by the personality of the Empress Eugénie. It became the scene of magnificent entertainments which made Paris the European centre of gaiety and fashion. The Imperial hunting parties held each year in the forest of Compiègne, the magnificence of the Paris Opera, the military parades—all these things gave an impression of "culture" and splendour.

Yet we must remember that some of the finest Frenchmen never accepted the new régime. The great novelist, Victor Hugo, lived in exile, while many leading Republicans were either in prison or banished to the French penal settlements.

Thus Napoleon III had crushed opposition, consolidated his power by dictatorship supported by the middle class and the peasantry, gained the unswerving loyalty of the army, and, up to 1860, carried out a successful foreign policy which, despite his difficulties, brought him considerable credit.

**Foreign Policy to 1860.** (a) *The Crimean War.* There is no doubt that Napoleon III was not the ruthless militarist which his uncle had been. Yet to gain support he had been compelled to strengthen the French Army and reintroduce much of the atmosphere of the First Empire. He had, in fact, encouraged many of the military leaders in France to look to glory for the army in the very near future. Napoleon III could not ignore the fact that without that glory the continued support of the army leaders for him was uncertain. This was one of the primary reasons for the Crimean War fought against Russia, 1854–1856.

The Czar Nicholas was claiming to protect the Christians of the Balkan peninsula against their overlords the Turks. Moreover, he was claiming protection of the Holy Places in Jerusalem for the Greek Orthodox Church as against the Catholic Church. And, above all, he had made his opinion quite clear to both Britain and France that the Turkish Empire was in decay and ought to have its life ended by the Great Powers as soon as possible. Traditional British policy was concerned to keep Russian influence out of the Mediterranean, to protect the route to India and therefore to bolster up the Turkish Empire. In all this Napoleon III saw the possibility of a successful war against Russia with the help of Britain, and he therefore urged the Sultan to resist Russian demands on Turkey. He also saw a clear opportunity to gain increased support from the Catholic Church by taking up the Catholic cause against the Greek Orthodox Church. Every Frenchman knew that Louis Philippe had been defeated by Russia and Britain over the Mehemet Ali affair, and now there was an opportunity to avenge both 1840—and 1812. But this time France's position was strengthened by the alliance with England. And had not the Czar Nicholas insulted Napoleon III by refusing to address him officially as "mon frère"?

When Russia attacked Turkey, Britain and France launched their joint attack on the Crimea. It was a war of terrible losses, of shocking mismanagement on the part of the allies, and of fierce resistance by the Russians. Only after 100,000 Frenchmen had been killed was the war brought to an end by the capture of Sebastopol and the Treaty of Paris imposed on Russia. The Black Sea was to be neutralised—no Russian warships were allowed on it and other Russian military establishments had to be dismantled. The Sultan promised to give better treatment to his Christian subjects, but, if anything, their treatment became worse as the years went on. However, Napoleon had won his war and Paris became the diplomatic centre of Europe. His prestige was strengthened, and this was recognised by the visit to Paris of Queen Victoria and several other crowned heads.

(b) *Napoleon III and Italy.* The Emperor's past career and promises continued to present him with a bewildering variety of problems. This is seen most clearly in his Italian policy. As a former Carbonaro, he was pledged to help the Italians in their struggle for freedom and national independence against Austria. Yet Austria was a great Catholic State and the protector of the Pope of Rome. Thus Catholic forces in France were mainly against assisting the Italians, while other forces, including Napoleon's cousin, the Prince Jerome, were in favour of assistance. However, the Sardinians had given considerable help to the French and British in the Crimean War, and at the Peace Conference, Cavour had drawn the attention of the allies to the grievances of the Italians against Austria. Napoleon was thus under considerable pressure to aid Italy, but he hesitated, and while he hesitated he earned the outright enmity of a number of Italian exiles in Paris who had expected him to act immediately. One of their leaders, Orsini, attempted to assassinate the Emperor and Empress by throwing bombs at their carriage while they were on the way to the Opera. The bombs killed several people, but Napoleon and the Empress escaped. From his prison and during his trial Orsini urged Napoleon to support Italy, but Napoleon's first reaction was to demand that Cavour suppress all revolutionaries in Italy. To this Cavour replied that the Italian people resented the French occupation of Rome and that there was danger of further attempts on the Emperor's life.

**The Compact of Plombières, July 20, 1858.** The final effect of the Orsini bomb was to make Napoleon come to an agreement with Cavour. His motives were partly fear of further attack on him and partly a genuine sympathy with Italian aims. A further motive was his desire not only to assist the Italian movement but also to control it in such a way that Italy would not become too strong. The interests of the Pope must not suffer. In other words, he was still hoping to satisfy everybody, from Catholics to Liberals.

It was four months after the Orsini plot that Napoleon III met Count Cavour secretly at Plombières. Here it was agreed that France and Piedmont should expel the Austrians from Italy, and in return for his help Napoleon III would receive Savoy and Nice. But there was no agreement for the complete unification of Italy under Piedmont. Instead, a Kingdom of Central Italy was to be formed independent of Sardinia, and the Pope was to be left as the ruler of Rome. But Cavour needed French support, and he was prepared to accept these terms in return for it. Even after the agreement, however, Cavour was so uncertain about Napoleon's promises that he did everything possible to provoke Austria to war. In particular, he mobilised large Sardinian forces on the frontier of Lombardy. Napoleon himself seems to have wavered in face of the opposition by the Empress and others at Court to any attack on Catholic Austria. When England intervened to prevent war, he agreed with her that Sardinia should demobilise and even sent such an order to Cavour. Thus, on the very brink of war which the Compact of Plombières was designed to bring about—he wavered! Nothing is more typical of the Emperor, and nothing shows how utterly different he was from the famous uncle whom he claimed to succeed.

Cavour refused the command from Napoleon to demobilise. The Austrians, thinking that Napoleon III was about to desert Piedmont, also ordered the Sardinians to demobilise. They refused. Austrian troops moved at once against Sardinia, and in doing so they played into Cavour's hands, for now Napoleon III had the justification he needed. The Austrians were the aggressors. European sympathy was with the Italians, and Napoleon would be fighting on the popular side. There was no fear of complications from other Powers. French troops poured into northern Italy to assist Sardinia, and they won two victories against the Austrians at the battles of Magenta and Solferino. Then, when everything was going well for Sardinia, and when the Austrians had already been driven from Lombardy, Napoleon withdrew from the war!

**The Truce of Villafranca, 1859.** The reasons for Napoleon III's sudden change of mind have always been a matter of dispute, but several factors seem to be certain. Firstly, the French casualties had been very high indeed, and he had to keep a close eye on French opinion and on his opponents among the friends of the Empress. Secondly, the successes in the north were encouraging people throughout Italy to demand union under Piedmont, which Napoleon, concerned above all for the Papacy and Catholic opinion in France, was anxious to avoid. In other words, he could not *control* the Italian movement as he had hoped. Thirdly, he saw a strong and united Italy as a danger to French interests in the Mediterranean. He gained the reward of Savoy and Nice for his assistance, but the outcome of the Italian intervention was not the clear-cut triumph which he had achieved in the Crimean War. He had offended all those Liberals in France who had expected him to live up to his avowed sympathy with movements of national liberation and carry the struggle through to the bitter end against Austria; while at the same time the Catholic interests in France were opposed to him for having gone as far as he did. In attempting to please all, he had succeeded in pleasing none.

**The Mexican Adventure.** While Napoleon III had only partly discredited himself by his Italian campaign, the next adventure was a complete fiasco, and a complete humiliation. In 1861 the Mexican government, which had borrowed large sums from certain European countries, refused to pay the interest on her debts. England, France and Spain sent an expedition against Mexico which forced her to resume payment. The British and Spanish troops left Mexico, but Napoleon maintained the French forces in the country. He had determined to establish a Catholic Empire in Mexico. His motives for this action were twofold:

(1) Military and imperialist glory which he thought could be cheaply won against the relatively weak government of Mexico.
(2) To regain the support of the Catholic party in France—a support which had been greatly weakened through his Italian policy.

In these circumstances, and urged on strongly by the Empress Eugénie, he persuaded Maximilian, brother of the Emperor of Austria, to accept the position of Emperor of Mexico. The struggle against the Mexicans under their great national leader Juarez was far more difficult than Marshal Bazaine, the French commander, had anticipated. However, Maximilian was able at last to enter Mexico City where he was crowned. But the triumph was short-lived. In

1865 the Civil War in the United States, which had kept that country occupied, came to an end, and a direct warning was given to Napoleon that he must give up his Mexican adventure or bear the consequences of infringing the Monroe Doctrine—war with the United States. Moreover, the situation in Europe was changing fast. Prussian strength was growing and Napoleon could not afford to have 40,000 French troops shut up in Mexico, nor could he afford the 14,000,000 francs a month which the campaign was costing. The outcome of the whole affair was that Napoleon withdrew his forces from Mexico, leaving Maximilian isolated. The wife of Maximilian went mad with anxiety and dismay at this betrayal. To crown the whole sordid edifice of betrayal and tragic failure, the Mexicans took Maximilian prisoner, had him tried, and finally shot him in 1867. This time, there was nothing whatever to compensate for Napoleon III's utter failure.

**Changes in the Government of France, 1860-1870.** The increasing difficulties abroad led to a corresponding increase in opposition to the Emperor at home. In 1860 he made a Commercial Treaty with Great Britain by which English coal, iron, machinery and textiles entered France with reduced import duties and in return England reduced duties on French wines and spirits. This treaty was in accord with the Emperor's Free Trade opinions, but it caused him to lose the support of the leading merchants and manufacturers of France. In order, therefore, to make up for the loss of support from manufacturers and the Catholics, he began to allow more political freedom in France with the purpose of gaining the support of the Liberals. In this way he hoped successfully to play off one political group against another. The period of the "Liberal Empire" begins, strictly speaking, in 1859 when he granted a political amnesty to all prisoners and allowed exiled politicians to return from abroad. He then issued decrees which allowed the publication in full of all parliamentary debates and also allowed the Senate and the Legislature to criticise the government. This greater freedom, however, led to an increase in the strength of his opponents, and in the elections of 1863 seventeen Republicans were returned.

There now developed in France a grouping of Liberal politicians, of whom Thiers was a prominent member, calling themselves the Third Party. They demanded the formation of a government responsible to the Assembly and not to the Emperor alone. As the foreign difficulties of the Emperor increased, so this group increased their own influence until in 1868 the Emperor was forced to make further concessions to liberty. The government lost its right to warn and

Fig. 15.—Paris' Link with the Outside World during the Siege of 1871.
(*See page 133.*)   A balloon at Montmartre.

suppress newspapers, and public meetings were again allowed. These concessions in their turn led to the increasing influence of the Republican newspapers, especially as the Socialists and Republicans had agreed upon an alliance against the Empire. The culmination of all these developments was the election of 1869 in which the opponents of the government gained 3,355,000 votes against 4,438,000 for the government. The Emperor was now suffering from a serious illness which made it increasingly difficult for him to keep a firm hold on events. He failed to hold together even his own supporters, while in foreign affairs things were reaching a critical stage. At last, under pressure of the Third Party, he agreed that the Legislature should introduce laws and vote on the budget, two fundamental needs for anything approaching parliamentary democracy. Thus, by 1870 the despotic Empire created in 1852 had already been seriously undermined. The final blow to the Empire came with the war against Prussia, the origins and course of which we must now consider.

### THE FRANCO-PRUSSIAN WAR OF 1870 AND THE FALL OF NAPOLEON III

By 1866 it had become obvious to Napoleon III that the rising state of Prussia under the leadership of her "Iron Chancellor" Bismarck was a challenge to the position of France in Europe. The war party in France, strongly supported by the Empress Eugénie, actually wanted a war against Prussia, for they considered that only by a victory over that country could the Second Empire continue. On the other side, Bismarck was also working towards war with France, and he played his cards so successfully that by the end of 1866 Napoleon III had already lost the initiative.

In 1864 Prussia and Austria had taken over control of the Danish provinces of Schleswig and Holstein and soon afterwards they quarrelled over the administration of the territories. This led to the Austro-Prussian war of 1866—the Seven Weeks' War—an overwhelming victory for Prussia. It was in this connection that Napoleon III made his most serious miscalculation in foreign policy. He had expected the war to be long and hard-fought, and he had imagined himself at the end dictating his own terms to two exhausted combatants. For this reason he had readily fallen victim to the wiles of Bismarck, who promised him the control of Luxemburg if he remained neutral. Thoroughly disconcerted by the rapid ending of the war, Napoleon now demanded the cession to him of part of the left bank of the Rhine, as well as Luxemburg and Belgium. Far from

FIG. 16.—DISCUSSING THE WAR IN A PARIS CAFÉ.

agreeing to assist in these aims, Bismarck let the South German states know of Napoleon's demands on German territory—with the result that the Southern German states now turned towards Prussia, whereas before they had inclined to regard France as a possible protector against Prussian aggression. Then, later, in 1870, Bismarck also published Napoleon's demands for Luxemburg and Belgium, which was a decisive factor in preventing Britain giving aid to France.

**The Spanish Succession.** The immediate cause of war was the question of the succession to the Spanish throne which had become vacant through the deposition of the reigning queen by a military rising. The new government offered the throne to Leopold of Hohenzollern-Sigmaringen, a relative of William I of Prussia. Bismarck persuaded him to accept the offer, knowing that the "encircling" of France which this would really amount to, would rouse tremendous indignation in that country. Bismarck's calculations were correct, and, in fact, William I persuaded Leopold to withdraw his candidature when France protested. For a time it appeared that William I, not wishing for an immediate war with France, had won the day against the Prussian supporters of Bismarck. But at this point the more aggressive party in the French government overstepped the bounds of common sense and even the wishes of Napoleon III himself. They now formulated the demand that the Hohenzollern candidature for the Spanish throne would never again be renewed, and the French Ambassador requested an interview with William I, who was at that time at Ems, the famous German spa. William informed Benedetti that he could not give such a promise, and regarded the matter as closed. William sent Bismarck a telegram from Ems describing these negotiations, and, before publishing it, Bismarck so altered the wording that it appeared that William I had insulted the French Ambassador by deliberately refusing to see him again when requested.

A wave of war hysteria, fiercely whipped up by the war party supported by the Empress Eugénie, swept over France. The Emperor himself was won over and war declared. Bismarck had achieved his object. He now made public Napoleon's demands against Belgium and Luxemburg, and this effectively isolated France from Great Britain. The war had been brought about, neither by the majority of French nor German opinion, but by Bismarck on the one hand and the war party in France on the other.

**The War of 1870** was a disaster for France from the beginning. Napoleon found his own troops ill-organised, transport broke down on several vital occasions and there was poor liaison work between the French armies. When Napoleon III arrived at Metz on July 28, 1870, to take command, not a single corps was properly equipped to take the field. None of these faults of poor organisation and delay characterised the Prussians. They won the war through their own efficiency and the weakness of the enemy. The French soldiers fought bravely and stubbornly in hopeless circumstances. Again, the Empress Eugénie and those who supported her refused to accept the idea of a French strategic retreat to concentrate on the defence of Paris and the rallying of the country after the first victories of the Prussians. When the main French army was being besieged in Metz, they insisted that Napoleon should move forward with another army to its relief. Too weak to resist this pressure, the Emperor moved to the relief of Metz, and was decisively defeated by the Prussians at Sedan, where he surrendered on September 3.

In Paris a Republic was proclaimed, the Empress fled to England, and the new Republic (the Third), inspired by the Republican leader

Gambetta, who escaped from the besieged Paris in a balloon to organise resistance from the provinces, continued the struggle. But after the fall of Metz, huge forces of Prussians were released for the attack on the capital which at last had to capitulate after every item of food, including cats and rats, had been eaten.

By the Treaty of Frankfurt, 1871, France was to pay 5,000,000,000 francs in three years, to have an army of occupation until the full reparations had been paid to Germany, and also to lose to Germany the valuable coal and iron areas of Alsace and Lorraine. With this complete humiliation imposed by the harshest peace treaty known up to that time, the Second Empire in France had crumbled.

FIG. 17.—KILLING AN ELEPHANT FOR FOOD IN THE JARDIN DES PLANTES.
(*The original of this drawing was flown out of Paris by balloon during the Siege.*)

# chapter seven

# THE AUSTRIAN EMPIRE, 1815–1850

**Introductory.** The history of the Austrian Empire and of Germany in the years 1815–1850 is dominated by the personality and aims of Prince Metternich, the Austrian Chancellor. He was utterly opposed to everything which the words "liberalism" and "nationalism" imply. Such liberal doctrines as the equality of all classes before the law, the right to free speech, the need for parliaments elected by the people—all these ideas Metternich regarded as a kind of poison brewed up by the democratic "rabble" for administration to the aristocracy. He had a similar detestation of nationalism, which implied the right of peoples of similar race, language and customs to form independent states of their own.

As an aristocrat and a member of one of the most distinguished Austrian families, Metternich was by tradition and upbringing opposed to liberal ideas. These opinions had been strengthened by his earlier career in the service of Austria. He had been an outright opponent of the French Revolution and came to regard its successor, Napoleon, as the propagator of the ideas of the Revolution and therefore the arch-enemy of the old feudal and aristocratic order in Europe.

Metternich's opposition to nationalism arose also from the peculiar position of the Austrian Empire, which was composed of numerous racial and language groups. If nationalism spread, the Empire would fall to pieces. In Bohemia and Moravia there were Czechs, Slovaks and Germans. In Hungary there were the Magyars, Serbs, Croats and Slovenes. In Galicia there were the Poles who had been wrenched from their native land to be included in the Austrian Empire during the Polish Partitions of the eighteenth century. Finally, the Austrian-controlled provinces of Lombardy and Venetia were completely Italian in language and traditions.

In his determination to prevent at all costs the spread of the liberal and national "poison", Metternich had the fervent and extremely bigoted support of his Emperor, Francis I. "I want," declared the Emperor, "not scholars but good citizens. Whosoever serves me must teach according to my orders. Whosoever is not able to do so or starts new ideas going, must go, or I shall eliminate him."

Fig. 18.—Prince Metternich.

These were the orders of the Emperor to the teachers in the schools and universities of the Empire, and in Metternich he had a servant far more cultured and brilliant than himself to carry them out.

There was very little likelihood or possibility of revolution within the Austrian Empire in 1815, and this situation continued right up to 1848. Nevertheless, during those years the grievances of the Liberals and Nationalists in the Empire slowly increased and the amazing crash of 1848 was the result of these developments. To understand the situation which arose in 1848, it is necessary to consider first the actual government of the Austrian Empire.

**The Government of the Hapsburg Empire.** Austria was an autocratic Empire—that is to say, every individual in the State was ultimately responsible to the Emperor alone. But it was not even an efficient autocracy. Austrian inefficiency in government made her the laughing-stock of Europe during the nineteenth century. For example, during the years 1815–1848 the expenditure of the government never once balanced its income. It was a permanently bankrupt empire. Metternich himself had made numerous proposals for reform, but in these matters his advice went unheeded, and he finally accepted the situation with his usual polished cynicism. "I have sometimes ruled Europe," he declared, "but I have never governed Austria."

**Grievances of the Bourgeoisie.** This inefficiency in economic and financial matters kept the industry and trade of Austria in a backward condition compared with that of England, France and Prussia. This backwardness caused considerable discontent among sections of the Austrian merchants, traders and capitalists—the middle class or bourgeoisie. There was nothing which could irritate them more than the wastage of economic resources. In Prague, in Brno, in Vienna and some other big cities it was the German element which was attempting to develop factories and heavy industries. It would have been in their interests to obtain raw materials from other countries in conditions of free trade, but the Emperor and his advisers clung for revenue purposes to a system of high protective duties on imports when that system was being swept away in many other countries. Thus, sections of the German capitalists in the Empire were discontented with the Emperor's economic policy, or lack of policy.

**Privileged Position of the Nobility.** Like the aristocracy of France before the Revolution of 1789, the Austrian aristocracy was also a highly privileged class. It controlled all the main activities of both town and countryside and held all the chief government posts in the Empire. The nobility were exempt from military service and had the right to administer their own feudal laws governing the peasantry in the manorial courts. In all these respects, the Austrian Empire was nearer to the condition of France before 1789 than to that of a modern state. It was natural enough that the middle class should feel this situation as a distinct grievance.

**The Censorship.** An elaborate system of censorship was imposed throughout the Empire in an attempt to seal off its peoples from all direct contact with the liberal ideas of western Europe. All books, newspapers, pamphlets and other publications came under this censorship. University and school books were the objects of special attention and had to receive the official approval of the censor's office in Vienna. It is difficult to say exactly what the results of this system were. It was, however, far less successful than Metternich hoped. It was said by some observers that books from western Europe reached Austrian university students in great numbers, and that the students of Vienna became far better informed about the state of the world than ministers of the Emperor. It is not surprising that the students of Vienna University took a very prominent part in the Revolution of 1848. The government's attempt to keep them in narrow ignorance was an insult to their intelligence and in the last resort the system defeated itself.

**Religious Intolerance.** Another source of irritation to many people in the Empire was religious intolerance. Only those who accepted the State Catholic religion could hold public appointments. Within the Empire there were the Slav peoples who were of the Greek Orthodox Church, while in Bohemia and Moravia the Protestant religion had been strong since the later Middle Ages.

But it was above all in the Hungarian part of the Empire that the worst social and political conditions were in evidence.

**The Condition of Hungary before 1848.** In Hungary the ruling class was the ancient Magyar nobility, and the Austrian Emperors had been forced to take some account of their independent spirit. Hungary had its own parliament or Diet, which consisted mainly of representatives of the Great Nobility, who inherited their positions, and of the Lesser Nobility who were elected to the Diet by the local or county courts. The Lesser Nobility were poorer and less educated than the Great Nobility and there was much antagonism between these two groups. But both of them felt strongly enough to work together to maintain the Hungarian Diet. For instance, between the years 1811 and 1825 the Emperor Francis 1 had suspended the Hungarian parliament altogether, but this caused such discontent that the Hungarian nobility forced the Emperor after 1825 to summon the Diet regularly to discuss affairs of State. This episode caused many of the nobility to fear that some such attack on their institutions might be made again in the future.

**The Croatian Movement.** The next success of the Magyars of Hungary was to get all official business and meetings of the Diet conducted in the Magyar language instead of the Latin in which it had up to this time been carried on. But this led to further complication, for the Magyars now enforced the use of the Magyar language upon certain minorities in Hungary, of whom the most important were the Croats. This in its turn led in the years 1830-1848 to an increased demand from the Croat people to be independent of Hungary. In general, the Croatian leaders wanted their country (which is part of modern Yugoslavia) to form a third part of the Empire with a considerable degree of self-government, such as that already enjoyed by Hungary. They wanted their own Diet and the official use of their own language. The Croatian movement was greatly stimulated by a revival of interest in the language, history and folk-lore of the Croatian people in the years up to 1848. This movement was aided by an important Croatian newspaper, the *Illyrian National Gazette*.

Thus we see that there was opposition between the Magyars and the Emperor, but at the same time other nationalities such as the Croats were coming into conflict both with the Austrians and the Magyars. There was one conflict within the other.

**Louis Kossuth and Hungarian Liberalism.** Inside Hungary there was developing another movement far wider than the narrow Magyar nationalism we have just noted. This was a Liberal movement headed by Louis Kossuth, a journalist who had been imprisoned for reporting debates in the Hungarian parliament and had become the editor of an influential newspaper. By illegal distribution of pamphlets, by journalistic and underground political work, he showed himself to be the most determined of all the opponents of the Austrian system.

But he brought forward other demands than those of the Magyars. Although a Magyar himself, he denounced the privileges of the Magyar nobility. He denounced their exemption from taxation and called for the abolition of their feudal law courts and their exaction

of forced labour from the peasants. In addition to this, his programme included a liberally-elected parliament with the vote given
to merchants, traders and professional people—the middle class. In
this last demand he was voicing the resentment felt by the middle
class against the aristocracy, for in the Hungarian Diet all the cities
of Hungary were represented only by two members. He demanded
equality for all classes before the law and the introduction of the jury
system.

In this way Kossuth went further than Magyar nationalism, for he
voiced the demands of other classes in Hungary, especially the middle
class and the peasants. He succeeded in 1847 in being elected a
member of the Hungarian Diet for Budapest.

**The Hungarian Revolution.** When the news of the revolution in
France against Louis Philippe reached the Hungarian Diet, which
was meeting at Pressburg, Kossuth immediately took the lead in
demanding the most drastic changes in Hungary. Public opinion was
strongly in his favour and those among the Magyars who might have
opposed him were forced to accept the popular demands, which
Kossuth put forward in a famous speech in the Diet on March 3,
1848. Kossuth also encouraged the revolutionaries who had risen in
Vienna itself. By March 15, the Emperor had been forced to accept
the Hungarian demands and to establish a constitutional government
in Vienna.

**The March Laws, 1848.** The programme of Kossuth and his
supporters was now adopted in the Hungarian Diet. The March
Laws, put forward by Francis Deák, created a Hungarian government which was responsible to the Hungarian Diet alone and not to
the Emperor. All the departments of government by which Vienna
had controlled Hungarian affairs were now swept away, and the
Hungarian government gained complete control for the first time of
foreign affairs, of the army and of taxation. Important social reforms
were introduced. Serfdom and the manorial courts were abolished
and the nobility were now forced to pay their share of taxation. A
more democratic form of election to the Diet was arranged, which
gave the vote to the middle class and a section of the peasantry.
Voting was to be direct instead of by the old method of indirect
election through the local courts. Complete religious toleration and
liberty of the press were declared. To safeguard all these gains, a
National Guard was formed. All this was the work of a few enthusiastic days, and everything looked extremely bright for the future
liberties of the people.

**The Minorities Problem and the Failure of the Hungarian Liberal Revolution.** The revolution was essentially a victory for the more progressive elements among the Magyars led by Kossuth. But this fact, that it was a Magyar victory, led to further complications with the Croatians and the Slovenes, who were now demanding from Hungary independent governments of their own. Some of the Hungarian leaders, especially Francis Deák and Count Szechenyi, wished to grant these demands, but Kossuth opposed them. This was the curious—and fatal—contradiction in his career: he was unwilling to grant to the other peoples the rights which the Magyars had won from Austria. Kossuth clearly wished to maintain Magyar domination in the new state. Count Szechenyi especially warned him that he was "goading into madness" the other nationalities against the Magyars.

**Count Jellacic and the Croat Movement.** The Croatians had elected their own parliament which met at Agram, and one of the first acts of this parliament was to refuse to accept the Magyar language as the official tongue of Croatia. Their leader was Count Jellacic, who was governor of Croatia for the Emperor. His outstanding characteristic was his hatred of the Magyars, and he was now able to convince the assembly at Agram that if the Croatians opposed the Magyars, then the grateful Emperor would give them their main demands. The Emperor gave his direct support to Jellacic and was thus able to exploit this fatal antagonism between the Magyars and Croats. In July, 1848, the Croat Army under Jellacic began an invasion of Hungary, supported by an invasion of Austrian forces under General Windischgrätz. The latter succeeded in capturing Budapest, only to be driven out again by Kossuth's forces.

**Declaration of the Hungarian Republic.** Kossuth's reply to the Austrian and Croatian attack was to declare Hungary a completely separate Republic. He himself became President. He was opposed in this policy, however, by some of the Hungarian leaders. The other course he could have adopted was to negotiate from strength with the Emperor after the defeat of Windischgrätz at Budapest. But his complete break from Austria had two important results. Firstly, it hardened the Emperor's determination to defeat the Hungarians and, secondly, decided him to call in the aid of Nicholas I, Czar of Russia. The Czar was only too ready to oblige his fellow sovereign, for the last thing he wanted on the frontiers of serf-ridden Russia was a Republic from which liberal ideas could spread into his own dominions. Also, the Emperor of Austria was now assisted by the victories of Radetsky in Italy in July, 1848, which freed Austrian forces for the Hungarian campaign. The Hungarians resisted heroically, but against 200,000 Russian troops and against the ruthless determination of the Austrian General Haynau, the fight was hopeless. Eventually Kossuth fled to Turkey and the Hungarian generals laid down their arms unconditionally.

A terrible revenge was exacted against the Hungarians by General Haynau. Many Hungarian leaders were executed, including thirteen generals of the Hungarian Army, and many thousands exiled or imprisoned. The grimly-punning name of "Hyena" given to General Haynau expressed the widespread horror which his policy of revenge excited throughout Europe. Hungary now lost her separate constitution altogether and was completely ruled from Vienna. As for the Croats and Slovenes, who had been led by Jellacic against the Magyars, their demands were now ignored.

**The Revolution in Vienna.** The news of events in France and Hungary had given sudden life to the liberal movement in Vienna. It was from the University that the first determined movements of revolt originated. On March 12, 1848, the students and a number of the professors held a demonstration before the Parliament building or Landhaus. The Emperor Ferdinand was forced to receive the Students' Petition in which they demanded a new government, democratic elections, the formation of a National Guard and the removal of all censorship of books and other publications. These demonstrations gradually took on a more violent and determined character, and the Mayor of the city was himself compelled to demand the removal of Metternich. The Imperial troops had added to the general revolutionary feeling by firing upon and killing a number of the demonstrators, but in general the Imperial troops were proving too unreliable to suppress the whole movement. On March 15, Metternich at last resigned the Chancellorship, made his escape from Vienna and finally reached England. Meanwhile, the Italians had driven the Austrians from Venice and Milan. The Empire appeared to be falling rapidly to pieces. In Prague, the capital of Bohemia, the Czechs had also risen in revolt.

On April 14, 1848, the Emperor issued a decree establishing a constitutional monarchy and providing for the election of a parliament to which the ministers of the government would be responsible. Meanwhile a Revolutionary Committee of twenty-four members, including representatives of the Academic Legion (students) and of the National Guard, ruled the city of Vienna. In the suburbs the workmen, who were under Socialist influence, were demonstrating against their employers.

In May, 1848, the Emperor and his family suddenly left Vienna for Innsbruck with his principal political supporters and the main part of the Imperial forces in Vienna. This freed him from the control of the Revolutionary Committee in Vienna. In the provincial city of Innsbruck there was no turbulent proletariat or student body to control him. A fatal error of the Viennese revolutionaries was to have allowed the Emperor to leave the capital at all.

The tide now began to turn rapidly against the revolution. In Italy, Radetsky defeated the Italians at Custozza and recaptured Milan. A Polish rising in Galicia was stamped out by Count Stadion, while in Prague, the Czechs, after failing to gain arms from the governor Windischgrätz, were bombarded into submission.

**Opposition of Slavs and Germans.** The military success of the Imperialists was made easier by serious divisions within the revolutionary movement. In Vienna the new parliament elected by universal suffrage contained far more Slavs than Germans, for we must remember that the Austrian Empire was mainly a Slav Empire. The main dispute between Slavs and Germans was over the question of a united Germany. The Slavs were opposed to Austria being part of a united Germany, for they feared that Slav interests would then have to give way to the German majority.

Once again the Imperial Court played the part of "divide and rule" as in the case of the Croats and the Hungarians. The Slavs were persuaded that the Emperor would support their demands provided they opposed the German representatives in the parliament. This led to complete turmoil in the City of Vienna, for attempts were now made by sections of the people to form another government for the City without any reference to the parliament where the Slav-German quarrel was reducing the revolution to a tragic farce. Finally, the Slav representatives left Vienna altogether, and the German revolutionary elements were left to face alone the Imperial armies now advancing on the capital. The outcome was the capture of the city by General Windischgrätz and the revolution was brought to an end.

The new Chancellor, Prince Schwarzenberg, now ruled with an iron hand and nearly all the gains of the revolution were lost. One gain of exceptional importance was not lost however, for serfdom, which the revolution had abolished, had gone for ever.

**The Dual Monarchy.** The system adopted by Schwarzenberg lasted till the year 1859, when further complications for Austria in the international field forced upon her certain important changes in government. In that year the Austrians were defeated in northern Italy by Napoleon III and his Italian allies (see pages 127, 180), and the weakness of the Austrian Empire was demonstrated to all. The Magyars of Hungary renewed their demands for a separate parliament for their part of the Empire. The Emperor Francis Joseph and his German advisers thought it advisable to make some concessions: the Hungarian Diet was restored as before 1848 and the Magyar language once again replaced the German language which Schwarzenberg had imposed as the official tongue in Hungary. In 1866, after the next defeat of Austria (by the Prussians), the Magyars went further and demanded the rights which Kossuth had obtained by the March Laws of 1848. Once again, the Austrians thought it advisable to conciliate the Magyars if the Empire was to have any chance of recovering strength after its serious military defeats.

**The "Ausgleich".** The Dual Monarchy was now established by a new agreement between Austria and Hungary. By this agreement, known as the "Ausgleich" or "compromise", Hungary was placed on an absolute equality with Austria in the Empire. She now had both her own parliament and government, and the Magyars controlled the State. For matters of common interest, such as foreign affairs, finance and war, special committees consisting of equal numbers of representatives from Austria and Hungary were set up. The old term "Austrian Empire" was now replaced by "Austro-Hungarian Empire" to signify the spirit of the important changes now made.

From 1866 till the fall of the Empire in 1918 this system was maintained. But it had many of the defects of the system which Kossuth attempted to set up. The Magyars were the all-powerful influence in Hungary and minorities such as the Slovaks were not accorded the same freedoms. This led to various forms of discontent within Hungary which partly contributed to the final break-up of the Austro-Hungarian Empire, after its defeat in the Great War of 1914–1918.

# chapter eight
# GERMANY, 1815–1850

**Introductory.** The Congress of Vienna restored a Germany comprising thirty-nine states. Before 1789 the German states had numbered over two hundred. At first glance it seemed that the 1815 arrangement was a move towards simplification and unity, but this was only an appearance. For one thing, many of the thirty-nine states were in possession of more territory after 1815 than they had ever had before, and they were far more interested in maintaining these gains than in any schemes for a single German government in which their own identity might be lost. Germany after 1815 was still a much divided territory.

This division of Germany exactly suited the aims of the Austrian Chancellor, Metternich, who had had a decisive voice in the settlement. Austria could control a disunited Germany far more easily than a united one. While the German princes were divided by political jealousy and distrust, the Austrians would have no united opposition to their policies and could exert a decisive influence in the affairs of Germany.

**The German Diet.** An Assembly for the whole of Germany was created after 1815, but this was by no means an effective German parliament. It represented the princes, not the people, of Germany, and was not in any way elected by popular vote. The Diet of the German Confederation met at Frankfurt and consisted of 17 members. Eleven of the big states had one member each, and various groups of the smaller states each had one member. Metternich secured the permanent presidency of the Diet for Austria, a position of decisive importance, for the President decided upon the business to be discussed and the procedure to be adopted. The Diet did discuss in 1816 the creation of a single German Army, but nothing came of these discussions, mainly because of jealousy between the states, and especially between the two largest states, Austria and Prussia. A scheme for the building of federal fortresses for the defence of Germany was also abandoned. Lastly, whenever fundamental laws of the Confederation or the Federative Act itself were to be enacted, the Diet was expanded into a General Assembly of 69 members.

Fig. 19.—Great Barricade in the Breitnestrasse, Berlin, 1848. (*See page* 150.)

Those elements in Germany who had looked forward to real unity, the Nationalists, were intensely disappointed by this state of affairs.

The Liberals, who had hoped at least for elected parliaments and governments responsible to the people in each of the German states, leading on to a united Liberal Germany, were also frustrated. A certain number of the German princes did introduce more liberal forms of government, especially in Bavaria, where in 1818 a parliament was set up which represented the peasants, townspeople and nobles, and also in Baden, Würtemberg and Saxe-Weimar. But the great majority of the thirty-nine states were governed by their princes in alliance with a highly privileged class of nobility, and politically the middle and peasant classes were ignored.

**Liberalism in Germany.** It must not be thought that the majority of German people were clamouring at this time either for liberalism or a united Germany. They were scarcely interested. Liberalism had its strongest hold amongst the intellectual class of writers, poets, scholars, university professors, lecturers and students. In the universities of Germany a number of student movements developed in these years, such as the Gymnastic Clubs and the Students' Unions or Burschenschaften, many of which advocated liberal ideas. It was this situation in the universities of which Metternich was particularly afraid. The German system of university education, by which students moved from one university to another during the course of their studies, greatly aided the spread of these liberal ideas.

**The Wartburg Festival and the Carlsbad Decrees.** In the year 1817 the conflict between Metternich and liberalism came to a head over the Wartburg Festival, held at Wartburg in Saxony and organised by the students of Jena University. The festival was a celebration of the German Reformation of the sixteenth century and also of the battle of Leipzig in 1813 which had been a decisive defeat for Napoleon. Besides celebrating these events, however, the students threw on a bonfire a number of Prussian jackboots, reactionary pamphlets and other symbols of anti-liberalism, including an effigy of Metternich himself. Metternich used these demonstrations as evidence of a widespread conspiracy. This was a deliberate exaggeration on his part of the importance of the students' celebration. He succeeded in playing upon the fears of the princes of Germany, and in 1819 another occurrence gave him even more opportunity for these tactics. A university student named Karl Sand assassinated the anti-liberal journalist and playwright Kotzebue, who was also a secret agent of the Czar Alexander in Germany. Metternich exploited this crime to spread further alarm among the despotic rulers of Germany, and he now found it easy to win over the Czar Alexander completely to his viewpoint. He was also successful in persuading Frederick William III of Prussia not to grant the constitution which he had promised his people towards the end of the war against Napoleon. The victory of Metternich was made complete by the Carlsbad Decrees which he persuaded the German Diet to accept in 1819. By these decrees all German universities were to have a government supervisor, students' societies were to be abolished and any student expelled from one university for his political opinions was not allowed to study at any other. The press was also to come under strict censorship. A permanent committee was set up at Mainz whose duty it was to see that these rules were applied and to collect evidence against liberals and other revolutionaries. Under this system some of Germany's most famous poets and writers were subject to "investigation". In general, despite the protests of the more liberal states, such as Baden, Bavaria, Würtemberg and Saxe-Weimar, this was a great triumph for Metternich, and it effectively checked the development not only of liberalism but of nationalism for thirty years. In 1820 further measures were passed by which the German Diet was given powers to use armed force to suppress revolution in any of the states of Germany.

**Germany and the Revolution in France, 1830.** The revolution against Charles X in France in 1830 stimulated a number of liberal protests in Germany. At a celebration in the castle of Hambach the flag of the Burschenschaften was unfurled and revolutionary speeches made, demanding the unification of Germany and a liberal form of government. The same results followed as in the case of the Wartburg Festival thirteen years earlier. Metternich secured the imposition of decrees which went even further than those of Carlsbad. All political meetings were made illegal and it was a crime for the Burschenschaften colours of red, black and gold to be worn even in scarves or neckties. Repression in Germany was stronger than ever. The liberals had succeeded in gaining a constitution in Hanover, but this was suppressed in 1837 by the Duke of Cumberland, who was King of Hanover. Several prominent professors of Göttingen University, including the brothers Jacob and Wilhelm Grimm, the famous writers of fairy tales and historians of German folk-lore, were expelled, to the accompaniment of student riots and protests. Under the Metternich system political progress in Germany came to a standstill.

**The Zollverein.** One important development of these years which was to have great future significance was the Zollverein or Customs Union. This originated in Prussia itself, where an extensive reform of her internal and external trading system was undertaken in 1818. Up to that time Prussia imposed customs duties on nearly 4,000 different kinds of goods entering the country. As Prussia had frontiers with 28 other states after 1815, it became an extremely complicated business to collect these customs duties, whose rates varied considerably from one type of import to another. In 1818 all duties between the Prussian provinces were abolished, raw materials entered the country free and an import duty of ten per cent was imposed on manufactured articles. This simplified the whole system and made it easy for other states to trade with Prussia. In 1820 one other German state came completely into the Prussian trading system and in 1834 nearly all the South German states entered the economic union. By 1854 the Zollverein included the whole of Germany except Austria and one or two small territories. Thus a uniform free-trading system developed for the whole of Germany under Prussian leadership. Prussian prosperity continued to grow and the Zollverein was undoubtedly one factor which caused many of the German states to begin to look to Prussia instead of Austria for the *political* lead in Germany.

**Prussia, 1815-1848.** After 1815 no liberal progress was made in Prussia. The further liberal reforms wanted by Stein and Hardenberg, who had roused the middle classes and peasantry against Napoleon, were not introduced. Up to 1818 Frederick William III was inclined to accept the idea of an elected assembly, but by that time Metternich had brought Alexander round to his viewpoint, and a combination of Russia and Austria against Prussia would in any case have been too strong. The King and government of Prussia therefore concentrated upon the *administration* of the country. Prussia became a state governed by the king and a host of extremely capable officials, a bureaucracy. Officialdom ruled the state. In the Prussian Army the Junkers or great landlord class of East Prussia, who were outright opponents of liberalism and all it stood for, gained control. Thus Prussia was ruled by a combination of bureaucracy and the Junkers. There was no place for liberalism—and no apparent need.

**Frederick William IV (1840-1861).** For a time in 1840, with the accession of Frederick William IV, the possibilities of liberal change seemed greater. It was thought that he would give the middle class some voice in political affairs, for with the development of big industries, especially in Berlin, and with the growth of the railway system, the middle trading class was becoming increasingly important, and was beginning to demand some part in the government of the state. But it soon became obvious that the new king had no intention of giving way to liberalism or democracy. In any case he had a firm belief in the divine right of kings to rule, and he regarded himself as answerable to God alone.

**The Parliament of 1847.** However, in 1847 an elected parliament was called. The circumstances were that the government needed money for railway development and thought it advisable to consult the monied classes from whom they wanted the cash. But even now the assembly was still divided into two houses, one consisting of the middle class and peasants and the other the nobility. The assembly was only allowed to vote taxation and present petitions to the King. It had no real law-making powers. This was most unsatisfactory to the liberals, to whom the king remained stubbornly opposed. However, a representative assembly had at least met, and this encouraged the liberals to hope that more political rights could be obtained from the King. The year 1847 was one of considerable agitation in Germany and saw the revival of liberal demands. There were numerous demonstrations of a liberal and nationalist character. There had also been a revolt somewhat earlier of the Silesian weavers against their employers on account of the terrible conditions in the industry. The revolt was brutally suppressed by the Prussian Army and this undoubtedly contributed to the growth of popular unrest, especially in Prussia.

**The Revolution of 1848 in Prussia.** It was the revolution of February, 1848, in France against Louis Philippe that stimulated renewed activity among the liberals of Germany. Risings quickly followed in most of the smaller states of Germany, and their rulers were forced to grant the typical liberal demands for freedom of the press and of speech, representative government, and trial by jury. But it was in Prussia that the most important movements occurred.

Between March 12 and 17 demonstrations in the streets of Berlin were constantly occurring, and clashes took place between the demonstrators and the soldiers. On March 17 a number of people were killed. The next day a demonstration before the King's palace demanded the withdrawal of the soldiers from the streets.

The King's reply was to order the soldiers to clear the crowd away, and this was done without any casualties. But almost immediately after the dispersal of the demonstration, people in various parts of the city began to build barricades and seize arms from the gunsmiths' shops. At this time there were 20,000 royal troops in Berlin, and they succeeded in regaining control of part of the city, but only at the cost of bloodshed and the destruction of many houses and administrative buildings.

At this point in the struggle King Frederick William IV shrank from the prospect of an outright civil war which would result in making Berlin a smoking ruin and would possibly arouse even further opposition to him. He now ordered the troops to withdraw and issued a proclamation granting freedom of the press and of speech and calling together the Prussian Diet to consider a new constitution. When the bodies of the victims of the fighting were paraded before the King and his family in the palace courtyard, the King stood bareheaded. At the funeral, nearly every class in the capital was represented—workmen, middle class, university authori-

FIG. 20.—CAVALRY CHARGE THE DEMONSTRATORS AT THE ROYAL PALACE, BERLIN.

ties, the clergy and members of the King's government. Never before had there been such a united demonstration against the King of Prussia, and it is not surprising that he left Berlin and took up his residence in the royal palace at Potsdam outside the city. He could no longer trust the people of his capital.

**Failure of the Revolution in Prussia.** The political fate of Prussia was decided between May and November, 1848. A Constituent Assembly met in May at Berlin to decide on the future form of government for Prussia. This was the greatest chance the Prussians ever had of forming a more liberal and democratic government, and yet it failed to achieve any of its objectives. The reasons for this can in part be found in the very composition of the Assembly itself. Of the 400 members only about 100 were drawn from the workers and peasants, while the remainder consisted of a large majority of middle-class representatives (mainly lawyers and other professional people) and of a group of Junkers. The latter group represented the most violently anti-liberal elements in Prussia and considered that the King had already betrayed them. The Junkers were highly organised and held their own meetings in Berlin to decide on their policy in the Assembly. One of their most violently-spoken supporters was Otto von Bismarck, of whom the world was to hear much more in the future.

The situation was this: the Prussian Army was still intact and the King could rely on it, and he was determined to regain his former powers as soon as possible. The King resisted all attempts of the middle class in the Assembly to get his consent to a liberal form of government in which he and his ministers would be responsible to an elected parliament. In the first days of the revolution he had been forced to accept as his ministers men of liberal sympathies, but he dismissed his liberal government in September, 1848. This was a direct challenge to the Assembly, and led to further furious debate there, as the King had anticipated. Demands arose from the representatives of the workmen and peasants for the arming of the people against the royal forces and, from some of them, demands were made for a Republic. The extreme Left in the Assembly also put forward a programme which involved granting rights to trade unions and heavy taxation of the wealthy classes. These demands led to a state of conflict between the workmen's and peasants' representatives on the one side and the middle class on the other. In Berlin, where there were already more than 50,000 factory workers, there was strong agitation under Socialist and Communist leadership both against the employers and against the Prussian monarchy. The middle class became increasingly alarmed by the extreme Left and the working-class elements in Berlin and other centres, and feared the development of Socialist ideas which would lead to an attack on private property. This division between the extreme Left and the middle class destroyed the possibility of their combined resistance to the King and the Junkers. Frederick William IV was now preparing to take full advantage of this division when he was aided by events outside Prussia. On October 31 the troops of the Emperor of Austria recaptured Vienna and the popular revolution in Austria was at an end. In France the popular revolt had been suppressed and General Cavaignac was now a temporary dictator. In Italy likewise the movement for liberation was meeting with great difficulties. In these circumstances Frederick William IV felt confident enough to use his army against the Assembly in Berlin. On November 9 the royal army reoccupied Berlin and on December 5 the Assembly was dissolved.

**The Prussian Constitution of 1850.** The King now introduced a constitution which provided for a Lower House elected by universal suffrage and a House of Lords partly hereditary and partly nominated by the crown. The King had power to introduce laws himself and to appoint his own government which was responsible to him alone and not to parliament. The voting system was altered in such a way that voters were divided into three classes according to the taxation they paid. Under this system the richer classes had the greater proportion of the votes. The secret ballot was abolished and open voting was introduced.

In this way the King had re-established his power with the support of the army, the State officials and the wealthier classes—especially the Junkers who had played a leading part in the events of 1848 in Berlin.

**The Nationalist Movement and the Frankfurt Parliament, 1848–1849.** At the same time as the liberal revolution was being attempted in Prussia the German Nationalists were trying to create a united Germany. As we have seen, the Prussian Zollverein had greatly encouraged the hopes of the Nationalists. In 1847 a meeting of representatives of all member states of the Zollverein had taken place to discuss the *political* union of Germany. Then, after the events of March, 1848, in Berlin, Frederick William IV had himself issued a proclamation supporting the idea of a united Germany. The next important event was a meeting held at Frankfurt of all those who were, or had been, members of their own assemblies in the various states. This meeting, attended by over 600 delegates, was known as the "Vorparlament" or Preliminary Parliament. The "Vorparlament" arranged elections to a national parliament whose purpose would be to decide on the form which a united Germany should take. In the voting for this parliament there was to be universal male suffrage and each member was to represent about 50,000 inhabitants of Germany.

**The Frankfurt Parliament.** The parliament was duly elected and met at Frankfurt-on-the-Main on May 18, 1848. It consisted of 831 members. It contained only 20 farmers and about 150 traders and merchants, while the remainder were lawyers, teachers, university professors, writers and other professional people. Such a composition of the parliament meant that the great majority of its members were people with no previous experience of practical politics and administration. This meant that the task of establishing a united Germany was all the more difficult. It was certainly necessary to

Fig. 21.—Session of the Frankfurt Parliament.

discuss the rights and freedoms of the individual in a future Germany, but these discussions of a theoretical nature were far too prolonged in the Frankfurt Parliament and wasted valuable time.

**Activities of the Parliament.** The parliament offered the position of Regent or head of a temporary German government to the Archduke John of Austria, who was acceptable to the princes and at the same time had a real sympathy with the idea of a united Germany. This was a good move by the parliament, but it was almost immediately cancelled out by the parliament's failure over the question of Schleswig-Holstein. These two provinces, which were attached to the Danish Crown, objected to changes in their constitution which would have meant closer union with Denmark. As many of their inhabitants were German, they had strong support from the German Nationalists. The Prussian King, Frederick William IV, supported them, but his army failed to defeat the Danes and the other Great Powers forced him to make a truce with them. This was a great humiliation for the Nationalists at Frankfurt, who should by this time have created their own army—to be ready to resist Prussia and Austria if necessary and also to support Schleswig-Holstein. But this question of a new army for Germany, which might have guaranteed success for the Frankfurt parliament, was never properly considered. The Schleswig-Holstein failure caused a popular riot against the Assembly at Frankfurt and two of its members were murdered. Prussian troops were used to restore order—a very ominous situation indeed, for if the Prussians had the power to protect the Assembly they would also have the power to act against it if Frederick William IV decided to do so.

After the Schleswig-Holstein affair the Assembly began a debate on the future membership of Germany. The Parliament came to grief over two important questions:

(1) Whether to include the whole of Austria or only its German parts in the new state.

(2) To whom to offer the crown of a united Germany, and on what terms?

Eventually the delegates agreed on the inclusion of the German part of the Austrian Empire only. The Austrian Emperor would have been in the peculiar position of complete ruler over the non-German part of his dominions but not entirely over that part included in the new Germany. The Austrians had up to this time been willing to accept the membership of the whole Empire in Germany, but they refused the final offer of the Parliament. The Frankfurt Parliament replied by deciding to keep Austria out of Germany altogether, a decision which the Emperor was bound to work against with all his might. His immediate reply was to withdraw the Austrian delegates altogether. The Parliament now offered the crown of a united Germany to Frederick William IV of Prussia. Why this choice? The reasons were many. Prussia had played a leading part in the defeat of Napoleon and had helped to rouse a truly national spirit in Germany at that time. Again, when Prussia obtained the Rhine Provinces in 1815 this made her the main guardian of Germany against any future attack from France. On the other hand, the only interest which Metternich and the Austrians had in Germany was to keep her weak and divided, impose the Carlsbad Decrees and maintain the complete domination of Austria.

But Frederick William IV refused the offer of the German Crown from the Frankfurt Parliament. He had two main reasons for this decision. He was afraid of offending Austria, for he himself still regarded her as the real leader of Germany, and he intensely disliked accepting the Crown from the popularly elected Frankfurt Parliament. He declared that he would not "pick a crown from the gutter" but would only accept it if offered by the princes of Germany. He was also opposed to the constitution for Germany put forward by the Frankfurt Assembly. This constitution would have given him the right to suspend laws proposed by the German Parliament, but not the right to veto them.

The next action of Frederick William IV was to withdraw the Prussian delegates from Frankfurt. By this time the delegates of Austria and the South German states had already withdrawn. The Frankfurt Parliament was thus deprived of the support of the principal German states.

**Austria *v.* Prussia, 1850–1851, and the Treaty of Olmütz.** Frederick William IV of Prussia had not given up the idea of some union of the German states under his own leadership and on his own terms. A Prussian League was now formed with Hanover, Saxony, Hesse and some other small German states as members. A parliament was elected for the League and it met at Erfurt in 1850. However, both Saxony and Hanover deserted the system and then another complication arose. In the State of Hesse the ruling prince cancelled a liberal constitution to which he had given an earlier consent. The people rebelled and asked for the assistance of the head of the League, Prussia. Austria, who had looked upon the creation of the Prussian

League with great disfavour, now declared her support for the ruler of Hesse and an army of 200,000 men was mobilised to support him against Prussia. Frederick William IV drew back from such a conflict, for his army was not strong enough for such a challenge. He gave in to the Austrian demands, and by the Treaty of Olmütz, 1850, he agreed to give up his support of the people of Hesse and to abandon the Prussian League.

In the meantime the old German Confederation and the Diet of 1815 were restored.

Thus by 1851 Austria had regained her position in Germany, had humiliated Prussia and had suppressed revolution in her own territory. By the use of her armed forces at Frankfurt, Prussia had dissolved the Assembly and brought to an end the attempt of the ill-fated Frankfurt Parliament to create a united Germany. In the other states of Germany the liberal constitutions were abolished by their rulers and many liberals were imprisoned, exiled or executed.

In the years 1848–1851 both nationalism and liberalism had utterly failed in Germany, and this failure was to have a profound effect not only on the destiny of Germany but on that of the whole of Europe.

# chapter nine

# THE UNIFICATION OF GERMANY, 1850–1870

**Introductory.** The supremacy of Austria in Germany had been re-established by the Treaty of Olmütz, which was humiliating both to the national idealists represented by the Frankfurt Parliament and to the Prussian monarchy. Yet between the years 1850 and 1870 one of the most remarkable changes in European history in the nineteenth century took place. Prussia arose as the unifier of Germany—on her own terms.

**Prince Otto von Bismarck.** The man most responsible for this remarkable change was Otto von Bismarck. He was a Prussian aristocrat, a Junker. On the great landed estates of East Prussia the noble's word was law, and in this environment Bismarck gained his own ideas of authority. He despised the masses, loathed democracy, and spent a great part of his life in attempting to suppress socialism, communism and their milder contemporary, liberalism. After some years spent at the university, on his estates and then as a Prussian civil servant, he entered politics and became a member of the Prussian Parliament in 1847. He spoke violently against the liberals in Parliament, and his words were carefully noted by King Frederick William IV. In 1851, when the German Confederation had been revived on Austria's terms, the King appointed Bismarck as a Prussian representative in the Diet. Bismarck soon came to the conclusion that Prussia herself could never be strong in a divided Germany controlled by Austria. He further concluded that Germany must be united by force, but on Prussia's terms. However, while Frederick William was King, Bismarck was kept at a discreet distance from the politics of Berlin. He was first appointed as Prussian envoy to the Frankfurt Diet, 1851–1858, then as ambassador to Russia, 1859–1862, and then for a short time to France, 1862. The King was anxious to remain on good terms with Austria and he was afraid that Bismarck's outspokenness might lead to trouble for Prussia. In his own words he regarded Bismarck as "only to be employed when the bayonet reigns".

**Accession of William I.** This situation of judicious isolation imposed on Bismarck was, however, suddenly changed when Frederick William went mad in 1858. His brother William became Regent and finally King as William I on the death of Frederick William in 1861. He was a very different man from his brother: more authoritative, more decisive, and far less afraid of Austria. His training in the Prussian Army had given him the same views of authority and the same detestation of liberal and democratic ideas as Bismarck. Some of his first actions showed these tendencies clearly. He made two very significant military appointments. Von Roon became Minister of War and von Moltke was made Chief of the General Staff. These two ministers were strongly anti-liberal and anti-Austrian, and their immediate programme was to strengthen the Prussian Army by increasing its numbers from 500,000 to 750,000. For this purpose they demanded from the Prussian Parliament a considerable increase of taxation.

**The Liberal Opposition in Prussia.** In the Prussian Parliament in Berlin the Liberals succeeded in gaining a majority against the proposed taxation, and the King's demands were rejected. The reason for this was not any opposition by the Liberals to militarism, but their demand that the Prussian Parliament should control the King and not merely accept the demands of himself and his military advisers. They therefore proposed certain amendments to the military laws as a condition of their accepting the new taxes.

**Bismarck called to Office.** If William I gave in, he would be accepting what was to him the loathsome principle that the King of Prussia should be controlled by the representatives of the Prussian people. A very tense situation now developed between the King and the Liberal opposition, and at one point William I contemplated abdication rather than see civil war break out. But von Roon persuaded the King to recall Bismarck from Paris and appoint him head of the government as Minister-President. Bismarck's first task was to maintain the morale of the King and persuade him to carry through the struggle with the Liberal opposition to the bitter end.

**Bismarck's Suppression of the Liberals.** Bismarck now showed no compromise with the Liberals whatever. He had a growing Prussian army at hand officered by Junkers who were men after his own heart. Might was to decide the issue, not right. "Germany", declared Bismarck, "has its eyes not on Prussia's liberalism, but on its might. The great questions of the day will not be decided by speeches and resolutions of majorities, but by blood and iron." In this statement to the Prussian Parliament Bismarck brutally summed up his hatred of democracy and his worship of might, power and success, however obtained.

But Bismarck was more than a mere worshipper of might. He was also one of the most astute political thinkers of the nineteenth century. He had calculated correctly that the Liberals in Prussia would no more make an appeal to force to gain their ends now than they had done in 1848 at Berlin and Frankfurt. This made his ruthless measures all the more certain of success. The newspapers were subjected to a close censorship and a strict purge of all Liberal elements from the Prussian civil service was undertaken. At the same time he proceeded to collect the taxes necessary for the increase of the Prussian Army. These measures met with only feeble resistance from the Prussian Liberals, and a few months after Bismarck's appointment as Minister-President the Liberals counted for nothing.

**Bismarck's Foreign Policy.** But he now had to justify these measures by carrying through to success the policy of uniting Germany under Prussian control. To achieve this he had firstly to defeat Austria and expel her from the German Confederation. Secondly, to consolidate such a position and make Germany the strongest state in Europe he would have to defeat the France of Napoleon III, for the latter would never allow German unity without a struggle. But before these two stages were reached there occurred the Bismarckian "curtain-raiser" of the war against Denmark.

**The Schleswig-Holstein Question and the War against Denmark.** The two provinces of Schleswig and Holstein formed the southern part of the possessions of the Danish Crown, but had their own constitutions. There was a substantial Danish population in Schleswig, but Holstein, which was mainly German in population, was a member of the German Confederation and there was a strong movement for a complete break-away from Denmark. In 1863 the Danish Government produced a new constitution which would have separated Schleswig entirely from Holstein and incorporated it completely in the Danish Kingdom. This action of the Danish Government was contrary to a previous agreement arrived at after an international conference in 1852. The German Holsteiners naturally resisted this move by the Danes and the opposition also developed strongly in Schleswig itself. An open clash developed between Denmark and the Duchies.

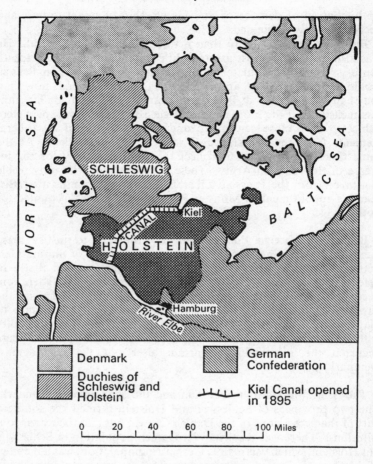

V.—SCHLESWIG-HOLSTEIN.

**Bismarck's Policy towards the Dispute.** Bismarck had no intention of standing aside from this controversy. It was, in fact, a most convenient development as far as his own aims were concerned. Firstly, he saw it as an opportunity to gain the support of the German Nationalists who wished to incorporate the two duchies into Germany. Secondly, by ultimately waging war against Austria and gaining complete control of the two duchies for Prussia he would drive home the lesson that the future of German nationalism really lay with Prussia, and not with Austria.

But before he could achieve these two aims Bismarck bent all his diplomatic skill to making certain that when the final conflict came Austria would have no allies. Firstly, there was Russia. Events in Poland in 1863 provided Bismarck with the opportunity of showing good will towards the Czar Alexander II. In that year the Poles rose in revolt against the Russians in an attempt to overthrow the Vienna settlement of 1815 and gain their independence. This revolt was crushed by the Russian armies, and refugees attempted to cross the Prussian frontiers in great numbers. Bismarck, however, had them turned back to the Czar's revenge. Several important leaders of the Polish revolt were in this way captured, and the Czar was grateful for Bismarck's assistance. It was a pledge of their common interest in the suppression of liberal revolution and was sufficient at this time to outweigh all other considerations in the Czar's mind.

Then there was that arch-adventurer Napoleon III. As Ambassador to France, Bismarck had gained an astute insight into the ambitions—and the weaknesses—of that ruler. There was no man in Europe who had a better understanding of Napoleon's character than Bismarck. Napoleon was already heavily involved in the Mexican campaign (see page 128), but, in order to make quite sure of French neutrality over the Danish question when it came to a conflict, Bismarck now hinted to Napoleon through the Prussian Ambassador that he would be willing to consider concessions of territory to Napoleon along the Rhine.

The British Prime Minister, Palmerston, was also outmatched by Bismarck. Palmerston had promised support to Denmark in her resistance to any attack, but Bismarck calculated that this was only bluff on Palmerston's part—at least, as far as military help went. In any case, with Napoleon III neutral and Russia on the best of terms with Prussia, Palmerston was isolated, and Bismarck was prepared to risk anything the British Prime Minister could do about it.

Bismarck now reached an agreement with Austria to settle the question of the duchies. This apparently friendly and co-operative attitude seems to have disarmed all Austrian suspicions about Bismarck's ultimate aims. Then Bismarck posed as the good European by proposing to the Danes that the question of the duchies should be settled by a European conference of the Great Powers. As he had expected, the Danes refused. The outcome of this refusal was the entry of Prussian and Austrian armies into the duchies of Schleswig and Holstein and the defeat of the Danes. After some minor disputes, the Convention of Gastein was arranged by which Prussia was to administer Schleswig and Austria administer Holstein. The Convention of Gastein was signed between Austria and Prussia in August, 1865.

**The Seven Weeks' War, 1866.** Bismarck merely regarded the Convention as a temporary agreement with Austria. He now used the Schleswig-Holstein question as a means of driving Austria from the German Confederation altogether. As we have seen, he was on good terms with France and Russia, but in order to keep Napoleon III from intervening on the side of Austria in the coming struggle, he had a meeting with the French Emperor at Biarritz in October, 1865. No one knows for certain what occurred, but Napoleon came away with the impression that Bismarck had promised him compensation in the Rhineland in return for the neutrality of France during a war between Prussia and Austria. But nothing was written down which could in any way be used in the future to make Bismarck keep his promises.

Now Bismarck obtained an active ally against Austria: he skilfully played upon the hatred between the new Kingdom of Italy and Austria, who still held the territory of Venetia. He promised the Italians the territory of Venetia as the result of a successful war against Austria. The Italians were to assist Bismarck if war was declared within three months of the agreement.

It now remained for Bismarck to provoke Austria into war—for it was a cardinal principle of his policy to make his opponents the aggressors. The Austrians had supported the claims of the Duke of Augustenburg to rule the duchies of Schleswig-Holstein, but by the Convention of Gastein Bismarck had managed to overrule the Austrian candidate. He now accused the Austrians of continuing to support Augustenburg (and there was truth in the accusation) and also of stirring up trouble for Prussia in Schleswig. In June, 1866, Prussian troops marched into Holstein and took over control. Austria now appealed to the Confederation against Prussia and was supported by the majority of the German states. This amounted to a declaration of war by Austria against Prussia, and the latter, already mobilised, began to move at once against the North German states, such as Hanover and Saxony, who had supported Austria. The lesser German states were overrun in quick time and with very little resistance, and the final battle of the war took place at Sadowa in Bohemia. Although the Austrians defeated the Italians,

150,000 Austrian troops had nevertheless been drawn away to the Italian front and this considerably weakened the Austrian forces facing the Prussians. Again, the Prussian armament was far more up-to-date. The Austrians used the old muzzle-loading rifles, while the Prussians had the new breech-loading needle-gun. The battle of Sadowa proved an overwhelming victory for the Prussians. After only seven weeks' campaign, Bismarck's first great military success had been cheaply obtained. It was in great part the result of an astute diplomacy which had caught the Austrians unawares and isolated.

**Bismarck's Policy after the Seven Weeks' War.** Far from imposing on Austria a crushing indemnity or seizing part of her territory, Bismarck now followed a very moderate course. This was typical of his intelligence and statesmanship which, however unscrupulous, was never rash. He had his eye on the reactions of Napoleon III. The latter had hoped that the Austro-Prussian War would be a long and exhausting one for both sides and that he would be able eventually to step in as arbiter between the two contestants and make his much-coveted gains in Belgium and Luxemburg and the left bank of the Rhine. But in all these calculations he now saw himself mistaken and unable to challenge Prussia who was armed to the teeth and victorious. Nevertheless, Bismarck thought it prudent to reduce the hostility of France, and to do this he wished to persuade Napoleon III that he had no intention of uniting Germany on Prussia's terms. He still left their independence to the South German states who had supported Austria. Furthermore, in order not to drive Austria into the arms of Napoleon III, he imposed on her only very moderate terms.

**The Treaty of Prague, 1866.** By the peace treaty Bismarck annexed to Prussia the duchies of Schleswig and Holstein. The small North German states who had supported Austria were also annexed, and this resulted in the Rhine territories gained by Prussia in 1815 being joined with the eastern lands in a continuous territory. In this way Bismarck consolidated Prussian territory and added another 4,000,000 inhabitants to the state. Finally, he handed over Venetia to the Italians as promised.

Bismarck now formed all the states north of the River Main into the North German Confederation which had a Federal Assembly for the discussions of matters common to all the states. The President of this Confederation was the King of Prussia and the Chancellor was Bismarck himself.

In this settlement Bismarck had shown great restraint and intelligence. He had resisted the demand of William I for a triumphal Prussian parade through Vienna, had left the South German states alone, and had succeeded in reducing the alarm of Napoleon III. Bismarck wished to wage war against France in his own time and on his own terms.

**Bismarck and Napoleon III after 1866.** The first aim of Bismarck after 1866 was to win over the South German states of Bavaria, Würtemberg and Baden before any conflict with France began. This was all the more important to Bismarck because Napoleon III had made strenuous efforts to secure the alliance of these states for France. Napoleon renewed his demands for compensation on the Rhine in 1866. He instructed his Ambassador in Berlin, Benedetti, to ask for territory taken from France in 1815 to be returned, and for territory on the left bank of the Rhine to be handed over to France by Bavaria. Bismarck had these demands published in order to convince the South German states of Napoleon's aggressive designs. The result of Napoleon's naïve willingness to submit these demands in writing was now seen. The South German states entered into an agreement with Bismarck by which the Prussians would have complete control of their armies in time of war. This was the next blow to Napoleon after 1866.

In 1867 Napoleon III put forward a demand for the purchase of Luxemburg from Holland and also proposed that Bismarck should help him to obtain Belgium. Bismarck refused these demands, and proceeded to rouse the opposition of the German states to them. Eventually, he agreed to the suggestion of Austria that a European Conference should be held. Bismarck appeared in a very moderate and accommodating rôle when he agreed at this conference to withdraw some Prussian garrisons from Luxemburg where they had been stationed as a safeguard against French aggression under the settlements of the Congress of Vienna, 1815. At the same time he secured an agreement to keep Luxemburg neutral—rather similar to the guarantee of Belgian neutrality under the Treaty of London, 1839. Here, then, Bismarck had used the European Conference to thwart the aims of Napoleon III.

**Isolation of Napoleon III.** Napoleon III, through his failures on the Rhine, in Luxemburg and in Mexico (pages 128, 130), was now being driven into the position where the only hope of his survival in France itself was a successful war against Prussia. His failures had already forced him to "liberalise" the political system in France and thus allow much more open criticism of his government. He was driven to the hope that he would be able to defeat his internal critics by defeating the external enemy, Prussia.

In these circumstances, Napoleon III looked round for allies. But already Bismarck had been at work: he promised the Russians that he would support them when they decided to repudiate the Black Sea clauses of the Treaty of Paris, 1856 (see page 231). In return for this support, Russia was to remain neutral in the event of war between France and Prussia. Italy was on the best of terms with Prussia after 1866, while Austria could not forget that Napoleon III had assisted the Italians against her in 1859. Bismarck's previous schemings and Napoleon III's own policy in the past were all leading to the complete isolation of France.

**The Spanish Succession Question.** By 1868 Bismarck was in such a strong position, both politically and militarily, that he only needed some convenient pretext for war against France. By 1869 the Prussian Army was fully prepared, and a plan of campaign against France had already been mapped out by von Roon and von Moltke. And then in 1869 there came one of those convenient European complications which Bismarck was a past-master at exploiting.

In that year a revolution occurred in Spain, the ruling queen was expelled and a constitutional government with a new sovereign was demanded by the revolutionary party. They offered the throne to Prince Leopold of Hohenzollern-Sigmaringen, a relative of the Prussian King. Bismarck encouraged the prince to accept the Spanish offer. But at this point Bismarck suffered a setback, for King William himself was doubtful about provoking Napoleon III through what would be the "encirclement" of France by German influence. The King persuaded Prince Leopold to withdraw his candidature. This, of course, appeared a distinct victory for Napoleon III, who was now encouraged to make a further demand, namely, that the German candidature should never again be renewed. This demand, which William I received from the French Ambassador at the German spa of Ems, was politely refused, and William sent a telegram to Bismarck in Berlin describing what had occurred. It appeared that the whole affair had been reasonably settled, but Bismarck determined that this should not be the result. He hit upon the unscrupulous ruse of altering the wording of the telegram so that it appeared that William I had insulted the French Ambassador by refusing to see him. This version was then sent to both the German and French press for publication. The ruse had its

intended effect. A war hysteria broke out in France, strongly supported by the Empress Eugénie and the war party. As we have
seen in the account given in Chapter VI, France declared war on
July 14, 1870—and suffered overwhelming defeat. The German
Empire was proclaimed by Bismarck at Versailles in 1871. He had
achieved not only the complete unification of Germany but its
establishment as the most powerful state in Europe.

**German Economic Growth, 1850-1870.** It was not only Bismarck's
political skill that had brought about this result. The basic source
of Germany's increased strength lay in its rapid economic growth.
During these two decades, Germany underwent an industrial revolution which made her (after Britain) the most powerful industrial
nation in Europe. In two respects, Germany's industrialisation differed from that of the other nations of Western Europe. First, the
German government deliberately fostered industrialisation as part
of its policy for building up the political power of Germany.
Secondly, Germany was the last of the great powers of Western
Europe to enter the industrial field, and so was able from the outset
to take advantage of the latest technical developments.

Coal mines and steel works now sprang up in Western Germany,
in Saxony and Silesia. Coal output doubled between 1860 and 1870,
and doubled again in the following decade. Great industrialists
appeared, like Alfred Krupp, the steel king, whose 250 employees in
1850 had grown to 16,000 by 1873. By 1870 railways were being
rapidly built all over Germany, the locomotives being provided by
the German firm of Borsig. Similar advances were made in the
production of cotton and woollen goods. In at least two new industries, Germany jumped into the foremost position: the inventions
of Siemens made his firm outstanding in electrical engineering, then
in its infancy; and Germany was the pioneer in the foundation and
development of the new chemical industry.

Side by side with this industrial transformation went a great commercial expansion. New banks arose and overseas trade grew fast.
The population also grew rapidly, overtaking that of France. In
the nineteenth century the German population increased from 23 to
56 millions, as compared with France's increase from 27 to 39
millions and Britain's 10 to 37 millions.

It was this economic growth which was now to put Germany forward as a participant in the scramble for overseas colonies (see pages
260-264), and was later to enable her to carry the tremendous
strains of two world wars.

FIG. 22.—PROCLAIMING THE KING OF PRUSSIA AS GERMAN EMPEROR AT
VERSAILLES.

# chapter ten

# THE UNIFICATION OF ITALY, 1815–1870

**Introductory.** For many centuries Italy had been divided into petty states, and her soil had been constantly fought over by contending armies in mediaeval and modern times. In the Middle Ages there took place a fierce struggle between the claims of the Pope and the Holy Roman Emperors—a struggle in which the petty princedoms took now one side, now the other, according to calculations of gain and victory. This struggle between the Ghibellines (supporters of the Emperor) and the Guelphs (supporters of the Pope) weakened the whole country and made it the subject of intrigues by foreign states. Then, when modern states had been formed and feudalism was giving way to strong despotic monarchies in Europe, the trouble began again. Italy became the object of plundering attacks, such as those of the King of France, Charles VIII, in 1494, and of his successors Louis XII and Francis I. Indeed, for the greater part of the sixteenth century, a fierce struggle went on between Germans, French and Spanish for the control of the Italian peninsula. This struggle was renewed from time to time up to the end of the eighteenth century.

The most powerful influences which affected Italy in the late eighteenth and early nineteenth centuries were the French Revolution of 1789, Napoleon and the Austrian Empire. The Revolution had a direct influence in Italy, and there were revolts against various despotic rulers. Indeed, when Napoleon, claiming to be the standard-bearer of the Revolution, invaded Italy in his first campaign, 1796, he had an active "fifth column" of Italians ready to welcome him against their own rulers. Napoleon expelled the Bourbon Monarchy from Naples, imprisoned the Pope in 1808, and the Austrians were completely driven out.

The country came completely under French domination, and this control had very definite effects on Italian life. The laws were reformed and made fairer for all classes, many aristocratic privileges were swept away, and the industrious middle classes were promoted to positions of equality with the aristocracy. After Joseph Bonaparte became King of Spain, Marshal Murat, one of the most brilliant of Napoleon's generals, was made King of Naples and enjoyed a considerable amount of support among Italians. Great material

FIG. 23.—THE ARCHITECTS OF ITALIAN UNIFICATION.
VICTOR EMMANUEL II, CAVOUR AND GARIBALDI.

progress was made, but at the same time Italian art treasures (including the famous bronze horses of the Cathedral of St. Mark in Venice) were removed to France.

In general, we can say that for the first time in hundreds of years, Italians learnt to work and think with other Italians beyond the boundaries of the former petty states. In this way the idea of *unification* was promoted at the same time as the idea of opposition to aristocratic privilege. Then, as the Empire of Napoleon became more and more a plundering concern, the Italians began to resist French domination and various secret societies were formed which carried on into the nineteenth century. Napoleon's occupation of Italy gave rise eventually to a new tendency—opposition to foreign domination of any kind, which is the very essence of nineteenth-century *nationalism*. In fact, the very propaganda of liberty which the French had used in 1796 was being turned against themselves long before the end of the Napoleonic Wars in 1815.

**The Congress of Vienna, 1815.** The newly-felt pride of the Italians was gravely injured, however, by the Vienna settlement. "Throughout Italy," wrote a famous Italian, Mazzini, "one stroke of the pen has erased all our liberties, all our reform, all our hope."

Austria was given control of Venetia and Lombardy in compensation for her loss of Belgium. These territories were a thriving and important part of the Kingdom of Italy, and without them it was impossible to establish a strong and united Italy. In Lombardy and Venetia the Austrians ruled with a ruthlessness unsurpassed in the nineteenth century. Active criticism of the Austrian government resulted in torture, imprisonment and death for Italian patriots. Even the street names were Germanised, while German was made the official language of the law courts and government administration. All school books were carefully censored, the press was rigidly controlled, and all this was supported by an efficient army of police spies. The trade and industry of Lombardy and Venetia were further developed by the Austrians, but this improvement was offset by the weight of taxation imposed for the benefit of the Austrian government. It has been estimated that one quarter of the whole Empire's revenue was derived from Lombardy and Venetia, although they had only one-eighth of the population.

In northern Italy the old Kingdom of Piedmont was restored under the rule of Victor Emmanuel I. He proceeded to undo every true element of progress which the French administration had introduced. Even the old exemption of the aristocracy from taxation was reintroduced and the special privileges of the Church were restored. Many of the improvements made by the French in the City of Turin were destroyed in a fit of reactionary spite, parks and gardens being dug up and roadways destroyed.

The same despotic policies were carried out in Naples and in the Papal States. In fact, the only states in which the despotic system with its apparatus of privilege, of censorship and police control were not restored were the small states of Parma and Tuscany. The general picture of Italy in 1815 is of a country forced back to the bad elements of the past and not led forward to a better future. "We Italians", said Mazzini, "have neither Parliament nor hustings, nor liberty of the press, nor liberty of speech, nor possibility of lawful public assemblage, nor a single means of expressing the opinions stirring within us."

**The Influence of Austria in Italy.** In 1815 the controlling influence in Italy became the Austrian Empire. This control was partly direct, partly indirect. Direct control was gained in Venetia and Lombardy and indirect control through the rulers of the various states who were subservient to Austria. The rulers of Parma, Modena and Tuscany were all connected by family ties with the Austrian Hapsburgs and would certainly do nothing to oppose Austria. In Modena, the police system was completely modelled upon that of Austria. Even the Pope looked for support to Austria which was the most important of the Catholic states of Europe. In regard to Naples and Sicily, Austrian influence was more direct, for the Bourbon King Ferdinand I had a treaty with Austria by which the latter was pledged to support him against revolution in Naples.

**Resistance in the Period 1815–1830.** The possibilities of open opposition to Austria were obviously very slender. Without freedom of publication and of speech the fighters for freedom and national unity had no open platform. Discontent was driven underground and took the form of a number of secret societies, of which the most important was the Carbonari. The Austrian reply to this was to set up secret societies pretending to support the Italian cause, but whose real purpose was to ensnare the leaders of the liberal and national movements. Austrian police agents also managed to penetrate the Carbonari.

Despite the difficulties involved, there were two important movements of revolt in these years—in 1820 and 1830 respectively. The first occurred in Naples, where the Carbonari Society had strong support. It was partly inspired by the success of the revolution of

1818 in Spain where a constitutional government had been secured, with the further result that the Spanish American colonies also broke away and formed their own national governments. In Naples the revolt was led by officers of the Neapolitan Army, and the King was forced to grant a constitution. The new government was weak enough, however, to trust the word of Ferdinand I and even allowed him to attend the Congress of Laibach, where he straightway asked Metternich for Austrian assistance (see page 88). Austrian troops marched south, defeated the rebels and restored Ferdinand to his former power.

At the same time a movement for constitutional government in Piedmont broke out into open rebellion and King Victor Emmanuel I abdicated. His successor was to be his son, Charles Felix, who at that time was absent from the country. In the meantime, the King's nephew, Charles Albert, became Regent and accepted the constitution demanded by the people. No sooner had Charles Felix returned, however, than he cancelled the constitution and called in 20,000 Austrian troops to assist him to suppress the rebellion.

A similar fate befell the movements of 1830. This time the external revolution which affected Italy was that against Charles X in France, and many of the Italian revolutionaries hoped for the support of the new King, Louis Philippe. Revolts broke out in Parma, Modena and the Papal States. Louis Philippe, however, was more cautious than the rebels had expected. He was, in any case, already involved in complications with Palmerston and the other Great Powers over Belgium. Austrian forces again suppressed all these movements with little real difficulty.

By 1832 the heroism of the Carbonari had failed lamentably. It was leading to useless bloodshed and reprisals, and each rebellion had been stamped out in depressing isolation. The situation, from the point of view of the Italian patriots, was gloomy, to say the least. Nevertheless, certain of the leaders were able to draw valuable conclusions from these defeats.

**Giuseppe Mazzini and the Young Italy Movement.** Giuseppe Mazzini, whose influence on Italian unification was great, inspired new efforts in the years 1830–1848. He was exiled from Italy in 1830 for his activities in the revolutionary movements, went to Switzerland and began to organise a new movement based on broader and grander ideals than the Carbonari. This movement, known as Young Italy, was, as its title implies, a direct appeal to Italian youth. Mazzini wished to overcome the weaknesses of the

Carbonari, which had been lack of preparation, lack of co-ordination between the various revolts and a narrowness of appeal to the middle class. The Young Italy Society appealed to all classes on a truly national basis. It was to be a movement extending far beyond a few army officers, university professors and the middle class, to the working people of the towns and the labourers and peasants of the countryside. Mazzini urged his followers to go out among the working people and arouse in them a desire for liberty. The Young Italy Society gave an almost religious fervour to the cause of unity and independence. It is estimated that the society numbered over 60,000 by the year 1833.

Mazzini very early came to the conclusion that no kings were to be trusted to produce the great united, free and democratic Italian nation of which he dreamt. When Charles Albert became King of Piedmont in 1831, Mazzini appealed to him to place himself at the head of the nation. His refusal was a decisive influence in making Mazzini a republican. To Charles Albert the time was not yet ripe for war against the powerful forces of Austria, but he declared that, when the time was opportune, he would act. It is possible that, in the conditions of 1831, he had more real political understanding of the situation than Mazzini, for one of Mazzini's greatest defects was that he let his romantic idealism run away with him.

In 1833, Mazzini decided to attempt the raising of a revolt in Piedmont against Charles Albert, to establish a constitutional government which would take the lead in a general rising throughout Italy against the Austrians. Gathering a few hundred armed supporters in Switzerland he attempted an invasion of Savoy. This invasion was to be the signal for a revolt in Piedmont led by the more fanatical wing of the Young Italy movement. The expedition itself was completely betrayed by the treachery of one of its leaders in whom Mazzini had had the greatest confidence. The government of Charles Albert was able to stamp out the movement and arrest a number of the leaders. Mazzini himself escaped, but he was now exiled by the Swiss, went to Marseilles from where he continued his organisation of Young Italy. He was then expelled by Louis Philippe and eventually came to England, where he maintained himself by conducting a school for the children of Italian exiles in the Tottenham Court Road district of London.

**Ideas on Unification.** There were other ideas than those of Mazzini as to the best means of securing Italian unification. In these years a number of writers and philosophers hoped to see the power and influence of the Pope restored to something like the extent it had enjoyed in the Middle Ages. The most influential of these writers was Gioberti, who wished to see the Pope take the leadership of Italy into his own hands and remove the Austrian influence. The supporters of this idea became known as the Federalists because they wished to see all the separate states of Italy leagued together in a federation presided over by the Pope. They saw in it also a great opportunity for the revival of the Catholic Church in the whole of Europe.

**Pope Pius IX.** In 1846 the supporters of this idea were greatly encouraged by the election to the papacy of Pius IX. He had been genuinely horrified by the rule of the previous Pope and decided to make amends. He at once released hundreds of political prisoners and created a Council of State to share power with the College of Cardinals. Then he formed a municipal council for the city of Rome itself and a special citizens' guard was enrolled. Naturally, Metternich was displeased by this turn of events. "We were prepared for everything," he remarked, "except a liberal Pope. Now we have got one there is no accounting for anything." The Italian supporters of the Pope were further encouraged by the fact that Pius IX ignored the actual protests made to him by the Austrians.

**The Risings of 1848.** During the two years 1846–1848 the liberal movements in Europe began to assert themselves more forcibly in the German states, in Austria, and in France against Louis Philippe. In Italy the first rising took place in 1848 on the island of Sicily, part of the Kingdom of Ferdinand II. The island demanded its own constitutional government apart from the mainland. In January, a rising in the capital, Palermo, succeeded in driving the troops of Ferdinand out of the town. Ferdinand was forced to grant the islanders self-government, because the Austrians, with many difficulties of their own, could not be relied upon as in 1820 and 1830.

The Sicilian revolt had important results. It encouraged the movement of revolt in the Austrian northern provinces of Lombardy and Venetia. In Milan the people rose against the 20,000 troops of the Austrian General Radetsky and forced him to withdraw from the city. He was compelled to abandon every Austrian position in the two provinces, with the important exception of the Quadrilateral fortresses of Verona, Peschiera, Mantua and Legnango. With considerable skill, he managed to retire his main forces into these key fortress towns, and the Italians never succeeded in getting him out.

The rising in Milan had been given further encouragement by news of the downfall of Metternich in Vienna, and Charles Albert now published a liberal constitution for Piedmont.

**Policy of Charles Albert.** The King of Piedmont hesitated to attack Austria. He was doubtful of success, but was under great pressure from his own people to take up the Italian cause. At last, after several days' hesitation and the loss of valuable time, he decided to support the Milanese rising and place himself at the head of the whole Italian movement. The new governments in the other Italian states (for they had each had their own successful popular movements) now decided to support Charles Albert. Pope Pius IX also gave his support. Forces began to move up from Naples and the Papal States to the assistance of Charles Albert.

Unfortunately, Charles Albert could not match the military skill of Radetsky. The King achieved a few successes on a small scale, but Radetsky's main forces were intact in the Quadrilateral. These armies were reinforced from Austria, and when, in July, 1848, Charles Albert attacked the Quadrilateral, he was defeated at the Battle of Custozza and was forced to conclude an armistice with the Austrians. Pope Pius IX had suddenly declared himself against the war, and his forces were withdrawn.

The armistice lasted some months, but, in an attempt to compensate for a bad start, Charles Albert launched another offensive against the Austrians in the following year, but was defeated at the Battle of Novara. He abdicated in favour of his son Victor Emmanuel II and retired to a monastery in Portugal where he died some months later.

**The Roman Republic.** Despite the Pope's desertion of the war against Austria, many of his subjects had fought for Charles Albert, while in Rome itself revolutionary feeling was high. A new prime minister appointed by the Pope, Count Rossi, was murdered and a republic proclaimed. Mazzini and Garibaldi gained control of the movement in the city and the Pope fled to Gaeta to the protection of Ferdinand II of Naples. The "Roman Republic" was destined to last only a very short time. The Pope appealed for support to Louis Bonaparte, the newly-elected President of the French Republic, who hoped to gain Catholic support by reinstating the Pope in Rome. A French force under General Oudinot was dispatched by sea and, despite an early success by Garibaldi against the French, was finally successful in defeating the forces of the Republic. The Pope then returned to the city under French protection, which continued till 1870.

In the meantime the Austrians had besieged and bombarded the city of Venice into submission, and in the south Ferdinand had succeeded in rallying his forces against the revolution and reconquering Sicily.

**Reasons for Italian Failure, 1848.** The Italian failure of 1848 can be ascribed to a number of important causes. Among these were the early hesitation of Charles Albert, the greater military skill of Radetsky, the sudden defection of the Pope and the demoralising effect of this upon many ardent Catholics. Many of the Pope's admirers in 1846 had made the mistake of thinking he was more liberally-minded than he really was. Another important factor was the intervention of Louis Bonaparte against the Roman Republic, which effectively prevented Mazzini and Garibaldi from rallying the movement. A complicated cause of failure was the variety of political opinion among the Italians themselves. Charles Albert was afraid of the Republicans, who had strong support in Lombardy and in the city of Venice, where, in fact, a republic had been proclaimed under their leader, Daniele Manin. These divisions made it extremely difficult to achieve a properly co-ordinated plan of campaign against the Austrians. Lastly, the failure of the revolutions in Austria itself had liberated many troops for operations against the Italians and had enabled the key fortresses of the Quadrilateral to be reinforced.

**Giuseppe Garibaldi.** Another of the heroic figures of the Italian movement had appeared on the scene—Garibaldi. A native of Nice, in Savoy, he was won over to the Young Italy movement when a youth. On the occasion of Mazzini's expedition from Switzerland in 1834 he had attempted to raise a revolt in the Piedmontese navy. After this failure, Garibaldi had fled to South America where he fought for Uruguay against Brazil and Argentina. It was during these adventures that he developed the art of guerrilla warfare which he was later to employ against the Austrians in Italy. In 1848 he returned to Italy and fought in Lombardy and then for the Roman Republic against the French. However, all ended in failure and he was forced to make his escape from the mainland after being hunted by the Austrians across the peninsula. He spent the next few years in Europe and the New World and then settled as a farmer on the island of Caprera off the north-east coast of Sardinia.

**The Kingdom of Piedmont after 1848.** Most of the rulers of the Italian states had regained their former powers after the failure of the movements of 1848, and they took a heavy revenge upon their disloyal subjects. But gloomy as things were, at least one important lesson had been learnt. The Kingdom of Sardinia must play the leading rôle in any united Italian movement, and foreign aid must be obtained.

The new King, Victor Emmanuel II, while having to pursue a very cautious policy for some years, was eager to put Piedmont once again at the head of the liberation movement as soon as the time was ripe. But before Piedmont could again take the lead it was essential to strengthen the country in every possible way. This strengthening was to be achieved above all by maintaining the new liberal constitution and by the development of the economic power of the country. Political liberalism and economic prosperity were to give the driving force needed for successful leadership in the Italian cause.

**Count Camillo Cavour.** The man who was to guide Piedmont on this new course, in co-operation with Victor Emmanuel II, was Count Camillo Cavour. He was an aristocrat by birth, but this did not prevent him having strong liberal sympathies. He had given up his commission in the army in 1830 because of a quarrel with the authorities over his openly avowed support for the revolution of 1830 against the Bourbon King of France, Charles X. For a time he had given his attention to the improvement of his estates and the introduction of the newest agricultural methods. He travelled widely in Europe. He knew England well, and greatly admired her methods of government. In 1847 he established an important newspaper, *Il Risorgimento*, devoted to the cause of Italian unity and freedom. In 1848 he was elected a member of parliament under the new constitution accepted by Charles Albert. After the events of 1848–1849 he strongly supported the policy of Victor Emmanuel II towards the Catholic Church in Piedmont. The government strove to reduce the political power of the Church, and this was in great part the result of the sudden change of policy by Pius IX which we have already noted. The government wished to make sure that in the future its policy was not in any way obstructed by the political influence of the Pope in Piedmont. Consequently, laws were passed which deprived the Church of its law courts in which alone clerics could be tried, and its right of inheriting property was now subjected to the approval of the state. This development naturally brought about a longstanding opposition between the Pope and Piedmont, and later between the Kingdom of Italy and the Pope. But the government was determined that there should be no "state within the state"

Cavour had strongly supported the anti-clerical policy in Piedmont, and in 1850 was made Minister of Commerce and Agriculture, of the Navy and Finance in 1851, and Prime Minister in 1852.

**Cavour's Domestic Policy.** Within a few years Cavour transformed Piedmont into a completely modern state. He did this by promoting above all the interest of the middle class of manufacturers and traders. It was from this class that he drew his most capable ministers. He created new state banks through which money could be invested in railways, in shipping lines, in agriculture. He supported this development by bringing about some important free trade treaties by which Piedmont was able to gain much-needed industrial goods from more advanced countries, especially England. Cavour had been much impressed by the Free Trade arguments of the "Manchester School" of Cobden and Bright in England. But besides these economic reforms, he gave much attention to the strengthening of the army of Piedmont. The whole force was re-equipped and the promotion of middle-class officers made easier.

**Cavour's Foreign Policy.** Cavour realised that Piedmont needed strong allies against Austria. But how was he to gain this support? Compared with England, France, Austria and Russia the Kingdom of Piedmont was insignificant and of little account in the eyes of the Great Powers.

But in 1854 Cavour saw an important chance for Piedmont to play an active part in the great contemporary question of the relationship of the Western Powers to Russia. When the Crimean War broke out in 1854 he offered the support of the Piedmontese Army to France and England. There was much opposition to this policy in Piedmont itself, for in fact the country had no quarrel whatever with Russia, but Cavour managed to get his way. Sardinian troops were sent to the Crimea and, unlike those of the other powers, they were prepared for the terrible conditions there and fought with great efficiency although only a small part of the allied force. Napoleon III especially could not fail to be impressed—which was one of the objects of Cavour. He had shown that the new army of Piedmont would give a good account of itself if Napoleon espoused the Italian cause against Austria.

At the Peace Conference at Paris, 1856, Cavour personally represented Piedmont and he brought before France and Britain the grievances of his country against Austria.

**The Compact of Plombières, 1858.** Cavour had now begun ac-

tively to seek allies for Piedmont. Britain, however, had serious problems of her own, for the Crimean War had shown up the grave defi-
ciencies of the British Army whose organisation in 1854 was the
same as it had been in 1815. Moreover, the Indian Mutiny had
been an experience which, coming immediately after the Crimean
War, had further disposed England towards a cautious policy
abroad. On the other hand, Napoleon III, so far successful both in
his home and foreign policy, was more likely to be interested in the
Italian question. In his younger days he had been a member of the
"Carbonari" and had taken part in the risings of 1830 in Italy. He
had professed a passionate interest in the rights of nations struggling
to be free. Moreover, dazzled by the fame of his uncle, Napoleon I,
he thought that the possibility of emulating him by a great campaign
in Northern Italy would remind the French of the campaigns of
1796 and 1800. Besides, such a campaign would be against the
same old enemy, the Austrian Empire. Successfully carried out,
it would please both his imperialist supporters in France and the
Liberals.

Yet Napoleon III hesitated to respond to Cavour's overtures.
There was one great opponent of his policy in France, the Catholic
Church. The Church's detestation of Cavour's anti-clerical policy
in Piedmont, its desire to protect the position of the Pope in the
Papal States, its opposition to any war against the great Catholic
power, Austria—all these factors presented a dangerous problem
for the Emperor.

In the midst of these hesitations and perplexities the Emperor
had his mind made up for him. The Italian patriot and anarchist,
Orsini, who had assisted Mazzini and Garibaldi at Rome in 1849
and had since been in exile, decided to make an end of the perfidious
Emperor who was failing to help the great Italian cause. Orsini
threw a bomb at the Emperor while the latter was on his way to the
Paris Opera. The Emperor and Empress escaped, but twelve other
persons were killed. Far from ruining the negotiations which Cavour
was already carrying on with the Emperor, this event had the opposite result. Napoleon realised the great dangers of *not* giving some
help to the Italians, and, in a private letter to the Emperor, Cavour
pointed out that the recurrence of such an attack was not impossible.

In June, 1858, the Emperor met Cavour secretly at the village of
Plombières in the Vosges Mountains. Here an important agreement
was arrived at. Napoleon III promised to support Piedmont against
Austria and, in return for these services, was to receive the important
city of Nice and the territory of Savoy. But the Pope was to retain

control of the Papal States and Ferdinand II was to remain in Naples.

**War against Austria, 1859.** Cavour's next aim was to work the Austrians into the position of aggressors. This manœuvre was necessary in order to make easier the entry of Napoleon III into the war—an arrangement which had really been made at Plombières. At the game of provocation Cavour was as masterly as Bismarck. He concentrated troops on the frontier of Lombardy, certain minor clashes between Austrian and Piedmontese troops were brought about, and a very tense atmosphere developed. Cavour increased his provocations and mobilised the army of Piedmont. Speed was all-important, for there were signs that the Emperor Napoleon III was already wavering. This was shown when the Emperor supported the suggestion of Great Britain that a conference should be called to discuss outstanding questions and prevent war. Cavour could scarcely oppose such demands openly, but he had no confidence that the Austrians would accept his demands and give up Lombardy and Venetia without fighting. However, just as the suggested conference was about to take place, the Austrians played into Cavour's hands by sending an ultimatum demanding the disbandment of the Piedmontese Army. Cavour rejected this demand, and Austria declared war in April, 1859. The campaign was brief and dramatic. Napoleon III entered Northern Italy at the head of the French forces and by midsummer, 1859, had won the important battles of Magenta and Solferino against the Austrians. Then, just as the overwhelming defeat of the Austrians seemed certain, there occurred one of the most astounding political events of the nineteenth century: Napoleon III made a truce with the Austrians at Villafranca on condition that Lombardy be left in the hands of Piedmont. Cavour, despairing of achieving his aims when Victor Emmanuel refused to carry on the war alone, resigned his position as Prime Minister. The actions of Napoleon III seemed fully to justify the distrust of him felt by Mazzini and Garibaldi, who were opposed to Cavour's reliance on foreign aid, especially from the Emperor.

Many explanations have been attempted of Napoleon's sudden change of policy. He was undoubtedly afraid that Prussia would make some move against him if his successes continued—a fear which the actual movement of Prussian troops towards the French frontiers seemed to justify. Again, he was not certain that he could control the actions of a Piedmont which was completely successful.

VI.—ITALY, 1859–1870, WITH SPECIAL REFERENCE TO GARIBALDI'S CAMPAIGNS.

If any moves were made against the Pope and Rome, as demanded by Mazzini and Garibaldi, then the Clerical party in France, strongly supported as it was by the Empress Eugénie herself, would turn against him, with possibly disastrous consequences for his régime in France. These considerations were reinforced by the fact that neither the battles of Magenta nor Solferino had been easy victories, for the French casualties had been very great. Napoleon's great problem was the French people themselves, and the various conflicting cliques and interests round the Imperial throne.

But the Italian people themselves now forced the pace and made up considerably for Napoleon III's partial desertion of the cause. There were popular revolts in the duchies of Modena, Parma and Tuscany and that part of the Papal States known as the Romagna. The demand was for union with Piedmont, and popular votes or plebiscites were demanded to decide the issue. Napoleon III, who had himself adopted the method of the plebiscite to justify his own seizure of power in France, could scarcely oppose this demand, and the Austrians feared that France would enter the war again if they intervened against the duchies. Moreover, Lord Palmerston, who had in the meantime become British Prime Minister, now intervened to warn both Austria and France that Britain would oppose any help being given by them to the rulers of the central duchies. This intervention carried considerable weight with both Austria and France. The plebiscites showed an overwhelming vote for union with Piedmont, and thus, despite Cavour's despair, very much had been won—much more than seemed possible at Villafranca. Nice and Savoy were handed over to Napoleon III as part of the bargain. This was the position reached by the year 1860.

**Garibaldi and the Thousand.** The next great event in the Italian struggle was the campaign of Garibaldi and the thousand "redshirts". In 1860 a popular revolt broke out in Naples, where the despotic government of Francis II was no better than that of his predecessors. Freedom was unknown and the dungeons of the city were crowded with political prisoners kept there in conditions of the utmost degradation—a state of things denounced by Mr. Gladstone who had visited Naples and seen the state of the dungeons and the oppressive nature of this Bourbon "police state".

The revolt, which actually began in the island of Sicily, was the signal to Garibaldi for action. He had settled as a farmer on the island of Caprera off the coast of Sardinia. The revolt in Sicily seemed to him the opportunity to carry the Italian movement

FIG. 24.—GARIBALDI'S MEN.

forward on his own initiative. He disliked Cavour's policy, especially the alliance with Napoleon III and the handing over of his
native city of Nice to the Emperor after Villafranca. Mazzini held
similar views and considered that the Italians should act on their
own account without foreign aid. He therefore strongly urged
Garibaldi to take action with the aid of the Sicilian movement, and
he himself took an active part in the preparations which were now
made. The Piedmontese port of Genoa was chosen as the assembly
point for the expedition to aid the Sicilians, and a secret subscription
list was opened to meet the expenses of the proposed expedition,
which would involve a landing of the volunteers on the island of
Sicily from the sea.

During this time, Cavour himself played a double game. He
openly opposed Garibaldi and prevented him gaining recruits from
the army of Piedmont. This policy was for the official consumption
of the Austrians, whom he was most anxious not to provoke into
an attack. Nevertheless, Cavour did not oppose the sailing of
Garibaldi and his volunteers from the port of Genoa, for he saw the
possibilities of gain for the Italian cause if the position was handled

with skill. Could he in any way use the expedition to further his own policy, and would Garibaldi be prepared to accept that situation? These questions could not be answered for certain when the red-shirts sailed from Genoa. Cavour's craft and diplomacy were about to be tested.

When the ship carrying Garibaldi's expedition arrived at Marsala on the western coast of Sicily he found a number of British war-ships anchored off the harbour and he was able to sail in under the cover of these vessels. The campaign in Sicily was a triumphal procession for Garibaldi, for he had the support of nearly the whole population. In two months he had conquered the island and driven out or captured the royalist forces.

Now difficulty came from another quarter. The French Emperor Napoleon III had become alarmed for the safety of the Pope in Rome as it became known that Garibaldi intended to carry his expedition to the mainland and up the Italian peninsula. The Emperor now proposed to Great Britain an arrangement by which their joint naval forces would prevent Garibaldi's forces passing over the straits of Messina. But on the whole, Palmerston's government, which included Gladstone, was favourably inclined towards Garibaldi and, in any case, it considered Cavour capable of handling the situation.

**Events on the Mainland.** As soon as Garibaldi landed on the mainland he gained the same enthusiastic support he had received in Sicily. He had the help of the revolutionary forces in the city of Naples itself, the King fled from his capital and Garibaldi entered the city. During this part of the campaign the Neapolitan troops of Francis II proved most unreliable—there were occasions when the very appearance of Garibaldi on his charger at the head of his forces was sufficient to make the royalist troops turn and run!

Mazzini had now joined Garibaldi in Naples and, working together as at Rome in 1848, they established their own government in the city. The critical point for Cavour and Victor Emmanuel II had now been reached, for it was not impossible that Garibaldi and Mazzini would gain control of the whole Italian movement, conquer the Papal States and establish an Italian republic. An attack on Rome would lead to fighting against the French garrison and might bring Napoleon III into action, and this in turn was most likely to produce Austrian intervention.

Cavour decided to send the army of Piedmont into the Papal States to forestall the threatened attack on Rome. Accordingly, the Piedmontese Army invaded the Papal States. This in itself was an attack on Papal territory, but on the other hand the protection of Rome was sufficient to keep Napoleon III quiet. Plebiscites were now held in the Papal States, which voted overwhelmingly for union with Piedmont. Cavour had protected the spiritual position of the Pope but had obtained his territory.

Soon after these events—towards the end of 1860—King Victor Emmanuel arrived in Naples and Garibaldi handed over the city to him, retiring to Caprera. His volunteers were disbanded by order of the King. The meeting between the King and Garibaldi had been friendly, but nothing could hide the fact that the policy of Cavour and Victor Emmanuel had won the day against the more romantic and impetuous policy of Garibaldi and Mazzini, who had shrunk from the possibilities of civil war.

**The Kingdom of Italy Created.** The Kingdom of Italy was now formally declared, and the first Parliament was opened at Turin in 1861. In the same year the Italian monarchy lost a valuable ally by the death of Count Cavour.

Venetia and Rome both remained outside the new Kingdom, but in 1862 Garibaldi crossed over from Sicily to Calabria with 1,000 men and marched on Rome with the purpose of capturing the City and incorporating it in the Italian Kingdom. However, he was met south of Rome by an Italian force sent to meet him by the Italian Prime Minister, Rattazzi. At Aspromonte he was wounded and taken prisoner and held for a considerable time while the Italian government discussed the question of his trial. This possibility aroused such violent popular feeling against the government that it was forced to grant him a pardon and Rattazzi was compelled to resign.

In 1864 the Italian government made a secret agreement with Napoleon III by which French troops were to be withdrawn from Rome on condition that no attack on Rome would be allowed, and that the Italians would move their capital from Turin to some other city as a preliminary. Once again there was popular violence against the government when the details of this agreement leaked out. The government was again forced to resign, but the new Prime Minister, La Marmora, ratified the agreement, despite opposition, and in 1865 the capital of Italy was transferred to Florence.

In 1865 Napoleon III withdrew French forces from the City of Rome, but the Pope's own forces were still largely commanded by French officers, and Garibaldi began a further agitation for a military attack on Rome. At this point he was arrested by order of the Italian Prime Minister and confined to the island of

Caprera. However, he managed to escape, and in October, 1867, led another expedition from Tuscany against Rome. In the meantime Napoleon III had sent back regular French forces into the City, and at Mentana they met about 4,000 of Garibaldi's men. The latter suffered severely and were forced to retreat, leaving several hundred prisoners in French hands.

After the battle of Mentana, the French Prime Minister, Rouher, declared that France could never allow the Italians to occupy Rome.

In 1866 Garibaldi had fought against the Austrians when the Italian government had entered into alliance with Bismarck. With the victory of Bismarck over Austria, Venetia was handed over to the Italians.

In 1871 Italian forces entered Rome when Napoleon III withdrew the garrison for service against the Prussians. The Pope's own forces made a token resistance and he retired to the Vatican Palace. It was not till 1929 that a definite treaty was made between the Papacy and the Italian State by which the Pope was given full sovereignty over the Vatican City.

# chapter eleven

# BISMARCK AND GERMANY, 1870–1890

**Introductory.** From 1871 to 1890 Bismarck effectively controlled the history of the new German Empire. Having achieved the territorial unification, he now gave his colossal energy to the task of strengthening still further the internal cohesion of the new state, now the greatest industrial country on the European mainland (see page 166). Any challenge to his own views of the future of Germany was to be resisted by a combination of political guile and outright force. He transferred the methods he had used in the earlier phase of German foreign policy to the internal problems of Germany. A long period is taken up with his struggle against what he regarded as the disruptive forces of Socialism and Roman Catholicism, but against them his success is only partial. The new German Constitution, which was essentially the work of himself and the Emperor William I, gave a certain veneer of half-liberalism to the German political system, but the real power still lay with the Army, the aristocracy and the highly efficient bureaucratic machine centred in Berlin. In foreign policy he played a masterly hand which successfully maintained German power without real challenge on the continent of Europe. On matters of colonial and trading policy his views changed in his later years and Germany entered on the path of high protection and colonial expansion. The sharp conflict of views between the forces in Germany representing the outlook of Kaiser William II and those supporting Bismarck led to the latter's downfall in 1890. Germany had entered on "the new course".

**Constitution of the German Empire.** The victory of Prussia over France in 1870 had finally united Germany and given Prussia the governing voice in the new state. The constitution adopted had a certain number of democratic-looking characteristics, but that is all that can be claimed. The effective control was Prussian.

The constitution established two assemblies, the Bundesrat and the Reichstag. The Bundesrat consisted of 58 members only who were nominated by the governments or rulers of the states of the federation. It was this small body which had the main law-making functions. But even the powers of the Bundesrat were seriously limited, for a vote of fourteen against any measure meant its rejection. This gave a decisive veto to the Prussians if they wished to exercise it, for there were seventeen Prussian members in the Bundesrat.

The Reichstag was the assembly elected by universal manhood suffrage. It contained about 400 members, of whom more than half were Prussians. Its powers were extremely limited, and it was mainly concerned with debating and suggesting amendments to the laws sent to it from the Bundesrat. It could be dissolved by the Emperor at any time. Moreover, the ministers of the government were in no way responsible for it. Their responsibility was to the Emperor alone.

The King of Prussia, who was automatically German Emperor, controlled the armed forces and appointed all the principal officials, including the Chancellor.

It might naturally be asked why the Reichstag was ever created, if its powers were so slight. The answer is that it served as the means by which the Emperor and Chancellor could sound the opinions of the people and take the measures they considered necessary either to suppress opposition or to modify their own policies as the situation demanded. It provided, in fact, a far more flexible system than a dictatorship, although there were considerable elements of dictatorship in it.

Bismarck also compromised with the individual states by leaving them a good deal of local power in matters which did not affect the whole of Germany, but the army, navy, foreign affairs, taxation, trade and railways came under the control of the central government.

**Bismarck's Problems.** From the very beginning of the new Empire, Bismarck set out to watch, restrain or completely to suppress any movements which seemed to threaten his own policy or the new prussianised state system. In this respect he had some formidable opponents to deal with, and much of his political career was taken up with supporting now this party, now that, in the Bundesrat and Reichstag and manipulating the party system in the interests of his own policy. For instance, the party representing the Junker or great landlord interests in East Prussia, the Conservative Party, was opposed to much of the industrial development of Germany just as the landowners in England were in conflict with the manufacturing classes at the time of the Corn Law Repeal (1846). Bismarck, although a Junker himself, did not agree with their policy and at one time had to seek the alliance against them of the National Liberal Party which represented the interests of the rising industrialists of Germany. But no sooner had the Conservative Party been brought to heel than Bismarck used it to oppose the National Liberals who were demanding greater powers for the Reichstag in the conduct of the national affairs of Germany.

But Bismarck's two greatest problems were, firstly, that of the Roman Catholic Church and, secondly, socialism. The Catholic Church was deeply involved in political questions, and the Centre Party came to voice its interests. The demands of socialism were expressed by the German Social Democratic Party, which was opposed to Prussian militarism and demanded the creation of a socialist state, with the great national industries under government control. It had strong revolutionary tendencies and drew much of its theory from the communist doctrines of Karl Marx (see pages 190–191).

**Bismarck and the Catholic Church.** In 1870 the Vatican Council proclaimed the dogma of Papal Infallibility which declared that when the Pope, in discharge of his office, states a doctrine in regard to faith and morals, he is infallible, and does not require the consent of the Church. Such decisions were unalterable. However, a minority of German Catholics refused to accept the new doctrine, whereupon the bishops excommunicated them and demanded the removal of certain similarly-minded university professors and school-teachers from their posts. Bismarck refused to allow these dismissals to take place, for he saw the Pope's demands as an attempt to control educational matters in Germany, which he regarded as purely a matter for the German State. There was to be "no state within the state".

The Centre Party, which supported the Pope, now began a public campaign against Bismarck. His reply was to launch a direct attack on the Catholic Church with the aid of his allies in the Bundesrat and Reichstag, and he secured the passage of the May Laws of 1872. He expelled the Catholic Jesuit Society from Germany, prevented priests from inspecting schools (a right which they had exercised for some time), and forced the colleges of the Church to accept examinations set by the State. At the same time thousands of protesting priests were imprisoned.

This struggle between Church and State in Germany was known as the "Kulturkampf" or "struggle for civilisation". In other words, what exact form was German civilisation to take? Was there to be complete domination of everything, including the Catholic Church, by the State, or was the Church to exercise very considerable control of education, marriage and other moral questions? Bismarck had further exasperated the Papacy by making civil marriage legal and thus reducing to a certain extent the control of the Church over family matters. In many of these measures he had the support of the Prussian Conservatives, who were strongly Protestant. At the same time the National Liberals, representing industrial and commercial interests, had been influenced against the Papacy because of its declared opposition to the extension of science and scientific education.

Nevertheless, Bismarck failed to force the Catholic Church into subservience to the German State. In fact, the Centre Party increased its influence in the Reichstag. Bismarck realised that other forces were more dangerous to his position than the Catholic Church. Moreover, Pius IX died in 1878 and was succeeded by Leo XIII, who was prepared to accept some compromise. The result was the return of the German Ambassador to the Vatican in 1878 and the removal of most of the May Laws. All religious orders of the Catholic Church were allowed to function in Germany except the Jesuits, and the Catholic Church was allowed complete control of the education of its own priesthood. On the other hand, it did not regain its right of inspecting the State schools.

**Bismarck and Socialism.** The rather abrupt end of Bismarck's campaign against the Catholic Church is partly to be explained by his increasing preoccupation with the Socialist movement in Germany. Indeed, he hoped to gain support from Catholics for his attempts to crush the new movement.

Socialism in Germany at this time was essentially a revolutionary movement inspired by the doctrines of the founder of modern communism, Karl Marx (1818–1883). Marx had attended the University of Berlin, where he gained a Doctorate of Philosophy, dabbled in poetry, student politics and journalism and finally had to leave Germany for France when the German authorities expressed strong disapproval of his views. He had, however, succeeded in forming a secret working men's association known as the Communist League, which had some influence among the workers of the Rhineland. In 1847, the League held a meeting in London at which Marx and his life-long collaborator, Friedrich Engels, were given the task of working out the practical programme and the theory on which the League was to base its activities. The document they produced between them was the famous Communist Manifesto which has exercised such a wide influence on the affairs of Europe and Asia in the last hundred years. Its analysis of human history was based on the conception of the class struggle, that is, the struggle of oppressed classes to overthrow the forms of society which were retarding their progress. Thus, slavery, having outlived its usefulness, gave way to serfdom; and this in its turn gave way to modern capitalism with its masses of exploited workers—the "proletariat"—who in their turn would overthrow the capitalist system and own collectively all the factories, mines, transport systems, etc. Society would then be organised on a communist basis, with all profits returning to the society which produced them and not into the pockets of private capitalists. This theory was given a more elaborate economic statement by Marx in his book *Das Kapital*, the first volume of which was published in 1867.

In 1847 Marx managed to return to Germany and took some part in the German revolutionary movement which led up to the Frankfurt Parliament. Both Marx and Engels saw the German revolutionary movement as essentially a "bourgeois" or middle-class revolution in its origin, but believed it would give way to a revolution of the proletariat or working class and would then be a complete and effective revolution. He edited a Communist newspaper in Cologne and in it advocated the arming of the proletariat to consolidate and extend the gains of the revolution. But he failed to get adequate support for this programme and, after the collapse of the Frankfurt Parliament, he fled to England, where he remained till his death in 1883.

The German Social Democratic Party was established in 1869 by a disciple of Marx, but not all its members believed in the necessity of violently overthrowing the existing State, and an early rift developed (as in many other labour parties since) between the revolutionary and "reformist" (or gradualist) wings of the movement. The reformist wing gained the main control in Germany and considered that socialism could be victorious in Germany through the capturing by the workers of parliamentary power. Marx himself strongly disagreed with this deviation from the pure doctrine of communism which he and Engels had enunciated. Nevertheless, to Bismarck, both the revolutionary and the milder forms of socialism were equally dangerous to the German State as he wished to build it, and he was alarmed when the elections of 1877 gave half a million votes to the Social Democrats and they returned twelve members to the Reichstag.

**Campaign against the Social Democratic Party.** Bismarck aimed at completely crushing the Socialist movement. He was aided by the circumstance that in 1878 two attempts were made to assassinate the Emperor William I. The would-be assassins were not Socialists, although it was convenient to Bismarck to lay these attempts at the door of the Socialist movement. These unscrupulous tactics enabled him to justify the introduction of the Exceptional Law of 1878, by which the Social Democratic Party was outlawed. Its newspapers were suppressed and many of its known supporters and organisers were deported from Germany. Nevertheless, the party continued to function from abroad, mainly from Switzerland, and its propaganda continued to filter illegally into Germany. The suppression of the party had been supported by the Catholic Centre Party in gratitude to Bismarck for calling off the Kulturkampf. This, in fact, was exactly what Bismarck had wanted.

But Bismarck failed as dismally against socialism as against the Catholic Church. Indeed, a rather curious situation developed, for the Socialist representatives in the Reichstag enjoyed parliamentary immunity and could speak there without fear of arrest—one of the curious benefits of the partial democracy which Bismarck had introduced. By 1890 the Social Democratic vote in the country was over 1,500,000. By 1914 it was 4,250,000.

Bismarck hoped to undermine socialism as a party movement by introducing gradual doses of "State socialism" which would benefit the German workers. In 1884 he introduced compulsory sickness insurance in all the main industries (with contributions from both workers and employers), insurance against accidents (to which the employers and not the workers contributed), and finally in 1889 a system of old-age pensions with contributions from workers, employers and the government. But, judging by the strength of the Social Democrats in 1914, when they were the largest party in the Reichstag, the efforts of Bismarck can scarcely be regarded as successful.

**The Tariff Question.** Up to 1879 Bismarck had supported a free trade system for Germany, and on that account had the support of the National Liberal Party. However, by that year other countries had begun to aim at more self-sufficiency by imposing customs duties on imports which would compete with their own home manufactures. Bismarck now considered that Germany could strengthen herself by a similar policy, especially as the development of the iron and steel industry, using the iron ores of Lorraine since 1871, had greatly strengthened that side of German industry and made her far less dependent on imports from abroad. He also decided to give protection to the big landowners of East Prussia, the Junkers, who had always detested free trade as tending to lower prices of grain owing to competition from other countries.

Bismarck's new trade policy meant a break from the National Liberal Party, and he now unscrupulously began to undermine its influence as a party by encouraging many German newspapers to denounce the leaders of the party as Jews. This unscrupulous use of the anti-semitic campaign for political ends was typical of Bismarck's methods. Having made the National Liberal Party the centre of his political system for ten years, he now threw them over when they no longer served his own purposes. This was a blow at the possibilities of more democracy in Germany, for the National Liberals had demanded more power for the Reichstag over the Chancellor. Bismarck now succeeded in undermining their influence throughout Germany.

**Bismarck and Colonies.** The new protective tariff policy is connected with a change in Bismarck's colonial aspirations. He had always contended that Germany did not need overseas possessions, for he had a purely European view of Germany's future. But now things were different. The manufacturers who benefited from protection were demanding that German colonies be obtained for the supply of needed raw materials and that such colonies should be closed, under the tariff law, to the trade of other nations. Thus German industrialists would benefit both ways, gaining raw materials cheaply, and selling finished goods back to the colonies without competition. In 1884 Bismarck accepted these ideas, and from then on Germany began the acquisition of colonies, especially in Africa and the Pacific. But, as we shall see, this development brought Germany into conflict with other states at the beginning of the twentieth century. These conflicts were closely related to the First World War of 1914–1918.

**Bismarck's Foreign Policy, 1871–1890.** Having defeated France in the war of 1870, Bismarck's chief aim in foreign policy was to keep France isolated and thus unable to wage a war for the recovery of Alsace-Lorraine. At the same time, he was most anxious to keep on good terms with both Austria and Russia. He wished for peace in a Europe where Germany was supreme and where all the main strings of diplomacy were in his own hands. But to achieve this was by no means a simple task, and it says much for the subtlety of his policy that he was successful in all his main aims up to 1890 when the new Kaiser William II threw him over.

Curiously enough, he began with a serious miscalculation. The heavy indemnity of £200,000,000 imposed on France in 1871 was considered by Bismarck a sufficient guarantee that the German Army of occupation would be in France for many years until the indemnity was paid. All classes subscribed so heavily to the loans floated by the French government that the indemnity was paid off in two years and in 1873 the army of occupation was withdrawn. By introducing a short-term army service the French were now building a large reserve force. By 1873 the available force was in the region of 2,000,000 men. These developments alarmed and infuriated Bismarck—an outburst of bad temper which was not lessened by the fact that the French Catholic Bishops were openly supporting the German Catholic opposition to him. In 1875 certain newspapers in Germany which were under Bismarck's influence began to discuss the question of another war against France. Things looked extremely black until the Czar of Russia, Alexander II, in a visit to Berlin, warned Bismarck against such action, while Queen Victoria herself wrote a similar warning to the Emperor William I. Bismarck's campaign of threats and bluster against France suddenly stopped, for he saw that France might have allies, and one of the main purposes of his diplomacy was to prevent such a development. The Russian policy is explained by the Czar's fear that if France were permanently weakened by another defeat at the hands of Germany, then Russia herself would be faced by an even stronger Germany. This Russian intervention shows how difficult it was for Bismarck to reconcile German and Russian interests—a problem which became increasingly difficult.

**The Dreikaiserbund or League of the Three Emperors.** Three years previously, in 1872, Bismarck, pursuing his purpose of keeping on good terms with both Austria and Russia, had achieved an agreement between William I, the Emperor Francis Joseph of Austria and Czar Alexander II. One thing they all had in common was fear of Socialist revolution, and Bismarck knew well how to play upon it. The agreement was known as the League of the Three Emperors and was a verbal understanding only. They all agreed to suppress Socialist revolution and to give common assistance if necessary, to consult one another on all important international questions and to attempt to settle the Eastern Question.

**The Eastern Question.** In 1875 national revolts broke out in the Balkan Peninsula against Turkish rule (see page 231). Serbia and the tiny state of Montenegro were both involved, but the movement which finally brought in the Great Powers was the rising of the

Bulgarian people. Here the Turks behaved at their worst. In their efforts to stamp out the national rising, whole villages were razed to the ground and the inhabitants murdered. Bulgarian prisoners were shot after being subjected to the most barbarous tortures. In England Mr. Gladstone came out strongly against the Turks and urged the government of Disraeli to make Britain's voice heard. However, despite the attempts of the Great Powers to reach some

VII.—The "Big Bulgaria", 1878, created by the Treaty of San Stefano.

settlement of the Balkan Question, no real satisfaction could be obtained from the Sultan Abdul Hamid II. At last the Russians abandoning all attempts at negotiation, formed an alliance with the Rumanian people who had also risen against the Turks, launched a campaign against the Sultan, defeated his forces and made him sign the Treaty of San Stefano. Disraeli had already sent British war-

VIII.—ALTERATION OF THE TREATY OF SAN STEFANO
MADE BY TREATY OF BERLIN, 1878.

ships to the Dardanelles, for Britain feared that the Russians intended to seize Constantinople itself.

By the San Stefano Treaty a new Bulgarian state was created virtually independent of the Turks, but at this point the Great Powers intervened against Russia. Disraeli threatened war against Russia unless she agreed to a meeting of the Great Powers at Berlin to revise the Treaty of San Stefano. He was strongly supported in this by the Austrian Empire, which had the greatest interest in preventing Russian expansion in the Balkans. Both Britain and Austria feared that the new Bulgaria would not in reality be independent, but under Russian control. They saw the Treaty of San Stefano as all part of the Russian march towards Constantinople and the Mediterranean.

**The Congress of Berlin, 1878.** The Russians, unprepared for a war against the other Great Powers, agreed to the Berlin Congress. This meeting drastically altered the arrangements of San Stefano, for the frontiers of Bulgaria were so reduced that half the territory returned to Turkish control. In other words, the Great Powers ranged against Russia had decided to bolster up the Turkish Empire. The Austrians also gained a protectorate over Bosnia and Herzegovina, which strengthened their position in the Balkans as against the Slav peoples under the influence of Russia. Of course, the Turks gave their usual promises of better treatment to the Christian minorities in their Empire.

**Bismarck's Policy at Berlin.** The German Chancellor had presided at the Congress, and his powerful personality had much to do with the results. He had brought Germany squarely down on the side of Austria and Great Britain. Once again, as in the Franco-German crisis of 1875, the possibility of any permanent friendship between Germany and Russia was shown to be very slender indeed. In 1875 Russia had intervened to stop Bismarck, and now Bismarck intervened decisively to stop Russia. Bismarck's reasons for this decision are reasonably clear. Firstly, if he supported Russia he would have the outright opposition of both Austria and Great Britain whose governments both feared and hated Russia. It might even be sufficient to bring England out of her "splendid isolation" into alliance with France. Secondly, if he supported Russia, there was a possibility that Germany would be involved in all the intrigues of the Slav movements supported by Russia in the Balkan Peninsula. Such a situation could only lead to trouble with both Britain and Austria, with France waiting to spring on the western frontier.

Thirdly, if he could form an alliance with Austria, he hoped to be able to control Austrian policy and thus have the great Danube River open to German commerce. Lastly, he hoped to increase German influence over Turkey by being one of the "bolstering" powers.

**The Dual Alliance, 1879.** Bismarck's policy at Berlin led naturally to the Dual Alliance of Germany and Austria. He saw clearly that his policy had risked the possibility of an alliance between Russia and France, and he therefore hastened his negotiations with Austria. He did not have everything his own way however, for Austria refused to promise armed assistance to Germany in the case of a war between Germany and France alone. Austria's only obligation if that occurred was to remain neutral. However, if Russia and France combined for an attack on Germany (or any other power in alliance with Russia), then Austria would support Germany. This obligation on Austria also applied to an attack by Russia alone on Germany. The alliance, which was renewed from time to time right up to 1914, was the central feature of Bismarck's system of international agreements. It will, of course, be noted that Austria was to assist Germany only if the latter were attacked, but Bismarck had no doubt that he could at any critical moment show Germany to be the aggrieved party.

**The Triple Alliance.** In 1882 Bismarck succeeded in bringing Italy into the Dual Alliance and thus converting it into the Triple Alliance which lasted till 1914. This success was brought about in a typically Bismarckian manner, and was closely related to the scramble for overseas colonies which was taking place at this time. In 1881 the French occupied Tunis in North Africa. This was the result in part of Bismarck's encouragement, for he had indicated secretly to the French government that Germany would certainly not oppose such a move. Moreover, Bismarck hoped by this means to divert French attention from the lost provinces of Alsace-Lorraine. However, Tunis had for some years contained a considerable number of Italian settlers, and the Italian government also had its plans for taking over the territory. This aim of the Italians was well known to Bismarck. The French action made the rather isolated Italians all the more ready to join the Dual Alliance of Germany and Austria. By the articles of the Triple Alliance treaty the three powers Austria, Germany and Italy were pledged to support one another if any one of them was attacked by two other powers, but Italy could not be required to fight against Britain in any circumstances. (This latter article partly explains why Italy did not join Austria and Germany in the Great War of 1914–1918.)

By the Triple Alliance Bismarck had achieved a diplomatic union of Great Powers extending across Europe from the Baltic Sea to the Mediterranean and Adriatic. The German "sphere of influence" and security had been greatly extended. Important as this diplomatic achievement was, the Chancellor was still determined to do everything he could to prevent the very thing which the treaty was aimed against, namely, the alliance of France and Russia. Even Bismarck realised that prevention was better than war.

**The Dreikaiserbund Treaty, 1881.** In the year 1881 a new Czar, Alexander III, came to the throne of Russia after the assassination of Alexander II, whose reign had begun with a series of important reforms. The fate of his father strengthened the already reactionary ideas held by the new Czar, and made him willing to listen to Bismarck's suggestions for the renewal of the Old Dreikaiserbund understanding of 1872 which had given assurance of mutual help against revolution. Bismarck also offered the neutrality of Germany if Russia was involved in war with a fourth party, which in those years might easily have been Great Britain. Russia in her turn gave a similar assurance to Austria and Germany, which meant that in case of a war between the Triple Alliance and France, Russia would not support the French. Bismarck made an important concession to Russia, for he agreed that the Big Bulgaria could be created again whenever Russia chose. In return for this assurance, Russia agreed that Austria could take over complete control of Bosnia and Herzegovina whenever she decided.

The Dreikaiserbund Treaty was in force till 1887, but was not renewed mainly owing to further complications in the Balkan Peninsula involving both Austria and Russia. As we shall see, Bismarck had a way of getting round even that difficulty.

**The Balkan Peninsula, 1885–1887.** Events in the Balkan Peninsula now took a turn most unexpected to the statesmen of Europe. In 1885 a revolt against Turkish rule in Eastern Rumelia led to the union of that territory with Bulgaria—the very thing which the Congress of Berlin seven years before had forced the Russians and Bulgarians to abandon. Now, however, the Bulgarian government decided upon real independence, and the Russian advisers who had controlled Bulgarian policy for some years were expelled from the country. This turn of events naturally delighted Britain, Germany and Austria, who now, of course, were all in favour of the Big

Bulgaria. When a German, Ferdinand of Saxe-Coburg, was elected Prince of Bulgaria in 1887, Russia refused to recognise his election.

Once again, Russia was in direct conflict with Germany and Austria. At the same time General Boulanger, at the height of his popularity in France, was calling for an alliance of France and Russia against Germany. And at this point also the Russians refused to renew the Dreikaiserbund Treaty of 1881. Bismarck had once again to face the old nightmare of a Franco-Russian alliance.

**The Secret Reinsurance Treaty, 1887.** Bismarck dealt with the new situation by an agreement which was in a number of ways against the interests of his partner, Austria. For this reason, among others, the negotiations which he now undertook with the Czar's government were secret. The Russians were in a strong bargaining position, and Bismarck had to recognise this. He agreed that Russia should exercise the main influence in the affairs of the Balkan Peninsula and, more important, he promised German neutrality in case of Russia being involved in war with a third Great Power, and Russia made a similar promise. The clause, however, was not to apply if Germany attacked France or Russia attacked Austria-Hungary.

Bismarck had achieved his aims of controlling the diplomacy of Europe in the interests of Germany, and had even succeeded in establishing friendly relations with Russia at those critical moments when everything seemed to be impelling the great Eastern Power towards an understanding with France. But the very secrecy of the Reinsurance Treaty of 1887 shows how increasingly difficult it was becoming to reconcile Germany's obligations to the Triple Alliance with friendship towards Russia.

**Accession of William II and the Dismissal of Bismarck.** In 1888 the Emperor William I died and was succeeded by his son Frederick, who was, however, already suffering from cancer and died after being Emperor for only three months. He was succeeded by his son William II (1888–1918). Strong differences of opinion developed between the new Emperor and Bismarck during the next two years. In the first place, William II wished to adopt a fresh policy towards the Socialists. He was sincerely interested in the condition of the German workers, who were some of the poorest-paid in Europe. William wanted to do away with Bismarck's anti-socialist laws, but Bismarck, more arrogant and self-willed than ever in old age, was determined to maintain them. Another cause of difference between them arose over foreign policy, the Kaiser wishing to secure German-Austrian control in the Balkans even if it led to hostility from Russia.

Lastly, the new Kaiser wanted a policy of colonial expansion far greater than anything so far, to be supported by the construction of a great German navy.

On all these matters Bismarck and the Kaiser were completely at loggerheads, and in 1890 Bismarck resigned, and a new—and dangerous—era began in the history of Germany and of Europe.

Fig. 25.—"Farewell."
Prince Bismarck leaving the Imperial Palace after his final interview with the Kaiser.
(*See page* 201.)

# chapter twelve

# FRANCE, 1870–1914

**Introductory.** The years 1870–1914 are years of instability and difficulty for the new French State. Difficulties which arise in the first years of the Republic are the legacy of the Franco-Prussian War and the Paris Commune. The Boulangist attempt to overthrow the constitution of 1875, the Panama scandal, the Dreyfus affair, are all symptoms of a political malaise which arose from the violent clash of such opposed interests as Church and State, imperialists and anti-imperialists, of capital and labour, of the Royalist remnants of 1870 and the Republicans. Towards the end of the period the clash between capital and labour becomes increasingly severe. Socialists, communists, syndicalists—all vie for the control of the rapidly-developing labour movement in France. The twentieth century opens with the inclusion of Socialists (of the milder brand) in the government. At the same time the economic development of France makes great strides, and it is not surprising that many groups of French industrialists look forward to the day when Alsace-Lorraine would once again be incorporated in France. The idea of "revanche" for 1870 is allied closely to the interests of these groups and provides a good deal of the basis for French national feeling in this period.

The surrender to the Germans of the last fully organised French army at Metz in October, 1870, was not the end of the Franco-Prussian War. Paris was put under siege by the enemy, but the great Republican leader Léon Gambetta escaped from the city in a balloon in order to organise further resistance from the French provinces. His enthusiasm and determination were strong enough to raise new volunteer forces, but there was such defeatism in France as a result of the humiliating blows already dealt by the Germans that he was unable to rally the whole nation. The new forces which Gambetta did manage to raise found the Prussians too much for them. Then, in January, 1871, the French army which had been sent to the relief of the great frontier fortress of Belfort which was being besieged by the Germans, was defeated, and an armistice followed. Elections were now held in France for a new Assembly, which met in Bordeaux.

FIG. 26.—THE LAST STAND OF THE COMMUNE. (*See page* 207.)

This Assembly set up a provisional government in February, 1871, under Adolphe Thiers.

The Bordeaux Assembly and Government were overwhelmingly monarchist. The Republicans were outnumbered by about two to one. The Bordeaux Assembly represented above all the interests of the wealthier classes of France and the peasantry who had been such strong supporters of Napoleon III. Some of them even hoped for the restoration of the Bonapartes in the person of the Prince Imperial, son of Napoleon III. However, before these matters could be discussed in any detail, the peace negotiations with Bismarck had to be concluded, and in May, 1871, the German peace terms were accepted. In the meantime the Bordeaux Assembly had moved to Versailles, the grandiose home of the French royal family and government before the Revolution of 1789. Here, of course, the Royalist deputies felt more at home than they would have been in the midst of the turbulent Republicans of Paris.

**The Paris Commune.** In March, 1871, there took place one of the most violent and tragic episodes in recent history—an event which has left a deep mark on the political life of France. This was the revolt of Paris against the Assembly at Versailles. In the first place, Paris had a strong revolutionary and republican tradition and was naturally hostile to the monarchist Assembly at Versailles. The very fact that the Assembly had moved from Bordeaux to the old centre of royal power was sufficient to arouse the suspicions of the Parisians that a royalist restoration was intended. Thiers himself favoured a constitutional monarchy, but did not consider monarchy possible in 1871. Another humiliation for the city was the triumphal parade of the German forces in March, 1871. This was a humiliation associated in the minds of the people of Paris with the Versailles Assembly which had accepted this German demand. The Assembly could have done nothing to resist the German demand, but this was never considered by the people of Paris, who associated the whole defeat of France with the politicians in control at Versailles. The working class of Paris especially felt that the "capitalists" of Versailles were the very people who had brought France down to corruption and defeat under Napoleon III. The old socialist revolutionaries of 1848 who had been in exile, hiding or in prison, appeared once again on the scene and took an active, leading part in the revolt.

The further actions of the Versailles government added to the fury of Paris. During the German siege of the city the people had suffered terribly—they had been reduced to eating rats from the Paris sewers. Factories and workshops closed down and unemployment was widespread. In these circumstances, the government had suspended the payment of all debts in order to give some relief to the people. But in March, 1871, the Versailles government ordered the payment of all back rent and all commercial debts with full interest. It followed up this order by a demand for the disarmament of the Paris National Guard and the stopping of its wartime pay. A small force was sent to Paris to remove the guns from the heights of Montmartre, but resistance to this demand was led by a section of the Paris National Guard, and the negotiators sent by the Versailles government were murdered. Shortly after this, Paris set up its own elected government or Commune (local council) of Paris. The struggle with the Versailles government had begun.

**Character of the Commune.** The ninety-two members of the Commune of Paris were by no means all Socialists or Communists, and there is no necessary connection between the terms "communist" and "commune". The majority were anti-Versailles republicans who wished for a republic which would give justice and security to the working people and to the small capitalist or "little man" in business. The Commune of Paris was in fact the union of working and middle class which we saw in the early part of the revolution of 1848. In order to secure adequate protection for their own interests they demanded for Paris the right to complete local self-government with scarcely any control by the central government. They were supported in this demand by several other big cities of France, of which the most important were Lyons and Marseilles where communes were also set up at this time. During its control of the city, the Commune began a certain amount of economic organisation of a socialist type—for example, it established work schemes rather similar to the National Workshops of 1848, and it took measures to control the price of foodstuffs to prevent profiteering. But its main energies were absorbed in the ferocious struggle against the army of Versailles.

**The Suppression of the Commune.** After the resistance at Montmartre Thiers gave Marshal MacMahon the task of subduing the capital. This task took two months, from the middle of March to the middle of May, 1871, to accomplish. During this period the German occupation forces stood aside while Frenchman fought against Frenchman. The only direct interference by the Germans was permission given to Thiers by Bismarck to increase the forces under MacMahon's command for the assault on Paris. For six weeks

MacMahon conducted an artillery bombardment against the positions held by the Commune, and at the beginning of May he managed to force an entry into the western suburbs of the city. Then another week of ferocious street and barricade fighting followed, until the forces of the Commune were driven back to their last stand behind the gravestones of the cemetery of Père Lachaise. The most appalling reprisals followed. Over 20,000 had already been killed either in the fighting or by the firing squad, and now 7,000 were transported to the French penal settlements overseas. Altogether, taking into account the great number of communards who fled from France, the population of Paris is considered by some authorities to have fallen by at least 100,000. Large parts of the most beautiful city in Europe were smoking ruins, for MacMahon had used incendiary shells in his bombardments. The communards themselves had also destroyed a number of buildings and monuments which were offensive to their political ideas.

**Effects of the Commune.** Besides the material damage, there were other effects of the Commune which were not so easily repaired.

IG. 27.—THE IRON HEEL: German Soldiers drawing up a "Receipt" for Property looted from a Paris Café.

In the first place, a section of the French working class was turned permanently "against the government"—it became a permanent enemy of the republic through the harshness of the reprisals undertaken by Thiers. The divisions between the wealthier and poorer classes of France became almost unbridgeable, and from this division arose the political opposition of the parties of the Right and the extreme Left, the latter following in the main the militant ideas of Marx. Another effect of the Commune was to make Bismarck's task of isolating France internationally much easier, for the horror felt by the governments and upper classes of Europe at the revolt played conveniently into his hands. The suppression of the Commune strengthened the position of Thiers in the esteem of the wealthier classes, who were now willing to subscribe freely to the special loans which he raised in order to pay off the immense indemnity which Bismarck had demanded. Within three years the indemnity had been fully paid and the Prussian Army removed from French soil. Bismarck had hoped to keep France occupied by German troops for at least ten years, and he was disconcerted by this achievement of Thiers' government, and especially by the speedy rebuilding of the French Army. He even contemplated the possibility of another war against France, but, as we have seen, was restrained by the Czar of Russia and Queen Victoria (see page 194).

**The Republic Established.** The question now to be settled was the form of government for France. Thiers, who was President from 1871 to 1873, wanted a form of government on British lines, but even by 1873 the parties in the Assembly were still unable to reach agreement. However, in 1873 the Royalists succeeded in voting Marshal MacMahon as President in place of Thiers. The new President was an ardent Royalist, and it seemed likely that a monarchist restoration would take place. At this time there were three claimants to the French throne—the Prince Imperial, aged seventeen, son of Napoleon III; the Comte de Paris (grandson of Louis Philippe); and the Comte de Chambord, representing the former Bourbon line of Charles X. The chances of the Prince Imperial were never very bright and the Royalists bent all their efforts to achieving some agreement between the Orleanist Comte de Paris and the Bourbon Comte de Chambord. After much intrigue and scheming in Royalist circles an agreed plan was arrived at by which the Comte de Chambord was to be elected and then he was to adopt the much younger Comte de Paris as his heir. But at this critical point for the Royalist cause, the narrowness and bigotry of the

Bourbon family ruined the agreement, for the Comte de Chambord refused to accept the tricolour flag as the emblem of the State in place of the white flag of the Bourbons. This appears, of course, a very childish dispute over which to wreck an important issue, but it was not quite so childish as it appears. Some very important principles were involved. In effect, the Comte de Chambord was saying that he would not recognise the control of the Assembly over him—he would rule as an absolute monarch—or something very near to it. He would not compromise with the Revolution of 1789. On the other hand, the Comte de Paris would have accepted the position of a constitutional monarch controlled by the Assembly on lines similar to those of England.

**The Defeat of MacMahon.** This undignified dispute between the Royalists was of great assistance to the Republican cause. All Republicans now united under the leadership of Gambetta to organise an anti-Royalist campaign throughout the country. In the highly critical debate in the Assembly in June, 1875, a decision in favour of a Republic was reached by a majority of one vote. This was not regarded by the Royalists as a decisive blow to their cause, and their hopes were now pinned on the President, MacMahon. He was determined to do everything he could to ensure the reversal of the Assembly's decision. For this purpose he used his powers of dissolving the Chamber of Deputies and ordering new elections in 1876 when the country returned a Republican majority. In the new elections he demanded for the President powers which would even have given him the right to appoint governments without reference to the Chamber of Deputies. Once again, however, the electors returned a Republican majority, and by 1879 there was also a Republican majority in the Senate. MacMahon, having been reduced to the position of a powerless figurehead, resigned. The Republic had been established.

**The Constitution of 1875.** The Constitution which had been voted by a majority of one in 1875 lasted, with minor alterations, until the German invasion of France in 1940. On reaching the age of twenty, all men were entitled to a vote in general elections for the Chamber of Deputies, the elections being held every four years. The Senate, or Upper House, was elected for nine years by a special electoral college in each Department of France. The Chamber of Deputies and the Senate together then elected the President for seven years. The ministers of the government were to be directly responsible to the Chamber of Deputies and the Senate. It did not follow automatically under the Constitution that new elections were held when the government was defeated, as was the practice in England. France has always had a considerable number of political parties, and this situation can lead to constant changes of government as a result of a change in policy or tactics of only one of the parties in the Chamber of Deputies. Thus, in the first forty years after 1875 there were fifty changes of government.

**The Ministries of Jules Ferry.** During the years 1880–1885 very important social developments took place in France—mainly due to the efforts of Jules Ferry who was Prime Minister in 1880–1881 and again in 1883–1885. Ferry was determined to adopt a constructive policy and to heal the wounds left by the régime of Napoleon III, the Franco-Prussian War and the Paris Commune. The exiled communards were allowed to return, and the workers' trade unions were made legal. Newspapers were entirely freed from censorship, and there was a new outburst of journalistic and literary life in France. Ferry also had very strong convictions about the need for education, especially elementary education, which had long been neglected in France. With the right to vote at the age of twenty, every Frenchman needed some elementary education, and Ferry established a system of primary schools for all children between six and thirteen. These reforms also raised the delicate question of the position of the Catholic Church in the State. Ferry's ideas were strongly anti-clerical and he wished by every possible means to reduce the influence of the Church in education. The measures which he took were drastic. The Jesuits and other Catholic teaching orders were banned and their members forbidden to teach in State schools. New State secondary schools or "lycées" were also set up and were intended to improve upon the work of Catholic schools, especially in their greater emphasis on science as a subject of the curriculum. In the universities the teaching of science was greatly increased, while the Catholic colleges were no longer given full University status, which allowed the holding of examinations and the granting of degrees. These measures, of course, did not increase the loyalty of Catholics to the Republic, and there was a strong tendency in these years for many Catholics to support those movements which wished to overthrow the Third Republic.

**Colonial Policy.** Jules Ferry was also a strong promoter of colonisation. Of course, many Frenchmen wished to recover Alsace-Lorraine, which had been lost to Germany in 1871, but Ferry realised the hopelessness of attempting this in the isolated position to which Bismarck's policy was reducing France. To him the best alternative appeared to be overseas expansion which would not bring France into conflict with Germany or her allies. He saw the best opportunities in Africa and the Far East. France took over Tunis in 1881 (as we have seen, directly encouraged by Bismarck), while the valuable island of Madagascar was brought under French control in 1883. At the same time the government carried forward Napoleon III's policy in Indo-China by sending French forces there and bringing large parts of the country under French control.

Naturally, traders and financiers eagerly supported Ferry's policy, for it meant more markets, and more valuable raw materials for France. Also it satisfied national pride by keeping France well in the colonial race with other great powers, and compensated her for the loss of French power in Egypt, incurred when Dual Control ended there, and Britain took over completely in 1881. However, there was considerable opposition to Ferry's policy, especially from the extreme Left in the Chamber of Deputies under the Socialist leadership of Georges Clemenceau. Ferry's policy was denounced as one of robbery and exploitation of the natives and a waste of the taxpayers' money. Ferry's position as Prime Minister depended on success in the colonial field, and when French forces suffered a reverse in a Far Eastern expedition in 1885 he was defeated in the Chamber of Deputies and resigned.

**General Boulanger.** The Third Republic was rocked to its foundations between 1875 and 1914 by a series of crises which aroused political passions to fever heat. One of the most serious of these crises arose from the personal ambitions of the Minister of War, General Boulanger, who was undoubtedly aiming at a dictatorship. Certain serious events had shaken public confidence in leading statesmen of the Republic, and this played right into his hands. For example, Daniel Wilson, the son-in-law of the President of the Republic, was receiving bribes from individuals wishing to be nominated for the Legion of Honour. Corruption of this kind is, of course, the very thing on which a would-be dictator can thrive, and Boulanger used it in his attacks on the constitution, which he wished to see revised in such a way as to give the President effective control of the State. Like Louis Bonaparte in 1848, Boulanger was a handsome, dashing, attractive individual who appeared genuinely honourable and virtuous compared with the corrupt politicians whom the current scandals had incriminated. Moreover, he wanted a glorious foreign policy and the recovery of Alsace-Lorraine. Ferry's defeat over the colonial question aided Boulanger's arguments. He even went so far as to suggest something which greatly alarmed Bismarck, namely, an alliance between France and Russia. Naturally, he had many allies among those discontented with the state of things. Many Catholics supported him, as also did those sections of the working class opposed to the colonial policy of Ferry, those industrialists or capitalists who wished to regain the iron and coal of Alsace-Lorraine, and many army leaders.

In 1888 Boulanger was elected to the Chamber of Deputies by six constituencies. It seemed that he was about to gain power by a "coup d'état" on Napoleonic lines. But at this point the extreme Left and the Republicans, realising that they would be the first victims of such a "coup" and that the whole constitution was in danger, united their forces, attacked Boulanger in debates in the Chamber of Deputies and finally persuaded the government to demand his trial on a charge of treason. At this point Boulanger's nerve gave way before the uncertain prospect, and he fled to Belgium, where he committed suicide in 1891.

**The Panama Scandal.** No sooner was Boulanger out of the way than another storm struck the Republic. This arose from the somewhat colourful career of the distinguished French diplomatist who had inspired the building of the Suez Canal, Ferdinand de Lesseps. In his later life he worked out a scheme for the Panama Canal and floated a company to raise the required capital. The money was raised and the work was undertaken, but owing to a serious underestimation of the natural difficulties of the project, the whole thing failed. An official investigation was held into the finances of the company and it was found that a large proportion of the money subscribed by the shareholders had been spent in bribing leading politicians to support the scheme in the Chamber of Deputies. Politicians of nearly all parties were involved. Public confidence in leading statesmen was seriously shaken. There was also another serious result of the Panama Scandal, for it led to an outburst of anti-Jewish or anti-semitic feeling when it was found that certain Jewish financiers had organised the bribery. Jewish financiers were not the only people involved, but anti-semitism had already become the stock-in-trade of some movements in France which wished to overthrow the Republic.

**The Case of Captain Dreyfus.** The anti-semitic motive figured strongly in another event which caused tremendous public controversy from 1894 to 1906. This affair involved a certain Jewish

officer from Alsace called Dreyfus, employed in the French War
Office. In 1894 he was accused of having sold military secrets to a
foreign power—by which was meant Germany. He was convicted
and sent to the notorious penal settlement of Devil's Island. However, this was not the end of the matter, for the conduct of the case
had aroused the suspicions of many intelligent people, among whom
the most influential were the leader of the extreme Left, Clemenceau,
and the famous novelist, Emile Zola. Generally speaking, the Left-
wing parties, Radicals, Republicans, and Socialists, supported Dreyfus, while the Right-wing parties, the Catholic Church and the army
leaders, were against him. At last, in 1896, it was admitted by the
culprit concerned that the document on which the condemnation of
Dreyfus had been based was a forgery, and soon after this admission the actual forger, a certain Colonel Henry, committed suicide.
It was now clear that Dreyfus had been victimised to cover up the
treason of other people in the French army, and they had worked
out the plot just at the time when an official inquiry into the
leakage of army secrets to Germany was about to be made. Yet
even after these disclosures it was not till 1899 that Dreyfus was
pardoned and not till 1906 that he was given back his commission.

Fig. 28.—Breaking Dreyfus' Sword in the Court of L'Ecole Militaire,
January 5th, 1895.

**Effects of the Dreyfus Case.** The whole affair had been most dis-creditable to the army, the government and to the public institutions of the Republic. It was becoming increasingly difficult for French-men to have any faith in the real integrity and honour of those to whom their fate was entrusted. No wonder that extremist move-ments of all kinds made great headway in these years. There was even a plot in 1899 by a society known as the League of Patriots to murder the President. The Dreyfus affair had other important results. The Left-wing parties, especially the Socialists, had gained considerably by coming down on the side of Dreyfus, whereas the Catholic Church and the Right-wing parties had lost heavily. The political struggle in France became more violent, and the part played by the Catholic Church enabled its opponents further to reduce its privileges.

**Developments of the Years 1899–1914.** The Dreyfus affair had helped the Socialist movement in France, and in the years 1899 to 1905 a number of moderate (or non-Marxist) Socialists were in-cluded in the government. The Socialist leader, Jean Jaurès, gave the support of his party to the measures taken against the Catholic Church. All the religious orders in France were now made to submit their rules to the government for approval, and a number were entirely suppressed. This was followed by a law preventing the Catholic Orders from teaching in France, and all teachers came under state supervision. In 1905, the Separation Law—that is, the law separating Church and State—withdrew all financial help formerly given by the State to the Church, and special committees known as "Associations Cultuelles" were set up to manage the property of the Church.

**The Growth of the "Left" in France, 1900–1914.** The years 1900–1914 witnessed a great increase of the "Left" in French politics. The term "Left" or "Left-wing" as applied to French politics in these years includes a number of movements which demanded Socialism of one kind or another but were much divided on the methods of bringing it about. The syndicalists wanted the workers to control industry under a regional system and they wished to remove political control from industry altogether. The moderate Socialists such as Millerand, who was a member of the government in 1899–1902, succeeded in securing the reduction of the working day to 9½ hours, and in 1901 special boards were set up to secure arbitration between capitalists and workers. However, Millerand did not satisfy the more extreme Socialists who, thinking on typically

Marxist lines, wanted a socialist revolution and the expropriation of all capitalists. Millerand was expelled from the Revolutionary Socialist Party in 1902 because he was too moderate. There was a great outbreak of strikes and social disturbances in these years. A great strike of railway workers in 1910 was under syndicalist leadership and this strike was suppressed by the Prime Minister Briand, who was himself a moderate Socialist. The Radicals also played an important part in these years, and a Radical government in 1911 imposed heavy taxation on big financial companies in order to finance various social services—a move rather similar to Lloyd George's so-called People's Budget of 1909 in Britain.

These social conflicts were partly the result of the growing prosperity of the wealthier classes in France. The years 1900–1914 saw a tremendous development of all the economic resources of the country. The government gave direct financial assistance to various industries, especially to the important silk industry. Iron production between 1870 and 1904 increased six times and coal output almost as much. The French farmer was also given financial help to improve methods of farming. All these developments were greatly aided by improvements in transport. Many thousands of miles of roads, railways and canals were added to France's transport system between 1870 and 1914 and all the important French harbours were improved. Industrial prosperity produced such a surplus of wealth that not only did radical and socialist attacks on the privileges of wealth increase, but France became one of the principal sources of loans to other countries. We shall see, for example, the great financial aid given to Czarist Russia in these years.

# chapter thirteen

# THE EASTERN QUESTION, 1815–1878

**Introductory.** In the nineteenth century the Eastern Question was generally understood to refer to the problems arising from the affairs of the Balkan Peninsula—problems which especially involved Turkey and the Great Powers.

The Turks were an Asiatic Moslem people who had entered Europe in 1356 and conquered Constantinople, the capital of the Eastern Roman Empire, in 1453. For another two centuries they were a menace to Europe, for they were essentially an aggressive and expansionist power. In the course of their expansion they conquered the peoples of the Balkan Peninsula—the Serbs, Rumanians, Greeks and Bulgarians—and on several occasions threatened the Hapsburg dominions and the heart of Europe, the last occasion being in 1683 when they unsuccessfully laid siege to Vienna. This was a serious check to their power on land. They also suffered serious defeats at sea, which greatly reduced their naval power in the Mediterranean, especially after the destruction of their fleet by the Austrians at the battle of Lepanto, 1571. These reverses had the effect of preventing further direct threats to Europe and causing the Sultan to consolidate his hold on the Balkan peoples.

**Decline of Turkey as a Great Power.** In the eighteenth and nineteenth centuries the Turks were a declining power. Their government became more and more corrupt and inefficient, with the result that the peoples under their control began to struggle for independence. The first to rebel in the nineteenth century were the Serbs, under their peasant leader Kara George. In 1804 they succeeded in driving the Turks out of their country, but were reconquered in 1813. In 1815 they rose again under another leader, Milosch Obrenovitch, who gained the title of "Prince of the Serbians" from the Sultan.

The Serbian revolt had the direct encouragement of the Czar Alexander I, for it was already an aim of Russian policy to hasten the break-up of the Turkish Empire, to take what spoils were going, and to replace Turkish control of the Balkans by Russian influence. Already, by the Treaty of Bucharest in 1812, the Czar had gained

Bessarabia from Turkey and thus brought the boundaries of Russia down to the River Pruth.

The Serbian revolt was the beginning of trouble for the Sultan in the nineteenth century, for the Serbian example soon spread and the next problem the Sultan had on his hands was the revolt of the Greeks.

**The Greek War of Independence.** The Greeks were by no means the worst treated of the Sultan's subject peoples. They were, for example, free from the burden of military service so long as they paid their annual taxes for the privilege of being exempt. There was very little persecution of the Christians, who could gain high office in the State. The peasants were owners of their land, and in this respect were in a far better position than the serf populations of Austria and Russia.

The real cause of Greek discontent was not derived so much from material grievances as from the fact that the Turks looked down on them as inferiors and infidels. This attitude of the Moslem Turks made it impossible to achieve any real compromise between the two peoples and the two religions. The Turks remained a conquering people, standing apart from the Greeks and never attempting to absorb them into their own civilisation. The Patriarch of the Greek Orthodox Church at Constantinople was made answerable for the good behaviour of the Christians of the Empire, but otherwise they were free to carry on their own forms of religion, education and social life. Within the same empire two different civilisations faced each other.

**The Revival of Greek Culture.** Many Greeks of the educated classes had never accepted the Turkish rule. Those who fled from the Turkish conquests to Europe attempted to keep alive the idea of Greek freedom, and towards the end of the eighteenth century there began a revival in Europe of interest in the Greeks of ancient times. The glories of ancient Greece were now used to support the demand for the freedom of the modern Greeks. This movement was given further strength by the outbreak of the French Revolution of 1789, which stimulated the thought and activities of the Greek patriots. The famous Greek revolutionary poet, Rhigas, was executed by the Turks in 1794 and immediately became a national hero. Attempts were made to spread the knowledge of the ancient Greek classics as widely as possible among the people, as a means of rousing their national pride. For this purpose important translations were made into the modern tongue.

This revival of interest in the great history of ancient Greece led on to other important developments. In 1814 a secret society known as the Hetairia Philike or Association of Friends was set up, with the purpose of spreading this interest in Greek culture and of rousing the national consciousness and preparing it for action against the Turks. The agents of the society became increasingly active in every part of Greece and by 1821 it had over 20,000 members.

**Conditions in the Turkish Empire in 1821.** At this time the Sultan was involved in great difficulties with some of his important Moslem subjects. On the Adriatic coast there was the Sultan of Janina, Ali Pasha, who, although nominally subject to the Sultan, was gradually gaining control over the coastal towns of Albania and carving out an almost independent state. This colourful ruffian and adventurer had in his earlier days adopted the tricolour flag of the French Revolution, had been encouraged by Napoleon in his activities against the Sultan and had eventually joined the allied side against Napoleon when he saw that the Emperor was on the downward path. Altogether, the Pasha of Janina was an embarrassment and nuisance to the Sultan.

In Egypt another adventurer, Mehemet Ali, was building up a powerful fleet, conquering the Sudan and Arabia with the help of his warlike son, Ibrahim, and reorganising and strengthening his army with the aid of French military advisers. Like the Sultan of Janina, he was nominally the vassal of the Sultan and ruled Egypt for his master, but in reality he was powerful enough to govern on his own terms.

These embarrassments of the Sultan, from Ali Pasha of Janina, from Mehemet Ali, from the Serbians and from the pressure of Russian aims as witnessed in the gaining of Bessarabia by Alexander I, seemed to favour an attempt by the Greeks to throw off Turkish rule. Another factor which seemed very much in their favour was the preference given by the Czar Alexander to Greek advisers. His foreign minister was Capodistrias, a Greek who had been present at the Congress of Vienna, while another Greek, Prince Hypsilanti, was the Czar's aide-de-camp and leader of the secret society the Hetairia Philike.

**Prince Hypsilanti and the Moldavian Revolt.** In March, 1821, Prince Hypsilanti moved across the River Pruth into Moldavia with a band of Greek officers who had been in the service of the Czar. He called upon the Moldavians to revolt against the Turks. The expedition was badly organised, Hypsilanti disgraced his cause by allowing the massacre of Moslems, and he had not even gained the support of the Hetairia Philike itself. He had led the Moldavians and the Greeks to believe that he had the support of Alexander, whereas in fact the latter was so much under the influence of Metternich that he quickly repudiated the aims of Hypsilanti. Another difficulty arose from the Moldavians themselves, who were not Greeks and distrusted Hypsilanti, and conflict soon broke out between the Prince's Greek followers and the Moldavian peasants. After a last desperate stand at Skaleni in June, 1821, the rebels were completely defeated by the Turks. Hypsilanti himself fled into Austria, where he was imprisoned by Metternich for seven years.

**The Revolt in the Morea.** No sooner had Hypsilanti's movement ended in tragic failure than insurrection broke out in the southern part of Greece known as the Morea. Here the agents of the Hetairia Philike had been extremely active and the revolt was more generally spread over the population than in the case of Moldavia. It was marred from the beginning by the most shocking ferocity, possibly to be expected from a people among whom brigandage had become almost a national pastime, but horrifying for all that. The Greeks killed every Moslem they could lay their hands on, and within six weeks there were scarcely any of the Moslem population of 25,000 still alive. This led at once to equally horrifying reprisals by the Turks, who murdered the Greeks in Thessaly and Macedonia to the north and in the Aegean Islands. The most horrible of these Aegean massacres was on the island of Chios, where the Turks killed 27,000 Greeks—men, women and children. One horror thus led to another, and on Easter Day, 1822, the Patriarch of the Greek Orthodox Church at Constantinople was hanged outside his cathedral and after a few days his body was taken down and thrown into the Bosphorus. The body of the Patriarch was picked up by a passing Greek vessel and taken to the port of Odessa, where it was given a martyr's burial.

The murder of the Patriarch horrified Europe and alarmed the ministers of the Great Powers, for it immediately produced serious political complications which made it very difficult for the Great Powers to stand aside from the conflict. The Czar Alexander concentrated 100,000 troops on the frontier with Moldavia, and it seemed likely that he would march against the Turks. Although Metternich and the British government persuaded Alexander to hold back, it was obviously becoming more and more difficult to confine the conflict to the Greeks and Turks alone. The policy of non-intervention was strongly denounced by many citizens of the European powers, and French and English officers now went out to assist the Greeks, while money and arms were supplied by voluntary subscriptions from sympathisers in Europe. The great English poet, Lord Byron, one of the most famous of these volunteers in the Greek cause, died of fever while fighting in the defence of the town of Missolonghi against the Turks.

**The Sultan calls in the Aid of Mehemet Ali.** Only by command of the sea could the Turks get sufficient forces into the Morea to suppress the revolt. But the Greeks, being a trading people, had a considerable fleet at their command. Their trading brigs, armed with thirty or forty guns apiece, were quite strong enough to defeat the Turks at sea and keep control of the Aegean islands. To overcome this difficulty, the Sultan now called on his Egyptian vassal, Mehemet Ali, for aid. On being promised the control of the Morea and the island of Crete for his services, Mehemet Ali sent his son, Ibrahim Pasha, with an army and fleet to the aid of the Turks. Ibrahim captured Crete and successfully landed his forces in the Morea, where he began to wipe out the Greek population.

This new, horrifying peak in the struggle was decisive in bringing intervention from the Great Powers. The new Czar Nicholas (1825–1855) was determined to assert the rights of Russia as the protector of the Christian population of the Turkish Empire, and the massacres being perpetrated by Ibrahim's troops seemed to justify his demand for intervention. Public opinion in Great Britain was also turning sharply in favour of aid to the Greeks, and the Foreign Secretary, George Canning, partly responding to this demand, and partly fearing that Russia would act alone, decided to reach an agreement with Russia. In 1826, English representatives went to St. Petersburg and the result was a proposal to the Sultan that Greece should be independent except for the payment of a yearly tribute to the Turks. However, the Sultan rejected these demands, and England, France and Russia renewed their demands in the Treaty of London, 1827. As the Sultan remained obdurate, a joint naval force consisting of English, French and Russian vessels was now ordered to blockade the Greek coast in order to prevent Ibrahim Pasha from gaining further supplies from Egypt. In the course of these operations the combined fleet under the command of Admiral Codrington came face to face with the Egyptian and Turkish fleets in Navarino Bay. Difficulties arose from the refusal of some of the Turkish vessels to move their anchorage, shots were

FIG. 29.—THE BATTLE OF NAVARINO, OCTOBER 27, 1827.

fired (who fired first is not certain), and soon a full-scale naval battle was in progress. The Turkish and Egyptian fleets were sunk.

The battle of Navarino was a decisive engagement in the political as well as the naval sense, for Ibrahim Pasha, unable to keep open his lines of communication with Egypt, was forced to withdraw his troops from the Morea. The Russians now invaded Moldavia and Wallachia and drove on against the Turks, whom they decisively defeated and forced to sign the Treaty of Adrianople, 1829. By this treaty the Turks recognised Greek independence, but tribute was still to be paid to them.

The Treaty of Adrianople was, naturally, unsatisfactory to the Greeks. It was also unsatisfactory to the other Great Powers, who considered that if any trouble arose over the payment of tribute to the Turks, then Russia would have an excuse for further intervention. Indeed, Britain and France suspected that this was the precise motive of Nicholas I in agreeing to the tribute clause of the Treaty. In these circumstances, the Great Powers, excluding Russia, now demanded the complete independence of Greece, and in 1832 the Sultan accepted these terms. Greece became an independent monarchy under a ruler acceptable to the Great Powers, Prince Otto of Bavaria.

**The Problem of Mehemet Ali.** No sooner had the Greek War of Independence been successfully concluded than the Great Powers were faced with the problems arising from the claims and pretensions of the ruler of Egypt, Mehemet Ali. As we have seen, he was promised the Morea and Crete for his services against the Greeks. Having lost the Morea he now demanded (1831) the cession to him of the greater part of Syria in compensation. The Sultan refused this demand and Mehemet's reply was to send his son Ibrahim with an army into Syria, which soon came under his control. Open war now developed between the Sultan and his rebellious vassal, and a Turkish army was sent against Ibrahim. The result was a crushing defeat of the Turks at the battle of Koniah. It now appeared possible, to the great alarm of all the states interested in the fate of Turkey, that Mehemet Ali himself might put paid to the Turkish Empire on his own account and install himself in the Sultan's place.

**Actions of the Great Powers.** The Sultan now appealed for the help of the Great Powers, but France and England were at this time, 1831, absorbed in the diplomatic tangles created by the Belgian Revolution and they therefore gave little attention to the cry of distress from Constantinople. This, of course, left the way open for Russia, who, in agreement with the Sultan, sent a large body of troops to Constantinople in readiness to defend the Turks against Mehemet Ali and Ibrahim.

This was, indeed, a remarkable change of front on the part both of Russia and of Turkey. The latter now accepted Russian protection, while the Russians were apparently ready to prop up the Turkish Empire instead of pull it down. This change is explained by the fact that Nicholas I had failed to obtain the settlement of the Greek question as he wanted it, and he now felt that nations whose independence was gained from the Turks were as likely to join the opponents of Russian policy as to come under Russian influence. It might be better, Nicholas considered, to sustain the Turkish Empire and also remain on good terms with Britain.

It was not long before Palmerston, British Foreign Secretary since 1830, decided that he could not allow Nicholas the dangerous privilege of "protecting" the Turkish Empire. The policy of Louis Philippe of France was to work closely with Great Britain, and at last in 1833 a joint British and French naval force was sent to the Aegean Sea. The Sultan Mahmoud was "advised" (with the Anglo-French Fleet not far away from Constantinople) to make peace with Mehemet Ali by handing over to him Syria, Damascus and Palestine. The Sultan reluctantly accepted these proposals and peace was made with Mehemet Ali. Palmerston had thus succeeded in making the presence of Russian troops on Turkish soil quite unjustifiable and had brought back the Sultan to the western fold. It was a diplomatic defeat for the new policy of the Czar Nicholas I.

**The Treaty of Unkiar-Skelessi.** On the other hand, the Czar Nicholas gained important treaty concessions from the Sultan in return for Russian help against Mehemet Ali. These were embodied in the Treaty of Unkiar-Skelessi, July, 1833, by which Russia and Turkey signed a defensive alliance pledging mutual assistance whenever peace and security might be endangered. The Sultan agreed to close the entrance to the Black Sea to the warships of all nations except Russia, whenever the Russians made the demand. This treaty was secret, but Palmerston soon got to know of it. It became one of his most determined aims to get this treaty cancelled as soon as possible, for he was resolved that Russia should never be able to control the Straits. In fact, Palmerston was extremely angry over the whole affair, for it was undoubtedly a great success for Nicholas I and a very great blow at British policy, which aimed consistently to keep the Russian fleet out of the Mediterranean. However, for some years the treaty remained in force, until new developments in 1839 enabled Palmerston to retrieve the situation as far as Britain was concerned.

**The Crisis of 1839–1841.** During the years 1833–1839 the Sultan Mahmoud concentrated all his efforts on preparations for revenge against Mehemet Ali. He was above all determined not to accept the permanent loss of Syria to the ruler of Egypt. His army was reorganised on western lines with the help of Prussian military advisers and in 1839 he launched his attack on Mehemet Ali. But Mehemet Ali himself had also been preparing for trouble and he was helped in his own army reforms by a number of French officers, for Thiers was now head of Louis Philippe's government and he was a strong and even violent supporter of an expansionist policy for France. By helping Mehemet Ali, Thiers was hoping to extend French trade with the Middle East and also to gain a part of Syria in return for French assistance.

The Sultan's attack on Syria in 1839 was crushingly defeated by

Mehemet Ali's forces, while the Turkish fleet sent against him deserted to his side.

**Palmerston's Policy.** Mehemet Ali was obviously as great a danger to the Turkish Empire in 1839 as he had been in 1833, and in 1840 Palmerston decided that it was time for Britain to act. His double task was to forestall intervention by Russia and to prevent Thiers' policy of support for Mehemet Ali becoming a menace to Britain's naval and trading power in the Eastern Mediterranean. He now called a conference of the Great Powers in London— deliberately omitting France. The Conference of London reached an agreement, known as the Convention of London, signed by the representatives of Britain, Russia and Austria. By this Convention Mehemet Ali was offered the southern half of Syria, was requested to make peace with the Sultan and was given ten days in which to agree to the terms. When he refused, an allied fleet was sent against Crete, which was captured, while a powerful English fleet was dispatched by Palmerston to Alexandria and Acre was taken by British troops. These demonstrations of naval force, the movement of Russian troops against him, and the dismissal of his ally Thiers by Louis Philippe, completely isolated Mehemet Ali. By the Second Convention of London (this time signed by France) he was forced to give up both Syria and Crete to the Sultan, but was confirmed as the hereditary ruler of Egypt.

**The Straits Convention, 1841.** Palmerston also succeeded at this time in ending the Treaty of Unkiar-Skelessi by securing another agreement known as the Straits Convention, 1841. The Sultan, having been strongly supported by Palmerston and having regained his lost territory from Mehemet Ali mainly through the initiative of Palmerston in calling the London Conferences, was under a strong obligation to accept Palmerston's terms. By the Straits Convention Turkey agreed to close the Bosphorus to the warships of all nations in time of peace, thus making it impossible for Russia to send her warships into the Mediterranean when she pleased.

Altogether, the crisis of 1839–1841 turned out a great triumph for Palmerston. He had defeated Mehemet Ali, regained British influence with the Sultan as against Russia, and had defeated the policy of Thiers. British foreign policy in relation to the Eastern Question had never been more successful.

**The Crimean War, 1854–1856.** The next most important development of the Eastern Question was the Crimean War of 1854–1856.

This war, apparently one of the most useless and wasteful ever fought, arose partly from the ambitions of Napoleon III, Emperor of France, and partly from Russian policy towards Turkey and the fears of that policy felt by the other Great Powers, especially Britain.

**Russian Policy.** After 1841 the policy of Czar Nicholas I became outspokenly opposed to the continued existence of the Turkish Empire. Various statements made by the Czar seemed to indicate to the other Powers concerned that he was determined to break the Empire for good and all. He referred to Turkey as "the sick man of Europe", and gave it as his opinion that no amount of doctoring would do the patient any good. On a visit to Britain in 1844 Nicholas suggested to various British statesmen that Britain and Russia should settle the fate of Turkey between them—Britain to take Egypt and Crete and Russia to occupy Constantinople temporarily. The independence of Wallachia and Moldavia, of Bulgaria and Serbia was to be guaranteed by the Powers, while the immediate "protector" of these states was to be Russia. In 1853 Nicholas again made rather similar proposals.

**British Policy.** The British government had two main reasons for opposing the Czar's suggestions:

(1) Russia would obviously become the most influential state in the Balkans and the Middle East and, with the control of Constantinople, would be able to dominate the entrance to the Black Sea and the Aegean. In fact, Russian warships would have completely free access to the Mediterranean.

(2) They considered Turkey to be stronger than the Czar suggested. There was a suspicion in British circles that the Czar was exaggerating the weakness of the Turkish Empire in his own interests. For these reasons (not always explicitly stated) the government of Lord Aberdeen remained unresponsive to the Czar's proposals for partitioning the Turkish Empire made in 1853.

**The Immediate Causes of the War.** In 1853 the antagonism between Russia and France flared up over a comparatively unimportant question, the guardianship in Palestine of the Holy Places sacred to all Christians. In the sixteenth century the French had been given the guardianship of the Church of Bethlehem and the sacred manger, but these duties had become neglected in the eighteenth century and the Russian Greek Orthodox Church took

over the guardianship. Napoleon III, with an eye to the full support
of the Catholic Church at home, revived the French claims, and in
1853 the Sultan agreed to recognise the French monks as the guar-
dians of the Holy Places. Russia naturally protested against this
agreement and sent as ambassador to Constantinople an aggressive and blustering individual, Prince Menschikoff, who now
put forward the demand that Russia should be recognised as the
protector of all the Orthodox Christians in the Turkish Empire.
This demand, if accepted, would have enabled Russia to intervene
in Turkish affairs almost at will.

Facing Prince Menschikoff in Constantinople was the British
Ambassador, Lord Stratford de Redcliffe, determined to frustrate
the designs of Russia at all costs. He encouraged the Sultan to stand
firm against the Russian proposals, and in this he was supported by
the government of Lord Aberdeen. At last, in July, 1853, Russia
replied by moving troops into the provinces of Moldavia and
Wallachia. This was a step towards war, but at this point the other
Powers made efforts to prevent the situation getting worse. A conference of Austria, Prussia, France and Great Britain was called in
Vienna and drew up proposals which were sent to Nicholas and to the
Sultan. The Russian interpretation of these proposals was that they
gave her almost everything she was demanding, including the right
to act as protector of the Orthodox Christians, and she accepted
them. On the other hand, Lord Stratford de Redcliffe urged the
Sultan to claim the sole right to act as protector of the Christians.
Russia refused to accept this proposed change, the Turks demanded
that she withdraw her forces from Moldavia and Wallachia and,
when she refused, declared war.

**Responsibility for the War.** The attempt to apportion responsibility for the Crimean War has been made many times, with very
little success. Everyone was to blame and everyone involved had
some plausible case. Napoleon III was determined on glory and on
the defeat of the enemy of 1812. Moreover, he wished to promote
French trading interests in the Eastern Mediterranean, to gain the
support of Catholicism in France and to humiliate the Czar Nicholas I who was rudely refusing to recognise the equal status of Napoleon III with the other rulers of Europe and would not address him
as "brother". The Czar himself acted impetuously and was misled
into thinking that the British government, under the peacefully-
inclined Lord Aberdeen, would not go to war. He therefore pressed
his claims against the Turks relentlessly. In November, 1853, the

Fig. 30.—A Quiet Night on the Batteries, Sebastopol.

Russians sank the Turkish fleet at Sinope, and this led on to a declaration of war by Britain and France.

It must not be thought that the Crimean War was unpopular either in France or Britain—far from it. In fact, popular anti-Russian hysteria after the battle of Sinope gave definite encouragement to both Napoleon III and the British government. It must be remembered that Russia at that time was regarded in radical and liberal circles in the West as the very embodiment of black, reactionary oppression, and therefore what could be healthier than a resounding defeat for Czar Nicholas? The cause of liberty in Europe would be served by keeping the Russian despotism as far away from Europe as possible. This line of thought counted for much more than considerations for the safety of the British overland route to India, which was very little used at this time and, in the words of a modern historian, only "catered for a few travellers in a hurry".

**Characteristics of the Crimean War.** Never was a more fantastic war fought than the Crimean. It was a tragi-comedy on the grand scale. There was a considerable "tourist traffic" out to the Crimea. It became an adventurous jaunt for the wives of officers who went with their husbands to the very scene of battle or gave out hampers of provisions for the troops; they were all entirely free to go where they pleased. Lord Cardigan, the commander of the famous Light Brigade, had his private yacht, the *Dryad*, taken out to the Crimea, and he dined and slept on it every night, seven miles away from the troops under his command. Strange things also occurred on the Russian side. Prince Menschikoff, now commander of the Russian forces, invited a party of young Russian society ladies from Sebastopol to a summer picnic on the heights overlooking the River Alma, whence they would be able to get a grand-stand view of the expected repulse of the British who were about to attempt the crossing against the fire from the Russian guns on the heights. The picnic was brought to a hasty end when, in fact, the British succeeded in crossing the river.

What has been aptly described as "the general insanity of the Crimea" was even more apparent in the breakdown of supplies for the troops, the appalling military bungling which led to the ill-fated charge of the Light Brigade and, worst of all, the shocking conditions at the hospital across the Black Sea at Scutari. When Florence Nightingale arrived to take charge of the hospital arrangements she found, in the words of Lytton Strachey, "Want, neglect, confusion, misery. . . . There were not enough bedsteads; the sheets were of

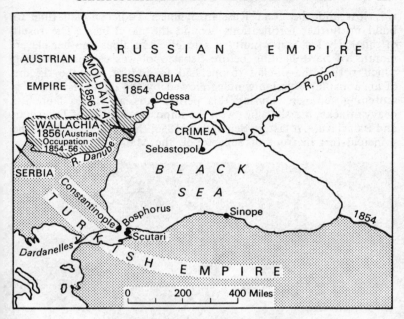

IX.—THE CRIMEAN WAR, 1854–1856.

canvas, and so coarse that the wounded men recoiled from them, begging to be left in their blankets; there was no bedroom furniture of any kind, and empty beer bottles were used as candlesticks. There were no basins, no towels, no soap, no brooms, no mops, no trays, no plates . . . there were no knives or forks or spoons." With the support of Lord Palmerston, who became British Prime Minister in 1855, Florence Nightingale and her band of nurses broke through the stupidity and obstruction of the allied commanders and thoroughly reorganised the medical services, with the result that the death-rate in the hospital at Scutari was reduced by forty per cent. In this campaign she had also been strongly supported by *The Times* newspaper, whose correspondent in the Crimea, William Russell, was the first ever to report war news directly from the field of battle.

The war itself needs only brief reference. In September, 1854, an allied force landed at Eupatoria in the Crimea, and soon afterwards won the battle of the Alma River. Through a disagreement between the British and French commanders the opportunity of immediately attacking the important Russian stronghold of Sebastopol was lost and the great Russian engineer Todleben had time to build up further fortifications around the naval base. The result of this early lost opportunity was to give the allies another eleven months of hard fighting before Sebastopol was captured, during which period the ill-clad troops had to endure first the rigours of an appalling Russian winter followed by the equal rigours of a scorching summer. During this period Russian forces launched heavy attacks, but the allies won the important battles of Inkerman and Balaclava. At last, in September, 1855, the French captured the principal fort in front of Sebastopol, the Malakoff, and this was

MISS NIGHTINGALE, IN THE HOSPITAL, AT SCUTARI.

Wherever there is disease in its most dangerous form, and the hand of the spoiler distressingly nigh, there is that incomparable woman sure to be seen; her benignant presence is an influence for good comfort even amid the struggles of expiring nature. She is a "ministering angel" without any exaggeration, in these hospitals, and as her slender form glides quietly along each corridor, every poor fellow's face softens with gratitude at the sight of her. When all the medical officers have retired for the night, and silence and darkness have settled upon all those miles of prostrate sick, she may be observed, alone, with a little lamp in her han[d] making her solitary rounds. With the heart of [a] true woman and the manner of a lady, accomplish[ed] and refined beyond most of her sex, she combin[es] a surprising calmness of judgement, and prompt[i]tude and decision of character. The popular de[ci]sion was not mistaken, which, when she set out fro[m] England on her mission of mercy, hailed her as heroine; I trust that she may not earn her title t[o] higher, though sadder, appellation. No one w[ho] has observed her fragile figure and delicate heal[th] can avoid misgivings lest these should fail.

FIG. 31.—EXTRACT FROM ONE OF WILLIAM RUSSELL'S DESPATCHES TO "THE TIMES".

followed by the surrender of Sebastopol itself. In March, 1855, Nicholas I died and was succeeded by his son Alexander II who was anxious to bring about important internal reforms in Russia and, after the fall of Sebastopol, was prepared to accept what terms he could get from the French and British. Negotiations were begun and the final treaty was signed at Paris on March 30, 1856, at a conference presided over by the Emperor Napoleon III.

**Terms of the Treaty of Paris, 1856.** By the Treaty of Paris the Black Sea was neutralised. That is, no warships of any nation were allowed on it nor were the Russians to build any military or naval fortifications. The Black Sea was to be free to the merchant vessels of all nations and the Danube was also internationalised. Moldavia and Wallachia were to be self-governing but to recognise the suzerainty of Turkey, and Russia was to abandon her claim to protect the Orthodox Christians within the Turkish Empire. The Sultan was made to promise better treatment of his Christian subjects.

The allied aims had been achieved. Russia had been defeated and her influence in the Balkan Peninsula decisively checked, while her naval power could not now threaten the power of Britain and France in the Mediterranean. But this achievement was of a most temporary nature. In 1870 the Russians, encouraged by Bismarck, repudiated the Black Sea clauses of the treaty, while the Sultan's promise to give true equality to Christians and Moslems was never carried out. In fact, things got much worse in this respect, as we shall see when we come to consider the Armenian massacres of the year 1896.

**Events Leading to the Congress of Berlin, 1878.** The promises of good conduct made by the Sultan in the Treaty of Paris proved completely worthless. The Turkish Empire continued to go from bad to worse. Administration was chaotic, government funds were misused, taxation continued to be grossly unfair as between Christian and Moslem, and outright persecution of the Christian minorities became increasingly common. The government attempted to stave off bankruptcy by huge borrowings from other countries, but even this failed to prop up the tottering finances of the Empire.

In 1875 a national revolt broke out in the Turkish Balkan provinces of Bosnia and Herzegovina, where serfdom still existed, and where the taxation of the peasantry was a crushing burden. In the same year the Turkish government repudiated part of its foreign debt and, of course, this was of even more immediate concern to the other powers than the revolt in Bosnia and Herzegovina. Austria, Germany and Russia presented to the Sultan certain proposals of reform in a communication known as the Andrassy Note, from the name of the Austrian Foreign Minister who was responsible for drawing it up. However, the people of Bosnia and Herzegovina were not prepared to put their trust in the Sultan's promises of reform, while the area of revolt was suddenly widened by an outbreak of rebellion in Bulgaria. The new Sultan, Abdul Hamid II (known appropriately in history as the "red Sultan"), gave no quarter whatever to the insurgents. As we have seen (page 195), he waged a war of brutal extermination against the Bulgarians, to the horror not only of Mr. Gladstone but of the whole of Europe. Once again, a situation had been reached in which Russia was certain to intervene alone unless the other Great Powers acted. By this time Serbia and Montenegro had risen in revolt in support of Bosnia and Herzegovina.

The British Prime Minister, Disraeli, called a conference of the Great Powers at Constantinople. This conference demanded equality for Moslems and Christians in the Turkish Empire and a guarantee by the Sultan of self-government for Bosnia and Herzegovina. But the new Sultan countered this move by going even further and granting a parliamentary system on western lines for the whole Empire. This, however, was only a manœuvre to forestall allied intervention against him, and after a few months he dismissed the minister who had framed the new constitution and restored despotic rule.

**Russian Intervention and the Treaty of San Stefano.** At this point the Russians decided that only the outright defeat of the Sultan would enforce the needed reforms and secure the independence of the peoples in revolt. Therefore, when the Turkish government refused to give guarantees of good faith demanded in another ultimatum from the Great Powers, Russia declared war on Turkey. She was joined in this declaration by Rumania, Serbia, Montenegro and Bulgaria.

The Russians found the campaign against the Turks more difficult than they had anticipated. The Turks, under Osman Pasha, defended the town of Plevna for five months, thus tying down 120,000 Russian troops. But after the fall of the town, the Russians advanced rapidly to Adrianople, and it appeared likely that they would go on to the capture of Constantinople itself.

At this point the antagonism of Britain and Austria to Russian aims came clearly into the open. Austria's interest lay in the fact that she already had a secret agreement with Russia by which she was to gain a protectorate over Bosnia and Herzegovina if Russia regained that part of Bessarabia taken away by the Treaty of Paris in 1856. But if Russia now occupied Constantinople she might feel powerful enough to repudiate this agreement. At the same time Disraeli, anxious to maintain the Turkish Empire as a restraint on Russian expansion, now ordered the British fleet to the Dardanelles. Both Austria and Britain demanded that the Russians should halt their advance at Adrianople and sign an armistice.

This pressure had the desired effect, and Russia made the Treaty of San Stefano with the Sultan. By this treaty Russia made certain gains of territory at the mouth of the Danube. Bessarabia, Bosnia and Herzegovina were to administer their own affairs, and the tiny state of Montenegro doubled its population and gained two small ports on the Adriatic Sea. But the most important clauses of this treaty, and the ones which most alarmed the governments of Austria and Great Britain, were those settling the future of Bulgaria, which now became the largest of the Balkan states. Its territory now stretched from the Danube River to the Aegean Sea and from the Black Sea to within fifty miles of the Adriatic. Thus the new Bulgaria completely cut in two the Turkish Empire in the Balkans. This "Big Bulgaria" was created by Russia, and it was thought that as a result it was likely to accept a certain amount of Russian control of both its home and foreign policy. This would mean, in fact, that Russia would become the dominating power in the Balkan Peninsula, and to this Britain and Austria were strongly opposed. They now demanded that the whole question should be decided by a European Congress and that the Treaty of San Stefano should be revised. Disraeli made warlike moves, the most dramatic being the sending of 7,000 Indian troops to Malta. But what really decided the Russians to agree to a Congress was the fact that Bismarck now came down on the side of Austria and Britain. A Congress was therefore summoned at Berlin in March, 1878.

**The Congress of Berlin, 1878.** Long before the Congress assembled various secret agreements had been arrived at between Britain and Russia and between Britain, Austria and Turkey. The Congress, under the chairmanship of the "honest broker", Bismarck, merely settled publicly certain outstanding details. The Big Bulgaria was divided in three, the northernmost part being virtually independent under a Bulgarian prince. The central district, Eastern Rumelia, was placed under a Christian Governor-General but was under the direct political and military authority of the Sultan; the southernmost part, including Macedonia, reverted to Turkey, which once again had a continuous territory stretching across the peninsula from the Aegean to the Adriatic (see map, page 196). Britain gained Cyprus from Turkey as compensation for the retention by Russia of Bessarabia and the territory of Kars, Batoum and Ardahan in Asia Minor. Austria was also given the administration of Bosnia and Herzegovina, which did not mean that they became part of the Austrian Empire, for Austria was answerable for her administration to the Treaty Powers of 1878. The Sultan made his usual promises of reform in his treatment of the Christian populations of the Empire.

**Results of the Treaty of Berlin.** Like so many other "settlements" of the Eastern Question, the treaty had very few lasting results. Within seven years the Bulgarians gained control of Eastern Rumelia and (contrary to Disraeli's fears) they carried out a policy completely independent of Russia. The Montenegrins and the Serbs never accepted the Austrian control of Bosnia and Herzegovina, and, as will be seen, the antagonism between Serbia and Austria had much to do with the outbreak of the Great War of 1914-1918. England had gained a Mediterranean base in Cyprus, but Disraeli's claim that he had returned from Berlin bringing "peace with honour" seems, in the light of after events, a rather smug and unsubstantial claim. In one respect honour was soon violated, for the Sultan Abdul Hamid II completely ignored his undertaking to treat humanely the non-Moslem minorities in his Empire, as the Armenian massacres of 1896 brutally witness (see page 267).

# chapter fourteen
# RUSSIA, 1789–1914

**Introductory.** For over a hundred years before our period begins Russia had greatly increased her interest in, and contacts with, the West. This policy had above all been carried through with ruthless and untiring determination by Czar Peter the Great (1689–1725). His aim had been to secure for Russia any benefits which Western Europe could bestow and thus to bring Russia as a nation to a higher level of culture and political power. With the help of a Scotsman, General Gordon, he built up a powerful army on western lines and defeated the great military power of Sweden—a victory which brought into the Russian Empire the Baltic provinces of Latvia, Esthonia, Ingria, Karelia and a part of Finland. With the conscripted labour of the serfs (who died in their thousands during the course of the work) he built his new capital of St. Petersburg (now Leningrad). He himself travelled and worked in Western Europe, especially in Holland and England. While in England he worked as a labourer in the shipbuilding yards at Deptford. On his return to Russia after two years in Europe (1697–1699) he had to face strong opposition from those who disliked his "westernising" policy, but he managed to suppress a revolt among the Imperial Guards or "Streltsi" in Moscow. He forced his wife Eudoxia to enter a nunnery because she was under the influence of the Russian Orthodox Church which was opposed to Peter's ideas. A man of colossal energy and brutality, Peter himself on occasion flogged his convicted enemies, while his own son was tortured and killed for opposing his father's aims.

In general, Peter was successful in his policies and the results were seen in a greatly strengthened army and navy, considerable improvements in education, the establishment of an Academy of Sciences on Western lines, the building of roads and canals and a general improvement of the actual administration of the country. He greatly reduced the powers of the "boyars" or hereditary landowners, abolished their own assembly or Duma and appointed new State officials who were loyal to his aims. Peter attacked a number of institutions which symbolised the old, unchanging past of Russia—he even ordered his boyars to cut off their beards, and he himself wielded the scissors (mainly as a form of amusement) on the more reluctant.

235

During the whole of the eighteenth century Peter the Great's influence was felt in the policies of his successors, especially in the reign of the Czarina Catherine the Great (1762-1796). She was a woman of strong, dictatorial character and considerable intellectual power. She was widely read in the literature and science of Western Europe and numbered among her friends and correspondents the great French philosopher Voltaire. She continued Peter's aggressive foreign policy and gained further territory for Russia, notably the Crimea, which was conquered from Turkey, and a considerable part of the kingdom of Poland. The latter country was the victim of its own internal chaos. The monarchy of Poland was an elective one, and this gave rise to violent struggles for the kingship between certain great Polish families, some of whom did not hesitate to call in the assistance of foreign powers. The government of the country itself was chaotic, for in the Polish assembly any one noble could by his vote prevent a law being passed—a right known as the "liberum veto". All these factors led on to civil war, and the Great Powers— Austria, Prussia and Russia—were soon involved in the affairs of Poland. The details of these intrigues and conflicts do not concern us here, but we must note that there were three divisions or partitions of Poland between the Great Powers in the eighteenth century—in 1772, 1793 and 1795. Further Russian gains by the last partition of 1795 meant that she now controlled more than half the territory of the former Polish Kingdom.

**Alexander I (1801-1825).** Catherine the Great was succeeded by her son Paul I, whose sanity was doubtful. His character and policy were so changeable and uncertain that he made enemies on every hand. He made himself extremely unpopular by deserting the coalition against Napoleon and forming an alliance with France. In 1801 Count Pahlen, the Governor of Moscow, formed a plot against Paul with the encouragement of the British Ambassador, and the Czar was murdered. His son Alexander was fully prepared to take his father's place.

During the reign of Alexander I, the most famous and the most enigmatic of the Czars of the nineteenth century, the power of Russia as a force in international affairs continued to grow. Even after Napoleon's victories at Austerlitz, 1805, and at Friedland, 1807, Russia was strong enough to make her own bargain with the Emperor from which she gained advantages in other directions. By his agreement with Napoleon at Tilsit, 1807, Alexander was free to direct his campaign against Turkey, from whom he seized the territory of Bessarabia in 1812. In 1808–1809 the whole of Finland was incorporated in the Russian Empire. Then in 1812, after the break between the Czar and Napoleon, there came the crushing defeat of the Emperor's forces in the Moscow Campaign. No wonder that Alexander began to feel something of a " divine mission" for himself and Russia. The defeat of Napoleon in 1812 produced that outburst of religious fervour on the part of Alexander which was to lead on to his proposals for a "Holy Alliance" of the European sovereigns in 1815 (see page 83). "The fires of Moscow lit up my soul," he declared afterwards. "I got to know God and became another man."

**Alexander's Liberalism.** From the commencement of his reign in 1801 to the year 1819, when he came strongly under the influence of Metternich, Alexander appeared to favour liberal ideas. In the court of his grandmother, Catherine the Great, he had had as his tutors men of western, liberal education, the chief of whom was the Swiss, Laharpe, who exercised an important influence over the impressionable mind of Alexander. The works of Voltaire, Rousseau and other great thinkers of the eighteenth-century "Enlightenment" were well known to Alexander and he was sincerely anxious to apply his knowledge to the benefit of Russia. Besides this liberal element in his character there was also a deeply religious tendency which had been stimulated by the teachings of a Christian mystic by the name of Madame Krudener who held religious sway for a time at the Russian court.

**Alexander's Domestic Policy.** One of the first significant actions of Alexander I on becoming Czar was to appoint a special committee, known as the Informal Committee, to advise him on policy. On this committee were represented some younger men who were sympathetic towards Alexander's liberal ideas and wished to see important changes in Russian government. They succeeded in suppressing the special political police which the Czar Paul had formed. Many exiles were recalled from Siberia and many political prisoners released. The use of torture by the police was forbidden and foreign books were allowed to be imported. Three new universities were established and a system of elementary schools begun. Alexander also approved a law enabling the great landowners to liberate their serfs, and about 50,000 (out of nearly 50,000,000) were released from personal bondage to their lords during his reign. Although the serf law only touched the fringe of the question, it was at least a recognition that the problem of the degradation of millions of human beings did exist and that the new Czar was not blind to the problem. The great

Russian gentry watched all these reforms with a jealous eye and did everything they could to obstruct what reforms the Czar attempted. He was by no means master in his own house when it came to the privileges of the old nobility. Indeed, the power of the serf-owning landlords and the State officials (the "bureaucracy") was shown in the fate of a would-be reformer whom Alexander supported for a time, Michael Speransky. In 1809 he produced a complicated but definitely progressive scheme by which elections were to be held for an imperial "duma" or parliament, and in these elections the peasants or serfs were to have a definite voice. These proposals were too much for the Russian gentry, especially when Speransky also proposed an income tax in order to improve the shockingly chaotic finances of the government. At this time the Czar's relations with Napoleon had become strained and he dared not risk the opposition of the gentry if a war with France developed. Alexander therefore dismissed Speransky and had him deported to the Russian provinces where he was put under police surveillance for some years.

The very idea of "reform from above" thus met with the effective obstruction of the landlords and the State officials who regarded Speransky and his followers among the younger Russians as nothing less than Jacobins and revolutionaries. In this important sense, the Czar Alexander was a prisoner of his own state. On the other hand, the possibilities of "reform from below" were at this time most remote, for the peasantry were ignorant, oppressed and apathetic.

**Alexander and Poland.** In 1815 the other allies prevented Alexander gaining control of the whole of Poland, but the greater part of the former Grand Duchy of Warsaw, Napoleon's creation, passed to him. Alexander at once incurred the displeasure of his fellow-monarchs by introducing into Poland the most liberal form of government in Europe. The Kingdom of Poland thus formed was to be almost self-governing, the only direct connection with Russia being the presence in Warsaw of a Russian Viceroy. A National Assembly was to be elected and to control all affairs relating directly to Poland. At the same time Alexander accorded the right of freedom of religion and of speech to all citizens. Even after 1819, when his reactionary phase in other matters set in strongly under the influence of Metternich, Alexander maintained the Polish constitution. However, his popularity with his Polish subjects was rather less at the end of his reign than in 1816. The reason for this was to be found in a vague promise which he had made to the Poles that certain territories which had formerly belonged to the old Polish Kingdom of the seventeenth century would be returned to them, especially part of Ukraine, White Russia and Lithuania. But Alexander was strongly opposed on this question by the Russian nobility and his vague promises were never made good.

**Alexander turns from Liberalism, 1819–1825.** The last years of Alexander's reign are marked by the growth of a reform movement among sections of the officer class in the Russian Imperial Army, in co-operation with a number of Russian intellectuals. The officers concerned with this movement were mostly men who had served in the Russian forces in Western Europe during the last years of the struggle against Napoleon. They had made contact not only with Western liberal movements of thought, but with the culture, customs and literature of France and the German states. Returning to Russia, they were horrified at the contrast between what they had seen in France and Germany and the backwardness of serf-ridden Russia with its ignorant, cruelly-treated peasantry, its narrow and bigoted gentry without true refinement and culture, its undemocratic government of police officials and reactionary civil servants. They looked first to Alexander to bring about important improvements and they were especially encouraged by the liberal constitution he introduced into Poland. They hoped that this would be followed by a parliamentary system for Russia.

Their hopes were soon disappointed, for in 1819, after the murder of the Czar's agent, Kotzebue (page 147), Metternich convinced Alexander that all reform movements meant nothing less than revolution against crowned heads. The revolutions in Spain (1818) and Naples (1820) were also used by Metternich to turn the Czar from liberalism. Alexander now instituted a censorship of all school textbooks, gave up schemes which he had had in mind for freeing more of the serfs, and gave the Russian Orthodox Church control of education, which meant that liberal and Western ideas would be rigidly excluded from the universities and schools. It also led to the persecution of other religious groups in Russia. Even in Poland similar measures of control were introduced. An attempted revolt of one of the Guards regiments in Moscow in 1820 only hardened Alexander in his policy.

**The Decembrist Conspiracy.** The would-be reformers were now driven to organise in secret. A number of secret societies were formed and the most important of these was under the leadership of an officer of the Imperial Army, Colonel Paul Pestel. His aim was to bring about a military revolt which would force the Czar to grant a liberal constitution for Russia. The principal society was known as the Society of the Public Good and was modelled on that of the Italian Carbonari.

On December 1, 1825, Alexander died at the early age of forty-eight. The plotters now considered that their opportunity had arrived. The situation that favoured them was this: Alexander having no children, his brother Constantine would normally have become Czar, but he had already renounced the throne in favour of his younger brother, Nicholas. Alexander had not made public this renunciation by Constantine and on December 24, 1825, the officers of the St. Petersburg garrison gave their oath of allegiance to Constantine. Soon afterwards, Nicholas learnt of Constantine's renunciation of the throne and he therefore ordered a new oath of loyalty to himself to be taken by the army officers. Nicholas was unpopular among the soldiers and Constantine was thought to be more favourable to liberal reform. Several regiments in St. Petersburg refused to give the oath of allegiance, but the leader whom the secret societies had agreed should act as temporary dictator failed to appear on the scene. Confusion followed, and the loyalists gained the upper hand. The revenge of Nicholas was severe. Five of the leaders, including Pestel, were executed and over a hundred exiled to Siberia.

Thus the reign of Alexander I ended in a "revolutionary" fiasco which is chiefly memorable for the desperate heroism of a handful of Russian officers and intellectual leaders such as the great Russian poet, Pushkin. The officers particularly had little contact with the Russian people and were therefore easily isolated and defeated.

The Czar Alexander is the most interesting and one of the most important of the Czars of the nineteenth century. His early zeal for liberalism was genuine, and he even encouraged various reform societies to spread their ideas abroad in Russia—ironically enough, some of the victims of Nicholas in 1825 had had the support of Alexander in his liberal years! Yet his mind was unstable and lacked the capacity to carry through a consistent policy which would have led to liberal government in Russia. He was impressionable and came too easily under the sway of Metternich, even though at the time of Napoleon's invasion of 1812 he had shown determined leadership and an iron purpose aided by the support of every class in the country. In the last resort, when it came to the possibility of his losing the position of despot over his own people, he faltered and turned back from the "spectre" of liberalism which he himself had helped to encourage.

**Nicholas I, 1825–1855.** The new Czar was determined to suppress all signs of liberalism in Russia. The Decembrist revolt had strengthened that determination. Nicholas had an idea of his position very similar to that of the "Divine Right of Kings" to govern their peoples according to their will alone. God had given him the mission to rule, and nobody was to be allowed to challenge his decisions. His mind was hard, narrow and inflexible.

Nicholas at once re-established the special secret police, and at the same time imposed the strictest government censorship over all publications. Nicholas himself was in the habit of reading the manuscripts of important Russian writers and deleting from them any passages which might be construed as an attack on his authority. The manuscripts of the most famous of all Russian poets of the nineteenth century, Alexander Pushkin, were treated in this way. Writers were also called to the Czar's presence to explain their shortcomings. Besides these changes, Nicholas restricted entry to the new secondary schools of Alexander I to the children of the gentry and of government officials only, and a close watch over university students was kept by the secret police. The teaching of certain "dangerous" subjects, such as history and philosophy, was completely forbidden in the universities. It became a serious crime to read prohibited literature, for which the penalty could be exile to Siberia.

After the attempted revolutions of 1848 and the dispatch of Russian troops to help the Emperor of Austria to quell the revolution in Hungary, Nicholas increased the severity of his rule. He especially directed his attention to the Russian intellectuals, many of whom were exiled to forced labour in Siberia, among them the great Russian novelist, Dostoievsky, the author of *Crime and Punishment*. Altogether, about 150,000 persons were exiled to Siberia in the reign of Nicholas I.

**Nicholas I and the Slavophils.** During the reign of Nicholas I there developed among the educated class in Russia two opposed lines of thought on the important question of the attitude that Russia should adopt towards the West. The thinkers known as the Slavophils were those who saw Russian culture and institutions as totally different from those of the Western world, and wished them to remain so. They pointed out, for example, that the typical peasant mode of life in Russia was the "mir" or village community (which, in fact, applied mainly to the royal estates, not to the whole of the land). In this "mir" the peasants had collective agreements among themselves on matters of village life and they were able to voice their opinions in the village meeting. This, said the Slavophils, was very different from the individual, private ownership or landholding of the Western peasant. Again, the Slavophils were opposed to Western "capitalism" of the type developing in England, with its factory and mineowners employing masses of free labourers working for wages. They wished to keep Russia under the control of the Czar, the Orthodox Church and the landowners. They wanted to preserve "Old Russia". Nicholas himself naturally came to support many of the Slavophil ideas, for they opposed the Western liberalism which he hated.

**Opponents of the Slavophils.** The opposite line of thought to the Slavophils was best represented by the Russian writer and socialist, Alexander Herzen. He attempted to show that there was no absolute division between Russia and the West, for many Russian traditions were, in fact, of Western origin. He wanted the Russian people to overthrow Czarism and establish a socialist state. He and his followers were naturally ardent supporters of the Western revolutions of 1848, and after their failure he became an exile from Russia and lived in England. From England he edited an important newspaper, the *Kolokol* (the *Bell*), which circulated secretly for a time in Russia until its failure. Herzen especially denounced serfdom, besides carrying on a lifelong literary propaganda against the Czarist policestate. His influence was felt among the Russian intellectuals who opposed the Slavophils.

**Peasant Unrest in the Reign of Nicholas.** Despite the ruthless police terror in the reign of Nicholas, the discontent of the Russian peasants broke out into open revolt during his reign. These revolts were isolated, despairing protests at the unjust exactions of the landlords, and we must remember that landlords in Russia could throw their serfs into prison and keep them in chains like any feudal baron in the Middle Ages. The peasant revolts resulted in the murder of landlords and bailiffs, but achieved nothing constructive. Yet, such was the widespread nature of the discontent, that more than four hundred peasant revolts broke out during the reign of Nicholas I and more than 300 of these occurred after 1840.

**Foreign Policy of Nicholas I.** In his foreign policy Nicholas aimed at the extension of Russian territory and influence. He waged a successful war against Persia and, in the Far East, gained important territory from China along the Amur River. Nicholas intervened actively in support of the Greeks, and by the Treaty of Adrianople, 1829, he gained the right of free navigation for Russian vessels in the Dardanelles and Bosphorus. The Treaty of Unkiar-Skelessi (see page 224) also gave Russia the main voice in the control of the entrance to the Black Sea. Nicholas made vigorous efforts to break up the Turkish Empire in agreement with Britain, but the failure to get agreement with Britain on this question led on to the Crimean War, 1854–1856, with which we have dealt in Chapter XIII. The failures of his forces in the war and the terrible mismanagement and incompetence which it revealed, really caused the death of the Czar Nicholas in 1855, before the war had finished. He died in complete despair for the future of Russia, feeling (with ominous foresight) that the system of government which he had attempted to develop was doomed to destruction.

**Nicholas I and Poland.** Nicholas had promised the Poles in 1825 that he would maintain the liberal constitution set up by Alexander I. But, despite his promise, many of his actions during the next five years were quite contrary to the constitution. For example, the censorship of books and other publications was greatly increased, Russian officials began to replace Polish officials in the government service, while in 1828 Nicholas ceased calling the Polish parliament together. He also abandoned the idea of adding Lithuania to the Polish territories.

In 1830, Nicholas determined to send an army to suppress the revolt of the Belgians. In November, 1830, the Polish troops in Warsaw, who were about to be sent westward for this purpose, rose in revolt and seized control of the city. The Russian Governor, the Grand Duke Constantine, was forced to flee from Poland.

The Polish revolt of 1830 was essentially a movement of the nobility and had insufficient support from the remainder of the population, especially the peasants. The nobility was also divided into two parties, the Whites, who wanted to negotiate with Nicholas after the first successes, and the Reds, who demanded that the struggle be carried through without any compromise with Nicholas. The Reds managed to gain control of the movement, declared Nicholas dethroned and Poland an independent State. Nicholas then prepared for a full-scale war against the Poles and sent an army of 120,000 against them. Outside Warsaw in September, 1831, the Poles were decisively defeated and the capital occupied by Russian troops. The divisions among the Poles, the lack of peasant support and tactical errors all produced a fatal weakness in the Polish movement. Some of the Polish forces were wasted in a fruitless expedition into Lithuania, whereas all available men should have been concentrated against the main Russian Army.

Nicholas I took a heavy revenge on the Polish patriots. The 1815 constitution was abolished and public meetings and political organisations banned throughout Poland. The University of Warsaw was closed down, all important posts in the country went to Russians, and about 80,000 Poles were exiled to Siberia. Poland sank to nothing more than a province of the Russian Empire.

**Alexander II, 1855–1881.** The new Czar was a man of more political insight and tolerance than his father. He came to the Russian

FIG. 32.—ALEXANDER II OF RUSSIA.

throne at a time when the fortunes of Russia were at a low ebb, and one of his first aims was to bring the Crimean War to an end by recognising defeat. After the conclusion of peace, Alexander turned his attention to the most serious problem facing Russia, that of serfdom.

We have seen how discontent among the serfs had led to numerous revolts in the reign of Nicholas. The latter had made some minor improvements in their conditions, but Alexander recognised that nothing short of the complete liberation of the serfs could offer any hope of a solution. In this view he was now supported by a section of the Russian gentry themselves. The change of opinion among them was due not only to humanitarian considerations, but also to the force of sheer necessity. Serf labour was becoming more and more unreliable and inefficient. This was especially the case in the cotton and woollen factories which were developing on the gentry's estates and in the larger towns. These factories could not find an adequate labour force unless the serfs were emancipated and thus enabled to move from the villages to the towns. Of course, these considerations were not the only ones that influenced Alexander II and the reformers. There were many enlightened Russians who realised that no country which held half its population as mere chattels could have an honourable and dignified future. They had come to realise that serfdom was a debasing force in the national life, for it involved cruelty and ignorance in the most horrible forms. Even then, Alexander had considerable opposition to his proposals and attempts were made by sections of the gentry to stop completely, or at least seriously limit, the proposed reforms. Despite this opposition, Alexander persisted in his purpose and by a law of March 3, 1861, the Russian serfs were freed. This was the famous Edict of Emancipation.

**Effects of the Edict of Emancipation.** By the terms of the Edict the serfs were set free without having to make any payment directly to their landlords. The peasants were now given about half the landlords' estates. Ownership of this land, however, was not vested in the individual peasants but in the "mirs", or village communities. The former landowners were compensated by the government, which was repaid by the villagers by annual payments spread over forty-nine years.

The Russian peasant did not become a completely free, individualist owner of his land on the Western pattern, for he was now grouped in village communities which elected their own Elders, responsible for the government of all village affairs. The peasant was not free to make any new legal arrangements or resell his land without the agreement of the Elders of the village council. Another important thing to note about the new arrangements was that the Elders now undertook much of the work which had been the previous responsibility of the local gentry. The result of this was that many of the gentry became socially useless and looked with envy and distrust on the new arrangements.

One of the government's main reasons for not allowing the serfs to wander away as they pleased from the land and drift into the towns was their fear of a town proletariat developing on Western lines and creating centres of socialist and revolutionary discontent which would threaten the Czar's government.

However, the drift to the towns did occur during the following years, for the peasants found the regular payments such a heavy burden that they had to abandon the land and seek work in the towns. Again, many of the peasants were dissatisfied that they had not been given the land outright by the government, for they claimed that in the distant past of Russia their ancestors had been recognised as the owners of the land in the old Russian communities.

These forms of discontent were produced by the way in which the Emancipation Edict worked, and it meant that the peasants made no great increase in the efficiency of agriculture and the production of food.

**Other Reforms of Alexander II: The Zemstvos, 1864.** An important reform of Alexander II was the introduction of a form of local government in Russia which was a considerable improvement on the previous system. Previous to the change, the nobles alone had dominated the provincial assemblies, but now this exclusiveness was broken down by giving not only the nobles but also townsmen and peasants the right to elect the District Councils or Zemstvos which were set up. The District Zemstvos then elected the Zemstvos of the Province. These new councils were responsible for the upkeep of roads and bridges, for education, public health and the election of Justices of the Peace.

In the administration of the law certain Western principles were adopted. For example, the judges and magistrates were made independent of the other departments of government, equality of all Russians before the law was recognised, court cases were now tried in public and the system of trial by jury was introduced. A number of important changes were made in the Russian Army in 1874, when all classes were declared liable for military service and the whole system was made less onerous by the reduction of service from twenty-five to fifteen years, six of which were to be spent in the regular army and five in the reserve or militia. The Russian press was given rather more freedom than before—the censorship was relaxed, though not abolished. A considerable advance in freedom of publication as compared with the previous reign is shown by the fact that in the reign of Nicholas I there were only 6 newspapers and 19 monthly magazines published in Russia, whereas in the reign of Alexander II these rose to 16 and 156 respectively.

**Increase of Discontent.** Yet, sound as many of these reforms appear, they did not go far enough to solve the social problems and ease the dangerous discontents existing in Russia. Fundamentally

Alexander was still an autocrat, intent only on introducing those piecemeal reforms which, by easing discontent, would strengthen his own autocratic position. It was still entirely "reform from above". His policy was "thus far, and no further". What many of the more educated Russians were demanding was a real democracy which would control the Czar from below, through a parliamentary system. Things were not made easier by the fact that Alexander's reforms had much opposition from the older civil servants or bureaucrats and from the "diehard" landlords. Alexander did not resist these reactionary forces with any determination and much of their power actually remained—for example, the Provincial Governors still had the right to veto the demands of the new Zemstvos; the editors of newspapers which offended the government could still be tried in special courts and did not have the right to speak in their own defence; political offenders were not tried by the new jury system, while peasants were tried in special courts and were thus still being treated in matters of the law as a class apart. The Secret Police were still able to arrest whom they pleased and such persons had no guarantee that they would receive proper trial.

To sum up, the main result of Alexander's reforms was to give Russians a slight taste of freedom and responsibility and to make them even more aware than before of the very limited nature of the reforms and the continued lack of real freedom. Again, many of the gentry never forgave Alexander for his liberation of the serfs, while the serfs themselves were dissatisfied by the new money burdens which Emancipation had imposed on them. We must remember, too, that Emancipation did nothing to solve the greatest problem of all as far as the peasant was concerned—his need for sufficient land to support himself and his family. A "land hunger" of a serious kind existed in Russia in these years. The most land a peasant could receive under the Edict of Emancipation was $17\frac{1}{2}$ acres, but in fact the majority received only between 8 and 12 acres. Only the barest existence (and sometimes not that, for famine and starvation were common) could be gained from such meagre holdings.

**Nihilism.** In view of the disappointment and frustration produced by Alexander's half-measures, it is no wonder that many of the younger generation of the 1860's began to take to various creeds of revolutionary violence. One of the earliest of these movements was known as Nihilism, derived from the Latin word "nihil", meaning "nothing". The ideas of the Nihilists were intensely destructive. Everything from the past was to be swept away before a new society

could be born. Everything that was not based on reason and science was to be destroyed. Such a doctrine meant that the Nihilists had declared war upon all the traditions of Russia and especially upon the Czar himself and the Russian Orthodox Church. The Nihilists gradually took to methods of terrorism to overthrow the Czar and his society. They directed their efforts especially against Alexander II and in 1866 made an attempt to assassinate him. The result of this attempt was that Alexander turned to severely repressive methods. As the Nihilists were mainly composed of young educated men from the universities, Alexander restricted entrance to the universities to those who could be proved "reliable", while new rules were introduced for the press by which editors who did not disclose the names of their contributors were to be dismissed. Increasing numbers of arrests, imprisonments and exiles to Siberia marked the later years of the reign of Alexander II. The Secret Police became increasingly brutal in their methods and torture became the regular method of extorting "confessions" and betrayals from their victims.

**Socialism and Anarchism.** A new line of attack on Czarism now developed. This was the Socialist movement, which aimed at the destruction of Czarism and the establishment of a truly democratic state in Russia under the effective control of the whole people. The Paris Commune of 1870 gave inspiration to the pioneers of Socialism in Russia. Another important force with which the Russian socialists were closely linked was the Socialist International, with its headquarters in Switzerland. The early socialist movement in Russia was in the main controlled by Lavroff, whose methods were educational and propagandist. He urged his followers to go amongst the Russian peasantry and educate them in the creed of Socialism. These methods were essentially non-violent. On the other hand, a more violent wing of the movement was under the domination of Michael Bakunin, the anarchist, who preached the doctrine of an immediate peasant revolution.

For some years the peaceful policy of Lavroff prevailed amongst the Russian socialists and hundreds of eager young socialists went out from the towns into the countryside to preach the new doctrines to the peasants. But these young people, derived mainly from the educated classes of the towns, found the Russian peasants unresponsive to their propaganda and full of distrust of people so very different from themselves. The peasants still clung to the idea that the Czar, the great father of his people, could be the reformer of all things and could solve their problems. This naïve, childlike faith in the Czar was the greatest obstacle to the progress of new ideas amongst the peasantry. Of course, many of the peasants were too abysmally ignorant and poverty-stricken even to listen to the propagandists from the towns. There was also the fear of the police, whose methods were ruthless.

**Terrorism.** As a result of the failure of more peaceful methods to make any headway, an atmosphere of dismay and frustration spread among the would-be reformers. Out of this frustration there arose more desperate and violent movements. Among the most important of these was the secret society known as "The Will of the People" under the leadership of Mikhailoff. By violence and terror against government officials and the Czar himself they hoped to force the Czar to give up his despotic rule. One of the most famous incidents of this terrorist campaign occurred in 1878 when a young woman terrorist, Vera Zasulich, shot and wounded the chief of the St. Petersburg police, General Trepoff. At her trial she denounced and exposed the brutal torturing and flogging of political prisoners by the secret police, and the jury acquitted her. Outside the court, the police attempted to rearrest her, but she was protected by a sympathetic crowd and made good her escape.

Alexander's reply to the terrorists was to use force against force. It has been estimated that between the years 1863 and 1874 more than 150,000 persons were exiled to the criminal settlements of Siberia. Alexander II also appealed to the Zemstvos to give him support against the terrorists, but in reply the members of the Zemstvos formed their own association or union and demanded the setting up of an elected parliament or "duma". But even this warning that the more intelligent and educated of his subjects throughout Russia were thoroughly dissatisfied with his rule had no effect upon the Czar other than that of making him even more obstinately opposed to the idea of an elected parliament with a government (and Czar) responsible to it.

**Alexander II and Poland.** Alexander II also had trouble with the Poles in 1863. They had been encouraged by the Czar's reforms in Russia, by the weakened position of Russia after the Crimean War, and by the success of the Italians in throwing off the Austrian yoke. Alexander tried hard to win the loyalty of the Poles by reopening Warsaw University, by reinstating Polish as the official language and by replacing many Russian officials by Poles. But these concessions could never reconcile the Polish nobility to dependence on Russia, especially as they had no hope of gaining from the Czar the coveted territories of Lithuania and the Ukraine. Secret revolutionary committees were set up in various parts of Poland, and in 1863 an insurrection broke out. The sorry story of 1831 was repeated. It was essentially a revolt of the nobility and their immediate supporters. The peasants, who had been freed from serfdom by Alexander on better terms even than the Russian serfs themselves, gave little support to the movement. As in 1831, there were divisions between the moderate Whites and extremely nationalist Reds. Once again, the Russian forces crushed the rising with ease. Alexander now divided Poland into provinces under Russian governors and the central government was transferred to St. Petersburg itself. The Poles were now more completely under Russian control than ever before in their history.

In the last years of his reign Alexander II was hunted by the terrorists with a persistence which at last resulted in his assassination in the streets of St. Petersburg in the year 1881.

**Alexander III, 1881–1894.** The assassination of his father only strengthened the determination of Alexander III to intensify the police action against revolutionaries and reformers of all kinds. The old policy of execution, torture and exile was taken up with renewed ferocity. The new Czar was determined to go back on the reforms of Alexander II. The universities were more strictly supervised than ever and many liberal teachers were dismissed. The secondary schools were entirely denied to children of the working class and of the peasants. Other measures included the suppression of fourteen newspapers, the appointment from the nobility of new officials known as Land Captains with despotic powers over all other local officials, whom they could dismiss at will. Another significant change was an alteration made in the composition of the Zemstvos or local councils set up by Alexander II. The Land Captains were now automatically members of the Zemstvos, while certain members of the "intelligentsia", such as school-teachers and doctors, who were regarded as "unreliable", were now prevented from standing as candidates. In the Baltic provinces of Esthonia, Latvia and Courland the Russian language was made compulsory and in Poland it was made a compulsory subject in all the schools. There also occurred new and ominous changes in religious policy. Alexander III's aim was to ensure that the Russian Orthodox Church had no competitors for the spiritual control of the people, and in the Baltic provinces especially the Lutheran protestant church was heavily persecuted and every possible obstacle put in its way. The persecution of the Jews was deliberately embarked upon, partly because many of the revolutionary leaders were Jewish and partly because it was a convenient way of turning the attention of the Russian people from the real state of things. Anti-semitism became a definite "policy" at this time, and terrible "pogroms" or massacres of the Jews were deliberately instigated by the police.

Despite some attempts of the government to improve the condition of the town workers by a number of factory acts, the reign of Alexander III shows the very worst aspects of Czarism. Religious and racial persecution, police terror of the most ruthless type, the suppression of liberty in the schools and universities and the "Russification" of the Baltic Provinces, Poland and Finland. The Czar went in terror of his life, surrounding himself with a permanent bodyguard of police, and shutting himself away in the royal palace without any personal contact with the ministers of his own government. On account of executions and exile, the ranks of the would-be assassins had, according to some authorities, been reduced to about forty persons in the reign of Alexander III, but this small group was sufficient to make the last years of the Czar resemble those of a somewhat desperate and hunted animal. He succeeded, however, in dying a natural death.

**Nicholas II (1894–1917).** The last of the Russian Czars began his reign by an open declaration to his subjects against any idea of a Russian parliament. "I will," he said, "preserve the principle of Autocracy as firmly and unswervingly as my late father."

Nicholas II was kindly in his personal relations, but narrow and bigoted in all his political ideas. He was the very last man to be able to grasp and deal with the social problems of Russia. He suffered the fate of a man who had the ideas of an autocrat but not a trace of the character required to be one. We must, however, consider more important matters at this point than the character and actions of Nicholas II.

**Changes in the Reform Movement in Russia.** After the assassination of Alexander II in 1881 (see page 251), and the ruthless measures taken by his successor against the revolutionary leaders, the more intelligent of the reformers began to see that terrorism was a hopeless weapon for the achievement of progress. They also came to realise the futility of attempting to get the revolutionary changes they wanted by appealing to the peasants who clung to their age-old faith in the Czar. Many of the revolutionaries had hoped that a revolution could be brought about by the educated classes in alliance with the peasants and that it was not necessary for Russia to develop a working class or proletariat of the towns under a capitalist system such as existed in Western Europe. Now, however, it became an article of faith with many of them that Russia needed a capitalist system which would inevitably produce an underpaid and discontented body of working people in the towns. These workers, it was argued, would be a stronger force for revolution than the peasants, for they worked together in masses, would be more educated than the peasants and would therefore be more open to revolutionary propaganda against Czarism. It became clear, therefore, that Russia needed a capitalist system to produce the conditions which would lead to some form of revolutionary change.

**Industrial Development in Russia.** This very development of a capitalist industry was in fact taking place rapidly in the last part of the nineteenth century in Russia. In 1855, at the end of the reign of Nicholas I, there was only one railway line in the whole of Russia, but during the reign of Alexander II railway construction went ahead rapidly and this in its turn aided industrial development. There was a drift from the countryside to the big towns and a town working class developed. Again, after 1893 and the alliance with France, a huge amount of French money was loaned to Russia for industrial development. By 1914 there were over 3,000,000 factory workers in Russia and she was fifth in order of production among the industrial nations.

**Sergei Witte.** The man most responsible for Russia's industrial development at this time was Sergei Witte who was appointed Minister of Finance and Commerce in 1892. Witte believed that Russia would always remain a lesser nation if she was mainly agricultural. He wanted Russia to become self-sufficient and for this ultimate purpose she would have to rely for a time on foreign assistance. He was the main organiser of foreign loans on which he guaranteed high rates of interest to French, English and German investors. He was responsible for raising the funds for the construction of the Trans-Siberian railway begun in 1892 and completed ten years later. As a result of Witte's policy the great industries of cotton, wool, coal, iron and steel made considerable progress in these years. Large manufacturing towns developed with masses of workers, and the same social movements arose as in Western Europe—demands for better working conditions, for the right of trade union organisation, for better wages. The clash between the new Russian capitalists and the workers developed as the revolutionaries had anticipated. These new capitalists themselves were far from being contented with the policies of Alexander III and Nicholas II, and they demanded a share in the government which was still dominated by the old civil servants and the nobility of the land. This development of Russian capitalism was, therefore, a most important change in the history of Russia in the reigns of Alexander III and Nicholas II.

**Political Developments in the Reign of Nicholas II.** These new conditions in the towns gave rise to new political movements, the most important of which for the future was the Russian Social Democratic Labour Party formed in 1898. One of the leaders of the new party was Vladimir Ulianov, known under the pseudonym of Lenin. Another prominent member of the party was Leon Trotsky who, together with Lenin and Stalin, was to play an important role in the Revolution of 1917. They all adopted the revolutionary theories of Karl Marx, although there were to be differences among the leadership as to the exact way in which the Communist revolution could be brought about in Russia and in Europe.

The Russian police began the arrest of the leaders of the Social Democratic Party as soon as it was formed, and it was decided to carry on its main propaganda from abroad. For this purpose Lenin became the editor of the revolutionary newspaper *Iskra* (the *Spark*) which he edited and published in England for distribution through underground channels in Russia. At a meeting of the party held in 1903 a split occurred between the Bolsheviks (literally the "majority") led by Lenin and the Mensheviks (the "minority"). Lenin and the Bolsheviks wished for a closely disciplined party comprised of active workers in the movement, whereas the Mensheviks wanted a mass party consisting of both active and non-active or sympathising members on the lines of the Western socialist parties. The Mensheviks were also opposed to the ruthless determination of Lenin to enforce a rigid discipline upon all members however small the majority on any decision might be.

Another extremely active party at this time was the Social Revolutionary Party which believed in the necessity of a peasant rising before anything else, and continued the practice of assassination. Another party was that of the Liberators or Liberals who aimed at a parliamentary system for Russia on Western lines and had great support among the professional classes. They saw a parliamentary system as a safeguard against the proletarian revolution which the Bolsheviks were working for. The members of the Zemstvos gave considerable support to this party.

Strikes among important sections of the Russian workers became far more frequent after the formation of the Social Democratic Labour Party, for the strike was not only the weapon of the party for forcing improvements in wages and living conditions, but also the means of educating the workers in the true meaning of the class struggle in the approved Marxist manner. The concentration of industrial workers in very large factories and in a few areas made such action the more effective. The government of Nicholas II was alarmed at the growing influence of the Social Democrats over the workers and attempted to combat this influence by sending secret agents into the factories to form trade unions and thus control the movement themselves, and at the same time ensure the arrest of real Social Democratic members. In order to get the support of the workers, however, it was sometimes necessary for these agents to foment strikes, a ruse which the workers soon discovered.

**The Russo-Japanese War, 1904–1905.** The difficulties of Nicholas II were tremendously increased by the disastrous war against Japan which broke out in 1904. The antagonism between these two countries dated back to 1895. In that year the Japanese waged a successful war against China and gained control of Korea and the naval base of Port Arthur. Russia, whose ambitions in Manchuria and the Far East generally were as great as those of Japan, formed an alliance with France and Germany which forced Japan to give up her conquest of Port Arthur, and in 1898 the Russians themselves leased the port from China. The Japanese imperialists were naturally infuriated at these developments and they concentrated even more vigorously than before on building up a powerful Japanese army and navy with the deliberate intention of revenge against Russia. In 1902 they made the treaty with Great Britain by which the latter would stand aside if Japan were at war with only one power, while if two powers were at war with Japan then Britain would come to her assistance. The way thus became clear for Japan to act.

In the years up to 1904 Russian trade and Russian arms had greatly increased in Manchuria and in Korea. The Japanese demanded in 1904 that the Czar should abandon these interests and come to a new agreement with Japan. The Czar Nicholas would have been well advised to negotiate with the Japanese, but he was encouraged by his more aggressive advisers to refuse all concessions, and he saw in the possibility of success against the Japanese a means of restoring the credit of his government at home. But Russia was not prepared. Her Far Eastern forces were weak in numbers and in training, both on sea and land.

The Japanese answer to the Czar's refusal to make concessions was a surprise attack on the Russian fleet at Port Arthur on February 8, 1904. The war was one long disaster for the Russians. Bad leadership and inefficiency, as in the case of the Crimea, made the heroism of the ordinary soldier and sailor utterly futile and led to colossal casualties. In the one battle on land which the Russians were actually winning, the commander lost courage and ordered a retreat. The Japanese besieged Port Arthur and captured it in January, 1905, the Russian Far Eastern Fleet was shattered by Admiral Togo, and on land the battle of Mukden resulted in a victory for the Japanese, who inflicted 90,000 casualties on the Russians and took 40,000 prisoners. In a last effort to retrieve the situation the Russians brought the whole of their Baltic fleet round from Europe into the Pacific, only to lose every ship except a few small vessels in the battle of Tsushima in May, 1905. After this disaster, the Russian position was hopeless, and the Czar accepted an offer by President Theodore Roosevelt of the U.S.A. to mediate. By the Treaty of Portsmouth (New Hampshire, U.S.A.), 1905, the Japanese gained control of Port Arthur and of Korea, while the Russians were compelled to move their forces from Manchuria.

**Effects of the War on the Internal State of Russia.** The results of the war were seen at once in a vast increase of discontent throughout Russia. The Russo-Japanese war was a disaster, not only to Russian arms but to the whole system of government which the Czar embodied. In 1904 the ruthless Minister of the Interior, Plehve, was assassinated by social revolutionaries, and in 1906 the same fate befell the Czar's uncle, the Grand Duke Sergius.

The union of the Zemstvos now put forward a number of important demands, including a guarantee by Nicholas of the rights of free speech and association, of fair trial and an end to the ruthless practices of the secret police. Above all, they demanded the calling of a properly elected Russian Parliament or Duma. In addition to these demands by the liberals, the working-class movement under the control of the Social Democrats began an intense campaign of strikes and demonstrations against the Czar in the big cities. Disorder broke out in the countryside and the gentry and government officials of a reactionary type were set upon and murdered.

**Red Sunday.** An event which intensified the general discontent occurred in St. Petersburg on January 22, 1905. A certain priest, Father Gapon, who had been one of the organisers of the government-approved trade unions among the workers (see page 254), decided that, in order to maintain his influence with the workers and in order to counteract the growing influence of the Social Democrats, he would lead a great procession of protest to the Czar's Winter Palace. The huge procession carried banners demanding an eight-hour day in the factories, improved wages and political freedom. The demonstration was entirely peaceful, but the answer it received was a series of devastating volleys from the soldiers guarding the Winter Palace and many were killed and wounded. Father Gapon himself escaped, but was killed by revolutionaries in 1906 because they suspected him of having been a government spy.

The results of this shocking affair were an intensification of the strike movement throughout Russia and a great increase in the influence of the Marxist Social Democrats over the workers.

The Zemstvos now took up again their plea for a representative parliament more urgently than ever, and the Czar could no longer resist the force of the demands made upon him. But even now he attempted deception and half measures, for when the new constitution was announced it only provided for a Duma for consultation with the Czar, but having no powers to introduce laws on its own account. Even the vote in the elections was to be restricted. For example, no factory worker was to receive the franchise.

**The General Strike and the October Manifesto, 1905.** The Social Democrats' reply to the Czar was to call a General Strike of the workers. The Soviets, or Workers' Councils, now made their appearance in the great industrial centres and were especially powerful in Moscow and St. Petersburg. Many people of the middle and professional classes—lawyers, schoolmasters, doctors—joined the strike movement. The pattern of 1917 began to take shape.

In December, 1905, the Soviets in Moscow began an armed uprising which was suppressed by the troops.

The very weight of the movement against him forced the Czar to make further concessions. By the October Manifesto of 1905, the Czar promised freedom of speech and organisation and the calling of an elected parliament which would have effective control over the laws. The vote was to be given to the workers and the professional classes. But even now, before the elections were held, the Czar issued further edicts which declared that he alone had control of the armed forces and of foreign policy. Moveover, the electoral laws were far from democratic. There was an elaborate system of indirect election, consisting of three stages. The first voters decided electors who elected further electors who finally elected the members of the Duma. The number of electors in the constituencies varied in opposite proportion to the size of the population. Thus the wage-earners who numbered over 12,000,000 returned only 112 electors, but the landlord class numbering about 200,000 chose over 2,500 electors. The whole system was thus designed to give overwhelming influence to the wealthier classes.

The First Russian Duma met in May, 1906. A majority of Liberals (or "Cadets") was returned and a dispute began with the Czar over the edicts. Attempts were made to force him to give the Parliament control of all affairs of State, including taxation. The Czar's reply was to dissolve the Duma and order fresh elections.

**The Elections for the Second Duma.** The situation which now developed showed the real forces at work in Russia. The police under Stolypin, the Minister of the Interior, took a direct hand in the elections. Many candidates were not allowed to stand on one pretext or another, many voters were struck off the registers and Jewish voters were threatened with their lives if they even dared to exercise their right to vote. In some places the reactionary gentry and the police actually imprisoned candidates whom they opposed.

Almost as soon as the Second Duma met in 1907, the Czar's government demanded that the Social Democrats be prevented from taking their seats (they had won about fifty), on the grounds that they were disloyal to the throne. The Duma was about to consider this demand when the Czar again dissolved it and ordered further elections. At the same time the government altered the law relating to the elections in such a way that many members of the Second Duma were not able to stand as candidates. The Social Democrats were prohibited altogether and the Liberals or Cadets were reduced to a minority in the Third Duma (1907-1912). The majority was now under the control of those politicians who were in general willing to follow the Czar.

**The Third Duma.** The work of the Third Duma is closely bound up with the activities of the Prime Minister, Stolypin. In many ways his policies were oppressive and unpopular. He deprived Finland of her last vestiges of independence and ruthlessly suppressed the Ukrainian national movement. He was also responsible for heavy persecution of the Jews. He depended on the support of the Nationalists in the Duma, but as this group was directly financed by the Czar's government Stolypin was little more than a ruthless stooge of the Court. During these years there were constant peasant rebellions and attacks on the property of the landed gentry. Stolypin's reply was to set up courts-martial in the countryside, and more than 4,500 persons were executed in these five years.

On the constructive side, Stolypin wished to put an end to the old peasant commune. He gave facilities for the purchase or renting by the peasantry of land from the gentry and the creation of compact holdings in place of the old communal strip system. He saw the individual ownership of land as a guarantee against unrest and revolution. The results were to be seen after the Bolshevik revolution of 1917 when the kulaks or richer peasants who mainly benefited from Stolypin's policy proved the backbone of resistance to the Communist Party in the countryside. However, Stolypin's cruelty and ruthlessness led to his assassination in 1911.

Thus the first attempts at parliamentary government in Russia were a grotesque failure. Police terror, intimidation of voters, pogroms against the Jews, disqualification of candidates and voters—all these methods were employed by the wealthy supporters of the old régime. The Czar and his supporters were determined that anything like a parliamentary system should be introduced entirely on their own terms, which were neither liberal nor democratic.

The result of this failure was that the workers of the towns increasingly placed their hopes on the revolutionary overthrow of the Czar. The Social Democrats prepared more actively than ever for the day of the proletarian revolution. Lenin had already denounced the Duma experiments as a fraud intended to deceive the workers. The Czar's policy had also turned against him large sections of the educated professional classes. These conditions of general unrest were already in existence when Russia entered the Great War of 1914–1918.

# chapter fifteen

# THE BACKGROUND TO THE FIRST WORLD WAR, 1914–1918

**Introductory. Economic Changes in the Late Nineteenth Century.**
By 1870 important economic changes were occurring in all the principal states of Europe. In place of the small concerns of the early
years of the century the modern "big business" was developing
rapidly. In Germany (page 166), in France, in Italy and even in backward Russia a new class of industrialist, supported by powerful bank-
ing interests, was pressing forward with the expansion of coal production, iron and steel, cotton and woollen cloth output, and transportation by land and sea. One business absorbed another either by
agreement or successful competition, and larger concerns were formed
until they took on the character of monopolies or "cartels" controf-
ling most of the production of a single industry or even a series of
industries linked together. These monopolies formed in one country
then faced the competition of similar great concerns formed in others,
and international rivalry intensified. This type of competition led to
a new struggle to gain sources of raw materials and fresh overseas
markets for the products of the home countries. In the rivalry for
overseas possessions, for colonies, for "protectorates" the governments of the various countries directly intervened in support of their
own industrialists. The rivalries between states intensified as the
century went on.

Travel and communications speeded up, and more and more unknown areas of the world were explored and claimed by the nations.
This process went on at such a pace up to 1914 that the whole of
what in 1850 was still known as "darkest Africa" had been explored
and the entire continent, with the exception of Abyssinia, had been
divided up among the European states. In the Far East and the
Pacific a similar expansion of the trade and "interests" of the European powers took place.

This expansion and competition was, in the main, a friendly business—at least, it involved very little warfare—until there was scarcely
any territory left to share out among the Great Powers. This was the
position reached by 1914.

**The Great Powers and Africa.** The opening up of Africa was the

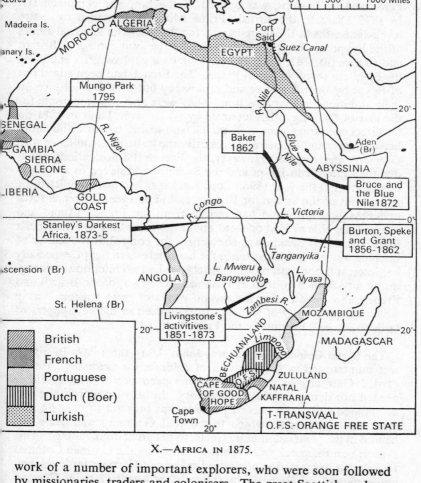

X.—AFRICA IN 1875.

work of a number of important explorers, who were soon followed
by missionaries, traders and colonisers. The great Scottish explorer
David Livingstone penetrated the vast areas of central Africa, covering more than 8,000 miles in his various journeys. Beginning in 1853,
he followed the course of the Zambesi River, discovering the Victoria
Falls and reaching the East coast near the mouth of the river. By
further expeditions in 1858 and 1866 he managed, before his death
in 1873, to map the greater part of Central Africa.

In 1869 the Suez Canal, the great project of the Frenchman Ferdinand de Lesseps, was opened by the Emperor Napoleon III. In 1875 Disraeli, the British Prime Minister, managed to secure seven-sixteenths of the share-capital for Britain. The financial affairs of the Egyptian Government came under the joint control of Britain and France till 1881, when Britain took over control, after subduing the Egyptian revolt of Arabi Pasha. The French had been edged out of Egypt by British money and diplomacy but they did not give up their ambitions in that direction. They were able to compensate for the loss of their Egyptian interests by taking over Tunis in 1881 on the direct encouragement of Bismarck who wished to cause difficulties between Italy and France and thus drive the Italians into alliance with Germany and Austria. However, the French did not entirely abandon their interest in Egypt and the Sudan, and this led to a dangerous incident in the year 1898. Lord Kitchener had just completed the reconquest of the Sudan for Britain, and in that year a French force under Major Marchand had moved from the French Congo and reached the Nile at Fashoda—at about the same time as Kitchener's force. As far as Britain was concerned, the control of the source of the Nile was of vital importance for her interests in Egypt, especially her interest in the cotton crop. Kitchener had no intention of recognising any French control at Fashoda. The two forces, British and French, faced each other for several weeks of great tension, during which the possibility of war was freely voiced in the newspapers of both countries. Eventually the French retired.

**The Berlin Colonial Conference, 1884.** Until the 1880's Bismarck was uninterested in the question of colonies for Germany. He regarded Germany as essentially a European power which neither needed nor demanded further territory. In his own words, she was a "satiated state". However, pressure was brought to bear on him from various quarters which feared that Germany was being left behind in the great colonial scramble, to her great disadvantage. This pressure on Bismarck was organised chiefly by the German Colonial League, an organisation composed mainly of German business men and explorers, of whom the most important was the famous German explorer Karl Peters. Bismarck was anxious to avoid involving Germany in quarrels with other states over African colonies, for such quarrels might upset his precious system of alliances by which he had isolated France. He was therefore most anxious to secure a peaceful division of Africa. For this purpose he called a conference in 1884 at Berlin of representatives of all the leading powers. At this conference

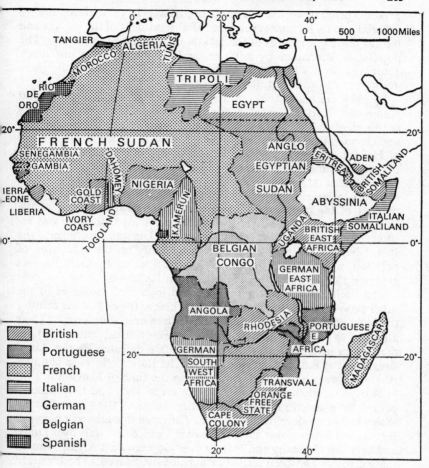

XI.—AFRICA IN 1914.

the great Powers decided on their main "spheres of influence" in Africa and attempted to settle such questions as fair trade practices and the treatment of the native populations. Various "gentlemen's agreements" were made on these questions. By a decision of the conference, the Congo Free State was set up mainly under Belgian control, and a Belgian monopoly in rubber and tin was quickly established. However, the Congo Free State became almost the personal property of King Leopold of the Belgians, and his reputation suffered greatly by later revelations of ill-treatment of the natives and the adoption of methods of forced labour amounting to slavery. The population decreased by millions, and conditions were not much improved until after the death of Leopold in 1909, when Belgium took over the administration.

In 1884 Germany took over South-West Africa, Togoland and Kameron. Karl Peters also conducted negotiations with various native chiefs of East Africa by which Germany gained Tanganyika and German East Africa. In 1890, Germany, in return for the cession of Heligoland, recognised the British protectorate of Zanzibar and the adjacent mainland, while Britain recognised German claims to German East Africa.

British expansion in Africa in 1850–1900 was undertaken by a number of big commercial concerns which had the blessing of the British Colonial Office. The British East Africa Company was responsible for the opening up of Kenya and Uganda. In Nigeria the Royal Niger Company built up its prosperity on the extraction of palm-oil, while the South Africa Company set up by Cecil Rhodes explored the territory which later became Rhodesia.

The Italians, lacking the military and industrial resources of the other powers, were late in the field, but before the end of the century they had gained a strong foothold in Eritrea and Somaliland. Their attempts to conquer Abyssinia were, however, a calamitous failure, the Italian invading army being completely defeated by the Abyssinians at the Battle of Adowa, 1896. The Italian efforts to conquer Abyssinia were only resumed in 1934 in the time of Mussolini.

This phase of the division of Africa up to 1900 had been accompanied by a certain amount of friction between the Great Powers which had never developed into war. The main trouble arose between Britain and France over Egypt, between France and Italy over Tunis, and between Germany and Britain over German East Africa. But all these disputes had been settled or judiciously ignored. There was, in fact, room for everyone in Africa.

**The Far East and the Pacific.** A similar expansion of trading and colonial power went on in the Far East. In that part of the world the main Powers involved were Russia, Japan, Britain, Germany, the U.S.A. and France. Britain's interests had been strengthened by the policy of Lord Palmerston who had forced the Chinese to grant Britain special trading facilities in the five treaty ports, and who at the same time had gained a lease of Hong Kong. In 1874 a British expedition occupied the Fiji Islands. Soon afterwards the Germans and Americans divided Samoa between them. Also in 1884 Germany gained control of part of New Guinea and followed this by the purchase from Spain of the Caroline Islands.

British governments in these years regarded Russian expansion in the Far East as a much more serious challenge to our trading rights in China than the activities of Germany, with whom Britain was on good terms. In 1860 Russia founded the port of Vladivostock and by 1902 had completed the Trans-Siberian Railway. These developments led to increasing Russian trade with Manchuria and North China. This Far Eastern policy of Russia arose from her failure to break up the Turkish Empire and make headway in the Balkans.

Japan was also entering on the colonial scramble. In the 1850's a revolution had occurred in her political and economic life. Not only did she open her ports to foreign traders after hundreds of years of exclusion, but her whole system of government was radically changed. She introduced a parliamentary system which was similar to that of Bismarck's constitution for the German Empire, and also developed great industries on modern lines. The real power was concentrated in the hands of the civil service and the armed services. A few great wealthy families also had considerable influence on policy. These wealthy families were naturally interested in securing new markets abroad for Japanese products and in gaining sources of raw materials. The Japanese army was organised by German, and her navy by British, officers. In the space of twenty years the armed forces of Japan passed from bows and arrows to rifles and field guns, and the country passed from feudalism to capitalism, from the complete despotism of the Emperor to a superficial imitation of Western liberal democracy.

The first pressures exercised by the new Japan were against China, whose suzerainty over Korea she was determined to break. Japan also sought to gain control of Formosa and Port Arthur. In all these objectives she was mainly successful. But no sooner had China been defeated than the Japanese had to reckon with the opposition of other Powers interested in the Far East, and a combination of Russia, France and Germany forced her to modify the treaty with China. In fact, she was forced to give up Port Arthur which, as we have seen (page 255), went to Russia in 1898. The Russian government also made loans to the Chinese by which they rapidly paid off the indemnity which the Japanese had imposed upon them. This intervention by Russia led Japan to concentrate on the further strengthening of her armed power for the day of revenge. The Russo-Japanese War of 1904–1905 was the result of this policy. The Japanese alliance with Britain in 1902 aided Japan in her aims, for it made almost certain that she would be fighting Russia only.

**The Pre-War Alliances.** The year 1870 marked a turning point in the relationships of the European states to one another. The defeat of France by Prussia left the French isolated, while British policy was already turning away from continental affairs. For the next thirty years Britain was more concerned with Imperial problems and internal social reform, with the one exception of the Congress of Berlin, 1878.

After 1870 Bismarck built up a system of alliances to suit the interests of German power and to keep France in the isolation into which her defeat had forced her. He was successful in his aims, except that difficulties with Russia were continually arising. By the time of Bismarck's dismissal by the Kaiser William II in 1890 it had become obvious that permanent friendship with Russia was impossible.

**The Dual Alliance of France and Russia, 1893.** In 1893 an alliance was formed between France and Russia, the first alliance which was in any sense a counterweight to the Triple Alliance of Austria, Germany and Italy. This was in many ways a most remarkable development and it is necessary to consider the various factors which brought it about. On the surface, it appeared that France and Russia had every reason to remain apart rather than form a diplomatic alliance. In the first place, France was the only Republic among the Great Powers and was generally regarded as the very centre of revolutionary influences in Europe—at least, her record in 1789, in 1848 and during the Paris Commune of 1871 seemed to justify that viewpoint. Certain it was that the autocratic Czars of Russia could scarcely be expected to look with favour upon the Republic. Again, the defeat of France in 1870 had shown her great military weakness, which made her of little value as an ally.

Certain important developments changed all this, however, and led to the alliance of France and Russia in 1893. These developments were

(1) The increasing antagonism of Germany and Russia, especially after the Berlin Congress of 1878 when Britain, Germany and Austria had united against Russia.

(2) The dismissal of Bismarck by William II in 1890 removed the only German statesman who stood any chance of keeping Germany on good terms with Russia. William II now deliberately ignored Russia and made no efforts to keep on good terms with her.

(3) The attitude of the Kaiser to Britain had further important results.

In 1888 the Russian government, pursuing the plans of economic development proposed by Sergei Witte, attempted to obtain loans from Germany, but the Kaiser's government prevented these loans being subscribed and Bismarck closed the Berlin Bourse to Russian loans. Russia then turned to France, and a huge French loan was, in fact, over-subscribed. Many more French loans were granted to Russia up to the outbreak of the Great War in 1914. The Russian Czars were grateful for this assistance, for it enabled them to keep their government from bankruptcy and thus fend off the nightmare of revolution. This development was also favourable to France, for the Russian government used part of these loans to buy armaments from France herself. In July, 1891, a significant event occurred when a French Fleet visited the Russian naval base of Kronstadt in the Baltic and the Czar Alexander III stood at attention, bareheaded, while a Russian band played "the Marseillaise"!

By the terms of the Dual Alliance of 1893, in case of an attack on France or Russia by a third power (Germany was clearly meant), then they would support each other.

**Results of the Dual Alliance.** What Bismarck had striven to avoid had thus been brought about. In case of war, Germany had now both an Eastern and Western front to consider. France had moved out of isolation and the position of Russia was also greatly strengthened. But the Dual Alliance had other important results, especially on the foreign policy of Great Britain. Britain was now more isolated than before, and, in the view of some observers, was now in *dangerous* isolation. Many observers in Britain thought that the Dual Alliance was directed more against Britain than Germany, for France and Britain were on very bad terms in these years, over Egypt and the Sudan—a state of affairs which led on to the Fashoda incident of 1898 (see page 262). British interests were also being challenged by Russia in Persia, Afghanistan and in the Far East.

Another event which emphasised the critical isolation of Britain was the Armenian Massacres of 1896 in Turkey. In that year the Turkish government carried out a frightful persecution of the

Armenian minority in its dominions, six thousand Armenians being killed in Constantinople alone. This barbarous action was a flagrant violation of promises of good conduct given by the Turks at the Congress of Berlin in 1878. In England, Mr. Gladstone came out of his retirement to lead another of his political campaigns against the Turks and to demand that the British government take action. But when the British government approached the other Powers on this question, there was no response. The moral authority of Britain counted for nothing.

Another disturbing fact for Britain was the attitude adopted by other countries when war broke out in South Africa between British and Boers (1899). Public opinion in most European countries was strongly against Britain. At the time of the Jameson raid (1896) Kaiser William II had sent a telegram to the Boer President, Kruger, in which he congratulated the Boers on having repelled this attack without foreign aid. This telegram implied that Germany was prepared to give aid to the Dutch against Britain in South Africa. During the Boer War, Kruger did not officially accept German aid, but British naval vessels intercepted a number of German ships which were carrying contraband of war to the Boers.

All these considerations made the British governments of the years 1895 to 1907 gradually turn from the old policy of "splendid isolation" which was no longer so splendid, but was now endangering England's security. But where was Britain to turn? Russia, Germany, France—all of them were most unfriendly to Britain in the late years of the nineteenth century.

**Britain and Germany.** The first efforts made by British statesmen towards a foreign alliance were directed to Germany. This is not so surprising as it seems at first sight. Britain was on far worse terms with France and Russia than with Germany. In fact, Britain had co-operated with Germany over Africa, and in 1878 Bismarck had supported Britain against Russia. Queen Victoria was also strongly in favour of friendship between Britain and Germany.

The British Foreign Secretary in 1901 was Lord Lansdowne, and his approaches to Germany were strongly supported by the Colonial Secretary, Joseph Chamberlain. But Kaiser William II showed only lukewarm interest in the proceedings. All his actions seemed to indicate that he regarded Britain as the future enemy. In 1900, at the very time that the British soundings for an alliance were being made, the German battle fleet was doubled by the new Navy Law and the Kaiser and his advisers deliberately engineered an outburst

FIG. 34.—KAISER WILLIAM II AT TANGIER, 1905. (*See page* 271.)

of Anglophobia (hatred of England) in Germany in order to get the Navy Law accepted by the Reichstag. At the same time the Kaiser was making a number of aggressive statements which could only be interpreted as attacks on Britain's naval supremacy. "Neptune with the trident," he declared, "is a symbol that we have new tasks to perform . . . and that trident must be in our hands." The Kaiser was also intent on pushing on with his plans for the Berlin–Baghdad Railway which would have connected Germany directly with the Middle East. The British Foreign Office came to suspect that the ultimate aim of the Kaiser was to control Egypt and India. In these circumstances, the overtures of Lansdowne and Chamberlain to Germany proved fruitless and Britain turned elsewhere.

**The Anglo-Japanese Alliance, 1902.** One effect on Britain of the German attitude was to make her look for an ally in the Far East who could be relied upon to resist German and Russian expansion in that part of the world. The aims of Japan at that time fitted in well with British objectives, and in 1902 an alliance was signed between the two governments. It provided that Britain would support Japan, if the latter were involved in war in the Far East, against the two other Powers who were attempting to gain economic and military advantages which would turn the balance of power decidedly in their favour. In 1900 a violently nationalist movement had broken out in China, the Boxer Rebellion, and the international force which suppressed it had been put under German command. Britain had agreed to this arrangement on the understanding that Germany would attempt to warn Russia off her policy of Far Eastern expansion, but Germany had done nothing of the kind. In fact, some members of the British government feared that Germany and Russia might combine in the Far East against Britain, and this fear was another reason for the alliance with Japan.

**The Anglo-French Entente, 1904.** But a far more important effect of the Kaiser's refusal of an alliance with Britain was to drive Britain towards an understanding with France. Certain events of the first years of the twentieth century assisted this tendency. Queen Victoria died in 1901 and was succeeded by Edward VII who was suspicious of the Kaiser and was eager to build better relationships between Britain and France. Edward VII was popular with the French people, and in 1903 he paid an official visit to France which was returned by the French Foreign Minister, Delcassé, and by President Loubet. Discussions were held during these visits between representatives of the two governments, and they were agreed on the danger to Britain and France of the somewhat aggressive and unstable Kaiser. "The Kaiser," remarked a French statesman, "is like a cat in a cupboard. He may jump out anywhere." This common fear of German intentions was the main factor in bringing Britain and France closer in foreign policy—a change strongly advocated by Delcassé.

**The "Entente Cordiale", 1904.** The first agreements reached between Britain and France attempted to settle old grievances. Firstly, France agreed to recognise the British occupation of Egypt. Secondly, Britain agreed not to oppose French policy in another important "sphere of influence" in Africa—namely, Morocco. Thirdly, Britain and France would support each other in their policies in Egypt and Morocco against the objections of any other Powers. Fourthly, arrangements were made for regular consultation on naval and military matters between the two governments and for special consultations if they thought that any attack on them by any other Power was about to occur. This was an "entente" or understanding, not an alliance which bound either Power to assist the other automatically in case of war. It was, nevertheless, an obvious counterweight to German power, and made it most unlikely that Britain would stand aside if France and Germany were involved in war. It should be noted that France and Britain had no legal right whatever to make the third arrangement concerning Morocco, for in fact the territory of Morocco had been under the joint supervision of the Great Powers since 1880. This clause in the "entente" was therefore kept secret— a piece of deception typical of the power politics of the pre-1914 vintage. However, the secret leaked out in the next two years, and the Kaiser had much to say about the matter.

**The First Moroccan Crisis, 1905–1906.** As soon as the Kaiser gained information of the secret clause of the Dual Entente, which would have meant the exclusion of German interests from Morocco, he brought the strongest diplomatic pressure to bear on France. Both the Kaiser and his Chancellor von Bülow visited Tangier in 1905 and assured the Sultan of Morocco that Germany would support the independence of Morocco and did not intend to recognise any other agreements. At the same time he demanded the calling of a European Conference on Morocco. The French Foreign Minister, Delcassé, wanted to reject the Kaiser's demand, but the French government eventually agreed to it and Delcassé was dismissed.

**The Conference of Algeciras, 1906.** The Great Powers met in conference at Algeciras in Spain in January, 1906. This conference was the scene of the first direct conflict between Germany and her opponents, and this time the Kaiser came off second best. After lengthy discussion and even lengthier secret intrigues and bargaining, the conference decided that the policing of Morocco should be undertaken by France and Spain, while France should have control of the customs and arms supply. The only concession gained by Germany was an equal control with France, Spain and Britain in the State bank of Morocco, which would also give Germany trading rights. During the conference sessions the three Powers, France, Britain and Russia, had constantly outvoted Germany, and the result was a decided defeat for the Kaiser.

**The Anglo-Russian Agreement and the Formation of the Triple Entente.** The support given by Russia to France and Britain at Algeciras showed clearly that these three Powers were by this time being drawn together against the Kaiser's policy. The French government had for the last two years been trying to persuade the Czar Nicholas II to come to a definite understanding with Britain over disputed questions. The Dual Alliance of France and Russia, as well as the substantial fact of continual French loans to prop up the Czar's government, gave the French considerable influence. Moreover, the Czar was as much opposed to the Berlin–Baghdad project of Germany as was Britain, for the scheme, if successful, would bring German trade and arms right up to the Middle East frontiers of the Russian Empire. On the Russian side, the member of the government most in favour of an agreement with Britain was the foreign minister, Izvolsky. In 1907 he eased Britain's suspicions of Russian Far Eastern policy by making an agreement with Britain's ally, Japan, by which Russia and Japan guaranteed the independence of China. Another factor which influenced Britain favourably was the Russo-Japanese War of 1904–1905, for the victory of Japan showed clearly that she alone was strong enough to prevent Russian expansion in the Far East.

In regard to the Balkan peninsula, Britain was no longer worried about Russian aims, for the small Balkan kingdoms were showing a remarkable independence of all the Great Powers. Besides, it was Germany who was now gaining more and more influence in Turkey, where German officers were already reorganising the army—a fact equally displeasing to Britain and Russia.

All these considerations led on to discussions in 1907 between the representatives of the British and Russian governments. The Anglo-Russian agreement settled certain important causes of dispute between the two countries. Firstly, it settled the century-old dispute over Afghanistan and the Indian frontier; the Russians gave way, and Britain gained control of the foreign policy of Afghanistan, while Britain and Russia exercised equal trading rights in the country. Secondly, in another region of power dispute, namely, Persia, a settlement was arrived at. Russia gained control of northern Persia (containing most of the big towns), while Britain controlled the southeast and the Persian Gulf, where important British oil interests had already established themselves.

By the year 1907 Russia and France, France and Britain, Britain and Russia were all linked by certain important official understandings and the Triple Entente of Britain, France and Russia had come to stay.

**The Second Moroccan Crisis, 1911. The Agadir Incident, 1911.** The Kaiser William II had been thoroughly dissatisfied with the results of the Algeciras Conference, despite official German statements to the contrary. The crisis which came to a head in 1911 nearly brought about a general war.

In 1908 the French secured the election of a new Sultan of Morocco in place of the previous ruler who was not proving very amenable to French policy. Three years later, in 1911, a rising occurred against the new Sultan and in order to suppress it the French forces occupied Fez, the capital, at the Sultan's request. This at once involved a dangerous complication. Germany had already warned the French government that any such move by France was not in line with the Algeciras agreements of 1906, and as soon as the French Army had occupied Fez the Kaiser despatched the gunboat *Panther* to the Moroccan port of Agadir to protect German interests. The Kaiser's attitude was extremely warlike. At first he attempted to negotiate with France alone, but Britain also insisted on being consulted on the Moroccan question in co-operation with France. Preparations for war were now made in Germany, and similar preparations for mobilisation were made in both Britain and France. But once again the Kaiser drew back after a long period of tension in which Europe was on the brink of war. Germany agreed to abandon Morocco to the French in exchange for a part of the French Congo.

This crisis showed clearly the danger of war between the Great Powers. Armies had prepared, naval building programmes in all the principal countries concerned had been suddenly increased, the British Mediterranean Fleet had moved to the North Sea to give protection to the northern shores of France, while the French fleet was concentrated in the Mediterranean.

**The Balkan Problem, 1878–1914.** It was in the Balkan Peninsula that the Great War of 1914–1918 began, and we must trace the course of events in the Balkan Peninsula which led up to it.

In 1908 a section of the Turkish people had themselves attempted to put an end to the corruption and inefficiency of the Empire. This attempt was led by the Young Turk movement and was an outright rebellion against the rule of the corrupt and cruel Abdul Hamid, the real author of the earlier Bulgarian and Armenian Massacres. The Young Turk movement demanded constitutional, liberal government on Western lines and absolute equality between Christians and Mohammedans. On account of the movement's strong support in the Turkish Army, Abdul Hamid was forced to grant a parliamentary system, complete freedom of political organisation and discussion and the return of many exiled politicians. The Young Turk revolution had apparently succeeded with surprising ease.

**The Balkan Wars, 1912–1913.** The immediate result of the "Young Turk" revolution was to encourage the further break-up of the Empire in the Balkans. Bulgaria now declared her complete independence of Turkey and her ruler took the new title of Czar of the Bulgars to symbolise this change. To strengthen her own power along the Adriatic, Austria now ended the "protectorate" of Bosnia and Herzegovina given her by the Treaty of Berlin, 1878, and incorporated the two provinces completely in the Austrian Empire. Austrian administrators and Austrian armed forces now dominated the two provinces, and the tension between Serbia and Austria tremendously increased as a consequence. The annexation therefore had the most serious results in worsening the political atmosphere of Europe. Russia now began preparations for war in support of Serbia. The Turks themselves were far too weak internally to move against Austria, and the Kaiser now came forward with a declaration that if Austria were attacked "a knight in shining armour would be found by her side". This clear alignment of Germany with Austria was sufficient to deter Russia at that time, for she was still suffering from the results of her defeat at the hands of Japan and the internal unrest which it had produced.

The general attack on the weakening power of Turkey now went on apace. In 1912 the Greek statesman Venizelos formed the Balkan League, consisting of Greece, Serbia, Montenegro and Bulgaria. The Italians declared war in September, 1911, attacked the Turkish African province of Tripoli, and very quickly defeated the Turkish forces. While this campaign was going on the Balkan League also declared war against the Turks and gained an overwhelming victory. Every member of the League gained some important victory over the Turks, and when the Serbians and Bulgarians captured Adrianople, Turkey was forced to make peace. During the war, Germany and Austria had stood aside, fully expecting that the Turks would defeat the League, but both governments had gravely miscalculated. By the Treaty of London, Turkey lost nearly the whole of her territory in Europe. But in the same year the Second Balkan War broke out, this time because the Bulgarians claimed a part of Macedonia which the Serbians refused to give up. Bulgaria attacked Serbia but was overwhelmed by a combination of Serbia, Rumania and the Turks, who had seen in this dispute between their former enemies an opportunity of regaining some of their lost European territory. For their part in the war the Turks now regained Adrianople, and Serbia and Greece kept control of those parts of Macedonia which they had gained by the Treaty of London.

**Results of the Balkan Wars.** The most important result of the Balkan Wars was the intensifying of bad relations between the Austrian Empire and Serbia. As we have seen, Austria incorporated Bosnia and Herzegovina in her empire in 1908. The real purpose of this move was to forestall the Serbian ambition of forming a union with these two territories. The Serbs had for long aimed at forming a united Slav state not only incorporating Bosnia and Herzegovina, but also the tiny state of Montenegro (an aim achieved in 1919 by the formation of modern Yugoslavia). There was a strong movement in these small territories for union with Serbia, who could claim, therefore, that she was leading a strong racial and national movement. The Serbs regarded the Austrian move of 1908 as an act of hostility towards themselves and their perfectly justified aims.

Austria had also frustrated Serbian national aims in another direction when, after the Balkan Wars, she had insisted on the formation of Albania as an independent state on the Adriatic, thus closing another stretch of the Adriatic coastline to possible Serbian expansion. It appeared that the Austrians were determined to keep Serbia as a landlocked state, unable to expand her trade and power by the possession of an adequate port on the Adriatic.

However, Serbia emerged victorious from the Balkan Wars, with a greatly enlarged territory through her gains in Macedonia. The Serbs were now confident and aggressive, and Austria was correspondingly alarmed at the effects of Serbian propaganda on the 7,000,000 Serbs and Croats in her own Empire.

XII.—Expansion of Serbia, 1817–1913.

The Austrian Empire also had its own ambitions for expansion in the Balkan Peninsula, and it was not merely a question of "cooping up" the Serbs. The Austrians wanted to gain a continuous territory across the peninsula from the Adriatic to the Aegean Sea, and for this purpose Serbia, who stood directly in their path, would have to be conquered and removed from the map as an independent state. In 1913 the Austrians attempted to gain Italian support for an attack on Serbia, but were unsuccessful. The Kaiser, on the other hand, assured the Austrians of his support if they fought a war with Serbia. Turkey, of course, could be relied upon to support such a move. These aims and calculations of the Austrian government were such as to make war with Serbia almost inevitable at some future time.

**The Sarajevo Assassination, June 28, 1914.** The incident which brought about the fatal clash between Austria and Serbia occurred at Sarajevo, the capital of Bosnia, on June 28, 1914, the occasion of an official visit by the Archduke Ferdinand, heir to the Austrian throne. The Archduke and his wife were assassinated by a Bosnian student as they were being driven over the bridge of the town.

This tragic event presented a clear opportunity for Austria to bring pressure upon the Serbians, who were held responsible for the murder. It is thought by some historians that certain members of the Austrian government who were anxious to begin war against Serbia were quite pleased that the assassination had occurred. But Austria could not act without the clear assurance of German support, and it was not till three weeks later that this was certain. Then, on July 23, 1914, the Austrians sent an ultimatum to the Serbian capital, Belgrade, demanding a satisfactory answer within forty-eight hours. The Austrian ultimatum contained three demands:

(1) That Serbia was to suppress all societies organising anti-Austrian propaganda.
(2) That Serbia was to dismiss all officials to whom Austria objected, and
(3) That Austrian police and officials were to enter Serbia to ensure that these two demands were carried out.

Of these demands the Serbians accepted the first two, but the third they refused to accept. Serbia suggested, however, that the third demand should be the subject of arbitration by the International Court of Justice at The Hague. The Austrian government refused to consider this course, and on July 28, 1914, declared war on Serbia.

The first effect upon the other Great Powers of the Austrian declaration of war was to cause the immediate mobilisation of Russia's forces, for her government had promised support to Serbia. Germany then demanded that Russia demobilise her forces and, when this was rejected by the Czar's government, Germany declared war on Russia on August 1, 1914. Germany had also demanded that France should give a guarantee of her neutrality and, receiving a refusal, declared war on France, August 3, 1914.

Up to the very last moment the attitude of Britain was uncertain. It must be remembered that the Triple Entente was not a definite alliance between France, Britain and Russia, and did not come automatically into effect if one of the Powers were attacked. There was, therefore, division and hesitation in the British Cabinet. The British Foreign Secretary, Sir Edward Grey, made strenuous efforts to the very last to obtain some compromise agreement between the Powers which would have prevented war. But the Kaiser, urged on by his Austrian allies, determined on a policy of sudden, and what he hoped would be overwhelming, attack. On August 4, 1914, the German armies began the invasion of Belgium in complete defiance of the Treaty of 1839 which guaranteed the neutrality of Belgium—a treaty called by the German Chancellor a "scrap of paper" which was not worth Britain's defending. Britain declared war on Germany on August 4, 1914.

**Influences Opposed to War.** Many forces opposed to war had been gathering strength during the previous fifty or sixty years, yet they were powerless to prevent its outbreak. The final decisions were the responsibility of statesmen who were not entirely controlled by the "will of the people", however glibly people talked of democracy. As we have seen, in Germany the powers of the Reichstag were limited, while in Britain the general public had little knowledge of foreign affairs, which were still the close secret of the Foreign Office. Even members of the British Cabinet were not always well informed, and the Foreign Secretary still regarded it as a right to "play off his own bat".

**The Economic Argument.** Many writers of distinction have argued that the Great War of 1914–1918 had mainly economic causes. This line of argument declares that competition between nations for trade, for colonies and "spheres of influence" produced the conflicts of interest which resulted inevitably in war. Obviously, this economic factor played a great part in the Moroccan dispute, in the Far East and in the relations, for example, between the landlocked Serbia and the Austrian Empire. These conflicts of economic interest between nations became more severe as the area for peaceful expansion became less and less as the nations absorbed the remaining free territory.

Yet there is an argument against the theory that these economic conflicts *inevitably* produced war. By 1914 trade was not merely a question of separate nations competing; there were many huge business concerns known as "cartels" which extended far beyond the frontiers of any one state. In these great concerns English, French, German, American interests were all combined on the boards of directors and the investors were people of numerous nationalities. How, it is argued, could these people want war between their states? Surely such international capitalist combinations were conducive to peace rather than war? Again, in regard to trade, it has been pointed out that Germany had more trade with Britain than any other power, while in Europe Germany was Britain's best customer. In 1906, at the time of the first Moroccan crisis, many German industrialists had openly complained that the Kaiser's aggressive attitudes and the conflicts resulting had done tremendous harm to Germany's trade.

**Peace Movements before 1914.** There was a very great development before 1914 of various organisations of a pacifist kind entirely opposed to war. More than one hundred such societies were registered at the headquarters of the peace movement at Berne in Switzerland. International Law had also developed fast during the nineteenth century, and the International Red Cross had been set up in Switzerland at Geneva in 1864. Some of the world's greatest writers were convinced pacifists and they exercised a considerable influence on public opinion. Another fact of considerable interest and importance is that the Nobel Peace Prize, a special yearly award to the individual who has contributed most to the advancement of the cause of peace, was inaugurated towards the end of the nineteenth century. Even the Czar Nicholas II of Russia succeeded in calling The Hague Peace Conferences in an effort to secure some agreed measures of disarmament among the Great Powers. At the first conference in 1899, twenty-six countries were represented, but no progress was made, except with a number of new regulations for conducting warfare in as humane a way as possible. However, a second conference was called in 1907, and forty-four countries thought it worth while to send representatives. But the conference broke down when it came to the question of actual disarmament. The Kaiser had an especially dampening effect on the proceedings. He expressed his opinion that international agreements could only be arrived at when small and relatively unimportant matters were affected and that it was the "greatest nonsense" to think that any nation would give up its ideas in favour of another. He obviously thought general disarmament was an idealistic absurdity. He regarded the British offer of a certain amount of naval disarmament only as a trick to prevent the development of German naval power whilst maintaining British superiority.

**International Socialism.** Another important movement avowing the cause of peace was the International Socialist Movement. The First International was set up in 1864 under the guidance of Karl Marx, the founder of modern communism. The purpose of the International was to unite the workers of all countries in the bond of brotherhood. In the opinion of Marx wars in modern times are caused by the greed and ambitions of the capitalist class which uses the workers as mere pawns in the game. The First International not only aimed at international peace through the solidarity of the workers of all countries, but served as the organisation of the trade unions on an international scale. The First International lasted till 1876, when it broke up on account of differences between the anarchist wing, led by Bakunin, and the followers of Marx.

The Second International was established in 1889, and one of its leading and most influential members was the French Socialist leader, Jean Jaurès. While he was prepared to defend France from attack, he never ceased to advocate the union of the workers of all countries to make war impossible. At one of the last meetings of the Second International held at Basle in Switzerland in 1912 a resolution was passed urging the workers of all countries to bring about a general strike if war broke out and thus put a stop to the conflict before it could develop. In 1914, however, the general strike did not occur, and in fact most socialist parties lined up behind their own governments. Jean Jaurès was assassinated by a political opponent in July, 1914.

Thus the Second International had proved itself powerless to prevent war, and the strict Marxists denounced its failure as a betrayal of the working class. These disputes within the movement were some of the causes for the later break-away of a section of the International to form the Third, or Communist International in 1919, which came strongly under the influence of Lenin and the Russian Communists.

**The Kaiser's Policy.** The apportionment of the blame for the war of 1914–1918 has been the favourite pastime of many writers, but it is an extremely difficult question. German policy was very greatly to blame, but it would be wrong to think that all aggressiveness was centred in Germany. Even in Britain there were those in high places who advocated an attack on Germany before she was strong enough to attack Britain, while in France there were many who looked forward to the day of "revanche" for the defeat of 1870 and the loss of Alsace-Lorraine.

The Kaiser's policy was undoubtedly both blundering and aggressive. He gave the governments of Britain, Russia and France every cause to fear that their vital interests were threatened. He claimed that the German Navy was being built for defensive purposes only, but the German battle fleet quickly developed beyond the needs of mere defence. This growth of German naval power had been opposed by Bismarck. Germany was, he declared, a "land rat" and Britain a "water-rat", and he was quite prepared to leave it so. But after his dismissal in 1890 this policy was changed. At first the change was gradual, for even the Kaiser had to take into account the fact that the German Reichstag itself was opposed to naval building. In 1891 there was an increase in the German Navy, but naval expenditure was only about £4,000,000—a small sum compared with that spent by Britain and France. However, in 1897, Admiral von Tirpitz began a strong public campaign for the creation of a larger German fleet, and the Kaiser now began to talk in terms of naval power—"the trident must be in our hands". The Navy Law of 1898 increased German battleships to 14 and cruisers to 4 (the figures for Britain were 54 and 34 respectively). During the Boer War an anti-British campaign was organised in Germany, and the Navy Law of 1900 just about doubled the fleet of 1898. The leading figure in all this development was the head of the German Navy, Admiral von Tirpitz. In 1906 Britain replied by producing a new type of battleship, the *Dreadnought*, more powerful than any existing battleship. The British aim was to keep ahead of German trends. The German reply was to commence similar building, and so naval competition went on till 1914. All efforts at disarmament failed, and the Kaiser refused to accept a British offer to reach an agreement by which the German fleet would remain at about sixty per cent of Britain's.

We have seen the other complications leading to the war, but we must also bear in mind the growing hostility of Germany and Russia, which flared into warfare over the Balkans and Serbia. Pan-Germanism, or the movement to spread German culture and power, was in direct conflict with Pan-Slavism, the movement to draw together all peoples of Slav race under the protection of Russia. The German "Drang nach Osten" or "drive towards the East", typified by the Berlin–Baghdad Railway project, was sure to produce hostility between Germany and Russia.

# chapter sixteen

# THE GREAT WAR, 1914–1918, AND THE POST-WAR SETTLEMENT

**Introductory.** The Great War was the first total war in modern times. Everyone in the belligerent states was involved, both soldiers and civilians. As the war went on and casualties mounted, more and more labour in all countries had to be diverted to the production of war materials, and for the first time women worked on an equality with men in munitions factories, on the land and in transport. Direct attack on civilians from the air also developed, and the German Zeppelin and the aeroplane became familiar features of the war. It was no longer possible to leave the waging of the struggle to the professional soldiers, as in the nineteenth century, for now the masses of men needed for the vast conflict involved forms of conscription in all countries—even in Great Britain, where it was adopted in 1916. New and deadly weapons were produced—tanks, flame-throwers, poison gas. The 40,000,000 men killed and wounded bear witness to the horrifying intensity of the struggle.

**The German Attack.** The German aim was to finish the war on the Western front quickly by an all-out blow against France and then to turn eastward against Russia. The Kaiser was confident of success, and the plan worked out as early as 1906 by the German strategist Count Schlieffen was put into operation. The first stage of the plan was to reach Paris by a thrust through Belgium and northern France, at the same time occupying the Channel ports to prevent the landing of British reinforcements. The initial attack on Belgium was extremely powerful, but the Belgians succeeded in delaying the German time-table long enough to enable a British Expeditionary Force under Sir John French to reach Belgium. At the Battle of Mons the British force succeeded in holding the German drive, but were compelled to retreat when the German armies further south broke through and threatened to envelop the British lines. On all fronts the retreat of the French and British forces went on apace. Belgium was completely overrun in three weeks and a German victory looked almost inevitable as the Kaiser's armies moved rapidly into France.

The moment of decision was reached when the Germans were within twenty miles of Paris and German shells were actually falling

Fig. 35.—Trench Warfare near Arras, March, 1917.

in the city. Troops were rushed from Paris in every available form of transport—lorries, omnibuses and even taxis. This was the counter-stroke decided upon by the French Commander-in-Chief, General Joffre. Between September 6 and 10 there was fought the First Battle of the Marne which saved France from what had looked like almost certain defeat. The Germans were thrust back to the River Aisne, but the effort and casualties involved had been so great that the French were unable to follow up the advantage gained.

**Trench Warfare.** The Germans now began to dig defensive positions along the whole Western front. The war in the West now became almost static, and eventually the lines of trenches and dug-outs extended from the Belgian frontier right down to Switzerland. For the next four years the war on the Western front became one of attack and counter-attack. Every gain of a few hundred yards resulted in such heavy casualties for the side attempting to move forward that it became a matter of furious debate between war leaders and strategists as to whether the war could be decided on the Western front at all.

**The Eastern Front.** On the Eastern front the war had opened with an invasion of East Prussia by the Russians, but at the battle of Tannenberg, August, 1914, they were heavily defeated by the German armies under von Hindenburg and Ludendorf. The German Western armies were at this time driving on towards Paris, and the Russian defeat meant that this drive could go on without any substantial forces being transferred to the Eastern front. On the other hand, the Russians scored important successes against the Austrians in Galicia, and the Serbs even managed to recapture their capital, Belgrade, from the Austrians.

In November, 1914, Turkey entered the War on the side of Germany. In May, 1915, Italy joined the Allies. King Ferdinand of Bulgaria, anxious to be on the winning side, and impressed by German victories over the Russians in Poland and Lithuania, threw in his lot with the Kaiser, October, 1915.

The entry of Turkey into the war on the German side was an event of great importance, for the Germans now had as allies a country of 21,000,000 inhabitants, holding a critical area of the Middle East—namely, Mesopotamia, Syria, Palestine and Arabia. Another result of this alliance between Turkey and Germany was that the Turks immediately opened the straits to German warships, which were thus able to operate against Russian ports and shipping in the Black Sea.

**The Naval War in 1914.** Right from the commencement of the war,

Britain's naval power told heavily in her favour on the seas. By the end of 1914 she had succeeded in sweeping most of the German navy and merchant shipping off the high seas. This result was in part due to the defeat of one of the few active German fleets at the battle of the Falkland Islands in December, 1914. The Allies were now able to transfer troops almost unhindered to any theatre of the war. In the Far East, the Japanese had given the Allies valuable aid by attacking and capturing the German naval base of Kiauchau. This was important because it enabled Britain to give unrestricted attention to the North Sea and the Atlantic. Besides this, most of the German colonies in Africa and elsewhere were quickly overrun.

**The Year 1915.** The year 1915 opened with a position of stalemate on the Western front, but in March the first big attempt was made to break through the German lines at Neuve Chapelle. This attempt was preceded by a terrific bombardment of the German positions by the British artillery along a front of only four miles, and then a massive infantry attack followed. The British advanced for about a mile, were then heavily counter-attacked by the Germans and were unable to make any further progress. The casualties on both sides were enormous—and the final positions were almost as before. In April the Germans launched an attack at Ypres and, with the aid of poison gas, broke through the French lines, but were then held by the heroic efforts of the Canadians. Subsequent attempts at offensives by the Allies achieved little at great cost. The result of these disasters was a change of command in the British forces. General Haig became British commander in place of Sir John French in December, 1915.

On the Eastern front disaster followed disaster for the Russians, and the allied cause received a calamitous setback. The German High Command had reversed their old policy and decided on an attempt to defeat Russia before turning West once more against France and Britain. Once again, as in 1914, it looked as if their campaign would force Russia out of the war. The Germans under Hindenburg and Mackensen defeated the Russians in East Prussia at the battle of the Mazurian Lakes, February, 1915. The Russian losses in killed and wounded were about a quarter of a million. The Germans followed up this success by driving the Russian armies out of Austrian Galicia, Lithuania, Courland and Poland, whose capital Warsaw fell to the Germans in August, 1915. The Russian line was still intact, however, although it had been driven back in places hundreds of miles. In these campaigns the Russians had lost altogether, in killed, wounded and prisoners, more than 2,000,000 men.

**The Dardanelles and Gallipoli.** The costly stalemate on the Western front and disasters in the East were now followed by further setbacks in a new theatre of fighting. The Allies had decided to attempt the capture of Constantinople by carrying the war against Turkey in the Balkans and the Aegean. If this plan were successful it was thought certain that the Balkan countries still hesitating between the two sides would throw in their lot with the allied Powers. A secret agreement was also made by which Russia would at last gain possession of Constantinople. The control of the entrance to the Black Sea by the Allies would greatly speed up communications with Russia and improve the allied prospects.

In March, 1915, the French and British fleets tried to fight their way through the Dardanelles, but the powerful shore batteries of the Turks sank several vessels and the attempt was a failure. The next effort to carry the new strategy into effect was made on the peninsula of Gallipoli, where Australian and New Zealand troops (the "Anzacs") made a landing. Here they held out only precariously against the Turks who were under the command of the German General Liman von Sanders, and eventually the British forces withdrew at the end of the year.

The result of the Gallipoli failure was that Bulgaria joined Germany and the combined German, Austrian and Bulgarian armies conquered Serbia and Montenegro. A British force did land at Salonica with the aim of giving assistance to Serbia, but this also eventually withdrew to its base after an unsuccessful campaign.

**The Years 1915-1916.** The critical position reached by the Allies in 1915-1916 led to important reorganisation in the leadership, both military and political. In Britain, Lloyd George, the most energetic of the cabinet members, now became Prime Minister in December, 1916, and he infused better organisation and spirit into every part of the British war effort.

**The Siege of Verdun and the Battle of the Somme, 1916.** The Germans, realising the heavy blows suffered by the French so far, decided to make another supreme effort to break through the French lines on a narrow front. The main defensive position of the French— the hub, as it were, on which their whole defensive system rested— was the fortress of Verdun. It was this defensive bastion which the German High Command decided must be taken, for then the whole allied front would be disorganised and nothing would stand in the way of a successful drive on Paris. On February 21, 1916, the Germans began an artillery bombardment of Verdun such as had never been experienced before. The French forces defending the perimeter were compelled gradually to give ground before the German infantry attacks which followed the bombardment. Everyone understood, however, that this was a decisive battle of the war: everything might depend on it. The inspiration behind the French defence was undoubtedly Marshal Pétain, who issued to his troops a stirring and confident call and poured in every reinforcement he could find. "They shall not pass" became the French rallying cry, and after six months of almost continuous fighting, the German onslaught was held. The

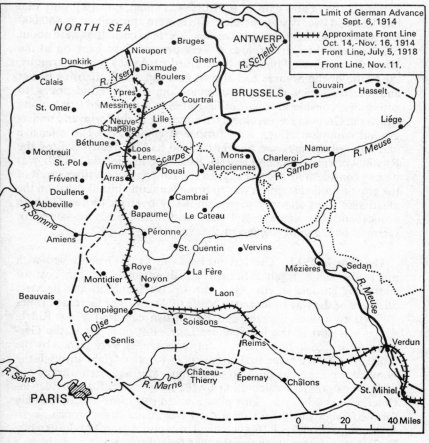

XIII.—THE WESTERN FRONT, 1914–1918.

French had achieved one of the greatest defensive victories in the history of war and had saved their country.

While the battle of Verdun was raging the Allies launched a huge offensive against the Germans in the battle of the Somme in which a new weapon—the tank—was first used by the British. The aim of this attack was to relieve the pressure on Verdun and to prevent the Germans sending further divisions to the Eastern front against Russia. By this time the strength of the British Army had grown tremendously and it was able to man on its own account a front of ninety miles extending from the sea coast down to the River Somme. The actual gain of territory was small, covering only one hundred and twenty square miles. There were approximately 450,000 British and 340,000 French casualties. German casualties were about 530,000, and the German armies were pressed right back on to the Hindenburg Line. Although these allied casualties were enormous, the battle of the Somme had shown growing allied offensive power and forced the new German Supreme Commander, Hindenburg, to withdraw a considerable part of his forces to a shortened front, along which the German emplacements of concrete, barbed wire and underground communications were further strengthened. The offensive had relieved the pressure on Verdun and had indirectly assisted the Russian offensive under General Brussilov in Galicia, which was having considerable success against the Austrians. Another result of the growing allied strength was to bring Rumania into the war on the allied side. But she was soon completely overrun by the German armies and her valuable oil-wells and wheat-fields remained in German hands until the end of the war.

**The War in 1917.** The war on land during 1917 continued with much the same results: limited allied advances at the cost of enormous casualties. In April the British launched the heaviest offensive of the war so far in the battle of Arras. The German armies suffered enormous damage and the British captured Vimy Ridge, which was part of the Hindenburg Line. But once again, the Germans were able to hold out and only a few miles were gained by the attackers. At the same time a new plan to break right through the Hindenburg Line was put into operation. This had been worked out with over-optimistic calculation by the new French Commander-in-Chief, General Nivelle. This plan entailed capturing the immensely fortified heights to the north of the River Aisne. The French began their offensive on April 16, succeeded in capturing most of the heights, but casualties were so enormous that the offensive was brought to a halt. Nivelle was replaced by Pétain as Commander-in-Chief, and the situation he had to face was extremely critical. A new factor was beginning to appear—the desperate discontent of the fighting men themselves. Serious trouble spread in the French Army which had suffered so greatly in Nivelle's offensive, and several mutinies broke out, a situation in which Pétain used the firing squads to suppress the mutineers. Another factor which was alarming both the Allied and German commanders was the increasing fraternisation of the troops. The British authorities had to issue an order banning the singing of a song the first line of which declared very emphatically "I want to go home! I want to go home!" This mood of frustration and disillusion with the war was scarcely relieved by the remaining events of 1917 on land. Firstly, the Russian Revolution broke out and by November Russia was completely out of the war. Secondly, two British offensives at Ypres and Cambrai were failures, despite the early success gained by British tanks, which had first appeared at the battle of the Somme, but were now used in much greater numbers. Thirdly, in Italy the Austrians had gained a decisive victory over the Italians at Caporetto in October. The allied Western front had to be weakened in order to rush French and British troops to Italy to assist in the defence of the new Italian line on the River Piave.

The only really bright spot for the Allies in 1917 was against the Turks in Palestine and Mesopotamia, where Baghdad was captured in March and Jerusalem entered by General Allenby's troops in December.

**The War at Sea. The United States joins the Allies, 1917.** The most important naval engagement of the war was the battle of Jutland, May 31, 1916, when the German Battle Fleet at last emerged into the North Sea. After a series of extremely complicated manœuvres, in which the German Admiral von Scheer showed very great brilliance of command, the British Fleet under Admiral Jellicoe lost 14 vessels (of which three were battle cruisers) and 6,274 men against the German loss of 11 vessels (of which one was a battle cruiser) and 2,545 men. The German losses were proportionately greater but Admiral Jellicoe was strongly criticised for not having prevented the escape of the German Fleet to its base. However, the fact remains that the German Fleet only made one more very brief appearance in the North Sea and remained cooped up for the rest of the war.

The Germans claimed the battle of Jutland as a victory, but they realised that German surface vessels would never succeed in defeating British naval power. This meant that the British blockade of

Germany, which was making it increasingly difficult for Germany to import food supplies, would now go on. The only hope was to retaliate in such a way that the British were starved out first. The German government now pinned its hopes on the submarine or U-boat. They had already declared in February, 1915, that the seas round the British Isles were a war zone in which all enemy vessels would be sunk, possibly without warning. German propaganda went on to denounce the British practice of seizing the cargoes of neutral vessels trading with Germany although these cargoes could not be classified as contraband under an international agreement arrived at in 1909 known as the Declaration of London. The German U-boat activities led to the torpedoing of the Cunard liner *Lusitania* off the coast of Ireland on May 7, 1915, with the loss of a thousand lives, including a hundred Americans. The Germans claimed that the *Lusitania* was a war auxiliary and was carrying ammunition. Another incident was the sinking in March, 1916, of a British ship, the *Sussex*, which was carrying American passengers. Early in 1917 the German government began completely unrestricted submarine warfare against all vessels trading with Great Britain. In April, 1917, the United States entered the war on the side of Great Britain. This change of policy by President Wilson and his supporters was dictated not only by the sinking of American vessels, but by the increasing activities of German agents in the U.S.A. and by a plot to get Mexico to attack the United States and take over Texas, New Mexico and Arizona.

In the meantime the German U-boat campaign took on an alarming intensity and Britain's position became extremely precarious. In April of 1917 the German submarines sank 450,000 tons of British shipping more than were actually constructed, and for the whole year the loss was about 2,000,000 tons more than construction. This was not only bringing Britain dangerously near to starvation, but was preventing the transportation of American troops. Through the energetic measures of the new British Prime Minister, Lloyd George, the position was gradually improved by the adoption of the convoy system, the Q-boats which were disguised to look like ordinary vessels but were armed to fire on surfacing U-boats, and the use of fleets of armed trawlers to attack the U-boats. In Britain rationing of foodstuffs was adopted in order to economise in food and ensure a fair distribution. However, the position was extremely difficult when the Germans began their last great offensive in March, 1918.

**The End of the War.** The German plan, mainly the work of Ludendorf, was to break through the Allied lines before substantial reinforcements could arrive from the United States. This powerful offensive began with an attack on the British lines at Arras on March 21, and spread along the whole Allied front. It lasted till the middle of July. The Germans had considerable success in the first stages of the onslaught, crossed the River Aisne and once again reached the Marne within forty miles of Paris. During this offensive the Germans captured more than a quarter of a million prisoners, and shells were fired into Paris from a distance of seventy miles.

For the Allies the position had never looked blacker, but in fact Ludendorf had exhausted the power of his drive (he lost more than 500,000 men by the time the Germans reached the Marne), and the arrival of 700,000 American troops by the end of June gave General Foch, who had been made Supreme Allied Commander in March, most valuable reserves. By August the Americans had their own army ready to take part in offensive operations. The Germans had lost their best reserves their new troops were very young and inexperienced, and, owing' to the poor food supplies, they suffered far more from the terrible flu epidemic of 1918 than did their opponents.

Marshal Foch began the Allied counter-offensive on August 21, 1918, when the British Army under General Haig attacked the German front near Amiens, using masses of tanks in the offensive. This British attack drove right into the Hindenburg Line in the North. The Americans also successfully attacked near Verdun. Then in September Foch converted these partial offensives into one great offensive along the whole front, beginning with a successful American advance in the Argonne forest, followed by a further British attack at Cambrai. With the addition of a great offensive by the French, the whole front of two hundred and fifty miles was in action. Despite a desperate German resistance, their position became hopeless, especially when Bulgaria, Austria and Turkey were knocked out of the war. Mutinies broke out in the German fleet and army and revolutionary movements developed in Germany itself. The Kaiser fled to Holland and an Armistice was signed on November 11, 1918.

Thus ended the most destructive and ferocious war the world had yet experienced. The killed alone amounted to about 13,000,000. For every minute of the fighting four soldiers were killed, nine wounded. The war left about 10,000,000 widows and orphans and 1,000,000 relatives without means of subsistence. The cost of the war in monetary terms was calculated as sufficient to provide every family in America, Canada, Australia, Great Britain, France, Belgium, Germany and Russia with a £500 house, £200 worth of furniture and £100 worth of land, and even then the "remainder" was equivalent to the whole capital value of France and Belgium! Such calculations may give some idea of the stupendous destruction caused by the war, but added to this was the vast problem of millions of starving people and refugees. New social and political forces were arising. Communism was already victorious in Russia and the movement was spreading to Europe. The old Empires of Germany, Austria-Hungary, Russia and Turkey had completely disintegrated, and the problem facing the Allied statesmen who met at Versailles was that of recasting the whole map of Europe and of bringing order out of untold chaos.

**The Versailles Peace Conference, January–June, 1919.** The final Treaty of Versailles with Germany was signed on June 28, 1919, in the Hall of Mirrors at Versailles. Other treaties were signed separately as part of the general settlement—namely, the Treaty of St. Germain with Austria (September), the Treaty of Neuilly with Bulgaria (November), and the Treaty of Trianon with Hungary (June, 1920). The later date of the treaty with Hungary is explained by the fact that a Communist government had seized power in Hungary and the Allies were unwilling to recognise it. It was not until this government had been overthrown and another installed that a final settlement was reached. Turkey was dealt with by the Treaty of Sèvres (August, 1920), the terms being later revised in the Treaty of Lausanne (1923). Generally speaking, the Treaty of Versailles or the Peace Settlement is usually accepted as meaning a reference to all the arrangements made.

**Leading Statesmen of the Conference.** The Versailles Conference was dominated from start to finish by three outstanding personalities: President Woodrow Wilson (U.S.A.), Lloyd George (British Prime Minister), and Georges Clemenceau (Prime Minister of France).

President Wilson, a Princeton University Professor who had late in life entered politics and become President of the U.S.A., was less a politician than a studious idealist who was absolutely certain that he alone had the answer to the world's problems. He found the hard-headed men of action such as Lloyd George and Clemenceau extremely difficult to fit into his scheme of things, and, indeed, eventually had to give way to them on a number of important questions. He was not a good negotiator, was extremely aloof in his dealings with others and was far less informed on the affairs of Europe than Lloyd George and Clemenceau. On the other hand, he was sincere in his desire to see real justice done at Versailles and was opposed to the policy of revenge against Germany which public opinion in Britain and in France, still affected by the violent passions of war, was de-

FIG. 36.—*Left to right:* CLEMENCEAU, WILSON, LLOYD GEORGE.

manding. He saw in such an attitude only the seeds of future war. As the author of the famous Fourteen Points and a strong advocate of the League of Nations, he brought fresh and progressive ideas into international affairs. Wilson was attempting to get the people of the U.S.A. to play a direct part in guaranteeing the peace settlement and in supporting the League of Nations. In these aims he failed to carry with him the Americans when he returned to the U.S.A. and this led to his death soon afterwards.

**The Fourteen Points.** In a speech in January, 1918, President Wilson had outlined the principles on which he thought a peace with Germany should be made. He had also made earlier efforts in 1917 to bring about peace between Germany and her opponents. The fourteen points were the result of his own analysis of the causes of international discontent and war and he made strenuous efforts to secure their acceptance by the Peace Conference. Briefly summarised they were

(1) All diplomacy and negotiation between States was to be carried on openly—"frankly and in public view".

(2) Absolute freedom of navigation on the seas both in peace and war—except in territorial waters.

(3) Equality of trade conditions between nations and the abolition of tariffs—"so far as possible".

(4) The nations to give guarantees that they would disarm to "the lowest point consistent with domestic safety".

(5) When the question of colonies was being settled the interests of the colonial peoples themselves must be given equal weight with those of the governments who put forward claims to mandates.

(6) Evacuation of all Russian territory and assistance "of every kind that she may need and may herself desire".

(7) Belgium to be completely freed.

(8) France to receive back Alsace-Lorraine.

(9) Italy to receive her proper "national" frontiers.

(10) The peoples of Austria-Hungary to be given the opportunity of independent development.

(11) Rumania, Serbia and Montenegro to be evacuated and Serbia given access to the sea.

(12) Peoples under Turkish rule to be autonomous and the Dardanelles to be open to the ships and commerce of all nations.

(13) An independent Poland to be established inhabited by "indisputably Polish populations".

(14) An international organisation to be formed to guarantee the independence of all States both great and small.

In dealing with the Treaty of Versailles it will be interesting to note to what extent it incorporates these high-minded principles and to what extent they were jettisoned by the Conference.

The attitude of mind of the French delegate at the Conference, Georges Clemenceau, is well shown by his cynical comment on Wilson's Fourteen Points: "The Good Lord himself had only ten." His only concern was the security of France; all other matters were of secondary importance. He was determined to wrench the fullest measure of retribution from Germany. His own political career went back to the Franco-Prussian War of 1870 and the Paris Commune of which he had been a member. Clemenceau was an intensely embittered opponent of everything German and an equally fanatical upholder of the idea of French glory and power. Germany was to be broken at all costs. His political nickname was, appropriately, "the Tiger".

Lloyd George, the British representative, was a far subtler politician than either Wilson or Clemenceau. His main task at the Conference was to secure some measure of compromise between Wilson and Clemenceau, although he himself had made a somewhat rash electioneering promise to the British public that he would "hang the Kaiser" and "make Germany pay".

The Great Powers decided to keep all discussion in the hands of the Supreme Council of the Conference or, as it was also known, the Council of Ten. Their decisions were only to be ratified by the full Conference, and the press and the representatives of the small powers were to be excluded from their discussions. So much for Wilson's first point! (See page 293.)

**Details of the Settlement.** (a) *Germany*. The French representative, Clemenceau, demanded that Germany should lose (in addition to Alsace-Lorraine) the Rhineland, the Saar, Upper Silesia, Danzig and East Prussia. This would have deprived her of the greater part of her coal and iron resources. Both Lloyd George and Wilson opposed this as too extreme and likely to produce dangerous discontent in

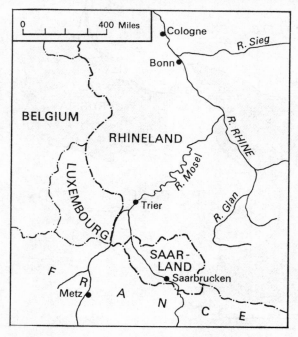

XIV.—THE SAARLAND.

Germany as time went on. The eventual settlement was a compromise between the French viewpoint and that represented by Lloyd George and Wilson. The Saar was put under international control for fifteen years, after which there was to be a plebiscite to decide its status. In the meantime France gained complete control of the Saar coal-mines. Danzig became a free city under the control of the League of Nations. The problem of Upper Silesia, where there was a mixed German and Polish population, was settled, on the insistence of Lloyd George, by means of a plebiscite, in which sixty per cent voted for incorporation in Germany, forty per cent for Poland. Eventually Poland received about a third of the territory, which contained most of its industries. The province of Posen, which was mainly Polish in population, was given to Poland, who now had a "corridor" running to the sea. This 'Polish corridor', however, divided East Prussia from the remainder

XV.—THE POLISH CORRIDOR, 1919–1939.

of Germany and created many future difficulties. By a plebiscite the preponderantly Danish part of Schleswig voted for return to Denmark. Belgium gained the small district of Eupen-Malmédy.

Germany lost all her colonies, was declared guilty of provoking the war, and by 1921 her payment in reparations to the Allies as worked out by a special Reparations Commission was fixed at the stupendous sum of £6,500,000,000 to be paid in instalments. She had to deliver to the Allies part of this sum in the form of ships (which she had to build for the Allies for five years), coal, chemicals, dyestuffs, cattle, etc. (The French flags captured in the Franco-Prussian War of 1870–1871 were also to be returned.) Germany was totally disarmed, except for a force of 100,000. The German General Staff of 1914–

XVI.—CzECHOSLOVAKIA, 1919–1939.

1918 was disbanded and was not to be re-formed. Germany was allowed no submarines and only six second-class battleships and a few smaller vessels. All German air forces were banned.

(b) *Eastern Europe*. Austria was reduced to a small country of 6,500,000 inhabitants, with its capital Vienna containing one-third of this population. Italy gained Istria, which was mainly Italian-speaking. Austria also had to give up Bosnia, Herzegovina and Dalmatia to the new Slav state of Yugoslavia. She also lost Bohemia and Moravia to Czechoslovakia, and Galicia to Poland. Hungary lost Croatia to Yugoslavia and also some territory to Czechoslovakia. The Turks were allowed to retain Constantinople and a small strip of territory in Europe north of the Sea of Marmora. The whole of the Turkish territory of Thrace was given to Greece, while Rumania gained Transylvania, Bukowina and Bessarabia. In the North the new states of Esthonia, Latvia and Lithuania were formed from the old Czarist Empire, while Finland gained complete independence of Russia—a settlement already established by Lenin and the Bolshevik government of Russia.

**Some Criticisms of the Treaties.** To pass any accurate judgments on the Treaty of Versailles is one of the most complicated of tasks, and there will always be many differences of opinion about it. We must above all realise the immensity of the task facing the statesmen gathered at Versailles. They literally had the task of reshaping the whole destiny of Europe and a great part of the world. Perfection was impossible. Wilson's Fourteen Points were an ideal, and before hard realities ideals have sometimes to be modified. Let us consider the treaty in relation to Wilson's principles. Point (1): This was abandoned at the Conference from the start. Point (2): Lloyd George refused to accept it and it was never incorporated in any articles of the Treaty or the League of Nations. Britain's interests were the deciding factor here. Point (3): Some efforts were made to have this discussed at the Conference, but nothing came of it and most of the new States created by the treaties put up huge tariff barriers to protect their own industries. Point (4): This was completely disregarded— no such guarantees were ever given. Point (5): Some attempt was made to give reality to this principle, and the German colonies were held as "mandates" by the occupying powers who were answerable for them to the League of Nations. This at least appeared better than the old colonialism of grab, but only in some of the colonies were the real wishes of the inhabitants considered. In the main, colonies continued to be governed purely in the interests of the occupying mandatory power. Point (6): The position was complicated by the outbreak of civil war in Russia between the Bolsheviks and the Whites. The leaders of the Whites refused an invitation to meet the Allied representatives and, despite the fact that diplomatic contacts were made with Lenin, who was willing to send representatives to such a conference, Wilson himself became opposed to it. Point (7): This was adopted. Point (8): Adopted. Point (9): Italy was given territories to which she had a just claim on grounds of language and population, for example, the Italian Trentino and the cities of Gorizia, Trieste and Pola; but the principle of truly "national" frontiers was not entirely maintained, for the Italians gained the Lower Tyrol (containing 250,000 Germans) and the Istrian Peninsula (containing 400,000 Yugoslavs). Point (10): This was carried out with reasonable fairness, as also was Point (11) and Point (12). Over the question of

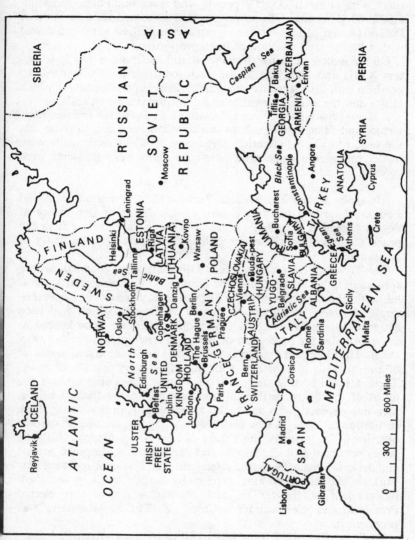

XVII.—Europe after the Peace Treaties.

Poland (Point 13) there is very much dispute, for in the new Poland there were some 10,000,000 people who were not Poles, including 2,500,000 Germans. The settlement had presented the new state of Poland (which, being new, had no experience of these great problems) with a "minority" question of huge proportions.

On the matter of Reparations we shall have more to say in Chapters XVIII and XIX, but, as we shall see, their main effect was to produce ruin for Germany and much of the social discontent which Hitler and the Nazis were able to exploit for their own ends.

It is not possible to give an exhaustive account of the treaties, their virtues and defects, but perhaps sufficient has been said to show that the task was almost superhuman; many excellent settlements were made, but at the same time nearly as many new problems were created.

**Mustapha Kemal and Modern Turkey.** The policy of the Allied Powers towards Turkey as shown by the terms of the Treaty of Sèvres proved a complete failure and was a very early rift in the peace settlement—a rift which had to be repaired by the treaty of Lausanne, 1923.

The Treaty of Sèvres attempted to divide most of Asia Minor into spheres of influence for the Allied Powers. Only a small portion was left under Turkish control. The Turks also lost control of Constantinople. In May, 1919, trouble began in Smyrna which had been assigned to the Greeks. In that month a Greek force landed at Smyrna under the protection of British, French and American warships. The Greeks at once began a ruthless persecution and massacre of the Turkish inhabitants, with the Allied warships standing by. These atrocities only succeeded in uniting the Turks against the terms of the Peace Settlement and brought to the front a leader, Mustapha Kemal, who had taken an active part in the Young Turk revolution of 1908. A new Nationalist Party was formed pledged to overthrow the terms of the Treaty of Sèvres. In March, 1920, the Allies occupied Constantinople and carried out widespread arrests and deportations of Nationalist leaders. The Nationalists in the new Turkish capital of Ankara replied by setting up a government independent of the Sultan, and Mustapha Kemal was elected President and Commander-in-Chief. A Turkish Republic was proclaimed.

By September, 1922, the Nationalist army under Kemal's leadership had defeated the Greeks and recaptured Smyrna. Kemal then decided on the invasion of Thrace, but was faced by a British force under General Harington at Chanak. The "Chanak incident" nearly brought about armed conflict between Britain and Turkey, but the British government decided to abandon the Treaty of Sèvres and resistance to the Turks when both the French and the Italians (who had been assigned the control of territory in Asia Minor) took this line. The Conference of Lausanne in 1923 gave to Turkey control of Asia Minor as well as Constantinople and that part of Europe which stretched beyond Adrianople to the Matesia River.

**Internal Reforms under Mustapha Kemal.** The complete victory of Kemal over the Allies had made him even more than previously the national hero of Turkey, and under the new constitution he was given almost dictatorial powers which enabled him for some years to use force against a number of his critics. He was able to make radical changes in the social life of Turkey. The alphabet was westernised, Sunday was proclaimed the day of rest in place of the old Islamic Friday, women were no longer to wear the veil, and the traditional fez worn by men was abolished. Elementary state schools were established, and, most remarkable of all, women were encouraged to participate in public life, and in 1929 were accorded the vote in elections to the National Assembly. All these changes, including the final removal of the Sultan, constituted a decisive break with the oriental past which had lingered on into the twentieth century. Modern Turkey arose in part from the serious mistakes of the settlement imposed by the peacemakers of 1919—mistakes of which the creator of modern Turkey, Mustapha Kemal, took full and effective advantage.

**The League of Nations.** Point (14) of the Wilson statement was carried out, and for the first time in human history an international organisation was deliberately created whose avowed purpose was the protection of independent nations from aggression and the preservation of peace. It was an integral part of the Treaty of Versailles.

The headquarters of the League were set up at Geneva. It consisted of a Council comprising representatives of five Great Powers and four lesser ones. The Great Powers were permanent members. The Council was to meet at least once a year and more often if serious international disputes arose which required action. In addition to the Council there was the Assembly, consisting of representatives of all the member states. The main officer of the League was the Secretary-General, a post first held by an Englishman, Sir Eric Drummond.

The famous Covenant of the League (like the present Charter of the United Nations which has replaced the old League) bound all its member states to certain principles of international conduct, especially the "acceptance of obligations not to resort to war", the adoption of the rules of international law, the respect for all treaties entered into. There were altogether twenty-six articles in the League Covenant, the most important of which was the famous "Sanctions" clause by which economic and, if necessary, military measures were to be taken by all other members of the League against any member nation which broke its obligations under the Covenant and resorted to aggression. Other important clauses bound the members to accept the settlement of disputes by arbitration, and recognised the need for the reduction of armaments and for the control of the private manufacture of arms. At the same time an International Labour Office (I.L.O.) was set up to attempt to secure international agreements on matters of wages, hours and general conditions of work for the mass of the population.

One last, and most important, fact remains to be mentioned. The Congress of the United States refused, despite the efforts of its President, either to guarantee the Peace Treaties or to enter the League of Nations of which Wilson had been a most fervent advocate. He returned to a United States which had become hostile to his ideals, and despite his campaigning efforts in the country (efforts which cost him his life) the United States retired into its old political isolation, refusing to put its vast power and resources behind the guaranteeing of peace in Europe. It was a bad beginning to the post-war period and to the League of Nations.

# chapter seventeen
# RUSSIA, 1914–1939

**Introductory.** The Great War of 1914–1918 led to the collapse of the Czarist system in Russia. Many ministers of the government were corrupt and inefficient, the soldiers at the front were badly armed and badly led, and the first great battle against the Germans (the battle of Tannenberg) was a Russian disaster. The Czar and his family came under the control of the evil monk, Rasputin, whose influence led them to rely on mystical religion and Rasputin's own doubtful advice on matters of State. Such were the evil results of Rasputin's hold over the Czar and Czarina that the monk was murdered in 1916 by a group of plotters led by Prince Felix Yussupov.

The plotters against Rasputin had hoped that his murder would lead to a complete reorganisation of the government, but this did not take place. By 1917 the Russian peasants were being sent into battle almost unarmed, and they died in their millions. The total Russian casualties in the war were about equal to the casualties of all her allies put together. The great wheat-growing area of the Ukraine was invaded by the armies of the Central Powers, agriculture was destroyed over a large area and famine was added to the other miseries of the war. The Czar himself attempted to conduct the war from his general headquarters, but his grasp of the military situation was poor and he was badly advised by those around him. After the murder of Rasputin the Czar spent nearly two months in attempting to make contact with the monk through spiritualistic séances. And meanwhile the Revolution had begun!

**The First Revolution, February, 1917.** The first centre of serious disturbances was Petrograd (formerly St. Petersburg). Demonstrations of students and workers took on more and more organised forms. Food was short, prices high, and unemployment was widespread. The position at the front was becoming hopeless. The demonstrations grew into a General Strike in the city before the end of the month. Then another very significant development occurred. The Cossack regiments, regarded by the Czar as his more reliable support, broke into mutiny when ordered out against the strikers and demonstrators. The strike movement was mainly under the control of the Bolsheviks, Mensheviks and Social Revolutionaries. The Cossack

Fig. 37.—Architects of the New Russia: Lenin and Stalin.

regiments joined the demonstrators, and other regiments in Petrograd followed their example. Representatives of the soldiers were appointed to the various Workers' Committees or "Soviets" which seized control of key points in the city. The Russian Duma or Parliament also refused the demand of the Czar that it should suspend its sessions. The result of these developments was that the Czar Nicholas, having also received news of widespread mutinies among the soldiers at the front, regarded his own position as hopeless and abdicated the throne on March 15, 1917.

**The Provisional Government and the Soviets.** A Provisional Government was now formed under the Premiership of Prince Lvov, a Liberal who had been an outspoken critic of the Czar's government. The first action of the Liberal Government was to issue a decree giving complete political freedom to the people—freedom of speech and association, the release of all political prisoners, and the right of workers to strike. The government also arranged for a Constituent Assembly to be elected by universal male suffrage for the purpose of working out a new system of government for Russia.

Parallel with this Liberal Government, however, there now existed the organisation of the workers in the form of the Petrograd Soviet. The Soviet declared that it would exercise control over all the armed forces in the capital and that it would only give support to the Provisional Government if the latter's actions had the approval of the soldiers' and workers' representatives. At this point in the Revolution, Lenin, Trotsky and other important revolutionary leaders were still abroad in exile.

**The Question of the War.** The fate of the new government was decided by its attitude to the war. Prince Lvov and his Ministers wished to continue the war against Germany. They considered themselves still bound to the Triple Entente, despite the enormous sufferings of Russia and the abdication of the Czar. A last desperate effort was made to retrieve the situation and counter-offensives were ordered against the Germans and Austrians. These moves were a complete failure and led to mass desertions at the front. At the same time soldiers' committees began to be formed under revolutionary control.

The attempt to continue the war was the fatal mistake made by the Liberal Government and resulted in its downfall. Alone among all the parties, the Bolsheviks came out with the demand for the ending of the war at any price. In this respect the Bolsheviks reflected the feelings of the mass of the people, whereas the Mensheviks and the Social Revolutionaries lost ground, especially among the workers of Petrograd and Moscow. The Social Revolutionary leader Kerensky had become a member of the government as Minister of War and was mainly responsible for the policy of continuing to send ill-organised, ill-armed and disillusioned troops into battle. The Mensheviks also had members in the government. These parties became identified with the war policy—a fact which the Bolsheviks were able to exploit to their own advantage.

**The Return of Lenin, April 16, 1917.** The most important event at this juncture was the return of Lenin from exile in Switzerland. He had been allowed by the Germans to travel across Germany in a closed train, and he arrived at the Finland Station, Petrograd, on April 16, 1917. In his first speech to the crowds outside the station he announced the need for the Socialist Revolution not only in Russia but throughout Europe. At the first important meeting of the Bolshevik leaders (both Trotsky and Stalin had now returned to Russia from exile in America and Siberia respectively), Lenin attacked the Provisional Government, demanded an end to the war and a seizure of power by the Soviets—but at the right moment, which he did not think had yet arrived. In fact, it soon looked as if disaster would overtake the Bolshevik cause, for a rising of the workers in July was a failure, Lenin had to flee to Finland, Trotsky and Stalin were arrested, and the Bolshevik newspaper, *Pravda*, was suppressed.

In July Kerensky became head of the Provisional Government, but the army offensive failed, the peasants began to take over the landlords' estates and general unrest continued. At this point, General Kornilov, who commanded the Russian armies, decided to attempt a military dictatorship to prevent a left-wing revolution and began to move his troops towards Moscow and Petrograd. This was a critical point for the Bolsheviks. They decided on the seizure of power to forestall Kornilov, and Lenin returned secretly to Petrograd at the beginning of October. In Petrograd, Trotsky was appointed chairman of the Revolutionary Committee and on November 6 all the key points in Petrograd were seized with very little opposition. The revolutionary cruiser *Aurora* bombarded the Winter Palace where the Provisional Government was holding its sessions but little damage was done. The Bolsheviks encountered more opposition in Moscow, but after about a week of fighting against the troops loyal to the Provisional Government, they gained control of the city. The revolution was a complete success. Lenin now became head of a

Bolshevik government, and Trotsky Commissar for Foreign Affairs. The Social Revolutionaries were also represented.

**Reasons for the Success of the Russian Revolution.** There were two revolutions in Russia in 1917—the first in February and the second in November (or October according to the old calendar, which was in force in Russia at the time; hence the description "the October Revolution"). The first revolution was of a type similar to those of the nineteenth century. It established a republic, guaranteed liberty of speech and political organisation to all gro ps and parties. A parliamentary system on Western lines was att empted. This first revolution had the support of wide sections of the people—professional workers, the middle class, the proletariat and the peasants. It succeeded because there was overwhelming discontent with the sufferings of Russia and the incompetence of the Czar. The leading men in the governments of Lvov and Kerensky were of the middle or "bourgeois" class. In this sense it was a "bourgeois" revolution. Their aim had been to continue the war, help in the defeat of Germany and thus be able to maintain the territory of Russia intact and to pay all Russia's foreign debts. Their mistake was to overestimate the capabilities of the Russian armies and to underestimate the influence of the Bolsheviks.

These mistakes of the government made the tactics of Lenin and his supporters all the more effective. Lenin had correctly analysed the situation whereas the Liberals had not. He realised that there was general war-weariness and that the party which demanded an end to the war was going to emerge victorious. Moreover, he promised the land to the peasants and the complete ending of landlordism, a promise which also had the support of the Mensheviks and Social Revolutionaries. Another aspect of the Bolshevik tactics was very important—Lenin prophesied a socialist revolution throughout Europe, beginning with the revolution in Russia. Thus it seemed possible to many of the Russian people that the seizure of power by the Soviets would lead to a general revolution which in its turn would mean general peace, with Russia living on the friendliest terms with her Socialist neighbours. By November, 1917, the Bolsheviks and the Mensheviks gained the loyalty of the majority of the troops in Petrograd and Moscow. This was the result of the tireless propaganda against the war policy of Lvov and Kerensky. The failure of the offensives against the Germans had above all added to the force of Bolshevik propaganda. The Soviets were mainly working-class organisations and their seizure of power turned the bourgeois revolution of February into the "proletarian" revolution of October.

**Events of the Years 1918–1927.** The first urgent question which faced the new Soviet government of Lenin was that of peace. The Germans were still fighting strongly on both the Eastern and Western fronts and were determined to exact the highest possible price from Russia. Léon Trotsky was given the task of negotiating peace with the Germans, but their demands for Russian territory were so great that he threw up the negotiations. Lenin, however, insisted on peace at any price, and at last this was brought about by the treaty of Brest-Litovsk, March, 1918. This Treaty was one of the most disastrous ever imposed on any people. The Russians lost to Germany one-third of their population and nine-tenths of their coal production. The Ukraine was made "independent", but was in fact under German control, for a German army occupied it in order to guarantee that its grain production was handed over to the Germans. Finland was also given her independence—a promise made by Lenin before the treaty of Brest-Litovsk.

The Treaty brought great dangers for Lenin's government, especially from those groups which had never agreed to peace at any price. This particularly applied to the Social Revolutionaries whose hold over the peasantry in parts of Russia was very strong. Risings occurred in various districts and an attempt to murder Lenin was made by a Social Revolutionary. Lenin was shot at and wounded, but recovered. Partly as a result of these activities by the Social Revolutionaries, the Bolshevik rule in Russia became more severe. The secret police, the Cheka, was enlarged and reorganised, a number of the Social Revolutionaries were arrested and shot and the party was suppressed. These struggles within Russia were also made more severe because of foreign intervention against the Communist government by Britain, America, France, Poland and Japan before the end of the war in Europe. For three years violence, terror and civil war raged. The former Czar Nicholas II, held a prisoner since March, 1917, was murdered with his family at Ekaterinburg in July, 1918. British forces occupied Archangel and the former Czarist Admiral Kolchak managed to secure the aid of Japan, America and Britain to seize control of the Trans-Siberian Railway. At the same time the British and French navies were active against Communist Russia in the Baltic and the Black Sea.

**Bolshevik Success in the Civil War.** In this critical situation the Bolshevik government showed remarkable powers of resistance.

The task of organising the Red Army to oppose the Whites (as the forces of Kolchak and the other Czarist Generals were called) was the work in great part of Léon Trotsky, while Stalin was also given important assignments by Lenin. The Whites helped to ruin their own cause by ruthless requisitioning of food from the peasants, the indiscriminate shooting of prisoners and a general disregard for humanity. The Whites were also hampered by the fact that there was much resistance in Europe to the idea of intervention against Russian Communism. In Britain, for example, the Labour Party and many Trade Unions were opposed to this policy and did everything possible to prevent supplies of arms going from Britain to the Whites. In the French Navy stationed in the Black Sea a mutiny broke out led by French Communists. All these circumstances combined to give victory to the Red Army and the policy of intervention collapsed when Kolchak was captured by the Red Army in 1920 and shot.

Meanwhile the Poles had set up their own national government. Their leaders were determined to gain back all territory they had lost since the first partition of their country in 1772. They wished to gain control of Southern Russia, including the city of Kiev, which their armies entered in 1921. The Red Army drove them back and moved on itself towards Warsaw. At this point the Polish armies under General Pilsudski received help in the form of arms from the Western Powers and in turn defeated the Red Army which was forced to withdraw. Lenin's government now had to make peace with the Poles by the treaty of Riga, 1921, by which about 4,000,000 Russians and Ukrainians came under Polish control. The peace treaty with Poland ended all hopes which the Whites might have had of defeating the Communist Government and the Civil War came to an end with Lenin's government definitely established.

**Developments in Russia, 1921-1934.** The Civil War and intervention left Russia in an appalling state, but the combination of genius and common sense which marked the character of Lenin enabled reasonable order to be achieved from chaos. The difficulties were immense. A mutiny broke out among the sailors at Kronstadt, the peasants forcibly resisted the requisitioning of food by the State, communist agents were murdered in the country-side, especially by the richer peasants or "kulaks". A system of ration cards was introduced to meet the food shortages which were the result of the civil war and of the failure of crops in the Ukraine. It has been estimated that in 1922 about 21,000,000 Russians were actually starving.

Appeals for help from other countries were at last sanctioned by Lenin, and food and clothing relief was sent from the U.S.A., Britain, France and other countries—collections mainly undertaken by voluntary organisations.

Lenin was a hard realist and not merely a rigid doctrinaire communist. He realised that private ownership and capitalism could not be swept away at once without dangerous resistance and the further lowering of food supplies. He therefore resisted the more extreme communists in his government and allowed the peasants to sell part of their grain in a free or non-government market. He also substituted a regular grain tax instead of the forced requisitions which had been imposed at any time the government decided. Small-scale businesses were allowed to function for private profit, but the main industries were controlled by the Soviets or Workers' Councils. Lenin's policy was successful. The production of food by the peasants rose steadily and by 1927 general production in Russia was already up to the level of 1914. It was this New Economic Policy (or N.E.P.) of Lenin which enabled Russia to recover from the worst effects of the years 1914–1921. In this policy he had to restrain the more fanatical communists who wished to force the peasants to give up their private holdings at once and enter collective farms. Altogether, the Bolsheviks showed great powers of leadership in these critical years, Lenin above all displaying a brilliant grasp of the situation.

**From the Death of Lenin, 1924–1939.** The effects of the earlier attempts on his life had weakened Lenin's physical powers and he died in January, 1924. His death was a great blow to Russia and to world communism. It created great internal difficulties for the Bolshevik Party. Joseph Stalin had already become General Secretary of the Russian Communist Party. Lenin, in his will, which at this time was kept secret, had criticised some of Stalin's personal qualities and in 1923 had added to the will a suggestion that someone else should be appointed in Stalin's place. Lenin had recognised Trotsky's great ability, but had also made some important qualifications. It is possible, therefore, that Lenin regarded neither Stalin nor Trotsky as the man fit to succeed him in the leadership of the country. The fact remains that in 1924 the friends of Stalin succeeded in preventing an open discussion of Lenin's will.

**Stalin versus Trotsky.** During the next three years a struggle for power developed between Stalin and Trotsky. This was not a mere personal struggle between two men of different temperaments, but involved important differences of policy. The two most important differences were that Stalin wished to build Socialism in Russia first before attempting to achieve world revolution, while Trotsky regarded the world communist revolution as a matter of immediate urgency. Trotsky held the view that Communism could not be successful in one country alone. The two men also differed on the policy to be adopted towards the peasants, Trotsky wishing to move more rapidly than Stalin towards a system of collective farms. The outcome of this struggle was success for the Stalinist line. In 1927 the Communist Party Congress accepted Stalin's policy, Trotsky was banished to Turkestan and later exiled from Russia, living the remainder of his life (till killed by an assassin) in Mexico.

**The Five Year Plans and Collectivisation.** Immediately after the end of the Trotsky episode, the first of the Five Year Plans was put into operation. The aim of this plan was to build up Russian heavy industry (coal, iron, steel, etc.) and to collectivise agriculture—that is, to do away with the individual farms of the peasants and to base Russian agriculture on the large farm run by a number of families. By this means the planners hoped to increase agricultural production through the efficient use of machinery and better organisation in general. The first Five Year Plan was a decisive step forward in the history of modern Russia. This was to be the means, not only of raising the general level of life in Russia, but also of resisting attack from any other states. In the view of Stalin, Russia was surrounded by hostile capitalist states, and with the rise to power of Hitler in Germany, Stalin realised that there was a special danger from that direction. There is little doubt that the Five Year Plans did eventually give Russia the power to resist the German attack of 1941 and, with Allied aid, to defeat Hitler's invasion.

**Trouble with the Peasants.** However, things did not go entirely smoothly with the first Five Year Plan. The attack on the richer peasants or kulaks was ruthless. They were heavily taxed, various requisitions were made on their property, and they were evicted from their farms. This campaign led to a situation of civil war in the Ukraine, where the kulaks murdered the communist agents and in reprisal hundreds of kulaks were herded by the police into forced labour camps. The kulaks also deliberately destroyed crops and farm buildings. Such was the state of confusion and loss of production that an enormous number of peasants died of starvation, and in 1930 Stalin himself had to call for a slower pace in collectivisation. However, by 1932 the government had won the day against its

opponents, and the collective farm in Russia had come to stay. Between 1932–1939 agricultural production rose steeply. With the system of allowing small private plots of land within the collective farms for each family and also allowing any surplus above the State needs to be sold on the free market, the peasants by 1941 had accepted the collective system and were working it with reasonable efficiency. Agricultural revival was greatly aided by an immense output of harvesting machines and tractors by Soviet industry.

**Industrial Progress.** The Five Year Plans also greatly increased industrial wealth, and huge industrial centres such as Magnitogorsk in the Urals and Stalingrad grew up in these years. The Moscow-Volga Canal was constructed, and a great dam completed on the Dnieper for the electrification of the countryside and towns of the Ukraine. The Five Year Plans converted Russia from a backward country into a great modern industrial state which made the condition of the old Czarist Russia look primitive in comparison. Russia in 1938 produced more than five times the amount of coal produced in 1913 and six times the amount of steel. Of course, this development meant that the people had to do without a great number of consumer goods in favour of the growth of heavy industry. Clothing was drab and dear and there was the absence of those luxuries which in the Western world add a certain amount of colour to life. But Stalin had to consider "first things first" and it was his policy which undoubtedly led to Russia's becoming one of the two most powerful States in the modern world.

**Political Events.** Parallel with the Five Year Plan, a considerable amount of drama (sometimes grim) continued to be played out on the political stage. A new constitution in 1936 created the first Soviet Parliament. The vote by secret ballot (for the first time) was given to all over eighteen. A separate House was to represent the various nationalities. In the 1936 election, both communist and non-party candidates were able to stand, but in all cases they had to be persons who accepted and worked ardently for the communist system. The new constitution, although it allowed no opposition parties in the Western sense at all, was an advance towards democracy. But meanwhile in Germany, Hitler had seized power and Stalin and other leaders realised the great danger to Russia. This and other developments led to complications inside the Soviet Union. In 1934, Kirov, a leading communist and the possible successor to Stalin, was assassinated, and as the result of investigations an opposition communist group was unearthed and a widespread "purge" of the Communist

FIG. 39.—THE NEW RUSSIA II: Industrialisation.

Party and civil service was undertaken. In 1936 some of the "old
guard" Bolsheviks of 1917 were tried and executed on a charge of
plotting to murder Stalin and to act in league with a foreign power
(Germany was really meant). Another purge, followed by shootings
and imprisonments, occurred in 1937 when certain leading communists were charged with plotting to overthrow Stalin in alliance
with Germany and other powers. Stalin and his supporters feared
the existence of any possible traitors inside Russia in the event of war
with Germany, and this partly accounts for the violence of the purges

and the ruthlessness which must have entailed a great deal of suffering to many innocent persons, whatever the "sins" of the more prominent individuals. However, the total effect of all the trials and purges was that the power of the Communist Party under Stalin's leadership remained supreme.

# chapter eighteen

# ITALY AND GERMANY, 1918–1939

**Introductory.** In October, 1922, Benito Mussolini and his "Black-shirts" marched on Rome from all parts of Italy. From then until the middle of the Second World War in 1943 the Fascist Party really controlled the Italian state. What were the circumstances which led up to this dictatorship?

Since the completion of unification in 1870, Italy had made very little social or political progress. The main problem was that of the sheer poverty of the people, of the industrial workers and, worst of all, of the peasants of Southern Italy. Successive governments had done very little to improve the lot of these two classes. The Italian Parliament was not in any way respected by the mass of the people. Party management and intrigue had replaced real concern for social conditions. By 1922 parliamentary life in Italy was at a low ebb.

The Great War added enormously to the suffering and discontent of the people. Over 600,000 Italians were killed in a war from which they gained a few territorial adjustments which meant very little to the man in the street. The end of the war left a huge unemployment problem in the industrial towns of Northern Italy. From the result-ant discontent all sorts of movements arose. The "arditi" were groups of young ex-service men (Black-shirts), while the Nationalists (Blue-shirts), the Liberals (Grey-shirts) and the Red Guards were all names of important political groups using violence of one kind or another against their opponents. In many of the factories of the northern industrial areas workmen's committees or soviets on the Russian model were set up and under socialist and communist leadership attempted to take control of industry away from the employers. An atmosphere of general violence reigned. Strikes by the workers, lockouts of the workers by the employers, riots and police violence were the order of the day. It was essentially from the midst of these conditions that fascism arose under Benito Mussolini.

**Origin of Fascism.** The word fascism is derived from the latin "fasces" or bundle of rods round an axe which was the magistrate's emblem of power in ancient Rome. The term "fascio" was the Italian form of the word meaning a group or squad. In the post-war period in Italy the term was used to denote groups organised to fight Socialism and Communism by violence. These groups or squads, to whose activities the name "Squadism" was given, were supported by a considerable number of the wealthier classes of Italy who feared Socialism and Communism. These squads attacked socialist and communist meetings, beating up their opponents and administering their own forms of torture. Benito Mussolini was the

FIG. 40.—THE FASCIST MARCH ON ROME, OCTOBER, 1922.
(*Mussolini second from right, front.*)

organiser of the Milan "fascio" in 1919. At first Mussolini's demands, in which he called on the workers for a revolution, sounded like Socialism or Communism itself, but in fact he nursed a violent hatred of the Socialist Party of which he had been an organiser up to 1914. In that year he had left the party because it would not support the entry of Italy into the war on the side of France and Britain.

In 1921 the National Fascist Party was formed and the black-shirt uniform and Roman salute adopted. This coincided with a state of extreme confusion in the Italian Parliament where a number of parties were so evenly balanced that stable government was almost impossible. (The position was very similar to that which has existed in France in recent years.) This was the situation which the fascists, under Mussolini, were sure to exploit for their own aims. By 1921 they had gained 22 seats in the Italian Parliament, and they now demanded representation in the actual government of the country. The government refused outright to accept this demand from the fascists and at this point Mussolini and his followers decided to make the challenge of force. On October 28, 1922, fascist columns converged on the city of Rome from various parts of the country. King Victor Emmanuel III and the army refused to resist them, and they entered Rome unopposed. The King then asked Mussolini to form a government and the first stage in the fascist revolution was accomplished. This was the famous March on Rome which really heralded the rise of fascism to importance in Italy. By their refusal to oppose it the King of Italy and the army showed where their true sympathies lay.

**The First Government of Mussolini, 1922–1925.** At first Mussolini continued to co-operate with other parties, and in fact there were only three outright fascists in his government. However, the violence of fascists against their opponents continued unabated, and in the elections of 1924 there were shooting incidents in which both fascists and others were killed. The general effect of these events was to strengthen the Socialist Party and increase its following. The leader of the Socialists in Parliament, Matteotti, continued his attacks on the government of Mussolini and demanded his resignation. Then, in June, 1924, one of the worst events in the recent history of Italy occurred—Matteotti was brutally murdered by fascists. A tremendous outcry arose in Italy against Mussolini, but he still refused to resign. The Italian Parliamentary system now literally fell to pieces, for the Opposition withdrew from Parliament altogether, and held their meetings in another building. At this point, with the opposition to him obviously increasing, Mussolini decided on the great gamble of force by which he could achieve a fascist dictatorship and completely suppress the Opposition. He appointed Farinacci, one of the most violent of his followers, as Secretary-General of the party. This was the signal for more intensive fascist violence. Opposition newspaper offices were attacked and closed down, many hundreds of anti-fascists were arrested on Mussolini's orders and sent into exile on the Lipari islands in the Mediterranean. University professors were forced to swear an oath of allegiance to the fascist government and to promise that they would teach according to fascist principles. Everywhere the organised bands of armed fascists under the control of Mussolini and Farinacci terrorised their opponents. The army, the police and the monarchy did nothing to oppose the establishment of the fascist dictatorship. Power was now completely in the hands of Mussolini

**The Corporate State.** The fascist seizure of power was followed by a complete reorganisation of Italian society. The relationship of workers and employers was established on a new basis. The old trade unions which had waged independent struggles against the employers for improved conditions were now abolished. A system of "corporations" was established in which workers and employers were represented. The worker-employer corporations were to settle, with the participation of the government and representatives of the fascist party, all matters relating to wages, hours of work and other conditions in industry. The special government department which had the task of supervising the industrial corporations was known as the Ministry of Corporations. The aim of this new system was, theoretically, to make both workers and capitalists support the State before their own interests. The fascist régime attempted to set up the State or Nation as being above selfish conflict, and therefore strikes by the workers and lockouts by the employers were now made illegal. In 1938 representatives of the twenty-two new industrial and professional corporations replaced parliament altogether, and Italy was then governed by an Assembly of Corporations. Over and above all was Mussolini the leader (Il Duce) and the Fascist Party. Italy became an authoritarian state in which life was supposed to be based on discipline and sacrifice in the interests of the State. Mussolini himself became very fond of praising warfare as the highest peak of human endeavour, in which man was at his very best. And the last of the Fascist Ten Commandments stated that "Mussolini is always right".

GERMANY: THE WEIMAR REPUBLIC AND THE RISE OF HITLER, 1918–1933

**The German Revolution of 1918.** The abdication of the Kaiser William II on November 9, 1918, was due to the complete collapse of his policy. War and aggression had failed. The working and middle classes in Germany were starving. The Russian revolution was encouraging the idea of revolution in Germany. In October a mutiny broke out in the German Navy and the socialists in the Reichstag took the lead in demanding the abdication of the Kaiser. The socialists, who had supported the war in 1914, also withdrew from the government, which then had scarcely any support among the people. These circumstances forced the Kaiser to give up the throne and Ebert, a socialist, became Chancellor.

At first it seemed that the German revolution would follow the same course as the Russian revolution in 1917. Workers' and soldiers' soviets were set up and a Council of Commissars was created. The German soviets declared that Germany was a Socialist Republic and that political power was in the hands of the workers' and soldiers' councils. But the old system of government (without the Kaiser) continued. The same civil servants and officials remained and a Cabinet was formed of mild socialists who were not genuinely in favour of the soviet system for Germany. This division between the German soviets and the socialist leaders led to further trouble. The Communist section of the socialists known as the "Spartacists", after the name of the leader, Spartacus, of a great slave revolt in ancient Rome, now attempted to rouse the masses to seize power. Their principal leaders were Karl Liebknecht and Rosa Luxemburg, a woman socialist who had always opposed the Kaiser's war. Under the leadership of the Spartacists and other socialist sympathisers, a huge mass of demonstrators numbering about 100,000 seized control of the main public buildings in Berlin on January 6, 1919.

A socialist Minister of the Interior, Noske, now undertook the task of suppressing the attempted Communist Revolution, and for this purpose he enlisted the help of a group of former German officers, the Free Corps. They attacked the communists, regained control of the centre of Berlin and murdered many prisoners among them both Karl Liebknecht and Rosa Luxemburg. Thus the German Republic began its career in a fierce clash between the socialists who opposed the workers' dictatorship on the Russian model and the communists. This opposition between the socialists and the communists in Germany continued over the next twelve years and made it impossible for them effectively to unite against Hitler.

**The Weimar Republic.** General elections were now held in Germany and all Germans over twenty-one had the vote. The elections resulted in the Social Democrats (Socialists) having the largest single representation, but several other important parties were represented.

Thus in Germany as in France a multiplicity of parties tended to make a steady government extremely difficult to achieve. As we have seen, a similar situation had also arisen in Italy. It is also important to bear in mind that the influences which had given the strongest support to the Kaiser were by no means eliminated, for the Nationalists, representing the Prussian Junkers and the big capitalists of Germany, had forty-two seats in the Assembly. The Free Corps was also a group of German officers who were determined to keep the old German policy alive. These influences were going to help in one form or another in the rise to power of Adolf Hitler.

A coalition government was now formed containing representatives of all the parties except the Nationalists and the Communists. The National Assembly established a new form of government for Germany. This was a far more liberal and democratic system than had existed under Bismarck and the Kaiser. In the first place, the Chancellor and the Ministers of the government were now completely answerable to the Reichstag for their actions. The Reichstag also gained complete control over taxation, as the Prussian Liberals had demanded as far back as 1860. The Upper House or Reichsrat was to represent the individual states of Germany, but it could not hold up the passing of any laws which had a two-thirds majority in the Reichstag. The President had, however, certain rights which gave him considerable power. He could dissolve the Reichstag, order new elections or use the armed forces to suppress revolution or restore order. The first President of the Weimar Republic, as it was known from the name of the ancient German town, where the National Assembly met, was, as we have seen, the socialist Ebert.

**Main Developments, 1920–1933.** No sooner had the Weimar Republic been established than attempts were made to overthrow it. There were communist risings in the Ruhr district and at Munich, where the communists controlled the city for more than a month. These movements were suppressed by armed force ordered by President Ebert. Then in March, 1920, a section of the old officers' group, the Free Corps, who wished to restore the Kaiser, seized control of Berlin. This rising was defeated by a general strike of the workers under socialist and communist leadership. In the elections to the Reichstag in the same year both the Nationalists (or extreme Right) and the Communists and Independent Socialists (or extreme Left) gained increased representation. Thus, in the conditions of unemployment and general social unrest, the extreme parties gained at the expense of the middle ones, and this tended to make the political and social clash in Germany more severe.

**Reparations.** Then, added to all these problems, was the allied demand for reparations which, as we have seen, was the utterly fantastic sum of £6,500,000,000. In various complicated ways, this demand led to an appalling economic situation in Germany. The French government complained that the yearly instalments were far below what Germany could pay and in 1923 French troops occupied the whole of the Ruhr district. The result was a decline in German industry and a calamitous fall in the value of German money, which became almost worthless. It eventually took 1,000,000,000 marks to buy a box of matches! The middle and professional classes in Germany suffered severely, for their pensions, investments and insurances were completely wiped out. In the Ruhr district the Germans declared a General Strike and refused in any way to co-operate with the French. No country had ever been in a more chaotic and desperate state than Germany in 1923.

**The Policy of Stresemann.** The position was temporarily saved when Stresemann (People's Party) became Foreign Minister in 1923—a position he subsequently held until his death in 1929. By the method of decree, sanctioned by the Reichstag, he succeeded in re-valuing the German mark. He secured easier instalments of reparations, and, after calling off the General Strike in the Ruhr, he persuaded the French to leave the Ruhr in 1925. In international affairs he raised the status of Germany by securing her admission to the League of Nations in 1926. By 1928 German industry had recovered, unemployment was on the decline, and the extreme parties (the Nazis, Communists and Nationalists) had lost ground in the elections. By the famous Locarno Treaty of 1925, Stresemann had secured from France and other countries a guarantee of the western frontiers of Germany, and relations between France and Germany were now far friendlier. Thus the years from 1924 to 1929 were a period of recovery for Germany and better international relations all round. For a short while it was felt throughout Europe that a new era of peace and progress was dawning. These hopes, however, were to have a very brief existence.

**The Rise of Adolf Hitler and the Nazi Party.** The Nazi or National Socialist Party arose in 1921, when it was set up by a small group in Munich. A few months after its foundation, Hitler was made its president. He was an Austrian of middle-class parents. He worked for a time as a sign-painter in Vienna, joined the German

Army in 1914 and rose to the rank of corporal. By all accounts, he was obsessed by a sense of his own power and destiny and at the same time felt the intense frustrations of his mediocre life—a feeling from which a fanatical power of hatred developed.

In the troubled state of Germany after 1918 which has been described, Hitler and his party hoped to gain rapid advancement. His main line of propaganda at this time, as later, was denunciation of the Versailles Treaty and the "traitors" (by which he meant Jews, Communists, Socialists, Pacifists and others) who had delivered a "stab in the back" to the German Army by starting a revolution. During the course of his career he was constantly to harp on this theme—according to Hitler, Germany was not "defeated", she was "betrayed".

It was against Stresemann's policy that Hitler and his party especially directed their early efforts. They denounced Stresemanns' negotiations with the French and his willingness to pay reparations. It was at this point that Hitler attempted to overthrow the Republic. In this conspiracy he was joined by Ludendorf. On November 8, 1923, he brought out his followers in Munich and proclaimed himself President of Germany. But the nerves of some of his disciples failed, and the commander of his forces went over to the other side. Hitler's "Munich putsch" was suppressed by the Bavarian government and he was put on trial. Hitler was sentenced to five years' imprisonment, but released after nine months. During his imprisonment he began the writing of his work *Mein Kampf* (*My Struggle*), which became the Nazi bible. During the next five years the Nazis lost ground in Germany. In 1924 they had 24 seats in the Reichstag, but in 1928 these had fallen to 12. Nevertheless, Hitler was preparing for another opportune moment. He had, however, decided that the old tactics were hopeless. He could not hope to win power by the Nazi movement alone—he must gain the support of the big industrialists in Germany and of the army. Conditions in Germany were soon to present him with his opportunity.

**Economic Collapse. Power passes to Hitler.** In 1929 a revised system of reparations payments by Germany was devised. It was known as the Young Plan from the name of the American financier responsible for the proposals. Germany had continued to be in arrears with her payments since 1921, and the new plan reduced the amount of her yearly payments, but she would still have to pay an annual sum in the region of £50,000,000 for the next fifty-nine years. Stresemann wished to accept these proposals, but the Nazis and Nationalists launched a violent campaign against him. At about the same time a colossal economic slump hit the whole world. It began in the U.S.A. with collapsing prices on the Wall Street Stock Exchange, followed by unemployment, falling-off of production in all industries, declining wages and general panic. This economic blizzard spread to Europe, and Germany herself was hit disastrously for the second time within ten years. By 1931 (when there were 3,000,000 unemployed in Britain) there were nearly 6,000,000 unemployed in Germany.

Fig. 41.—The Orator.

**The Growth of Violence in Germany.** In these circumstances social discontent and violence developed rapidly. On the one hand, the Communist Party of Germany was denouncing the capitalist system and the Nazis, while on the other hand, Hitler was laying the blame for everything at the door of the foreigners, Jews, Communists, Socialists, and Pacifists—the usual Nazi list. The Nazi "Storm Troopers", organised by Hitler's henchman, Captain Roehm, and now numbering 400,000, were parading everywhere. Violent clashes with bloodshed occurred between the Storm Troopers and their Communist and Socialist opponents. An atmosphere of terrific tension developed.

Hitler now began to appear to many Germans as the real hope—the man with a strong policy and purpose—unlike the incompetent

FIG. 42.—HITLER (*extreme left*), MOUNTING THE ROSTRUM TO ADDRESS A NAZI RALLY AT NUREMBERG, SEPTEMBER 1933.

politicians who had failed hopelessly to save Germany from calamity. In 1932 Hitler polled 11,000,000 votes for the Presidency as against Hindenburg's 18,000,000 and about 5,000,000 for the Communist candidate. In the general election of 1932 the Nazis won 230 seats in the Reichstag. After further intense Nazi campaigns in the country and much intrigue among the various party groups, Hindenburg agreed to the appointment of Hitler as Chancellor in January, 1933.

**The Seizure of Power.** The Nazis now prepared for another election. These preparations included a reign of terror against their opponents by the Nazi Storm Troopers. Goering, who was a member of the government and also head of the Prussian police, enrolled armed Nazis and Nationalists into the police force. On February 27, 1933, the Reichstag building in Berlin was burnt down and the Communist Party falsely accused of being the perpetrators. Leading members of the Communist Party were immediately arrested. Socialist and Communist newspapers were suppressed, and brutal attacks on the Jewish people began. In these conditions the election took place on March 5, 1933. The Nazis and their Nationalist allies gained 341 seats out of 647—a bare majority. They were dissatisfied with this result and stepped up the campaign of terror and violence against all their main opponents. The other German parties "voluntarily" dissolved themselves. Hitler was voted powers to govern for four years without summoning the Reichstag, and the Nazi dictatorship had begun.

Of the Nazi leaders, Goebbels was appointed Minister of Propaganda and Goering organised the "Gestapo" or Secret Police. The Concentration Camps for Nazi opponents became the order of the day, and by 1945 over 12,000,000 individuals had died in them in conditions of the most appalling ill-treatment. The trade unions were abolished and all workers were organised in the Nazi Labour Front. The dictatorship of the Nazi Party was complete by 1934 when, on the death of Hindenburg, Hitler became Head of the State and Commander of the Armed Forces. One of the most important rivals to Hitler himself, Captain Roehm, leader of the Storm Troopers, was shot on Hitler's orders on June 30, 1934, and a number of other prominent German politicians also died in the "purge". It is considered by some authorities that Hitler's aim in the removal of Roehm was to secure the full support of the German Army, whose leaders feared the rivalry of the Storm Troopers.

Certain it is that the mob-enthusiasm of the Storm Troopers was no longer needed, now that Hitler had come to power. In their place there now emerged a hand-picked and disciplined organisation known as the "S.S." (short for *Schutzstaffeln* or protection squads). Starting as a small personal bodyguard to Hitler, the S.S. became the security police of the Nazis during their rise to power, and grew into the principal agency for enforcing Nazi rule during the years of Hitler's ascendancy. Numbering half a million men by 1945, the S.S. ran the concentration camps and formed the special S.S. divisions of the German Army which spearheaded its campaigns. The S.S. was the most appalling instrument of political and military terror known to history.

**Some Reasons for the Rise of the Nazis.** We have seen how the Nazis were able to exploit for their own ends the sufferings of the German people. On the other hand, it must be remembered that their programme gained great support from a large section of the populace. This was particularly the case with large numbers of the middle class—professional people, tradesmen, civil servants and other "white collar" workers who had been ruined by the collapse of the German currency in 1923 and were facing a second dose of ruin in 1931. It was easy for the Nazis to promise this class a revived Germany and better conditions which would come with the repudiation of the Versailles Treaty, of reparations and of general enslavement to the foreigner. It is significant that a large proportion of the Storm Troopers of Roehm had been recruited from this class. The middle class was also easily swayed by Hitler's anti-Communism, for Communism meant the dictatorship of the working class, the end of capitalism and many of the rights of property. Hitler was also able to appeal to some of the unemployed, who found a new purpose in life and a discipline in their uniformed parades under the swastika flag.

The big capitalists of Germany also saw in Hitler the protection of their interests against Communism and Socialism. It must be remembered that Germany was now (after U.S.A.) the second most powerful industrial nation in the world, and the leaders of German industry wielded immense influence. Lastly, many of the Army leaders thoroughly sympathised with Hitler's demands for the full rearmament of Germany and the abolition of the Versailles Treaty. Some of them were under the illusion that the Army could control Hitler, whereas in fact the Nazi Party soon gained complete control of the Army. It must also be borne in mind that Hitler was the most powerful demagogic orator the twentieth century has produced. He exercised over vast numbers of the German people a hypnotic power, which he used to exploit their grievances and arouse their national feeling.

# chapter nineteen

# INTERNATIONAL AFFAIRS, 1919–1939

**France and Germany.** French foreign policy immediately after 1919 was dominated by the desire to keep Germany in a permanently weakened state. This was an attitude of mingled fear and hatred, above all typified by the policy of Poincaré, who became French Prime Minister in 1922. He was determined to prevent any rearmament of Germany and to exact every penny of reparations. This attitude created a rift between the official policies of France and Britain towards Germany, for Britain was prepared as early as 1924 to agree to a drastic scaling-down of German payments. French policy further aimed at building around Germany a strong defensive system of alliances. In 1921 France made a defensive treaty with Poland and supplied that country with arms for many years to come. The French also made a similar treaty with Belgium.

In addition, France encouraged the creation of the "Little Entente" between Czechoslovakia, Rumania and Yugoslavia. These three States had benefited most from the break-up of the Austro-Hungarian Empire, and the treaty was designed to give mutual protection against any attempts by Hungary to regain the territory which she had lost to the three Powers. France herself came to an agreement with the "Little Entente" Powers by which she would assist them against any attempt to alter the boundary settlements of 1919. In this way France regarded herself as the main guardian of the peace settlements not only in the West, but in Eastern Europe also.

**Reparations and the Crisis of 1923–1924.** A critical position arose in 1923 in connection with reparations payments. Since 1921 Germany had fallen far behind in her payments to the victors. This was due partly to the immense sums demanded and partly to deliberate evasion by German financiers and industrialists. The French government under Poincaré continued to insist that the yearly sums decided upon in 1921 by the Allied Reparations Commission must be paid. The French were also hardened in their attitude by the discovery by the Allied Commission of hidden stores of arms in Germany. In January, 1923, the French took drastic action on their own account and sent their forces to occupy the Ruhr industrial district, which

Fig. 43.—Stresemann addressing the League of Nations.

produced four-fifths of Germany's coal and iron. For eight months the German workers, supported by their government at first, went on strike. Despite the importation of French workers to work the mines, railways and steel works, industrial production slumped heavily. The whole of German industry and finance was thrown out of gear and the value of the German mark sank to a worthless level (see page 322). At this point Stresemann became German Foreign Minister and, as we have seen, his policy was one of compromise with the French. He called off the strike and promised to pay what Germany could find at once—and more later. The French Army eventually withdrew in 1925.

Relationships between France and Germany had never been worse (short of war) than they were in 1923 and 1924. Significantly, this was the time of Hitler's attempted Munich revolution (see page 320). The Nazis and the Nationalists gained considerable support for their denunciations of France, of reparations and of the Versailles Treaty under the terms of which, in fact, the French had occupied the Ruhr. In France, however, public opinion turned against Poincaré, who was regarded as mainly responsible for the bad situation that had arisen through his implacable attitude towards Germany. In 1924 the French electors turned out Poincaré. He was succeeded by Aristide Briand, who advocated a more moderate policy towards Germany and worked in considerable harmony with Stresemann.

**The League of Nations.** The first years of the League of Nations were difficult, but a certain amount of real constructive work was done. Austria, economically weak and unbalanced between town and country by the Peace Settlement, was given the assistance of loans which, with League supervision, she employed to develop her industry. A dispute was also settled between Sweden and Finland over the Aaland Islands, which were eventually handed to Finland. However, other events showed weakness in the League when faced by a real armed challenge. The city of Vilna had been assigned to the small state of Lithuania on the Baltic (created out of part of the old Russian Empire). But the city was also claimed by the Poles, who seized it by force. Eventually, the League accepted the Polish occupation. This was a dangerous acceptance of the result of armed force. But an even more serious challenge came from Mussolini in 1923, when, after the murder of four Italians on the Albanian-Greek frontier, the Italian navy bombarded the island of Corfu and seized it from Greece. The League remonstrated with Mussolini, but he held on to the island. Eventually the League ordered the Greeks to pay compensation for the murders, and Italy evacuated the island. Italy had used force before any other means, and had openly defied the League. These incidents were small ones, perhaps, but they were a real test of the willingness of members of the League to act against aggression.

The Corfu incident and some others brought up the whole question of what was really meant by "aggression". Attempts were now made through the League of Nations to get a clear definition of the term, so that an aggressor in the future could be clearly recognised. After prolonged discussion and debate, an agreement known as the Geneva Protocol was drawn up and approved by the League Assembly in 1924. By this agreement any state which refused arbitration and went to war was automatically an aggressor, and every member of the League was pledged to apply sanctions against her. The effectiveness of this agreement was partly destroyed by the unwillingness of the British Dominions to involve themselves automatically in war in Europe.

**The Locarno Treaty.** However, the failure of the Protocol was compensated for by another important arrangement proposed by the British Foreign Secretary, Austen Chamberlain, in 1925. This, the famous Locarno Treaty, was probably the most important treaty of the post-war period and it greatly strengthened the work which the League of Nations was attempting. The treaty met the difficulties raised by agreeing on the limitation of its scope to Europe alone. The frontiers of France and Belgium were guaranteed by Britain, France, Belgium, Italy and Germany herself. France also signed treaties of defence against aggression by Germany with both Poland and Czechoslovakia. Stresemann also brought about agreements for arbitration in case of disputes between Germany on the one hand, and France, Belgium, Britain and Poland on the other. This was a highly constructive treaty which made war in Europe far less likely in the future, and it marks the period when Germany under Stresemann was obviously prepared to renounce aggression, give guarantees to the other Powers and live on friendly terms with them. The German attitude had been made more possible by the Dawes Plan, 1924, by which reparations instalments from Germany had been made easier, and by the withdrawal of the French troops from the Ruhr in 1925. This plan was named after the American, General Dawes, who proposed it, and it included provisions for loans to Germany by the U.S.A. to assist German industrial recovery. It is of considerable significance that in 1926 Germany was made a member of the League of Nations with a permanent place on the Council. The years 1925–1929 witnessed an outburst of optimism in Europe.

This atmosphere, created by the Locarno Pact and better relations between Germany and her neighbours, greatly strengthened the work of the League of Nations which was able to stop a war which broke out in 1926 between Greece and Bulgaria. The Greeks had launched an invasion of Bulgaria after some Greek soldiers had been killed on the Bulgarian-Greek frontier. The Bulgarians appealed to the League, which ordered the Greeks to withdraw and pay compensation for the damage caused by their attack. Confronted by very strong League demands, the Greeks did as they were told. In this case the League had worked as intended, possibly aided by the fact that Greece had received a substantial loan for reconstruction through the League and was anxious not to lose this support.

Again in 1926 the League settled a dispute between Turkey and the new Arab state of Iraq over the possession of Mosul, the great oil centre on the frontier between the two countries. The Turks finally accepted the decision of a League Commission which gave the area to Iraq. Besides these activities, the League undertook the administration of the free port of Danzig and of the Saar territory (under the Versailles Treaty), and arranged important loans to Austria, Hungary, Greece and Bulgaria.

**The Kellogg Pact, 1928.** A resolution adopted by the Assembly of the League in 1927 to prohibit all wars of aggression led to another hopeful development of the years 1925-1929. This was the famous Kellogg Pact (1928), named after the American Secretary of State who, together with the French Foreign Minister Briand, was the principal exponent of the idea. All the signatories to the pact renounced war as an instrument of policy, and indeed all the Great Powers, including Russia (who was not admitted to the League until 1934), signed the agreement with a gold pen appropriately provided. In all, sixty-five countries pledged themselves to the renunciation of war, with the exception of a war in "self-defence"—but what exactly constituted self-defence was never clearly defined. However, despite this loophole, the Treaty was an important effort to further strengthen international peace and the work of the League of Nations.

**The Change for the Worse, 1929-1939.** From the peak of optimism reached in 1929 the relationships of the Great Powers fell away in painful stages towards the catastrophe of the Second World War, 1939-1945. In this tragic development, many aspects of which still remain unstudied by the historian, certain factors are clear.

**The Economic Crisis, 1929-1931.** As we have seen in the previous chapter, the economic collapse beginning in 1929 in the U.S.A. spread to all countries. The result was, everywhere, unemployment, hunger and social discontent. In Germany, the very key to the peaceful or warlike development of Europe, the Nazis under Hitler were able to exploit this situation for their own ends and to gain power in 1933. Their policy was based on the denunciation of the Versailles Treaty, the demand for German land, air and naval re-armament, the demand for colonies ("a place in the sun"), and the demand for the union of all Germans in one state. The latter demand, of course, referred particularly to Austria and to the German minority population in Czechoslovakia, the Sudeten Germans. This policy was closely connected with the Nazi "philosophy" which declared the Aryan race to be superior to all others, and laid harsh penalties on those who could not prove that their blood was free from non-Aryan (mainly Jewish) admixture since the year 1800. The brutal persecution of the Jews was also undertaken on the grounds that they, together with the communists, socialists and pacifists, had "stabbed Germany in the back" in 1918. All these attacks in Hitler's speeches were used to arouse the Germans to a state of racial and national hysteria. Combined with his anti-semitic line was another which Hitler exploited to the full, namely, the menace of Russian Communism. By constantly harping on the theme that Germany was Europe's real protector against Russian Communism, he gained the sympathy of many people in Europe who were by no means Nazis or Fascists. Right up to 1939 there were those who thought that, if war was to come, it could still be confined to a struggle between Germany and Russia. In fact, Hitler's anti-communist line was a disguise for his real purpose of eventually gaining what he called "Lebensraum", or living space, not only in the Russian Ukraine, but elsewhere.

**General Increase of Aggression and Weakening of the League of Nations.** Trouble began early in the Far East. Amongst the countries severely hit by the economic depression was Japan. With a rapidly growing population in a limited space and at the same time a huge unemployment problem, the Japanese solution was to look round for means of expanding foreign trade and gaining new sources of wealth. The army and navy leaders were the principal forces behind this Japanese policy, and in the serious economic position of 1929–1931 they gained the upper hand in the counsels of the Emperor. In 1931, in complete defiance of the League of Nations (of which she was a foundation member), Japan launched an attack on the rich province of Manchuria, which she wrested from Chinese hands, and established her own state of Manchukuo.

In the Western world and in the League of Nations there was

confusion and hesitation, and a number of Western statesmen even expressed a sympathetic "understanding" of Japan's needs. The League failed completely to act against Japan. This failure was in great part due to difficulties and conflicts already arising among the European nations themselves which made it increasingly unlikely that they would act together. Moreover, Russia, who alone could have used land forces against the Japanese in the Far East, was not yet a member of the League. Again, with unemployment everywhere in Europe and large sections of industry at a complete standstill, it was a very difficult time indeed in which to commence a trade embargo against Japan as well as war—for that is what resistance to Japan by the League would in all likelihood have entailed. Nevertheless, it remains a lamentable fact that Japan's successful aggression against China was the real beginning of the League of Nations' decline. When a Disarmament Conference met at Geneva in 1932 it is scarcely surprising that Japanese and German naval-building demands were an important cause of its failure. Aggression seemed to be already a paying proposition. After the seizure of power by Hitler, Germany left the League of Nations in October, 1933.

**Italian Policy under Mussolini.** The next successful aggression which further undermined the League of Nations was that of Mussolini against a fellow-member of the League, Abyssinia. Mussolini, like the Japanese, desired colonial expansion to relieve the problem of poverty at home. Also, a victory against Abyssinia would bring nationalistic credit to his government by avenging the Italian defeat at Adowa in 1896 (see page 264). Trouble began in 1934 on the border between Abyssinia and Italian Somaliland, when fighting resulted from Italian provocation. The Abyssinians appealed to the League, but nothing effective was done. There was much debate, many pious resolutions, and a commission was sent to the frontier and declared neither party to blame. But Mussolini was now preaching daily about the "vital needs of the Italian people and their security in East Africa", which he claimed was threatened by the Abyssinians. In October, 1935, the Italians began the invasion of Abyssinia, using, besides the usual weapons of war, poison gas sprayed from aeroplanes. By May, 1936, the capital, Addis Ababa, had been entered and the King of Italy proclaimed Emperor.

The invasion of Abyssinia was the most serious test case since the foundation of the League, and many of its member countries realised the momentousness of the position. This time something was done. An embargo on the sale of arms to Italy by League members was imposed. But then, during the course of the war, the Foreign Secretaries of both France and Britain proposed in December, 1935, a division of Abyssinia, with a great part of the country going to Italy. This led to a popular outcry in Britain and other countries, and Mr. Anthony Eden, who was in favour of more stringent sanctions against Mussolini, replaced Sir Samuel Hoare as Foreign Secretary. But the damage was already done, the Franco-British proposals having only encouraged Mussolini to carry on with his flagrant violation of the League Covenant.

**The Berlin–Rome Axis.** The success of Mussolini in Abyssinia had shown the weakness of the League and the willingness of some Western statesmen to compromise with him. This, of course, was a direct encouragement to Hitler. In 1936, German forces marched into the Rhineland, which had been demilitarised under the Versailles Treaty. This open violation of the treaty terms went completely unopposed by the other Powers. Soon afterwards, Hitler and Mussolini came to an understanding which meant that in future the two fascist states would work together in foreign policy, and which eventually brought Mussolini into the Second World War in 1940. This was the Berlin–Rome Axis, which by 1939 had brought the other great aggressor, Japan, into its fold and became known as the Berlin–Rome–Tokio Axis. The other term which the creators of this alliance gave to it was the Anti-Comintern Pact, the Comintern being the international Communist organisation of those years. It should also be noted that Japan had begun another attack on China in 1937.

**The Spanish Civil War.** The scene now shifts to Spain. In that country a Republican Revolution had ended the Spanish Monarchy in 1931, but there was continued strife between royalists and their socialist, communist and anarchist opponents. The left-wing governments had begun a series of reforms which reduced the powers of the big landowners, while the trade union movement was exerting constant pressure against the big business interests. Other reforms also reduced the powers of the Catholic Church over education. The Republic had therefore strong opponents among the army, the church, the big landowners and capitalists in general. However, in the election of 1936 the combined left-wing parties or Popular Front gained a majority in the Spanish parliament. At this point General Franco, who was in exile in the Canaries, crossed to Morocco, and became leader of a rebellion against the Popular Front government; soon the war spread to the mainland. Franco's forces

marched on Madrid, which, however, after a desperate resistance, succeeded in repulsing him. Franco's failure to capture Madrid with the help of Moorish troops enabled the Republican government to carry on the war for another two years.

Hitler and Mussolini assisted Franco from the beginning. German and Italian forces entered Spain, and arms flowed in to Franco from both these countries. Russia gave various forms of assistance to the Republican side, while an International Brigade (Britons, French, Germans, Americans, and other nationalities), who were anti-fascists, went to Spain to strengthen the government's resistance. The official attitude of the French and British governments was non-intervention, and Italy and Germany actually agreed to this policy. But in fact their intervention continued, and Italian submarines began to sink British and other vessels trading with Republican Spain. For two years the war went on, until in 1939 Franco, with the help of his Italian and German allies, captured Barcelona and Madrid and established his own fascist dictatorship. Thus another country had been won for fascism in Europe—and by the same technique of aggression against legally constituted authority.

**The Final Phase.** The final scenes leading to the Second World War, 1939–1945, are set in Austria, Czechoslovakia and Poland.

In Austria the Nazi party had campaigned violently for years for union with Germany. This campaign had been resisted by successive Austrian Chancellors, but by 1938 the Nazis had succeeded in being represented in the Austrian government of Chancellor Schuschnigg. Schuschnigg was opposed to the union of Austria and Germany and felt confident that a national plebiscite on this question would go in his favour. No sooner, however, had he voiced his intention of holding the plebiscite than he was forced to withdraw it by open threats of force from Hitler himself. Soon after this, in March, 1938, German troops entered Austria without resistance and the Nazis became the real rulers of the country for the next seven years. This was another defiance of the Treaty of Versailles, which had forbidden the union of Austria and Germany. It was another triumph for Hitler. Things were going from bad to worse, and Hitler, in the gamble of force which he had decided upon when occupying the Rhineland in 1936, was once again successful.

**Czechoslovakia.** The frontier area of Western Czechoslovakia (Map XVI, page 297) was the area known as the Sudetenland and was populated to a large extent by German-speaking people, who numbered about 3,000,000 out of a total population of 15,000,000.

One of Hitler's avowed aims was to unite all German elements with Germany herself and this cry was taken up by the Nazi party in the Sudetenland under their leader Henlein. To many people in Europe it seemed only natural that Germany should want to unite all German populations, but the future was to show that this was only an excuse for German aggression against the whole of Czechoslovakia.

After the seizure of Austria, the Nazi campaign against the President of Czechoslovakia, Dr. Beneš, was intensified. The Sudetenland became Hitler's demand and Henlein and his supporters responded by a violent campaign in the Sudeten areas.

Along the frontier with Germany the Czechs had established one of the strongest fortified lines in Europe, and if this frontier was once given up they would be completely open to further aggression from Hitler. The German Führer now intensified his campaign of threats against Czechoslovakia, which became the main object of hostility at the huge Nazi Nuremberg rally in the summer of 1938. The Czechs appealed to the Western powers and Russia for support, and there appeared to be an imminent danger of war.

France and Russia had already signed a treaty of mutual aid in 1934 and Russia also had a pact with Czechoslovakia. But Russia would take no action unless France did also; and in all the events of these critical months the Russians were almost completely ignored by Western statesmen.

**The Munich Agreement, 1938.** The Prime Minister of Great Britain was Neville Chamberlain, and in September, 1938, he made two flights to Germany to meet Hitler at Berchtesgaden and Godesberg. Then at Munich in the same month he had a meeting with Mussolini, Hitler and the French Prime Minister, Daladier. The outcome of these meetings, which the whole world was watching, was agreement between the four Powers to the German occupation of the Sudeten areas. This was the notorious Munich settlement, which was a matter of violent dispute at that time, as it has been ever since. Naturally, the whole of Czechoslovakia saw it as nothing but a betrayal, as did millions of other people in all parts of Europe. On the other hand, there was widespread relief that war had been avoided.

As the Czechs could now count on no support, the German armies marched into Czechoslovakia unresisted and occupied the whole Sudeten area. Mr. Chamberlain declared that the settlement meant "peace in our time", but he had been sadly deceived by Hitler's promises that he had no further claims to make. In March,

1939, the German Army swept into the western part of Czechoslovakia, occupied Prague, and installed a Nazi controlled government which remained in power till the liberation of the country in 1945. In the unoccupied Eastern part of the country, the Germans established the puppet state of Slovakia. The great prize of the Skoda armament works, one of the largest in Europe, now fell into the hands of Hitler, and he added the resources of a highly industrialised state to the Nazi system.

**Poland.** The final stage came with Hitler's claims against Poland. No sooner had Prague been occupied than the Nazis whipped up their campaign for the return of the Polish corridor and Danzig to Germany. But now the Chamberlain government in England signed a defensive treaty with Poland, as also did France. Negotiations for a pact between Russia and Britain had already begun, although very late in the day. These negotiations broke down for a variety of causes, one of them being the demand of Stalin for the right to send Russian troops into Esthonia, Latvia and Lithuania in case of a German attack along the Baltic coast. Immediately after the failure of these negotiations, Stalin made a non-aggression pact (the Soviet-German Pact) with Hitler, who was now freed from the fear of a war on two fronts. On September 1, 1939, German troops invaded Poland, and Warsaw was bombed from the air. On September 3 Britain and France (probably to the surprise of Hitler) declared war against Germany. It may never be known for certain whether Hitler expected Britain and France to hold back as they had done over the Rhineland, Austria and Czechoslovakia.

Thus began the Second World War which, in the course of various dramatic changes during the next two years, was to see the creation of the alliance of Britain, Russia and the United States which overwhelmed the Nazi system after the most destructive war yet fought by mankind.

# chapter twenty

# THE SECOND WORLD WAR

**The Nazi Attack on Poland.** When Hitler's attack began Poland was still not fully mobilised. Forty-five German divisions and 1,500 aircraft, launched with lightning rapidity and surprise, completely overwhelmed the Polish forces. Most of the Polish air force was destroyed on the ground within the first twenty-four hours, while German motorised and armoured divisions swept all before them on the road to Warsaw, which they reached on September 8. Although the city had already been subjected to a devastating aerial attack, its defenders resisted stubbornly until September 27. In the meantime, after September 16, Russian forces moved into eastern Poland under the terms of the Nazi-Soviet Pact. In a few weeks the Polish state had ceased to exist and leading members of the government were in exile.

**The "Winter War" and the "Phoney War".** All this time the Western front had remained quiet, for the French stayed defensively behind the Maginot Line, despite the fact that they had fifty-seven front-line divisions in the field. It was widely expected that the defeat of Poland would be followed by an attack in the west, but this did not occur until the spring of 1940. It seems that Hitler was held back by his General Staff, who were anxious to increase the strength of their armies before facing the Western allies. As a result the Germans were frustrated by the exceptionally harsh winter of 1939–1940 and they also became involved in a campaign in Norway. Even before this another "winter war" was being fought between Russia and Finland. The Russians had demanded territorial concessions from the Finns in order to improve the defences of Leningrad. When these demands were refused, the Russians launched an attack on November 30. Under the leadership of General Mannerheim, the Finns put up a surprising resistance and the Western allies were distracted from the menace of Hitler by their preparations to send help to Finland. However, before this could happen the Finns had been defeated in February, 1940, and Stalin's demands had been met.

In the meantime the allies had suffered further setbacks with the loss of the battleship *Royal Oak*, sunk in Scapa Flow by a German midget submarine, and the depredations of the German battleship,

*Graf Spee* in the allied shipping lanes of the Atlantic. Eventually the *Graf Spee* was forced into Montevideo harbour by three British cruisers, and scuttled by her captain.

Yet all this time there were no offensives in the west and the allies remained on the defensive. For the people of France and Britain the struggle still seemed quite unreal, a "phoney war".

**The Norwegian Campaign.** During the preparations to help the Finns, the British had drawn up plans to seize the port of Narvik, which handled vital iron exports from Sweden, and to destroy the Swedish iron mines themselves. However the defeat of the Finns put a stop to these plans and in the end Hitler moved into Scandinavia first. On April 9 German forces invaded Denmark and proceeded to seize the main Norwegian ports. In this they were helped by a Norwegian Nazi-sympathiser, Vidkund Quisling, and his henchmen, and Quisling's name soon became a widely used term to describe traitors and collaborators. However Hitler's actions were not completely unopposed. The allies immediately launched an expedition to Narvik and severely damaged German naval forces in the area. Yet in the long run the allied effort was in vain; the Germans demonstrated a superior use of air cover to support their land and sea forces and the British and French troops had to withdraw. The British suffered heavy naval losses and Hitler was left in command of the iron ore supplies, the entrance to the Baltic Sea, and many valuable naval and air bases. The immediate effect in Britain was a Parliamentary revolt against Neville Chamberlain, who was succeeded on May 10 by Winston Churchill at the head of a coalition government.

**The German Offensive in the West.** On the very day that Churchill became Prime Minister, German forces invaded the Netherlands, Belgium and Luxembourg. The French High Command had been completely deceived: the main French and British forces were ordered to face the enemy on this front, but the German attack came, not through the lowlands of Belgium, but through the Ardennes where there were only twelve allied divisions facing the forty-five divisions under von Runstedt. The conservative-minded, defensive thinking of the allies had been proved worthless, and the replacement of the French General Gamelin by General Weygand as Allied commander-in-chief made little difference. The allies were unable to stem the German advance, which soon threatened to cut the British off from the Channel ports. The British and French forces in the north made a rapid retreat to Dunkirk abandoning most of their heavy equipment

FIG. 45.—BRITISH AND FRENCH TROOPS WAIT TO BE EVACUATED FROM THE
BEACHES OF DUNKIRK.

as they went. Finally, under an intensive aerial bombardment, over a
quarter of a million British and over 100,000 French troops were
evacuated in small boats from Dunkirk to England. In one sense
this evacuation marked a major defeat for the allies in Europe and a
blow to their morale, but it was a remarkable achievement: the British
force had been kept intact and Hitler's plans had been partially frustrated.

**The Fall of France and the Establishment of the Vichy Régime.** On
June 14 the Germans entered Paris and the French government
which had moved to Bordeaux sought an armistice. Marshal Petain,
the hero of Verdun in the First World War, replaced Paul Reynaud
as Prime Minister, and delegates of his government met Hitler at
Compiègne on June 22. The armistice was signed in the very railway
carriage in which the Germans had accepted defeat in 1918, and it
was small wonder that Hitler literally danced for joy when the surrender was completed. Under its terms Germany took over the direct
administration of Alsace-Lorraine, northern France and the Atlantic
coastline. Petain and his government were allowed to administer
southern and central France from a new capital at Vichy. The Vichy
government were to retain control of the French colonies and navy,
which was, however, to be disarmed.

Once the Vichy government was established the premiership passed to Pierre Laval, while Petain became head of state. The immediate result of the naval agreement was that the British sought to seize all French ships in British controlled ports. The French warships in the north African ports of Oran and Mers-el-Kebir were attacked by British bombers, when their commanders refused to hand them over to the Free French forces. The régime at Vichy will be dealt with in more detail in Chapter Twenty-Six; it is sufficient to point out here that it had many similarities with the Fascist Corporate state and that Laval favoured increasing co-operation with Hitler. For a while he was replaced by the even more pro-German Admiral Darlan, who supported active co-operation with a German offensive in the Middle East. This made Vichy-controlled Syria a danger point for the allies in the Levant.

**Operation Sea-lion and the Battle of Britain.** With France beneath his heel, Hitler prepared for the invasion of Britain—Operation Sea-lion. He appears to have had no illusions about the difficulties of this formidable task. The invasion date, first set in August, was moved on to the middle of September. By that time Hermann Goering, the commander of the Luftwaffe, promised to have completed the destruction of the R.A.F. so that the German invasion force could be given unimpeded air cover.

In mid-August the struggle for the control of the skies over Britain began. The Germans' primary aim was to destroy British airfields in south-east England, but from the start the British enjoyed the enormous and decisive advantage of radar. It warned them of impending attacks and allowed them to make the best possible use of their limited supplies of men, fuel and aircraft. As a result the Germans suffered heavy losses, while, through an immense effort of production, the British had more fighters available at the end of the battle than at the beginning. In the first eleven days the Germans lost 290 planes against 114 British losses. At the end of August the Germans switched to daylight raids on London which continued until the end of October, but even before that, in September, Hitler had decided that the invasion would have to be indefinitely postponed.

Faced with increasingly heavy losses the Germans turned to night raids on London and other cities which continued until May, 1941, when the planes were redeployed on the Russian Front. But despite the enormous damage these terror raids caused in cities such as Coventry, they neither broke the spirit of the British people nor seriously reduced war production. In any case Britain's military resources were soon being swollen from another source, as the Americans moved decisively away from the strict neutrality they had announced at the beginning of the war.

President Roosevelt's Lend-Lease Act of March, 1941, enabled the Americans to provide Britain with desperately needed ships and equipment. This development led in turn to an intensification of Hitler's U-boat operations in the Atlantic, which were made immensely easier by his control of the French Atlantic coastline. In 1941 nearly four million tons of British shipping were sunk.

**North Africa and the Balkans.** Mussolini entered the war immediately after the collapse of France, but from the start he proved to be something of a liability to his Nazi allies. His armies in Africa scored a few short-lived victories: they seized French and British Somaliland and Marshal Graziani advanced into Egypt with 250,000 men as far as Sidi Barrani. Here however they were held by General Wavell's British and Commonwealth troops, although Wavell was heavily outnumbered. Between February and May, 1941, Wavell proceeded to drive the Italians out of Egypt and he captured Cyrenaica. Another morale-raising victory was the reconquest of Abyssinia and the restoration of the Emperor Haile Selassie, who had been in exile since 1935.

Mussolini was in equally great difficulties in Greece, which he had invaded in October, 1940. The Greeks threw the Italians far back into Albania, whence the invasion had come, and the British Fleet Air Arm destroyed half the Italian Navy at Taranto. These defeats dealt a hard blow to the myth of Fascist invincibility and Hitler had hastily to prop up his ally. Strong detachments of the Luftwaffe were sent to Sicily to join the Italian attack on Malta and, more important, the Afrika Korps under General Rommel was dispatched to North Africa. Rommel was able to drive Wavell back into Egypt and the whole British position in North Africa was endangered. However an Australian force held out for eight months in Tobruk and Rommel was hampered by the fact that Hitler was unwilling to commit more troops to the Middle East at a time when he was preparing to attack Russia. As a result the British with Free French help were able to suppress pro-Axis forces in Iraq, Syria and Lebanon. In March, 1941, they also inflicted another naval defeat on the Italians at Matapan.

On the other hand the British suffered a heavy setback in Greece, despite Churchill's controversial decision to support the Greeks at the expense of Wavell's forces in North Africa. In the spring of 1941 Hitler invaded first Yugoslavia and then Greece, and British forces avoided complete annihilation or capture only thanks to a successful evacuation by the Royal Navy in April, 1941. The story was repeated in Crete, which the Germans captured by a brilliant airborne invasion. This left Hitler in complete control of the Balkans, as pro-Nazi governments had already been established in both Rumania and Bulgaria.

**Operation Barbarossa.** With all opposition crushed on the continent of Europe, Hitler was now ready to launch his long planned attack on the Soviet Union. Despite the warnings of Churchill and others, Stalin was ill-prepared to face this offensive for his army had still not recovered from the purges of 1937–1939 and it did not possess the equipment to deal with Hitler's war of movement. As late as the beginning of June Stalin refused the offer of an alliance with Britain.

On June 22, 1941, the decision was taken out of his control for Hitler ordered an attack along the whole Russian frontier. In the first two days a third of Russia's 6,000 planes were destroyed on the ground and the Nazi forces, numbering some 3,000,000 men began a three pronged advance towards Leningrad, Moscow and Kiev. The mobile German forces carried all before them. By July they had reached Smolensk, two hundred miles from Moscow and by mid-September they were in the outskirts of Leningrad. Here they were held, by the Red Army, aided by workers battalions from the factories and supported by the efforts of the whole population, had to withstand a terrible siege that lasted until the German withdrawal in 1943. On all fronts the Russians had already lost a million men killed and captured, and the Germans continued their drive to Moscow, winning a crushing victory at Viazma. In the south the German armoured columns under Guderian captured Kiev and drove on towards Kharkov and the Caucasian oilfields.

Thus, by the autumn of 1941, the Soviet Union was in the most perilous position. But both Hitler, and those of the allies who doubted Russia's ability to survive, had underrated the amazing reserves of strength of the Russian people and the Red Army. Russian reinforcements under General Zhukov threw back the Germans from the outskirts of Moscow, and Rostov-on-Don in the south was recaptured. Moreover the German forces were ill-equipped to face a winter campaign and winter came early that year in Russia. The forward sweep of the Germans was checked and Stalin won time to draw on the country's enormous resources for the great battles to come. Through over-confidence and a lack of accurate information on

FIG. 46.—GERMAN SOLDIERS IN A BURNING RUSSIAN VILLAGE.

Russian reserves, Hitler had suffered a decisive setback to his plan for a lightning victory in the east.

Meanwhile, in North Africa, Commonwealth forces had once again driven the Axis armies out of Egypt and back into Cyrenaica. So although 1941 was a year of great victories for Hitler, it ended without him gaining all that he had hoped for.

**The Atlantic Charter, August, 1941.** In August 1941 President Roosevelt and Winston Churchill met on board the American cruiser *Augusta* off the coast of Newfoundland, and, as a result of the meeting, issued the Atlantic Charter. The Charter declared that during and after the war the basic human freedoms were to be respected and that no territory should change hands after the war without the consent of its inhabitants. The faith of both Nations in democracy was stressed, and the meeting clearly showed where the sympathies of the American government lay. The declaration was an important part of the process by which Roosevelt persuaded the American people to take a less detached view of the war, and although the United States remained neutral, more direct aid was given to the allies. American naval patrols were extended out to Iceland and Lend-Lease operations now included the Soviet Union.

**Pearl Harbor.** In July, 1941, the Japanese began to follow a more aggressive policy in South-east Asia. In that month they moved into French Indo-China partly to outflank the Chinese Nationalists under Chiang Kai-shek and partly with their eyes on the valuable mineral resources of South-east Asia. This obvious threat to British Malaya, the Dutch East Indies, and the American controlled Philippines was countered by a British, Dutch and American embargo on trade with Japan in such important war materials as oil, rubber, tin and shipping. The Americans also closed the Panama Canal to Japanese ships.

For some months there were negotiations between the Japanese and American governments, but in the Japanese cabinet the war party led by the War Minister, General Tojo, won support for a drastic policy to cut through the stalemate. On December 7 more than half the American Pacific fleet was put out of action by a sudden and totally unexpected aerial attack on the great naval base at Pearl Harbor. On December 8 the United States, Britain and the Netherlands declared war on Japan. At this stage however the Soviet Union was not involved in the war in Asia. The Russians had signed a treaty with Japan just before Operation Barbarossa and this remained in force until 1945. On the other hand both Hitler and Mussolini declared war on the United States soon after the Japanese attack.

The bombing of Pearl Harbor transformed the war. On the one hand it enormously extended its geographical scope and meant that Britain had to divert some of her resources to the Asian front. On the other hand it brought the vast potential power of the United States fully behind the allied efforts. For a while however, the Japanese carried all opposition before them. On December 10 the British battleships *Repulse* and *Prince of Wales*, unprotected by air cover, were sunk by Japanese aircraft. Japanese forces captured Hong Kong and swept down through Malaya to take the great naval base at Singapore. In a matter of weeks they occupied Burma, the Dutch East Indies, the Philippines and most of the western Pacific islands.

It was not until May, 1942, that they were checked, when an American fleet repulsed a Japanese force on its way to Port Moresby in New Guinea, the capture of which would have left Australia in danger of invasion. This battle of the Coral Sea was followed by an even more important victory in June, when American aircraft inflicted heavy losses on a Japanese fleet off Midway Island. In the meantime the Americans were preparing for a future counter-offensive by occupying the Solomon Islands and General MacArthur

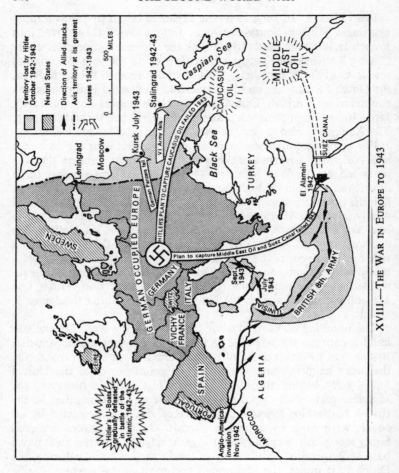

XVIII.—THE WAR IN EUROPE TO 1943

established a headquarters in Australia from which to direct the re-conquest of South-east Asia. Just as the Germans had hoped to knock Soviet Russia out of the war by a lightning blow in 1941–1942, so the Japanese had hoped to win the struggle in the Pacific by their startling victories in 1942. In fact neither of these plans quite suc-ceeded and once Russia and the United States were able to draw fully on their tremendous potential, the tide turned slowly but steadily against the Axis powers.

Fig. 47.—The Allied Advance in North Africa.

**El Alamein and Allied Victory in North Africa.** In June, 1942, Rommel captured Tobruk, a heavy blow to the Allies, and once again drove the Commonwealth forces back into Egypt. However, Britain's successful defence of Malta assured General Montgomery of a steady flow of reinforcements in Egypt, while Rommel was having to operate with dangerously extended lines of communication. By October Montgomery had built up a tank superiority of six to one over Rommel. On October 23 he launched a crushing offensive against the Germans and Italians at El Alamein which sent Rommel's armies reeling to the west. At the same time preparations had been made for an Anglo-American invasion of Morocco and Algeria and the first landings were made on November 7 at Safi, Casablanca, Oran and Algiers. Admiral Darlan, the Vichy commander in North Africa, now joined the allies. Later in the year he was assassinated and the allied leaders dealt instead with General Giraud. General de Gaulle's claims to command all French troops and territories were ignored at this time by both Churchill and Roosevelt, and not surprisingly de Gaulle felt extremely bitter towards his allies.

The war in North Africa now entered its final phase with the Axis forces trapped between allied advances from both east and west. However the Germans fought tenaciously especially around the

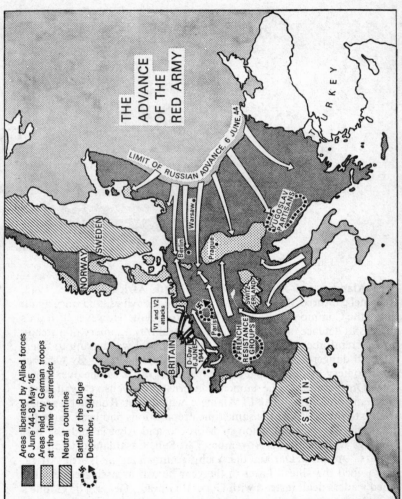

Areas liberated by Allied forces
6 June '44–8 May 45

Areas held by German troops
at the time of surrender.

Neutral countries

Battle of the Bulge
December, 1944

THE ADVANCE OF THE RED ARMY

LIMIT OF RUSSIAN ADVANCE, 6 JUNE, 44

NORWAY

SWEDEN

TURKEY

YUGOSLAV PARTISANS

Berlin

Warsaw

Prague

SWITZERLAND

V1 and V2 attacks

Paris

FRENCH RESISTANCE GROUPS

BRITAIN

D-Day 6 JUNE 1944

SPAIN

XIX.—THE WAR IN EUROPE 1944-5.

Mareth Line in Tunisia and it was not until May, 1943, that Rommel's Army, a quarter of a million strong, surrendered. In the months before, Hitler had tried desperately to get reinforcements to Rommel and had attempted to seize the Vichy French fleet at Toulon. In fact the fleet was scuttled before the Germans could reach it, but Hitler did take control of the whole Vichy area with the assistance of the government, now led once more by Laval.

**Stalingrad and the turn of the tide in the East.** In the meantime there had been a fantastic change of fortune on the Russian Front. In May, 1942, Hitler's summer offensive took the Germans as far as Rostov-on-Don, but the Russians held Voronezh and Stalingrad. The latter was the key to the whole south Russian front, for from there the Germans would be able to move either to the Caucasus or north towards Moscow. Soon it became the centre of a titanic struggle which was to play a key part in Hitler's downfall. By mid-September the Germans had reached the outskirts of Stalingrad, but the Russians were contesting every house in ferocious hand-to-hand fighting. Then, as the Germans moved slowly into the city, Stalin deployed a huge reserve army around the enemy, who found themselves under siege in the midst of the Russian winter. Hitler refused to allow a strategic retreat, but he could not prevent the loss of 300,000 men and the surrender of 100,000 survivors under Field-Marshal von Paulus in January–February, 1943.

The Russian victory at Stalingrad put new spirit into the allies. Moreover the war was now being carried into the very heart of Germany with the intensive bombing of German cities by British and American bombers. This controversial policy was the work of Air Vice-Marshal Harris. It was of doubtful effect on either German production or the morale of the German people, but it was certainly a sign of the increasing strength of the allies. The Germans also continued their attacks on British cities and both sides suffered heavy losses in men and aircraft. However in the spring of 1943 the allies were increasingly successful in bringing the U-boat menace under control with long-range aircraft operating from British bases.

**The Battle of Kursk, July 1943.** Despite Stalingrad, Hitler continued to be confident of German capacity to win the war. This attitude was reinforced by the success of General Manstein in recapturing Kharkov from the Russians in February 1943. Enormous preparations were now made for a great offensive on the Orel–Kursk–Byelgorod salient which was aimed at piercing the Russian defences and making a decisive thrust north to Moscow. It is clear that Hitler attached great importance to this offensive and that vital divisions were moved from the west. The German offensive was launched on July 5, employing seventeen armoured divisions, which was almost the total that could be used. The Russians were prepared —huge and intricate minefields had been laid, while masses of tanks and long-range guns were used on a scale which surpassed all previous battles of the war. The Soviet air force was also strongly engaged. Between July 5 and 15 the Germans maintained their pressure, and both sides sustained enormous casualties. But the hoped for German breakthrough was frustrated and the Soviet counter-offensive began to dislodge the Germans from the slight gains of territory they had been able to achieve. On July 24 the Russians announced the end of the Kursk battle and the recapture of all ground lost. German losses had been at least 70,000 men killed, 2,900 tanks and over 1,300 aircraft. The battle of Kursk thus ranks with Alamein and Stalingrad as one of the decisive turning points of the war.

**The Far East 1942–1943.** During 1942–1943 the allies started to recover ground in the Asian theatre of war as well. The British hit back at the Japanese from bases in India: a supply road was built into north Burma and the Chindits, a group of guerrilla fighters under the command of Orde Wingate, were sent into Burma to harass the Japanese from behind their own lines. There was a steady build up of troops along the India–Burma frontier, so that when the Japanese launched an offensive against India in 1944, they were decisively defeated at the battle of Kohima—a battle which is comparable in importance with El Alamein in the North African campaign.

During the same period the Americans staged a remarkable reconstitution of their naval power in the Pacific and from this time clearly outstripped Britain as the world's greatest naval power. The Pacific theatre was, in fact, left almost entirely in the hands of the Americans, while British naval forces were deployed in the Atlantic and Mediterranean. In 1943 General MacArthur's American and Australian troops won control of the eastern part of New Guinea. In the meantime Americans had overrun the Solomon Islands and isolated the key Japanese base at Rabaul. After the capture of Saipan in the Marianas it was possible to begin long-range bombing of Japan itself.

**The Italian Campaign.** With the defeat of the Axis in North Africa the Allies decided to launch an attack on Sicily. Their invasion force landed on July 10 and scored a more immediate success than they had expected. The invasion produced a political crisis in Italy during which the King dismissed Mussolini and replaced him by Marshal Badoglio with the object of making peace with the allies. After some discussion Churchill was able to persuade the Americans to carry the war on to the Italian mainland and landings were made in Calabria in September. Hitler's response was to flood Italy with German troops and take control of the administration of the country and the conduct of the war there. German airborne troops staged a daring raid to release Mussolini from prison and he set up a republican government in north Italy under German protection.

The Allied campaign in Italy proved to be both difficult and costly, and it was soon being widely criticised, especially by Stalin who was demanding a second front in northern France. German troops, helped by the difficult terrain, held out tenaciously in central Italy notably at Monte Cassino, which withstood a five months siege from January to May, 1944. To by-pass Monte Cassino the allies established a bridgehead farther north at Anzio, but it was not until June that they were able to enter Rome. Victor Emmanuel then abdicated in favour of his son Umberto, and Badoglio was replaced by the leader of the National Liberation Committee, Signor Bonomi.

**D-Day and the Liberation of France.** The main value of the Italian campaign was that it brought about the downfall of Mussolini and tied down at least twenty-four divisions of Germans while the allies prepared for the main attack on Hitler's Europe in the north. In 1943 General Eisenhower was made supreme commander of the allied invasion forces and the most elaborate preparations were made for the invasion of France. An oil-pipeline to be run under the channel (PLUTO) was designed and two enormous floating harbours were constructed to be brought to the beach-head in the wake of the invasion; huge forces were concentrated in southern England and many devices were employed to mislead the Germans about the true intentions of the allies. Dummy installations were built on the coast opposite Calais and naval forays made in that part of the Channel. At the same time air attacks were launched on Nazi lines of communication in northern France and most of the Seine bridges were destroyed.

On the morning of June 6, 1944, the allied armada crossed the Channel to the surprise of the Germans. Partly deceived by earlier allied feints, they had insufficient troops at the landing points chosen by the allies and a bridgehead was established. Despite heavy losses on some of the beaches, General Montgomery, in command of all land forces, was able to push inland and over one and a half million men had landed in France by the end of July. The operation was a triumph of close co-operation between all forces: an intense aerial and naval bombardment had played havoc with German lines of communication and coast defences, while a fleet of gliders had carried

FIG. 48.—THE LIBERATION OF EUROPE: Allied equipment pours ashore in Normandy.

troops inland beyond the beach-heads. The British advanced through Normandy to Caen by July 18, while the Americans captured St. Lo and drove into Brittany.

As at Stalingrad, Hitler refused to allow his generals to carry out strategic retreats and a large German force was surrounded and destroyed in the battle of the Falaise Gap. Mainly as a result of these setbacks a group of German military leaders attempted to assassinate Hitler and were very nearly successful. However he survived and carried out a brutal purge of the military leadership. Most of those involved in any way with the plot were executed, though Rommel was allowed the privilege of suicide.

The allies advanced steadily throughout the summer of 1944. The Free French under de Gaulle were given the privilege of liberating Paris, while other Free French troops landed in the south of France and advanced up the Rhone towards the Rhine. The allies then moved into Belgium and the Netherlands, overrunning the V1 flying-bomb bases from which London and south-east England had been bombarded. Soon afterwards the silent and deadly V2 rockets began to fall on London from other bases in the Low Countries with devastating results. However their use had been delayed and reduced by successful RAF attacks on the German rocket research establishment at Peenemunde on the Baltic coast.

**Arnhem and the Battle of the Bulge.** At this stage the allied leaders were divided on the best way to exploit their successes. Montgomery favoured an overwhelming attack on a narrow front which would drive rapidly through the German lines into the Ruhr and bring the war to a speedy end by the sheer disruption of the enemy that the breakthrough would cause. Eisenhower, on the other hand, preferred the strategy of a slower advance along a broad front.

In September an attempt was made to outflank the German defences along the Seigfried Line and gain a foothold across the River Arnhem. However, after some initial success, the airborne and ground attacks at Arnhem were unsuccessful and the allies turned instead to the capture of the port of Antwerp and the destruction of the V2 bases. In November they captured the island of Walcheren in the Scheldt and soon afterwards Antwerp fell.

The last German attempt to retrieve the situation in the west came in December, 1944, when von Runstedt launched a well-prepared counter-attack in the Ardennes. The allied line was flung back but not broken in the Battle of the Bulge, and once the fury of the Germans' attack was spent, they were incapable of any further initiative.

The German situation was now desperate and Goebbels, the Minister of Propaganda, was given the task of mobilising every German between sixteen and sixty for the defence of the fatherland. But the new contingents did not possess the fighting power of the old German divisions and the general mobilisation weakened German industrial effort still further. Hitler himself now retired to the bunker of the Reich Chancellery in Berlin and continued to order new armies into battle—armies which no longer existed.

**The Defeat of Germany.** After 1943 the Russians advanced steadily westwards with only minor and temporary reverses. Rumania, Bulgaria, Finland and Czechoslovakia were liberated, while Communist partisans under Tito helped to drive the Germans out of Yugoslavia.

FIG. 49.—PRISONERS IN DACHAU CONCENTRATION CAMP WELCOME THEIR
LIBERATORS.

In the spring of 1945 the Germans reached the river Oder while the
Western allies crossed the Rhine and occupied the devastated Ruhr.
The Russians entered Berlin and advance units of the Russian and
American forces met on the river Elbe on April 25. It was an historic
moment, though the goodwill expressed between the Eastern and
Western allies was to be dissipated in the post-war years. In the
course of their advances the allied troops had found horrifying evidence of the brutality of the Nazi régime. The British and Americans
had liberated ghastly concentration camps, such as Belsen and Buch-
enwald, while the Russians had found the yet more grim extermination camps, such as Auschwitz, where millions of Jews had been
wiped out.

But now the end had come for the Axis leaders. On April 30
Mussolini was captured and shot by Italian partisans and on the
same day, with the Russians only streets away, Hitler committed
suicide in the bunker and his body was burnt in the courtyard of
the Chancellery. Admiral Doenitz, his successor, agreed to an
unconditional surrender on May 7, 1945.

THE ADVANCE OF THE JAPANESE
ARMED FORCES, Dec.1941 - July 1942

Territory held by Japan
in December, 1941

Advances by Japan

Territory captured by
Japan to July, 1942

0   250   500   750   MILES

RUSSIA

OUTER
MONGOLIA

ALEUTIANS

C H I N A

Peking

J A P A N

Tokyo

to PEARL
HARBOR

Chungking

PACIFIC

BURMA ROAD

BURMA

FORMOSA

Hong Kong

OCEAN

WAKE Is.
(U.S.A.)

Air raids
on Ceylon

Saigon

PHILIPPINES
(U.S.A.)

GUAM
(U.S.A.)

Sinking of Repulse
& Prince of Wales

MALAYA

SUMATRA

Singapore

BORNEO

CELEBES

NEW GUINEA

DUTCH EAST INDIES

JAVA

Air raids
on Darwin

Darwin

AUSTRALIA

XX.—THE WAR IN ASIA, 1941–3.

**The Defeat of Japan.** In October, 1944, an American fleet destroyed
almost all that was left of the Japanese Navy at the battle of Leyte
Gulf and the Americans were soon once more in control of the Philippines. At Leyte and in the attacks on the islands of Okinawa and
Iwo Jima the Japanese also lost the bulk of their air force. From
island bases, such as Okinawa, the Americans were now able to
launch devastating bomber attacks on Japan. However, despite the
Japanese emperor's efforts to get a negotiated peace, it was obvious
that the Japanese Army would stage a last ditch defence which would
involve enormous casualties on both sides and the prolongation of the

war into 1946. In the light of this, the allies decided to drop the newly tested atomic bomb on a Japanese city. On August 6, 1945, an atomic bomb was dropped by an American Superfortress on the city of Hiroshima killing 78,000 people at one blast. A horrifying new dimension had been added to war. On August 8 the Russians declared war on Japan and invaded Manchuria; on August 9 the Americans dropped another atomic bomb, on Nagasaki; on August 14 the Japanese surrendered unconditionally. The war was over.

**The Allied Victory.** There are good reasons to believe that Hitler's original strategy was based on the expectation of a rapid victory over both France and Britain, after which he would have been able to wage war against the Soviet Union alone. After the fall of France some peace feelers were put out to Britain, but they were never seriously considered by Churchill. Hitler's failure to destroy the British Army at Dunkirk and the defeat of the Luftwaffe in the Battle of Britain destroyed his hopes of an early military victory over Britain; the operation on Lend-Lease helped to sustain Britain materially and morally against an Axis siege.

In the same way the great extension of the war after Operation Barbarossa and Pearl Harbor depended for its success on a speedy

Fig. 50.—The Americans and Russians meet on the Banks of the Elbe

and overwhelming victory. In neither case did the Germans and Japanese quite achieve their aims and, once the resources of the United States and the Soviet Union were fully mobilised, Hitler and his allies were at a permanent disadvantage in terms of manpower and industrial production.

The war was a total struggle which involved not just armed forces but the whole civilian population as well. On the home front both sides devoted great attention to the propaganda battle; in this the allies were fortunate that even in the darkest days of the war they scored morale-boosting victories against the Italians. An even greater advantage that they enjoyed was the operation of resistance movements in almost every country that the Germans overran. In some cases the resistance was able to pass on valuable military information and carry out acts of sabotage; in other cases, such as Yugoslavia, they were able to mount major guerilla campaigns which tied down thousands of Axis troops. This was also true in Asia, although the Japanese went to great lengths to try to win the co-operation of the Asian peoples in the struggle against their former imperial masters.

Account must also be taken of the conduct of the war by the leaderships on each side. Neither Mussolini nor his people had wanted to fight the war and Fascist Italy was an extremely weak link in the Axis alliance. Indeed the Italians fought much more effectively in the later stages of the war, when they had joined the allies than they ever did in 1940–1943. In contrast the Germans had at their command a superb fighting force, but on several occasions it was destroyed by Hitler's inflexibility. The outstanding example of this was at Stalingrad, but there were many other times when Hitler refused to follow his generals' advice and allow strategic withdrawals.

On the allied side the Russians bore the brunt of the land war and suffered perhaps twenty-five million casualties as a result. The Americans were responsible for the largest part of the Pacific war and made by far the largest contribution to the war in terms of materials. British and Commonwealth troops however sustained the war almost unaided in the vital period 1940–1941. Perhaps the most controversial decision of the allies was to press for unconditional surrender in Europe and Asia. It was a decision that led to a lengthening of the war and to the dropping of the atomic bombs. However, the allies were well aware that the Axis powers hoped to use a negotiated settlement to split Russia from her Western allies. They were also intent not only on the military defeat of Germany, Japan and their allies, but on the overthrow of the Nazi, Fascist and Japanese militarist régimes. This could only be achieved by total victory.

## chapter twenty-one

# EUROPE AND THE COLD WAR, 1945-1953

**The Wartime Conferences: 1. Yalta, February, 1945.** From the time of the Atlantic Charter onwards the allied leaders held regular meetings to discuss the conduct of the war. However, the first conference to map out the details of the post-war settlement was not held till February, 1945, when Stalin, Roosevelt and Churchill met at Yalta in the Crimea. The Yalta conference was important because it laid the foundations of post-war world and in particular of the domination of the Soviet Union in Central and Eastern Europe. During the conference Roosevelt played a mediatory role between Stalin and Churchill and refused to accept Churchill's plans to push western troops as far into Eastern Europe as possible. As a result of this, the agreement has subsequently been subjected to a good deal of criticism in the west.

The most important part of the conference was devoted to the treatment of liberated Europe. It was agreed that the liberated people should be helped to establish "democratic" governments, but just what this would mean in practice was not closely defined. In respect of Poland, which was already in the hands of the Russians, Stalin conceded that some non-Communists should be included in the provisional government. It was also agreed that the reconstituted Polish state should include considerable territory which was formerly part of Germany up to the line of the Oder and Neisse rivers, but that it should cede some of its own former territory in the east to Russia. The Russians agreed to declare war on Japan in the near future and in return were rewarded with the Kurile Islands, a lease of Port Arthur from China, and certain rights over Manchurian railways and Outer Mongolia. Finally it was settled that post-war Germany should be divided into allied zones of occupation and that a new international organisation should be set up to replace the discredited League of Nations.

**2. The San Francisco Conference, April–June, 1945.** The San Francisco Conference was not attended by any of the Big Three leaders, but it did lay the foundations of a new international organisation. On June 26, 1945, the Charter of the United Nations was signed by re-

XXI.—THE RESETTLEMENT OF CENTRAL EUROPE.

presentatives of fifty states and it came into force on October 24. The main organs of the United Nations Organisation were the General Assembly, made up of delegates from all the member states, and the

Security Council. The latter was to be the executive body of the organisation and initially had eleven members. Of these five were permanent: U.S.A., U.S.S.R., Britain, France and China. Any decision taken by the Council could be approved by a simple majority, but each of the permanent members had the right to veto decisions. This power was to be used on numerous occasions by U.S.S.R. during the cold war and has also been used by Britain, France and China. The other main arms of the organisation were the Economic and Social Council, the Trusteeship Council which took over responsibility for the old League Mandates, the International Court of Justice and the permanent secretariat under the direction of the Secretary General (for details see Chapter Twenty-six).

**3. The Potsdam (or Berlin) Conference July–August, 1945.** The last great conference of the war met at Potsdam, the old royal suburb of Berlin, between July 17 and August 2. The atmosphere had changed considerably since Yalta. In the first place Clement Attlee replaced Winston Churchill as British Prime Minister during July, and, following the death of Roosevelt in April, Vice-President Truman had taken over the Presidency of the United States. Of the wartime Big Three only Stalin remained. Relations between the wartime allies had also become much less friendly. The Western allies were highly suspicious of Russian activities in Eastern Europe particularly in Poland, where the Russians were installing a Communist controlled government. However the conference re-affirmed the Oder-Neisse line as the western boundary of Poland and agreed that East Prussia should be divided between Poland and Russia.

The conference also settled further details concerning the treatment of Germany. Berlin was split into four sectors and control over economic matters was vested in the Four-power Allied Control Commission, of which the first chairman was an American. German war industries were to be dismantled and war criminals brought to trial. Each power was to take reparations from its own zone as it saw fit, and, in recognition of the enormous losses that Russian industry had suffered, the Russians were allowed to ask for additional reparations from Western Germany. However the Western allies resisted Russian demands to share in the control of the Ruhr industrial area.

At this time it was the publicly declared policy of all powers that Germany should be reunited in the foreseeable future and a peace treaty signed with her. A generation later neither of these aims had been achieved.

**The Other Treaties.** The collapse of the Nazi empire involved a re-drawing of frontiers and a resettlement of people all over Europe, particularly in the east. In theory there were two sorts of states involved. On the one hand some, such as Poland, Czechoslovakia and Austria, were treated as liberated allies. Czechoslovakia and Poland are dealt with in more detail elsewhere (page 364). Austria was occupied by the four powers and divided between them, but a moderate Socialist government with powers over the country as a whole was established with Russian consent.

On the other hand Rumania, Bulgaria, Hungary, and Finland were all classed as defeated enemies. The first three were occupied by the Red Army, Communist or Communist-controlled governments set up, and some frontier adjustments made (see pages 386–9). Finland escaped occupation although the country was forced to give up some territory to the Russians, to grant economic privileges to them, and to allow the Russian occupation of the naval base at Porkkala. A moderate Socialist government was established and the country was able to develop close economic links with both Western and Eastern Europe.

The only other defeated belligerent state was Italy. Italy obviously enjoyed a rather different position, firstly because no part of the country was occupied by the Russians, and secondly because for the last part of the war Italians had fought alongside the allies against Germany. The Russians did demand very large reparations for the damage Italians were supposed to have done as Hitler's partners on the eastern front, but the Russians were not allowed any direct control in Italian affairs. However Italy did lose her African colonies and was forced to concede some disputed territory around Trieste to Yugoslavia.

**The Cold War.** By the time of the Potsdam conference it was clear that the post-war world would be dominated by the two super-powers, the Soviet Union and the United States. In the years after the war, relations between these powers deteriorated so rapidly that it seemed that a new war without bloodshed was being fought, a cold war which showed no signs of abating at least until the death of Stalin in 1953.

The Russians were in an overwhelmingly dominant position in the whole of Eastern Europe at the end of the war, with their troops in Poland, Hungary, Rumania, Bulgaria, Czechoslovakia and the eastern parts of both Germany and Austria. In all these areas, with the exception of Austria, they used this military control to impose

Communist or Communist-dominated governments and to direct both internal and external policies in these states. An early example of this process was Poland, where the People's Party which represented Peasant interests was suppressed in 1947 and other non-Communist parties were either broken up or absorbed into the National Front of the Polish Workers' Party (Communist) and the Polish Socialist Party. When it appeared that even the Polish Communists might seek to follow a line independent of that dictated from Moscow, some 75,000 Communists and Socialists whom the Russians regarded as unreliable were purged from their parties. The First Secretary of the Communist party, Gomulka, was forced to resign in 1948 because of his supposed sympathies with Tito in Yugoslavia (see page 365) and he was arrested and imprisoned in 1951.

There was also conflict between the State and the Roman Catholic Church which could claim the allegiance of 90 per cent of Polish people. In 1951 the Polish government abolished the papal administration of dioceses in the western territories which had been gained from Germany and in 1953 all clerical appointments came under the control of the State. However neither the independent spirit of the Church, nor the support of the mass of the people for Catholicism was broken.

The same sort of process occurred in Hungary: the Hungarian Smallholders (peasants) Party was suppressed and its leaders imprisoned; and there was conflict between the State and the Church.

**Czechoslovakia.** These developments certainly disturbed the Western allies and contributed to the mounting tension between Eastern and Western Europe. However they felt much more directly threatened by events in Czechoslovakia. Czechoslovakia was the most industrialised state of Eastern Europe and the one with the most successful experience of democratic government before the war. Because of the active role it had played in resisting the Nazis, the Communist Party gained wide support amongst the workers and intellectuals and after the war joined a coalition government of liberal and left-wing parties under the 'Stalinist' Klement Gottwald. The Communists soon gained control of key posts in the police, communications, and the armed forces. In February 1948 tension between the Communists and non-Communists led to the breakdown of the coalition and a new government was formed by the Communists and Social Democrats alone. This was followed by a purge of anti-Communists in government posts and in elections of May, 1948, a single list of National Front candidates was put before the electorate.

After the elections President Benes, who had been restored to his office in 1945, resigned and was replaced by Gottwald. Already in March of that year the last non-Communist member of the Cabinet, Foreign Minister Jan Masaryk son of the founder of Czechoslovakia, had been found dead in suspicious circumstances.

The Communist control of Czechoslovakia was followed by a purge of the Party itself. Only those leaders who had proved themselves completely loyal to Moscow were left in power, and amongst those who were executed was Rudolph Slansky, the secretary of the Czech Communist Party. As in Poland and Hungary, there was conflict between Church and State and the redoubtable Cardinal Beran was expelled in 1951.

**Tito and Yugoslav Communism.** Unlike most other countries in the area, Yugoslavia had not been liberated by the Red Army. The native Communist Party under Tito had won control of the country very much on its own initiative and for this reason the Yugoslavs were much less ready to take orders from Moscow. In 1948 disagreement between Tito and Stalin came into the open. The Russians accused Tito of betraying his fellow Slavs by giving up Yugoslav claims to Austrian Carinthia; the Russians also maintained that

FIG. 51.—PRESIDENT TITO INSPECTS HIS CRACK TROOPS.

Russian citizens were mistreated in Yugoslavia. Behind the flow of petty accusations and counter-accusations there were much more important issues. In particular Tito refused to accept Stalin's line in economic affairs and he also had plans to build up an alliance of Balkan states which did not suit Russian purposes. Tito was denounced as a traitor and an American collaborator, and Yugoslavia was expelled from the International Communist movement. However the Yugoslavs were loyal to their leader and the western powers were only too anxious to offer economic aid to the country. Within Yugoslavia Stalinist policies were soon abandoned. The consumer industries were not completely subordinated to the claims of heavy industry and the peasants were allowed to opt out of the collective farm system. Another distinctive feature of Yugoslav Communism was the absence of bureaucratic centralisation on the Russian model. In the villages and factories the workers enjoyed a genuine form of local self government, and the managing committee of each enterprise was drawn from an elected works council.

Tito's form of independent national Communism naturally won support in other Communist states, and it was to scotch a movement so dangerous to Russian interests that Stalin carried out his drastic purges of local Communist leaders in Hungary, Poland, Rumania, Bulgaria and Czechoslovakia between 1948 and 1952.

**The Greek Civil War.** The Communists had also taken a leading part in the resistance to Nazi rule in Greece and, after the German evacuation in 1944, they had joined the coalition government. However, when the government proposed to disarm the Communist guerrillas, fighting broke out in Athens and it was only controlled with the help of British troops. In March, 1946, the right-wing monarchist party was successful at the general elections and began to take repressive action against the Communists. The Communists reacted by organising guerrilla forces in Macedonia, where they could be supplied from neighbouring Communist states, especially Yugoslavia.

The civil war that followed was marked by appalling atrocities, but by 1949 the Communist guerrillas had been defeated. Tito had cut off the supply lines from the north and the monarchists had enjoyed support from the British, and after 1947 from the Americans. They also benefited from the economic aid that came into the country under the Marshall Plan (see page 371).

By the death of Stalin in 1953, the situation in Eastern Europe had been more or less stabilised with Stalinist governments in power in most countries, but with both Greece and Yugoslavia free, in their

FIG. 52.—RIOTING IN ATHENS, 1946.

different ways, from Russian domination. The Communist success in this part of Europe owed something to the great part that the Communists had played in organising resistance movements in the war. It owed even more to the fact that the area had been liberated by the Red Army. To many Western politicians the extension of Communist control had been a ruthless and aggressive policy through the exercise of propaganda, political manipulation and military power. On the other hand the Russians believed that it was part of a largely defensive policy which would secure the Soviet Union in the future from a repetition of Operation Barbarossa—whether launched by a revived Germany or by the western allies.

**The Revival of Western Europe.** The political development of Western Europe during this same period, 1945–1953, naturally followed a quite different course. Here communist parties established themselves quite successfully within the parliamentary systems, but middle of the road political movements remained in control.

In France the first coalition government was led by de Gaulle and included members of the French Communist Party. However the

Communists went into opposition in 1947. With the intensification of the Cold War co-operation with liberal and socialist parties became increasingly difficult and in particular the Communists were opposed to the acceptance of Marshall Aid (see page 371). In contrast to Czechoslovakia, the Communists in France did not manage to win over an important section of the Socialist movement, and coalition governments in France thereafter came to depend on combinations of the Socialists, M.R.P. (moderate catholic party), and Radicals. Unfortunately the proliferation of small parties and the rather even balance between the three or four main groups made stable government very difficult. Every government represented a combination of diverse political interests, which could easily split apart on any controversial piece of legislation. Only cautious reforms which had general support could be introduced and by 1947 General de Gaulle had already tired of the party manipulations which were necessary to hold a government together. He therefore resigned and retired to the country and thereafter he was to be a remote but powerful critic of the weakness of the whole political system of the Fourth Republic.

The Italian elections of 1946 also led to the formation of a coalition government led by the Christian Democrat (moderate catholic) leader, de Gasperi. It included the Socialists and until 1948 the powerful Italian Communist Party. Here the Communists did succeed in forming a working alliance with a group of Socialists under Signor Nenni and in the election of 1948 they won a third of the national vote. However the Christian Democrats with 40 per cent of the vote remained the largest single party and the basis of all post-war Italian governments. Unfortunately these administrations were never strong enough to take the decisive steps which were necessary to solve Italy's social and economic problems. The most troubled area was the poverty stricken south where the Communists encouraged the peasants to expropriate the lands of the southern landowners and set up "committees of the land" on the Russian model of 1917. In the end this movement failed, but it did highlight one of the unresolved problem of the country that the Christian Democrats had never really tackled.

**The Problems of Germany.** Germany was by far the most difficult area for political and economic reconstruction. The country as a whole was divided into four zones and the old capital, Berlin, into four sectors. The Allied Control Commission was supposed to co-ordinate matters of common interest to the country as a whole, but relations between the four occupying powers were very bad. The problem was made worse by the fact that Germany was suffering not only from the devastation of the war, but was being flooded with hundreds of thousands of refugees from Eastern Europe, including the expelled Sudeten Germans. The Russians dismantled and carried away much of the industrial equipment from their own zone and wanted to do the same from the Ruhr, but were refused permission by the British who controlled the area. In May, 1946, the Americans also refused to allow the Russians any more reparations from the American Zone.

Within Eastern Germany the Russians nationalised a third of all industry by 1948 and confiscated and redistributed all estates of over 250 acres. They encouraged the formation of the Social Unity Party made up of Communists and Social Democrats with the former really in control. However there was still no clear cut attempt to divide Germany permanently. The division hardened gradually during the "Cold War".

In 1947 the Americans and British united their zones for economic purposes. In 1948 by the London Agreement all three Western powers decided to establish a single government for Western Germany and two major political parties emerged, the Christian Democrats under Konrad Adenauer and the Social Democrats led by Kurt Schumacher. At the same time the Russians were establishing a central government in Eastern Germany; already by 1948 the hopes for a unified Germany were receding.

**The Berlin Blockade June, 1948, to May, 1949.** Relations between the occupying powers deteriorated throughout 1948. In February the Soviet Commander, Sokolovsky, claimed that the whole of Berlin was part of the Soviet Zone. In June, at a meeting in London, representatives of U.S.A., Britain, France, Belgium, the Netherlands and Luxembourg passed a resolution in favour of creating a federal government for Western Germany. The final step to an open confrontation came when the allied authorities in the West arranged for a revaluation of the currency to help economic reconstruction and defeat the "black market". The Russians claimed that the unilateral revaluation by the Western powers was contrary to the terms of the Potsdam agreement and would hinder economic relations between East and West Germany by disastrously depressing the value of the east German mark. They forbade the circulation of the new currency in their zone and throughout Berlin, thus re-iterating their claim to control the whole city, at least for economic purposes. In June they closed the land corridors into the Western sectors of Berlin in an attempt to drive the Western powers from Berlin altogether.

This land blockade lasted almost a year and the Western sectors were supplied for the whole of that time by a vast, costly, but ultimately successful airlift. At times during the crisis it seemed that the powers were on the brink of war, but in the end an agreement was reached in May, 1949, which led to the re-opening of the land routes. In effect the four powers recognised that both Germany and Berlin would be divided for the forseeable future. The status quo could only be altered by open war and neither side was prepared to face that choice.

FIG. 53.—UNLOADING COAL DURING THE BERLIN AIRLIFT.

The result in Germany itself was to hasten the establishment of two states and two governments. The Federal German Republic was set up in August, 1949, with its capital at Bonn and a Christian Democrat government led by Adenauer. In October, 1949, the German Democratic Republic was established with its capital in the Soviet sector of Berlin. Its first premier was the socialist Grotewohl, later to be superseded by the ardent Stalinist, Walter Ulbricht.

**The Truman Doctrine and the Marshall Plan.** In his famous speech at Fulton Ohio in 1946 Winston Churchill had warned that an "Iron Curtain" was descending through Europe, dividing the West from the area dominated by the Soviet Union. Not all Western statesmen agreed with Churchill at this time, but the division between East and West became increasingly clear as time passed. In the same year Truman accepted that it should be a part of United States policy to contain Communism by all possible means and in 1947 the U.S.A. took over Britain's commitment in Greece and Turkey to support the anti-Communist régimes.

An even more decisive point in the drawing of a hard and fast line between East and West came with the proposal by the American Secretary of State, George Marshall, that the United States would make a major contribution to the economic recovery of Europe, provided that the European states themselves would co-operate in the assessment and administration of the aid programme. Molotov, the Soviet Foreign Minister, joined the Western European leaders in the initial discussions, but in the end he rejected Marshall Aid because he claimed that it represented American interference in the internal affairs of other states. The arguments the Americans had used against the Russians were now thrown back at them and Molotov, on Stalin's orders, not only refused Marshall Aid for Russia, but forced the other Eastern European states to do the same.

In the end the Marshall plan was administered by the Organisation for European Economic Co-operation made up of sixteen European states and Canada and the United States. Enormous sums were pumped into Europe from North America and the European countries were given valuable experience in the benefits of economic co-operation.

The rejection of Marshall Aid was followed by the imposition of much tighter Communist control in Eastern Europe and of a strict Stalinist line within the Communist parties there. Stalin established the Cominform (Communist Information Bureau) to co-ordinate the work of the European Communist parties and enforce ideological conformity and the COMECON, an economic co-operative plan for Eastern Europe as an alternative to O.E.E.C. The results of Stalin's policies can be seen in the purge of the Communist leaders (p.364) as well as the Czech and Yugoslav crises.

**The Formation of NATO.** The post-war division of Europe was further emphasised by the Treaty of Brussels in March, 1948. By this treaty Britain, France, Belgium, the Netherlands and Luxembourg formed a defensive alliance against any form of aggression. The treaty was clearly aimed not only against a revived Germany, but also against the military presence of the Soviet Union in Europe. One of the leading figures in the formation of this alliance was Ernest

Bevin, the British Foreign Secretary and an ardent supporter of economic and military co-operation in Europe. However, it was clear to Bevin and the other European leaders that the Brussels group did not have the power to counter-balance the might of the Soviet Union. They therefore favoured closer long-term military co-operation with the United States and not only welcomed the Marshall plan, but also pressed for the inclusion of the United States in the Brussels Pact. Under the policy laid down in the Truman Doctrine this idea certainly appealed to the United States government, especially after the Communist takeover in Czechoslovakia and the Berlin Blockade. The result was the formation of the North Atlantic Treaty Organisation in March, 1949. It included not only the members of the Brussels Pact and the United States but also Canada, Denmark, Norway, Iceland, Italy and Portugal (Greece and Turkey became members in 1952). It had a permanent headquarters in Paris and the Supreme Headquarters Allied Powers in Europe (SHAPE) at Versailles initially commanded by General Eisenhower.

NATO was seen by some both as an essential defensive organisation against Communist aggression and as a successful step towards European co-operation. On the other hand the Soviet Union denounced it as an aggressive American dominated pact, the formation of which was a breach of the United Nations Charter. Russian denunciations of the Western military pacts increased in 1954 when the Brussels Pact was renamed the Western European Union and extended to include Italy and the Federal German Republic. As the Western European Union formed the core of NATO, this in turn led to development of the German armed forces as part of NATO. From the Western point of view this was a means by which Germany might develop her own forces once again, but under international control through NATO. It marked the final recognition of West German sovereignty by the Western allies and thereafter allied troops remained in Germany as the advance guard of NATO rather than an army of occupation. The Russians on the other hand bitterly criticised the redevelopment of German military strength less than ten years after the war.

However NATO itself was at no time an equal match for the forces of Russia and her satellites. The real strength of the alliance was that it had the support of the United States and her atomic weaponry. This became even more vital after September, 1949, when the Russians exploded their first atomic bomb, thus breaking the American monopoly of this terrifying weapon.

Although during this most intense phase of the Cold War the emphasis in Western Europe was on military co-operation, there were also signs that the economic work of O.E.E.C. could be extended. In particular in 1952 the European Coal and Steel Community was set up. Inspired by Robert Schumann, the French statesman, the Community established a joint authority over the iron, steel, and coal industries in France, Germany, Belgium, the Netherlands, and Luxembourg. Britain had also been invited to join the community, but had been unwilling to accept international control over parts of her economy. However the Community soon proved the great advantages of operating in a large market and it was to be an important step towards the creation of the Common Market later in the fifties (see page 390).

# chapter twenty-two

# NATIONALISM, COMMUNISM AND THE DECLINE OF THE ASIAN EMPIRES, 1945-1953

After 1945 it is impossible to consider European history in isolation. The struggle in Europe had been only part of a wider war fought in the Middle East, North Africa and the Far East, and in the aftermath of the war the affairs of Europe and the non-European world remained closely interconnected. In the first place, the war accelerated the desire of the subject peoples of the European empires to win their independence, so that the major European powers became deeply involved in the problems of nationalism in Asia and Africa. In the second place the "Cold War" between the Russian bloc and America and her allies was fought not only in Europe itself, but also in Asia and the Middle East. America and her allies became concerned to contain the Communist expansion in all parts of the world while the Russians were very ready to help and advise the nationalist leaders in the emergent states of Asia and Africa. Thirdly, the European nations had enormous economic interests in other parts of the world, and even where their direct colonial control was relinquished, they still sought to maintain areas of political and economic influence. An outstanding example of this was the desire of the British to protect their oil interests in the Middle East.

## THE MIDDLE EAST 1945-1953

**Britain and Palestine.** Britain had long regarded the Middle East as one of her spheres of influence and when, in 1945, the independent Arab states—Egypt, Transjordan, Lebanon, Saudi Arabia, Iraq, Yemen and Syria—formed the Arab League, the British hoped to maintain their influence despite the new nationalistic mood of the Arabs. However there were several barriers to good relations between Britain and the Arab world, the greatest of which was the situation in Palestine. Here Britain had control under a League of Nations Mandate and the British administration was struggling unsuccessfully to balance the interests of the Arabs and the Jewish immigrants, who flooded into the country both before and after the war. In the face of inter-communal violence the British decided to withdraw altogether in 1948 and hand over the problem to the United Nations. The U.N.

tried to get agreement on a partition of the country between Jews and Arabs, but the Jews proclaimed an independent state of Israel which was immediately attacked by its Arab neighbours. In the war that followed the Jews gained ground at the Arabs expense and in 1949 the U.N. was able to arrange a truce. However the Arab states never recognised the right of the state of Israel to exist. The settlement left a million Palestinian Arabs as refugees and over, 200,000 Jews were expelled from Arab states. Moreover there remained a dangerous situation which was to erupt into war on two more occasions within the next twenty years.

**Britain and Egypt.** Britain's other conflicts with the Arab world stemmed mainly from her control of the Suez Canal and her position in the Sudan. The Anglo-Egyptian Treaty of 1936 allowed Britain to maintain troops in the Canal Zone, while the Canal itself was run by a company in which the British government was by far the largest shareholder. The Egyptians resented this situation and harrassed the British by guerrilla attacks on the Zone. The Egyptians also wished to bring about the incorporation of the Sudan into Egypt while the British were intent upon leading the country to complete independence. In June, 1952, there were riots in Cairo in which British property was attacked and British civilians were killed. In July the violence turned against the corrupt government of King Farouk and he was overthrown in a military coup. General Neguib was the nominal leader of the revolution, but the real power behind it was Colonel Nasser. In fact, however, this turn of events seemed to offer Britain the chance to make a fresh start in her relations with Egypt.

**France and the Middle East.** The French at this time were experiencing even greater difficulties in the Arab world. In 1945 they had failed to re-establish their control in Syria and they were soon facing nationalist unrest in Morocco, Tunisia and Algeria. The Tunisian nationalist leader Habib Bourguiba was imprisoned, but there was a mounting campaign of terrorist attacks on French property and forces. In Morocco the French Resident, General Juin, imposed a policy of repression and when, in 1953, the Sultan refused to co-operate as a French puppet he was exiled to Madagascar. In Algeria, despite the granting of some local self-government, the French persisted in their policy of treating the territory as part of metropolitan France with representatives in the National Assembly in Paris. Effective local control remained in the hands of the large minority of French settlers, the "colons".

Fig. 54.—Colonel Nasser (*left centre*) and General Neguib (*right centre*)
soon after the Egyptian Revolution.

**Persia.** The conflict between nationalism and the interests of the
European nations was not restricted to the Arab lands. During the
war Persia had been jointly occupied by the Russians and the British
after the overthrow of a pro-Axis government. The Soviet Union
encouraged the growth of a local Communist Party (the Tudeh) in
the northern zone and the Persian government was forced to include
some Communist members in the administration. The Russians also
tried to set up a joint Soviet-Persian company to exploit oil in the
north of the country. However in 1947 agreements with Russia were
repudiated and the Tudeh was banned.

At the same time, however, the Persians sought to free themselves
from British control in the south and nationalised the Anglo-Iran-
ian Oil Company. The Shah himself was forced into exile by nationalists. However in 1953 the Shah was restored by a military coup and
a new agreement was reached with the Western oil companies. In all
these crises in the Middle East the Russians refrained from direct
intervention at this time. However there was a potentially dangerous
tension throughout the area between nationalism and European
interests in both the Suez Canal and the enormously valuable oil-fields.

## THE FAR EAST 1945–1953

**The British in Asia.** The pre-war situation in Asia, as in the Middle East, was disturbed by two closely related forces. In the first place the area had been a theatre of war and in large parts of it the European powers had been ejected from their colonies by the Japanese. In the second place, the forces of nationalism had become very much more powerful after 1945, while the old imperial nations were suffering from a relative decline as military and economic powers. The effect was immediately apparent in South Asia, which was completely freed from British control by 1948. In the Indian sub-continent this was only achieved after much greater communal violence between Muslims and Hindus, which was only partially resolved by the creation of the independent dominions of India and Pakistan in 1947. Both states remained within the British Commonwealth, however, although from the very first they showed that they had no intention of being closely bound by British foreign policy. In 1948 Ceylon made a peaceful transition to self-government and also remained a member of the Commonwealth. Burma, on the other hand, left the Commonwealth altogether on becoming independent in 1947.

Despite the bloodshed in India, the British had withdrawn from South Asia without a direct confrontation with local resistance forces. This pattern was not repeated in Malaya where, after 1947, British troops were to fight a long war against guerilla forces made up mainly of Communists drawn from the Chinese population of the Malay states. Ultimately the British campaign was to be successful because it won the support of the Malays themselves in return for a definite development towards self-government, which was to be achieved by the Federation of Malaya in 1957.

**The Other European Empires in Asia.** Apart from the British, the French and Dutch were the two main colonial powers in the Far East. The Dutch East Indies were completely overrun by the Japanese during the war and anti-Dutch feeling encouraged amongst the Indonesians. A strong nationalist movement developed with some Communist support and the Dutch were never really able to re-establish their control. They finally recognised this in 1949 by formally acknowledging the Republic of Indonesia under the leadership of President Sukarno.

In French Indo-China the Communist Viet-Minh, led by Ho Chi-Minh, had played a leading part in the struggle against the Japanese and at the end of the war they dominated northern Annam (Vietnam) including the major city of Hanoi. The French were prepared to

FIG 55.—MUSLIM REFUGEES FLEEING FROM THE HINDU SECTION OF CALCUTTA, 1946.

recognise Ho Chi Minh's republic north of the 18th parallel, but they resisted his claim that the whole of Vietnam should pass out of French control. In reply they set up a government in the south of Saigon and recognised the former Japanese puppet, Bao Dai, as ruler of the whole of Vietnam. However the Viet-Minh refused to accept this solution and, supported from the Soviet Union and Communist China, they began an open war with the French. The outcome of this struggle is dealt with on pages 423–28.

**Communist Victory in China.** In the 1930's the Nationalist government of China under Chiang Kai-shek had been challenged by Communist forces operating from a number of bases in the provinces and led, after 1934, by Mao Tse-tung. This conflict had been mainly suspended during the war with the Japanese, but in 1945 it soon developed into full-scale civil war, spreading from Manchuria over the rest of the country. By 1949 the Communists were triumphant and Chiang had been driven from the mainland to the island of Formosa

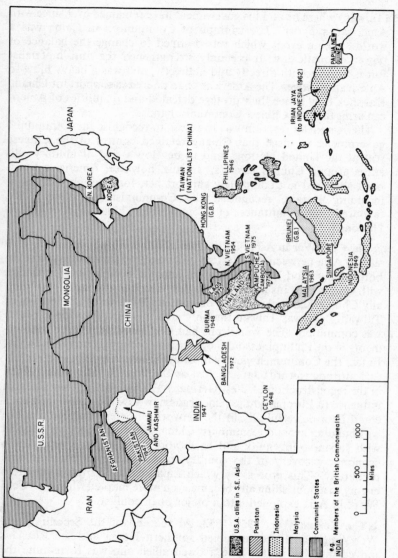

XXII.—Post-war Asia.

(Taiwan) where he and his government have remained ever since with American support. The triumph of Communism in China was a world shaking event which was destined to change the balance of power dramatically. It certainly strengthened the anti-imperialist forces in Asia both directly and indirectly, and was a heavy blow to American prestige. The Americans had poured in support for Chiang Kai-shek only to see their protégé defeated and quantities of American arms fall into Chinese Communist hands.

The American reaction was to refuse to recognise the Communist government, to insist that Chiang retained control of the Chinese seat at the United Nations, and to develop a ring of military alliances around China's borders. In this, however, America's European allies did not completely support her, for a number of them, including Britain, recognised the Communist government and favoured the admittance of Communist China to the United Nations.

**The Cold War in Asia.** By the late 1940's there was mounting tension in Asia between the Western allies and the Communist bloc. In both Malaya and Vietnam Western imperial powers were in conflict with Communist insurgents, while the Americans, in support of their ally Chiang Kai-shek, faced Communist China across the Straits of Taiwan. Nor was Taiwan the only area in which the United States was committed. The Americans had long standing defence commitments in the Philippines and they were the occupying power in Japan. In fact the Communist victory in China hastened a change in America's attitude towards Japan. Just as the Western allies had helped in the reconstruction of West Germany as a bulwark against Russian influence in Europe, so the Americans now saw that a revived Japan could be a powerful ally in the network of defence agreements she was building around Communist China. American support coupled with Japanese ingenuity and hard work soon led to a remarkable economic recovery in the country, now ruled by a constitutional monarchy. This process by which Japan changed from a prostrate enemy to a flourishing ally became even more marked when the "Cold War" in Asia exploded into a major open conflict.

**The Korean War, 1950-1953.** At the end of the Second World War American forces occupied southern Korea and the Russians moved into the north. The avowed allied aim was to re-unite the country into an independent state under the temporary trusteeship of the United Nations, a trusteeship to be administered by the Soviet Union, Nationalist China, the United States and Great Britain. However, attempts by the United Nations to hold national elections in 1948 failed and in February of that year the Democratic People's Republic of Korea was established in the north of the country. Shortly afterwards a separate government was established in the south under the presidency of Dr Syngman Rhee. With the departure of both Russian and American troops in 1948 and 1949 respectively the two Korean states were left facing each other across the 38th parallel. Both sides were supplied with arms by their former occupiers and the political situation in the south was very unstable. There was widespread sympathy for the Communists there, especially amongst the poorer people, and in 1948 there was a rebellion in Yosu province due to the slowness with which the government was carrying through the promised land reforms. The rebellion was crushed with great brutality, and Syngman Rhee's support fell markedly in the 1950 elections.

In June, 1950, after numerous frontier incidents, North Korean forces crossed the 38th parallel in strength. At the time the Soviet Union was boycotting the United Nations, so the Security Council was able to pass a resolution condemning the North Koreans as aggressors. American forces were immediately sent to South Korea and they were later joined by British, Commonwealth and Turkish troops as part of a United Nations army. The northerners were repulsed and the U.N. force under General MacArthur advanced over the 38th parallel. MacArthur wished to drive north to the Yalu frontier, which was the border with China, despite Chinese warnings against such action. In fact, even before he had advanced that far, MacArthur found his forces under attack from tens of thousands of Chinese troops who had been sent in to aid the North Koreans. The U.N. forces operating on extended lines of communication were heavily outnumbered and driven south again. In the face of this setback MacArthur wanted to bomb Chinese industrial installations in Manchuria and even to use the atomic bomb against the Chinese. These moves would probably have brought the Soviet Union, now also an atomic power, into the struggle and started a third world war. American and allied statesmen drew back from such a risk, and MacArthur was dismissed by President Truman.

The war continued with great ferocity and heavy casualties on both sides until, following Russian proposals at the United Nations, a truce was called in June, 1951. The negotiations that followed dragged on until 1953, due largely to the intransigence of both North and South Koreans. However, eventually it was agreed that the 38th parallel, with some adjustments, was once more to mark the boundary

FIG. 56.—TURKISH TROOPS IN THE U.N. FORCE SEARCH CHINESE PRISONERS IN KOREA.

between the two states and a permanent truce commission was set up at Panmunjon to deal with disputes between the two states. It was still in existence sixteen years later.

The effects of the war were felt far beyond the area of the conflict which was itself devastated and the scene of terrible military and civilian suffering. The war marked the period of most intense activity in the Cold War in the Far East. The Chinese accused the Americans of using germ warfare against them, an accusation which was taken up by anti-American movements in other countries. In America itself the war marked the high point in the career of Senator McCarthy, a fanatical anti-Communist who used his position in the Un-American Activities Committee to hound many innocent Americans with left-wing or liberal sympathies.

American support for Syngman Rhee and Chiang Kai-shek led Communists and nationalists in Asia to accuse the United States of propping up corrupt and reactionary governments. Certainly Syngman Rhee's government represented the right-wing and traditional forces in South Korea and Rhee himself was an unbending anti-Communist who saw war with Communist China as inevitable.

The diversion of resources to military expenditure and the development of atomic weapons in America had far reaching economic effects. The price of basic commodities increased, especially as Britain and other European powers also increased their military expenditure.

Perhaps the only good result of the war, especially at the time of MacArthur's dismissal, was that it focused attention on the danger of an atomic conflict. It did lead to efforts to control and limit the production and spread of atomic weapons, although in the long run it did not prevent the atomic powers developing even more powerful means of destruction.

## chapter twenty-three

# UNITY AND CONFLICT IN EUROPE, 1953–1978

**New Trends in Eastern Europe.** Stalin died on March 5, 1953. For a generation he had dominated Russia and since 1945 all the eastern European states except Yugoslavia had been rigidly controlled through his supporters and nominees. There was no one in Russia to take his place or maintain the monolithic nature of the Communist bloc.

In Czechoslovakia the Stalinist Gottwald also died in 1953 and there were signs of open discontent. The cost of living had been affected by current reform. Strikes and demonstrations, notably in Pilzen, put down by troops and police, showed that there was a strong current of opposition. Some steps were taken to meet these discontents by slowing down the process of collectivisation and by increasing production of consumer goods—both representing a break from Stalinist economics.

In East Berlin a dispute over the wages of building workers developed into rioting put down by Soviet tanks with heavy loss of life. Here and elsewhere in East Germany the demonstrations took on both an anti-Communist and an anti-Russian character.

In Hungary the Stalinist Rakosi was replaced by the more flexible Imre Nagy, more attention was paid to the provision of consumer goods and the peasants were allowed to opt out of the collectives. By the end of 1954 about 10 per cent of the collectives had been broken up and the peasants were being given more direct aid towards the modernisation of agriculture.

In Poland press and radio were allowed to operate more freely and the hated secret police had their activities curtailed. Collectivisation was limited and in Poland, as in Hungary, about two thirds of the land had remained in the peasants' hands in any case. There was an amnesty for many political prisoners amongst whom was Gomulka, who was re-instated as First Secretary of the Polish Communist Party in 1956.

Russia itself was also deeply affected by the death of Stalin. His two most powerful successors were Malenkov, the new Prime Minister, and Kruschev, the First Secretary of the Party. Beria, Stalin's chief of the secret police was executed and there were some attempts to reduce the powers of the secret police and strengthen the proper operation of the Soviet legal system. Malenkov placed a new emphasis on the production of consumer goods to meet the demands for an improved standard of living.

At the same time Russia's control over many aspects of life in the satellite states declined. By 1956 the joint companies, which had been set up with Russia in the Eastern European states to control trade and production, were wound up. The Soviet Union did, however, retain control of the production of uranium in Rumania, Bulgaria and East Germany.

Russia also began to develop the theory of peaceful co-existence, claiming that the Communists could engage the capitalist world in peaceful competition and thereby demonstrate the superiority of the Soviet system.

**Kruschev and the Twentieth Conference of the Soviet Communist Party.**    By 1956 Kruschev had emerged successfully from a power struggle in Russia with Malenkov and other members of the Soviet leadership. When the Soviet Communist Party held its Twentieth Conference in February, he announced a remarkable new line for the Communist movement. But the most remarkable part of the speech was a trenchant criticism of Stalin's policies and methods: it denounced his personal dictatorship which had led to the development of a "cult of personality"; it denounced the conduct of the early stages of the war. It also accused him of precipitating the Soviet–Yugoslav dispute.

Since Stalin had been regarded as one of the founding fathers of the Russian Revolution and of modern Communism, this change of policy was found to have far-reaching effects. Many political prisoners of the Stalinist era were released in Russia and the reputations of many of those executed in the purges were rehabilitated. The pattern was repeated elsewhere: in Czechoslovakia for instance the policies of Gottwald were denounced and in Poland some 30,000 political prisoners were freed.

**Poland and de-Stalinisation.**    Liberalisation in Poland, as elsewhere, did not go as far as many people hoped, while it did give them a greater opportunity to express their discontents. In June, 1956, the workers in Poznan staged a demonstration which had to be put down by police and soldiers. Unrest continued, and in October Gomulka was re-instated as First Secretary of the Communist Party. The Poznan riots forced the government to improve conditions. New arrangements were made with the Catholic Church and religious education was once more allowed in schools. The Polish parliament, the Seym, was given greater freedom in legislation and more authority was devolved upon local government. The workers were consulted more in the management of factories, and there was greater freedom for art and literature.

The Poles also took the opportunity to assert greater independence from the Russians. They dismissed Marshall Rokossovski, Stalin's Russian nominee as Polish Minister of Defence.

But the Poles insisted that they maintained their links with Russia and their membership of the Warsaw Pact. Power remained the monopoly of the Communist Party and indeed many of the liberalising reforms were to be eroded by Gomulka and his fellow Communist leaders in the years to come. Despite this the Russian leaders were worried by events in Poland, and might well have done more to try and check them had they not been faced with a much more serious challenge in Hungary.

**The Hungarian Rising, October, 1956.** Since 1953 there had been mounting pressure for reform in Hungary and the leaders of the Soviet Union had contributed towards this by their criticisms of Rakosi and by the new line at the Twentieth Congress. However the relaxation of the old Stalinist system only led to further unrest in the country which, combined with a very bad harvest in 1956, produced an atmosphere of political ferment in the autumn. On October 23 there were demonstrations in Budapest directed against collectivisation, the power of the secret police and the country's membership of the Warsaw Pact. Imre Nagy became Prime Minister once more with promises of free elections, a neutralist foreign policy and the release of Cardinal Mindszenty, the imprisoned head of the Catholic Church in Hungary.

At first the Russians accepted this dramatic development. On October 30 Red Army units moved out of the capital. However on November 4 tanks, infantry and armoured units poured over the Russian border and Budapest was re-occupied after street fighting with supporters of the Nagy government. Already a rival government had been formed by Janos Kadar, Secretary of the Hungarian Communist Party, and this pro-Soviet group was placed in power by the Russians. In the course of the fighting over 25,000 people were killed and 150,000 Hungarians fled to Western Europe. Nagy was later seized and executed.

The Soviet action was widely condemned by world opinion but the western world itself was deeply divided at that very moment

FIG. 57.—BATTERED BUILDINGS AND BURNT-OUT TANKS IN THE STREETS OF
BUDAPEST, 1956,

over the Anglo-French action at Suez. The Russians feared that
Nagy would lead Hungary right away from the Warsaw group and
that a dangerous wedge would thus be driven into their military
system in Eastern Europe. They also believed that right-wing
elements would destroy even a nationalist-Communist government
on the Polish model, and because of this danger they were able to
command the support of many members of the Hungarian
Communist Party.

Immediately after the insurrection the Kadar government carried
out a vigorous purge of the army and civil service. However after
1960 there was a general relaxation. Many political prisoners were
released and great efforts were made to improve the standards of
living. However Hungary remained a loyal member of the Warsaw
Pact.

**The Development of European Communism after 1956.**    In many western European countries the local Communist parties lost support as a result of the Soviet action in Hungary. In Eastern Europe the reaction was much harder to assess, but it is noticeable that there was very little sign of support for Hungary from Czechoslovakia even though, at this very time, many Czechs were also pressing for a more liberal government. The Czechs could not forget the part played by the Hungarians in the destruction of their country in 1938–1939.

It is even harder to know what the ordinary Russians felt about their country's action. However, they themselves were to enjoy a general improvement in living conditions over the next few years.

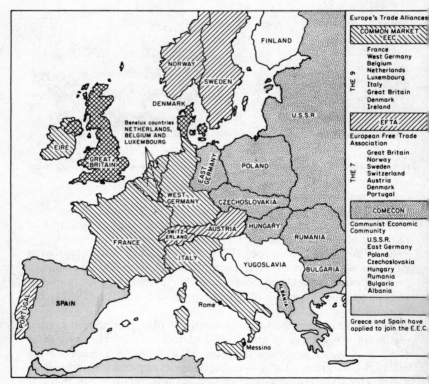

XXIII.—THE EUROPEAN TRADING ALLIANCES.

More emphasis was placed on the provision of consumer goods and many of the harsher features of the Communist system—such as the activities of the secret police and the use of forced labour—were curtailed. The country was at last beginning to enjoy the fruits of its industrial transformation since the revolution and it was soon to score notable prestige triumphs in space technology. In 1964 Kruschev was removed by other members of the Praesidium, but this bloodless change of control was not followed by any dramatic re-alignment of policy. Russia's new rulers, led by the triumvirate of Kosygin, Brezhnev and Podgorny have, however, been severe with any Russians who have been outspoken enough to offer a fundamental criticism of the Soviet system.

The Hungarian crisis certainly led to a new coolness in Soviet–Yugoslav relations which had improved after the death of Stalin. In any case the Yugoslavs with their own form of Communism were enjoying a tremendous economic growth. President Tito led the way in involving the people in their own government and in the control of factories and farms. The secret police and the party bureaucracy were severely restrained and there was a good deal of intellectual freedom. However, critics of the system as a whole were punished even when, as in the case of Milovan Djilas, they had close personal connections with Tito.

A different reaction again came in Communist China. After 1956 the Chinese leadership accused the Russians of betraying the Communist ideals both in their concentration on material progress and prosperity regardless of ideology, and in their closely connected policy of peaceful co-existence with the west, the policy which, ironically, they now pursue themselves. But in Europe China's only real ally was the backward and isolated state of Albania.

## WESTERN EUROPE 1953–1968

**The European Economic Community.** After 1953 the idea of economic co-operation became increasingly popular in Western Europe. The Coal and Steel Community had laid the foundations of the European Economic Community. In 1955 representatives of the six members of the ECSC appointed a special committee under the chairmanship of M. Spaak of Belgium. In April, 1956, this committee proposed that within twelve years the six states should abolish all mutual customs barriers. They also suggested that the six states should co-operate in the peaceful development of atomic power in an organisation that was to become known as Euratom. On March 24, 1957, the Treaty of Rome was signed by the Federal German

Republic, Italy, France, the Netherlands, Belgium and Luxembourg, a group whose total population topped 170,000,000. On January 1, 1958, the European Economic Community and Euratom Commission created by the treaty formally came into being.

The benefits of the economic association were soon felt by the member nations. Trade amongst themselves increased by 29 per cent in the year 1960–1961. Trade barriers were progressively lowered and the three co-operative bodies ECSC, EEC, and Euratom were merged in 1967. In that year common prices were fixed for agricultural products, notably wheat. A special agricultural fund was established to help support the price level of agricultural products.

Over the years the EEC certainly proved its success as a venture in economic development. There were difficulties, particularly in agreeing on a common agricultural policy, and there was some danger that those areas farthest from the centre of the Community, such as Brittany and southern Italy, would be put at an economic disadvantage. But these problems were overshadowed by the massive increase in productivity and the rise in the standards of living within the group. Nowhere was this more apparent than in Germany. The West German mark had become the most stable currency in the world by the 1960s and when the French franc, the dollar and the pound sterling all seemed in danger in the world currency crisis of 1968, it was to Germany that the world's financiers turned for help, as they did in other financial crises in 1974–1975 and 1978–1979.

**The European Free Trade Association.** After 1945 many British statesmen supported the idea of European unity, but British governments had opposed any scheme which would affect the country's sovereignty. Britain had not joined ECSC and so was not automatically involved in the Rome negotiations. However, even at this stage Britain would almost certainly have been welcomed as a member of the EEC. But Britain disliked the commitments affecting national sovereignty that were involved and remained aloof. However, the early success of the Community prompted her to form a rival trading group—the European Free Trade Association in December, 1959. The Association comprised Britain, Norway, Sweden, Denmark, Portugal, Austria and Switzerland and involved mutual trading benefits without the handing over of any sovereignty to an international authority. The Association was a limited success: it certainly increased trade between its members considerably, but its joint population was much smaller than that of EEC and it formed a much less natural and compact economic unit. Britain and other members of EFTA therefore became increasingly interested in joining EEC.

Britain made two efforts to join, the first in 1961–1962 under Harold Macmillan's Conservative government and the second in 1966–1967 under Harold Wilson's Labour government. Both attempts failed because of the French veto. In the first instance the French objected that Britain was not prepared to be truly "European" and sacrifice her imperial economic connections and that she was too closely tied in her military alignments with the United States. On the second occasion the French objection was again to the military link with America and to Britain's severe economic difficulties in the mid-Sixties which had made the pound very unstable and left the country heavily dependent on American and other international financial support. Basically President de Gaulle wished to see the Common Market as a third force in world affairs, between the Soviet and American blocs and led by France. British membership of EEC would certainly have threatened the achievement of these goals.

**Britain joins the Common Market.** The death of General de Gaulle in 1969 and the gradual change in the attitude of the French government to Britain's application were important new factors. The main problems arose from Britain's desire to give adequate protection to her dairy products from New Zealand and sugar from the West Indies. There was also the problem of the size of Britain's financial contribution to the Community. Matters moved forward decisively after a meeting on May 30 and 31, 1971 between President Pompidou and the British Prime Minister, Edward Heath. This was followed at Brussels by agreements satisfactory to the Commonwealth countries on their dairy and sugar exports to Britain. In Britain itself there was considerable opposition to entry especially from those who foresaw a serious diminution in Britain's sovereign powers and rule from Brussels. The trade unions also came out in opposition. Nevertheless, the Treaty of Accession was approved by the House of Commons by a narrow majority and Britain became a member of the Common Market on January 1, 1973. The Labour Government which succeeded that of Mr. Heath organised a referendum on Britain's entry; after a strong campaign by supporters and opponents, the result was a majority of two to one in favour of membership.

**The EEC 1973–1978.**   The majority of the member countries of the EEC continued to grow richer during this period, in spite of a world-wide trade recession brought on by the oil crises of 1973 and 1978. Britain alone failed to do so, due largely to internal policies and industrial defects. Greece (see page 405), Portugal (see page 406) and Spain (see page 406) became democracies and applied for membership of the EEC. It seems likely that their applications will be accepted in the near future.

But the EEC has failed to live up to the hopes of its founders; the member-countries have not sunk their national differences. France, for example, continues to "go it alone" in defence (see pages 393, 439). Likewise Britain, now a major oil-producing country, is insisting that it is her oil and that it is not a Community property. Nationalism is still a major factor in Europe.

Perhaps this is more clearly and frequently seen in the arguments over the Common Agricultural Policy (CAP). This policy aims to make Europe self-sufficient in food production as far as is possible. Farmers are guaranteed a certain price for their products, the price being fixed annually by the Ministers of Agriculture of the member-states. The political influence of farmers in France, Germany and Holland is very considerable and their Ministers seek to get as high a price as possible for their farmers. This has led to the creation of vast surpluses—of meat, milk, butter, wine and fruit—as farmers produce as much as they can in order to get the fullest benefit from the price system. Food-importing countries—and notably Britain—resent this system, since it is they who have to make the largest payments into the fund need to give farmers the promised prices. People also resent the vast amounts of these expensive foods sold, at low prices, to Russia and other Eastern-bloc states.

**The European Parliament.**   Since 1958 the EEC has been "ruled" by its Commission, which proposes rules and laws to the Council of Ministers who normally accept the proposals of their Civil Servants. The members of the European Parliament used to be appointed by the governments of the member-states. But this Parliament was a mere debating chamber since it had very little power over the Commission or the Council of Ministers. In 1978 each member-state held elections for European Members of Parliament. Britain, for example, was divided into eighty-one constituencies, as were France, Germany and Italy; the smaller countries were allocated fewer seats.

In France and Germany—but not in Britain—leading political figures became candidates, and, if elected, European Members. It is too soon to say what effect this will have on the nature of that Parliament. Powerful politicians may well seek to widen its powers—over the Commission and over the Council of Ministers. If they are successful, then we shall see the emergence of a powerful Parliament—and this might be a major step along the road to European unity.

**The Problems of NATO.**  During these same years the North Atlantic Treaty Organisation suffered considerable internal stresses. Some were the result of members' conflicting policies in military organisation; others were due to different attitudes in the international crises—at Suez in 1956, in the Turko–Greek conflict in Cyprus, and in the various confrontations around the world between the Western powers and the Communist states.

From the first the alliance never managed to raise its target force of men or a truly unified military command. In 1950 Britain proposed that member states should contribute to the alliance according to their resources, which meant that Britain and America would provide the nuclear deterrent while the other states would supply the bulk of conventional forces. This did not appeal to France where it was seen as another British proposal to "fight to the last Frenchman". In 1962, at a meeting at Nassau, President Kennedy of the U.S.A. and Britain's Prime Minister, Harold Macmillan, agreed that the Americans would provide Britain with Polaris submarines capable of firing nuclear warheads. To de Gaulle this appeared to be a strengthening of the special Anglo–American relationship and the policy of 1950. NATO members then discussed the possibility of a multinational nuclear force to which all members would contribute and in which Britain would include her nuclear bombers. However such a force would have remained American dominated and found little support in France or elsewhere. Close military organisation was not possible while there was deep political disagreement between the members.

The deepest division was between President de Gaulle of France and the Anglo-Saxon group—Britain and America. As soon as he came to power in 1958 he rejected the idea of a unified command and he withdrew both the French air force and the French Mediterranean fleet from NATO control. The French developed

Fig. 58.—Elder Statesmen of the new Europe, de Gaulle and Adenauer.

their own nuclear weapons and advanced military aircraft. They refused to subscribe to the Nuclear Test Ban Treaty of 1963 (see page 399) and for some years maintained only tenuous membership of the alliance. De Gaulle pursued a quite independent foreign policy, moving increasingly towards a neutral position between Russia and America and courting unaligned powers in Africa, Asia and South America. In 1967 the links with NATO were more or less finally broken with the removal of its headquarters from French soil. By the late 1960s, therefore, the alliance was considerably weakened and many people outside France were beginning to subscribe to de Gaulle's claim that it had outlived its usefulness.

**Russia and NATO.** One important reason for this change in attitude towards NATO was the gradual change in relations with the Soviet Union. Since 1956 Russia has become increasingly prosperous. Kruschev's announcement of the policy of peaceful co-existence was a public recognition of the fact that the Russians were less willing than formerly to spend their economic resources in an arms race with the United States. In practice this change in attitude was clearly reflected in the withdrawal from Cuba (see page 399) and the agreement to the Test Ban Treaty (see page 399). The new Russian line angered the Chinese but won approval in Eastern Europe. It also led many people in the West to believe that the Warsaw Pact and NATO were obsolete and that disputes could be settled by negotiation rather than confrontation.

**The Problem of German Re-unification.** Between 1945 and 1953 the allied aim of re-unifying Germany moved further and further from fulfilment. With the death of Stalin it seemed possible that the question might be reopened, but the East German risings (see page 384) led to a hardening of the Russian attitude once more.

However, in 1954 the four occupying powers met in Berlin to discuss re-unification. The three Western powers proposed: (1) the holding of free elections throughout Germany, (2) the subsequent establishment of a government which would sign a peace treaty with the four powers, (3) the creation of an independent Germany which would be free to align herself in international affairs as she pleased. The Russians, however, countered with their suggestions: (1) that a provisional government made up equally of members from East and West Germany should be appointed, (2) that elections should then be held, and (3) that the new state should maintain a policy of strict neutrality.

Neither side would compromise on the question of neutrality and the negotiations broke down. The Western powers gave full recognition to the Federal German Republic (see below), although they stipulated that the new republic should not attempt to seek to alter her frontiers or re-unify Germany by force. The Russians reacted by formalising their military alliances in Eastern Europe into the Warsaw Pact in May, 1955. Kruschev also visited Yugoslavia in an attempt to improve relations with Tito. In the same year the Russians extended diplomatic recognition to the German Federal Republic, a surprise move, made no doubt in the hope that the Western powers would recognise the German

Democratic Republic. The West did not however respond as Kruschev had hoped.

**The Berlin Crisis, 1958.**   The problem of Germany remained a constant threat to peace. Berlin was the focus of conflicts between East and West. In 1958 Kruschev demanded the withdrawal of the allies from Berlin and Western recognition for East Germany. If this was not forthcoming he threatened to grant unilateral recognition to the East Germans' right to control Berlin and sign a separate peace treaty with them. Eventually the deadline which he had laid down for the allied withdrawal, May, 1959, passed without action on either side, but it did serve to emphasise the need to settle the Berlin and German questions. In 1959, now on a peace offensive, Kruschev visited the United States and held talks with President Eisenhower at Camp David. Preparations were put in hand for a meeting of heads of state of the great powers in 1960, a summit meeting at which, it was hoped, the German question could be settled.

**The Paris Summit Conference, 1960.**   The agenda for the meeting which met in Paris in May extended far beyond Germany to the questions of disarmament and the relations of NATO and the Warsaw Pact. Eisenhower, Kruschev, de Gaulle and Macmillan came together. However, shortly before the meeting an American spy-plane, a U2, was shot down over Russia. The Russians accused the Americans of bad faith. The Americans claimed that the Russians were only using the U2 as an excuse to cancel the meeting.

Whatever the rights and wrongs of the case, Kruschev left Paris before anything could be achieved and all the hopes which had been built around the conference were left in ruins.

**The Berlin Crisis Again.**   In 1961 John Kennedy became President of the United States. He was determined to try to reach an agreement with Kruschev. They met in June, 1961 in Vienna and once again Kruschev demanded Western recognition for East Germany. The Russians were under some pressure from the East Germans to help them achieve the goal of international recognition and there was a mounting tension between East and West after the Vienna meeting failed to settle anything.

In August the East Germans began to construct a massive barrier through Berlin to check the flow of refugees from East to West which had reached the rate of 20,000 a month. The construction of

FIG. 59.—KRUSCHEV AND MACMILLAN IN PARIS, 1960 BEFORE THE SUMMIT
MEETING COLLAPSED.

FIG. 60.—AMERICAN TROOPS PATROL THE BERLIN WALL.

the Berlin Wall aroused intense hostility in West Berlin and there were massive demonstrations. It seemed that there might be a physical assault on the hated barrier. The Berliners were held in check however by their Social Democrat mayor, Herr Willi Brandt, while the Americans and their allies moved tanks up to the checkpoints to the East. The Western powers calculated, however, that the Wall was a defensive move rather than one intended to spark off a conflict with NATO.

In time the Wall became an almost accepted feature of life in Berlin. The problem of Germany however remained. The politicians of West Germany have faced a difficult choice. They were loath to accept the division of their country as a permanent settlement, but they could see no immediate prospect of unification. They have always also had to cope with extremist groups within the country who wanted not only re-unification, but also the repossession of East Prussia and the other lands beyond the Oder and Neisse rivers which had been lost to Poland and Russia in 1945. Such claims were unlikely to win support even from Germany's friends and allies especially as the emergence of a neo-Nazi movement in Germany in the mid-1960s reawoke fears of aggressive German nationalism.

**Crisis and Detente, Cuba.**   In the fifties and early sixties relations between the Communist bloc and the Western powers appeared to be growing a little easier. But the autumn of 1962 brought one of the most dangerous crises since the war. The Russians had one firm ally in the American continents, Fidel Castro of Cuba. The Americans found the existence of a Communist aligned state virtually on their doorstep almost intolerable and in 1961 they had helped an ill-fated attempt by Cuban exiles to overthrow Castro. The miserable failure of this expedition set Castro even more firmly into his alliance with Russia.

In the autumn of 1962 American spy-planes spotted rocket sites on Cuba and the Americans realised that Russia was equipping Cuba with missiles which could fire far into the United States. Kennedy at once demanded the removal of the rockets and as Russian ships approached Cuba the American fleet threw a blockade around the island. Had the Russians continued on their course a clash involving the two super-powers would have been inevitable. The world was suddenly faced with the very imminent threat of nuclear war. At the last moment Kruschev turned the Russian ships back and agreed to the removal of the rockets. The crisis had passed and one good result was the establishment of the "hot line" telephone communication between Washington and Moscow to speed the settlement of urgent crises and to prevent a nuclear war "by accident".

**The Test Ban Treaty.**   The development of nuclear weapons posed a threat to humanity for scientists had long been aware that repeated nuclear tests polluted the atmosphere with nuclear fall-out. To check this menace the United Nations and individual governments had been involved in a long series of negotiations. For some time these had been defeated by Russia's objection that it was very difficult to detect the trials and thus have the assurance of the good faith of all parties concerned. In time however methods of detection for tests in the atmosphere, though not for the less dangerous underground tests, were developed. The way was then clear for the signing by Russia, the United States and the United Kingdom of a treaty to ban all tests in the atmosphere. The treaty was endorsed by most other countries in the world and in 1968 the great powers also signed an agreement to try to prevent the spread of nuclear weapons to non-nuclear powers.

However, neither France nor Communist China agreed to the Test Ban Treaty and both countries pressed ahead with their own programmes for nuclear weapons, which involved testing in the atmosphere. The Test Ban Treaty was in any case a partial one since it did not affect underground tests. On the other hand, it was definitely a most important step towards checking the proliferation of weapons which endangered the very existence of mankind. It was also a sign that the Russian and American leaders were ready to co-operate on at least some world issues. However it did not lead to any general agreement on world armaments and the two super-powers were still deeply divided. There was evidence of this both in the Middle East (see page 407) and the Far East (see page 425), while Europe itself seemed to be threatened with a revival of Cold War at its most intense during 1968.

**The Crisis in Eastern Europe, 1968.**    After 1956, it was increasingly apparent that the Communist bloc was not a monolithic structure controlled from Moscow, but that there were deep divisions in it as there were in the Western alliances. On the one hand the Chinese and the Russians were increasingly at odds as Mao Tse-tung and his fellow leaders sought to wrest the leadership of the Communist movement in the underdeveloped world from the Russians, whom they suspected of betraying true Communism for the sake of material prosperity and peace with the West. On the other hand the former satellites in Eastern Europe were increasingly unwilling to subordinate their own interests to those of the Russians. On occasions these countries were able to exploit the Sino-Soviet struggle in order to win greater freedom from Moscow. An example of this was Rumania, a country which rejected the inferior role in the economic plan of Eastern Europe assigned to it by the Russians in the COMECON plan.

In Rumania the internal government of the country remained strictly authoritarian, even though the leadership was defying the Russians. Elsewhere, however, there were liberal stirrings both within and outside the Eastern European Communist parties. The most dramatic example of this came in Czechoslovakia.

During 1967 Czechoslovakia was involved in an inflationary crisis with rising wages, but a severe shortage of consumer goods. Productivity was not increasing as fast as it should have been, and there were many demands for the easing of central economic controls. But the creation of a free market in which the demands of the consumer would largely determine output was regarded as heresy by the old Communists led by President Novotny. There were other reasons for discontent as well. The Slovaks wished for

Fig. 61.—August 1968, Czechs Watch the Russian Tanks move into Prague.

greater local self-government and during the Arab–Israeli War of 1967 (see page 413) there was great sympathy for the Israelis in the populace at large, although official Soviet and Communist policy favoured the Arabs. The Writers' Union denounced the heavy-handed censorship of literature and young people showed less and less enthusiasm for the Communist Party, 40 per cent of whose members were over the age of sixty.

During 1967 Dubcek, a man quite opposed to the Stalinist line of Novotny, became First Secretary of the Czech Communist Party and in January, 1968, in the face of mounting public opposition Novotny himself was forced to resign and was replaced by General Svoboda, the distinguished commander of Czech forces in Russia during the Second World War. These men were supported by many others within the Party and State structure and in January, 1968, began to introduce sweeping reforms to liberalise many aspects of life in Czechoslovakia.

Firstly, the right to assemble and form voluntary associations was proclaimed. Secondly, in June, a law was passed abolishing press censorship. Thirdly, a law was passed guaranteeing the rights of the country's various nationalities, Czechs, Slovaks, Hungarians and so on (in October after the Russian intervention a law was passed making the country a federal state with a good deal of local self-government in the hands of the separate administrations in Bohemia and Slovakia). Fourthly, a more democratic electoral system was proposed. Fifthly, strict curbs were placed on the state security police. Sixthly, many victims of earlier purges were rehabilitated. Seventhly, the economy was freed from many controls and plans were made to increase trade outside the Communist bloc. Eighthly, there was to be freedom to travel outside the country. Ninthly, the parties forming the National Front were all to have the right to participate in the government of the country and the National Assembly was to be free to criticise the central government. There was no longer to be arbitrary government by decree.

These dramatic changes were carried out by the Communist leadership with massive popular support and the leaders were at pains to assure their neighbours that they did not intend to break with the bloc or to surrender the predominant position of the Communist party in the government. But the Russians and some other leaders in Eastern Europe, notably Ulbricht of East Germany, strongly disapproved of the changes. During the summer there were massive Warsaw Pact military manœuvres in and around Czechoslovakia. For a while it seemed that the Russians would have to accept the new situation, but suddenly in August they invaded the country in force. The Czech leaders tried to control their people and the army remained in its barracks as the Russians took Prague and other centres. However there were widespread demonstrations against the Russians and some loss of life. Dubcek was seized and flown to Moscow, but the Russians could find no alternative government for the country as they had done in Hungary in 1956. Svoboda refused to negotiate with the Russians without Dubcek and after a series of meetings a re-constituted government, which still included Dubcek and many other reformers was set up. However Dubcek and his sympathisers had to accept the repeal of many of their reforms and the continued occupation of the country by the Warsaw Pact troops. But this compromise was not acceptable to the people and in 1969 workers and intellectuals continued to demand the reintroduction of the basic reforms.

The crisis brought protests from not only capitalist governments, but also Communist parties outside Eastern Europe. It alarmed the other Communist rebels in the east—Yugoslavia and Rumania—countries which had made open gestures of sympathy to the Czech reformers. It appears that the Russians feared that the liberalisation programme would not only undermine the hold of the Communist party on Czechoslovakia, but shake it elsewhere in Eastern Europe and even in Russia itself. In this they were supported by the governments of East Germany and Poland. They held that the reformers were counter-revolutionaries in league with Western interventionists and they certainly totally underrated the support for the reforms both within the Czech Communist party and in the country at large.

The next stage of the Czech drama was the gradual assertion of the influence of the anti-Dubcek elements in the Czech Communist party and government. By 1970 Dubcek had lost all real influence and was conveniently removed by the "hardliners" to the innocuous post of Ambassador to Turkey. In his place as First Secretary of the Party was Dr. Husak, pledged to co-operation with the Soviet Union.

**Poland, 1970–1978.** The year 1970 proved extremely critical in Poland. Although there was considerable advance in Poland's international situation with the recognition of the Oder-Neisse frontier by West Germany, with the development of external trade and the signing of a treaty of friendship and co-operation with

France, the internal situation was unstable. The younger generation were dissatisfied with the stifling bureaucracy and officialdom. The question of freedom of speech was openly raised in sections of the Polish press. The economic condition of the country was stagnant. Rigid state planning of industry led to the production of goods for which there was no real public demand. Low agricultural production led to reliance on imports of grain from the Soviet Union, Canada, France and West Germany. Government revenue declined, and at the end of 1970 the government announced stringent increases in prices, ranging from 8 per cent to 60 per cent on food, fuel and clothing. This was followed by widespread outbreaks of violence. On December 15 rioters set fire to the Communist Party headquarters in Gdansk, and rioting spread to several other large industrial towns and seaports. Heavy fighting occurred between the state militia and demonstrators. The government sealed off the whole coastal area and rail traffic was suspended. Clearly, the government was faced with a major internal upheaval. Rapid changes now occurred in the communist hierarchy. Gomulka was replaced as Secretary-General of the Communist Party of Poland by Edward Gierek—a less dogmatic, more empirical communist. Several of Gomulka's followers were also removed from the government in favour of a number of younger men. Gierek also cancelled all the emergency decrees, froze food prices for two years and ordered large wage increases for lower-paid workers. At the same time he toured the country and encouraged an open discussion of the faults in Polish society. The Catholic Church played a large part in these discussions and condemned the methods used by the old "hard-liners" to suppress discontent. The Church also demanded the democratic freedom of discussion in the press and throughout the country.

This political ferment continued in Poland throughout 1971. Drastic changes were made by Gierek in the state institutions, involving the replacement of older by younger, more democratic and not necessarily Marxist personnel. This coincided with Gierek's declaration that it was not necessary to be a Marxist to be of value to society. In general, conditions improved in Poland during 1971–1976. Many large enterprises were given more freedom from government control and proved more successful in their marketing than the completely state-controlled factories. There also developed a number of joint East–West enterprises in Poland, and there were large loans of western capital. The year 1973 proved one of the most successful economically—real wages rose by 24 per cent, industrial production by 33 per cent and agricultural production by 19 per cent. However, efforts by the government to increase basic consumer prices in 1976 aroused renewed resistance and the government was once again compelled to modify its demands.

The problems of Poland in these years were typical of the problems arising in countries of the eastern communist bloc—the problem of the nature of freedom. Could democratic freedom be reconciled with, or tolerated by, a communist government? Was the rigid state control of industry the best form of economic organisation, even in a communist state? How far could a communist government go in allowing the powerful Catholic Church the freedoms it demanded—to preach, to teach in its own schools and universities and to operate its own newspapers? In October 1978 the world in general and the government of Poland in particular, was made aware of this State–Church clash when the Archbishop of Cracow, Cardinal Wojtyla, was elected Pope of the Catholic Church. He took the name of Pope John Paul II in memory of his two predecessors, and he reminded the world of his working class background, his resistance first to occupying Nazi troops, and later as a priest to Communist governments. His election was welcomed by Poles who viewed it with nationalist and anti-Communist eyes. His visit to his home country in 1979 showed how popular he was—and how important the Church is in Poland.

**International Developments, 1974–1978.**  During these years important political changes occurred in several European and non-European states. In Greece, for example, the military dictatorship which had existed since 1967 collapsed in 1975. The most important reason for this was the failure of its ill-judged efforts to bring about Greek control in Cyprus in the face of opposition from Turkey and the Turkish minority in Cyprus. These efforts resulted in the invasion of Cyprus by Turkish forces and the division of the island into Turkish and Greek zones.

In Italy the thirty-year rule of the Christian Democrats was challenged by the continued growth of the Italian Communist party. In 1976 the internal condition of Italy was weak, hampered by corruption, by a slow-moving bureaucracy and by economic and financial problems which brought the international value of her currency to a very low level. Despite the Pope's demand that Catholics should not vote for Communist candidates, the Italian elections in June 1976 showed a great increase in Communist support 'although the Christian Democrats succeeded in maintaining their position as the largest party). A communist was elected President of the lower house of the Italian parliament and the communists claimed the right to be consulted on all matters affecting the national interest. This communist advance in Italy is accounted for by (1) the excellent record of a number of communist-controlled local councils, (2) the scandal of the receipt by some political parties of payments by international oil concerns, and (3) the critical attitude taken by the Italian Communist party towards Russia. But the experience of shared government has not been a success. Communist support was needed to push through unpopular measures intended to halt inflation—and rank-and-file members of the Party condemned their parliamentary representatives as "capitalist stooges". There are signs that the Party may well split over this matter in the future. In France also a move was being made away from the Moscow-dominated policies which had existed in the days of Stalin and his immediate successors in Russia. Thus the two largest communist parties in Western Europe were moving towards a communist line which would put national interests above international dogma. In the 1978 elections the Communists formed a broad alliance of the Left with other Socialist groups. It was an uneasy alliance, its members quarrelling publicly over its aims. And it was an unsuccessful alliance, the Left doing much worse in the elections than pollsters had predicted. Here, as in Italy, Euro-Communism took a hard knock.

In 1975 the fifty-year fascist-type dictatorship of Dr. Salazar in Portugal ended. The first important challenge to the old regime came from within the armed forces—hence the apparent ease with which the change-over was brought about. There was an immediate outburst of political activity by the newly-legalised Socialist, Communist and other parties. In the autumn of 1975 an attempt by the communists to gain complete control failed, despite considerable support for them within the armed forces. This attempt was accompanied by an outbreak of violence between communists and their opponents, but by 1978 Portugal appeared to be on the road to a democratic form of government.

Startling changes occurred in Spain after the death of General Franco in 1975. He had decided that Don Juan Carlos should become king, but this naturally produced strong resistance from the Falange, the national movement which had governed Spain since the end of the civil war in 1939. However, in 1976 the Cortes debated and accepted the need for Spain to make the transition to a liberal form of constitutional monarchy. This decision meant the legalising of some political parties—for example, the Spanish Socialist Party but not the Spanish Communist Party or the Basque Separatist movement. The press in Spain began to be more outspoken on all national matters as much of the former censorship was relaxed. The changes were, however, too few and too slow for the extremists of the Left, led by the still illegal Communist Party of Spain. But to most West European observers what was happening in both Portugal and Spain was most significant for the future of Europe and liberal democracy.

These events in Europe were closely linked with the end of the remnants of colonialism in Africa. By 1976 after years of guerrilla activity Portuguese control of Angola and Mozambique was ended. Economic aid and military supplies had come from communist-controlled Eastern Europe, and in Angola the eventual victory of the MPLA over its internal rivals was substantially aided by the presence of forces from General Castro's Cuba.

One important consequence of these changes was the closing of the border between the former Portuguese colonies and Rhodesia and the organisation of guerrilla warfare against Rhodesia. There is no doubt that the 1970s saw a great strengthening of communist power in Africa and Asia—a trend which constituted a serious setback for the policies of the United States. At the same time, however, the Soviet Union declared its interest in reaching a situation of *détente* between Warsaw Pact and NATO powers. Various negotiations were put in hand to secure an agreed reduction of armed forces in Europe and limits to be placed on the production of intercontinental nuclear missiles. Negotiations between the United States and Russia were put in hand at Helsinki. In 1972 these led to the signing of the first of the Strategic Arms Limitations Talks agreements. In return for agreements on arms limitation the Russians promised to allower greater freedom to dissidents, Jews and other critical minorities in their country. They have failed to live up to that promise. But they have not failed to take advantage of opportunities to win increased power in Africa, Asia and Latin America. Negotiations for a SALT agreement continue, but in Europe and the USA there are many who fear that the Russians will once again be the main beneficiaries of such an agreement.

During the 1970s the Middle East became increasingly disturbed. This centre of instability was a major cause of concern to the Soviet Union and the United States. The general tendency that developed was for the Soviet Union to support the Arab and Palestinian cause and for the United States to redress the balance by its support of Israel. But in 1975 another complication arose which divided the Arab world itself. In Lebanon a fierce military struggle broke out between the Christian right wing forces and the Moslem left wing. Increasing casualties and devastation in the capital (Beirut) led to numerous efforts to achieve a ceasefire, all of which had proved abortive by the summer of 1976. At that time a joint Arab peace-keeping force entered Lebanon in an effort to secure stability, but Syrian troops found themselves in conflict with the forces of the Palestinian Liberation Organisation which had demanded their withdrawal. Thus, with Arab fighting Arab the Israeli–Arab conflict sank into the background. Nevertheless, Israel was also concerned about the type of government which would ultimately prevail in Lebanon, where much Palestinian guerrilla activity against Israel had been organised in the past.

In June 1976 Palestinian guerrillas seized an Air France plane and diverted it to Entebbe airport in Uganda. Here the skyjackers demanded the release of a large number of Palestinian guerrilla prisoners held in Israel and elsewhere. The non-Israeli passengers were released, but the Israeli passengers were held hostage in the old airport building at Entebbe. While negotiations continued, an Israeli airborne force flew to Entebbe, killed most of the skyjackers and the Ugandan guards whom General Amin had placed around the airport, released and took back to Israel nearly all the hostages. This brilliant expedition was a serious defeat for skyjacking policies.

# chapter twenty-four

# EUROPE AND THE THIRD WORLD, 1953–1978

By 1953 the forces of nationalism were spreading to other parts of the underdeveloped world. The revolution in Egypt was the prelude to a more militant and revolutionary form of nationalism throughout the Arab nations. In Africa, too, both north and south of the Sahara, nationalist leaders were emerging determined to establish the political independence of their countries and end the privileges of the European minorities. Even where independence had been achieved there were still many disputes between the former colonies and the European powers, which continued to have a major economic stake in the old colonial areas.

Relations between European states and the new nations of Africa and Asia were complicated by the fact that the Communist powers were interested in increasing their political influence in, and their economic contact with, these countries, especially in the Middle East. The new nations, not anxious to exchange their colonial masters for new Communist ones, sought to create a Third World between East and West. Nevertheless they were dragged into world political rivalries, as both the Western powers and the Russians built up systems of alliances.

**The Baghdad Pact.** The Western powers tried to contain Communism in Asia and the Middle East by military alliances with pro-Western governments. In 1952 Greece and Turkey joined NATO and the Americans later established rocket bases on the Turkish–Soviet border. They adopted the anti-Russian role once held by Britain. Elsewhere in the Middle East Britain remained the most involved Western power. British military advisers remained in Iraq and Jordan, and in 1955 Iraq was encouraged to form an alliance with Turkey which was later enlarged to include Pakistan, Persia and Britain. This anti-Communist alliance was disliked by neutralist states. India feared that it might be turned against her in her disputes with Pakistan, although Britain said she would not ally against another Commonwealth country. Although the United States was not a member of the Pact she encouraged it, and the Baghdad Pact was linked to both NATO through Britain and Turkey and the South East Asia Treaty Organisation through

Britain and Pakistan. SEATO was an anti-Communist Pact made up of the United States, Britain, France, Australia, New Zealand, the Philippines, Thailand and Pakistan, and was formed in September, 1954, to counter aggression in the South West Pacific area below the latitude 21° 30′.

**Egypt and the Western Powers.**    Soon after the fall of Farouk (see page 375) the old Egyptian political parties, including the nationalist Wafd, which had opposed British influence for over sixty years, were dissolved. They were replaced by the National Liberation Rally, a new nationalist movement controlled by the army officers who had staged the revolution and commanding widespread popular support. In 1954 Nasser became Prime Minister (and later President). A passionate nationalist, he strongly opposed Britain's presence in the Canal Zone and Sudan. In 1953 the Egyptians had agreed that the Sudanese should decide their own future, although wanting a union of Egypt and Sudan. In fact the Sudanese chose complete independence in 1956.

Britain's continued occupation of the Canal Zone was a more difficult problem. Nasser demanded that Britain leave the Zone, while conceding her right to return in time of war. After negotiations the British agreed to evacuate the Zone in 1954. But this friendly period in Anglo–Egyptian relations was short lived.

The Russians sought to outflank the Baghdad Pact by giving economic and military aid to Egypt. In September, 1955, Nasser announced an arms deal with the Communist bloc. Many people in America and Western Europe believed that Nasser would now come under Russian domination. This led to the withdrawal of Western offers of aid for the construction of the Aswan High Dam with which Nasser hoped to begin the economic transformation of his country.

Nasser's response was dramatic. On July 26, 1956, he announced the nationalisation of the Suez Canal, promising that the shareholders, mainly the British government and private French investors, would be compensated. Britain, the United States and France were deeply disturbed and imposed various financial and trading sanctions on Egypt. Britain took a leading part in forming a Canal Users Association to try to force Nasser to reverse his action. It was widely believed that the Egyptians would not be able to run the Canal, but they recruited foreign pilots. Soon the ships of many nations, including the United States, were instructed by their governments to pay their canal tolls to the Egyptian government.

FIG. 62.—FRENCH AND BRITISH TROOPS ON GUARD IN PORT SAID, 1956

The British did not accept the situation. Anthony Eden, the Prime Minister, denounced Nasser as another Hitler. French reactions were equally strong. The French disliked Nasser's support for anti-French activities in Algeria (see page 435).

On October 29 Israel launched a surprise attack on the Egyptians and advanced rapidly through the Sinai Peninsula. On October 30 Britain and France vetoed a United Nations Security Council resolution urging all parties to refrain from the use of force. Instead they issued an ultimatum to the Israelis and Egyptians to withdraw their forces to either side of the Canal. When this was rejected the British and French launched an attack on Port Said with troops they had been assembling in the Eastern Mediterranean. The United Nations now condemned Britain, France and Israel, and the Russians, fresh from their victory in Hungary, threatened to intervene. The United States refused to support Britain and France in the financial crisis that followed and voted against them at the United Nations. As a result of these developments, Britain and France called a ceasefire on November 6. They handed over to a United Nations Emergency Force which was to patrol the Israel-Egypt border and clear the damaged canal.

The Suez affair was a sensational international incident. Britain, France and Israel were condemned as aggressors and accused, apparently correctly, of conspiring to bring about the crisis. For Egypt it was a victory, even though her troops had been worsted by the Israelis. It damaged the prestige of the two leading powers in Europe and led the new Afro–Asian states to look to Russia for help.

**The Middle East after Suez.**   The Suez affair led to a rapid decline in British power in the Middle East. Even before 1956 she had lost much of her influence in Jordan, where the nationalists looked increasingly to Egypt for guidance. In 1958 a nationalist revolution in Iraq led to the overthrow of the monarchy and the withdrawal of that country from the Baghdad Pact (now renamed CENTO). Growing unrest in south Arabia led eventually to a nationalist guerrilla campaign in Aden and the Aden Protectorate and the withdrawal of the British in 1967.

Nasser was in the ascendant. The linking of Syria and Egypt in the United Arab Republic lasted only from 1958 till 1961, but Nasser remained far and away the most influential Arab nationalist. He committed his troops to a costly and indecisive campaign in the civil war in the Yemen and kept up a stream of propaganda against Western interference in the Middle East and even more against the existence of Israel. Even those Arab rulers, such as King Hussain of Jordan, who had little reason to like Nasser found that nationalist pressures in their own countries made it unwise to oppose him openly, especially on the Israeli question.

**Arab–Israeli Relations, 1956–1968.**   Nasser's influence was clearly a threat to Israel. He and other leaders constantly repeated their desire to destroy Israel altogether. However, the most immediate threat to peace in the area came from the Palestinian Liberation Front which operated from the Arab countries on Israel's borders and especially from Jordan, where they pressed Hussein to abandon his moderate policies towards Israel. In November, 1966, an Israeli attack on Hebron led to still greater pressure on Hussein and he was only saved by Western support from a nationalist revolution. He accepted jet fighters from Britain and America to strengthen his forces. However he now adopted a

FIG. 63. ISRAELI CHILDREN IN THEIR SCHOOLROOM; THE ARABS REFUSE TO RECOGNISE THE STATE OF ISRAEL SHOWN ON THE WALLMAP.

hard line towards Israel. In the meantime there were major clashes along the Israel–Syria border.

In the early months of 1967, the clashes intensified. In April, Syria and Egypt declared the destruction of Israel as their main policy. In reply the Israelis took an increasingly tough line, massing troops on the Syrian border. Events now moved rapidly. President Nasser ordered the United Nations Emergency Force, which had stood between Israel and Egypt since 1956, to evacuate Sinai and under the terms of the 1956 agreement they complied. On May 22, Nasser closed the gulf of Aqaba to Israeli shipping, thus denying the Israelis access to their only southern port, Eilat. He was now demanding a return to the pre-1948 position and he was joined by Hussein in a five-year military pact. When Hussein flew to Cairo to sign the pact he was accompanied by the leader of the Palestinian Liberation Army, who had sought his overthrow in 1966.

On June 5, 1967, the Israelis struck first. On the first day they put airfields in Egypt, Jordan, Syria and Iraq out of action, destroying many planes on the ground. The Jordanian and Egyptian armies were left without cover. Israeli forces drove through Sinai to the Suez Canal by June 8. In the meantime all the towns on the west bank of the Jordan were captured from the Jordanians including the Arab area of Jerusalem. On June 8 Hussein and Nasser accepted a ceasefire. On June 9, the Syrians, who had been driven from the Syrian heights also capitulated.

In a matter of six days the Arabs had suffered a humiliating defeat which they were unable to disguise by accusing the British and Americans of aiding the Israelis. Even so the Arab leaders refused to negotiate with Israel. Indeed Nasser and Hussein were pushed even harder by extremist nationalists anxious for revenge. In the meantime the Israelis remained defiantly in control of the Jordanian, Egyptian and Syrian territory and the Suez Canal remained closed. Within months the old pattern of raids and counter-attacks had begun again. In this crisis Israel had the sympathy of most Western powers while the Communist countries had sided with the Arabs. After the war Russia and her allies made good Egyptian losses of planes and tanks, while the Israelis were sold new weapons by the Americans—supposedly to maintain the balance of power in the area. This was all the more important to Israel because President de Gaulle denied them replacements for the French equipment on which they had previously relied. However perhaps the most obvious lesson of the war was that not even Russia and America, let alone the other European powers, could really control their allies in the Middle East, either through secret negotiations or through the United Nations.

A further development of the situation arising from the war was a United Nations resolution of 1967 which required the withdrawal of Israeli forces from occupied territory, thus opening the way to peace negotiations. However, hostilities of an irregular kind soon resumed both across the Suez Canal and on the Israeli frontiers. Guerrilla activities from Syria, Jordan and Lebanon were frequent, with Israeli reprisal raids. The main developments of 1970 were the increasing supply of Russian arms and military advisory personnel to Egypt and the stepping-up of anti-Israel propaganda by the Soviet Union and its increasing pressures against the Jewish community in the Soviet Union itself. It became increasingly difficult for Jews wishing to go to Israel to leave the Soviet Union. However, some slight breakthrough was achieved by the acceptance of a cease-fire by both sides, which was further extended into 1971. In the meantime the sudden death of President Nasser created widespread dismay in the Arab world. Another serious complication for the Arabs was the outbreak of civil war in Jordan between King Hussein's forces and those of the guerrilla movement pledged to outright opposition to peace with Israel. The result was to leave the guerrilla movement intact and in effective command of certain towns in north Jordan. In Amman itself the King's authority was re-asserted. During the autumn of 1970 peace negotiations under the auspices of the United Nations at last began, but were broken off by Israel on the grounds that Egypt had broken the agreement by which military preparations in an agreed zone each side of the Suez Canal were to cease. However, despite this setback, Israel agreed to the resumption of negotiations in January, 1971.

**Arab–Israeli Conflict, 1971–1978.** No progress was made in 1971 despite the efforts of the United Nations mediator, Dr. Jarring. A new treaty was signed between Russia and Egypt in May 1971 and Russian military supplies to Egypt greatly increased. Soviet MIG-23s flew over Israeli airspace on at least two occasions. Israel feared another attack and was unwilling to issue a declaration of intent (as requested by the United Nations) to withdraw from the territories she had won. The United States brought pressure to bear on Israel by holding back supplies of planes. The answer to this was given by Mrs. Meir, the Israeli Prime Minister: "No planes, no talks". During 1972 the U.S.A. held back military supplies to Israel for eight months with the aim of persuading Israel to accept the United States as a mediator in talks with Egypt. Guerrilla attacks continued against Israel from Lebanon, and Israel counter-attacked guerrilla posts across the border. Skyjacking of aircraft by Palestinian groups also occurred, and Palestinian terrorists massacred Jewish sportsmen at the Munich Olympic village before the opening of the 1972 Olympic Games.

**The Yom Kippur War, 1973.** On October 6, 1973 (the Day of Atonement, Yom Kippur), when Israeli business was closed down and activity in Israel was at a standstill, Egypt and Syria launched massive attacks—across the Suez Canal and the Golan Heights respectively. Israel, despite intelligence warnings, had not mobilised her defence forces. At first the Arab attack swept everything before it—the Egyptians were particularly successful in moving large forces over the Suez Canal. However, by October 10 the Israelis began to hold and repulse the Arab attacks. Some of the greatest tank battles ever known were fought east of the Suez Canal—more fierce even than those at Alamein or on the Russian front during the Second World War. On October 16 Israeli forces crossed the Suez Canal near the Great Bitter Lake and began operations on Egyptian soil, destroying numerous Soviet-installed SAM missile sites. The Egyptian Third Army was trapped east of the canal. Both the U.S.A. and the Soviet Union supported a United Nations resolution calling for a ceasefire. Eventually, on November 11, direct negotiations began between Israel and Egypt for the exchange of prisoners and the disentangling of the armies. This process was achieved, and was followed in 1975 by a further mutual withdrawal and the stationing of United Nations forces between the former combatants with the purpose of preventing surprise attack.

The Yom Kippur War was a shattering experience for Israel and produced great financial burdens. It had shown the falsity of the idea that military strength made Israel immune to Arab attack. It appeared also that Israel's unwillingness to accept United Nations directives was losing her a good deal of western support just at the moment when the western powers were in any case becoming embarrassed by their dependence on Arab oil diplomacy. Another blow to Israel was the massive majority in the United Nations Assembly in 1975 to allow the leader of the Palestinian Liberation Organisation, Yassir Arafat, to address the Assembly in November. The type of reception he received was similar to that given to a head of state. This amounted to a recognition of the PLO as leading the cause of the Palestinian refugees in their demands for the establishment of a Palestinian state and the withdrawal of the Israelis from the occupied West Bank of the Jordan.

**Arab oil diplomacy.**    The oil industries of the Oil Producing and Exporting Countries (OPEC) had once been controlled by foreign oil companies. However, since 1953 the governments of these countries had gained increasing control of their major natural resource. By 1972 the foreign oil companies had lost their control of the industry and were forced to deal with well-trained and able Arab ministers. In 1972–1973 these quadrupled the prices charged for their oil—which pushed up prices in the Western World, led to a flow of money into the Arab countries and to a slow-down in world trade. Since then the OPEC governments have increased their prices whenever they thought it advantageous to do so.

Western dependence on Arab oil allowed the OPEC governments

to use their oil as a diplomatic weapon. They threatened to cut off the supply of oil to any country which supported Israel. Fortunately for the West there is a division inside OPEC with Saudi Arabia and Kuwait standing against the more belligerent and anti-monarchist governments of Libya and Iraq. But the West has had to begin learning to consume less very expensive oil and to try to develop new methods of energy conservation as well as new sources of energy.

**Egyptian-Israeli peace.** The Nixon and Ford governments of the United States had tried to bring peace to the Middle East. But in the event it was left to the opposing countries to arrange their own futures. In October 1977 President Sadat of Egypt (Nasser's successor) flew to Jerusalem on what was described as "the most significant journey of the year". He met Prime Minister Begin of Israel, the rest of the Israeli Cabinet and addressed the Israeli Parliament. He asked that the two countries, sharing a common Semitic origin and having the same interests in the peaceful development of their countries, should arrange a peace in the Middle East.

Sadat's journey was followed by a return visit by Begin to Cairo. But while the Western world welcomed these initiatives, the Communist governments and the bulk of the Arab governments condemned Sadat for having "betrayed the Arab cause". OPEC governments cut off the aid they were accustomed to give to Egypt; the PLO and other nationalist movements asked for a holy war against both Egypt and Israel.

This meant that Sadat and Begin could, at best, arrange an Egyptian–Israeli peace and not as they hoped a settlement in the Middle East as a whole. Israel withdrew her forces in the Sinai desert and handed the territory back to Egypt, which in turn allowed free access through the Gulf of Aqaba. Israel also promised to withdraw her forces and settlers from the Gaza strip. But militant religious and nationalist groups in Israel supported those settlers who refused to leave, claiming that theirs was the ancient land of Galilee.

There remains a number of major problems in the Middle East area. Israel claims the right to settle her people on the West bank of the Jordan—and so rouses Jordanian hostility. She also maintains her forces on the Golan Heights—and remains at enmity with Syria. The PLO is still determined to regain "the lost lands of Palestine" and to "wipe Israel off the map".

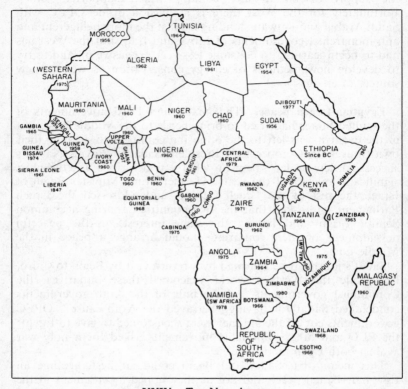

XXIV.—THE NEW AFRICA.

**The End of the African Empires.**  The decline of European political influence came later in Africa than in Asia and the Middle East, but it was completed more rapidly. There was less than a dozen years from the granting of independence to Sudan in 1956 until the establishment of independent governments in the High Commission territories of South Africa (Bechuanaland, Swaziland and Basutoland).

During that period the whole British African empire was handed over to government by indigenous populations with the exception of Rhodesia in which the white settler government declared independence unilaterally in 1965. This process was completed with very little violence though the post-independence history of many of these territories has been troubled. The disappearance of the French African empire was even swifter, being completed almost entirely in the years 1958–1960 (see Chapter 25). The year 1960 also witnessed the establishment of independence in the former Belgian Congo—an event which was followed almost immediately by one of the greatest tragedies in African history (see page 453). Apart from the comparatively small Spanish territories, this left Portugal alone in possession of a major African empire. The Portuguese refused to follow the path of decolonisation which the other European powers had chosen and so became embroiled with African resistance movements in all her colonies. Finding little sympathy from the former colonial powers, she turned instead to the white supremacist governments of the Republic of South Africa and Rhodesia.

**Rhodesia 1965–1978.** In 1965 Ian Smith, the Prime Minister of Rhodesia, gained widespread support among the Rhodesian whites when he announced the Unilateral Declaration of Independence of his country. Britain obtained United Nations support for a policy of sanctions (see page 452) which was meant to bring down the rebellious government "in weeks rather than months". The policy failed to achieve anything in the short run. Even by 1978 the Rhodesian whites enjoyed almost as high a standard of living as they had enjoyed before UDI and sanctions.

But the governments of neighbouring countries, notably Zambia and Tanzania, provided training grounds for black Rhodesian guerrilla armies. The effects of the constant and increasingly successful attacks by guerrilla forces and of the diplomatic pressure from Britain and the United States finally wore down the Smith government's will to resist. In spite of several abortive negotiations, the white government finally announced that it was changing the constitution so that blacks could vote in parliamentary elections, would be allowed to stand as candidates and, if they gained a majority of seats, would be allowed to hold office. However, the whites retained the right to twenty-five seats in the small Parliament—giving them the power to prevent the passing of important laws (which constitutionally would require a two-thirds majority). The whites also retained control of the army, police, foreign office and other important posts.

Bishop Abel Muzorewa became the first black Prime Minister of the first freely-elected government of Rhodesia. But more militant blacks, led by Joshua Nkomo and Robert Mugabe continued the guerrilla war. They argued that the whites were still really in control and that the Bishop and his fellow ministers were mere stooges. Smith, an important minister in the Bishop's government, hoped that the election of a Conservative government in Britain in 1979 might lead to a British move to give diplomatic recognition to the government. However, pressure from the United States and from black Africa forced the Thatcher government to withhold that recognition. In September 1979 the British called a Conference where the Foreign Secretary, Lord Carrington, worked with Muzorewa, Smith and the guerrilla leaders, Nkomo and Mugabe, to hammer out a new constitution, giving the blacks more power than they had been granted under Smith's constitution.

**The Power Struggles in Asia.**    In the years after the Korean armistice, conflict was to break out in many parts of Asia. Sometimes the struggles were of only regional importance, but others drew in contenders from outside Asia.

Relations between India and Pakistan have never been good and on several occasions there has been open war between them. The main cause for conflict is the disputed territory of Kashmir which is still partitioned between them. Both sides have received military aid from outside, but their position in the struggle between Communism and Capitalism has not been a clear-cut one. India, following a neutralist foreign policy, has drawn economic and military aid from both Russia and the West, while Pakistan, a founder member of the South East Asia Treaty Organisation, sometimes aligned with China against India in the early 1960s. Russia has shown no desire to exploit their differences, and indeed it was at Tashkent under Kosygin's mediation that some progress was made towards a settlement after the 1964 Indo-Pakistan War. On the other hand India's relations with China have deteriorated and there have been a number of clashes between them along their mutual border, and a short war in 1962 in which India suffered a sharp defeat.

Further south, Britain tried to draw her former colonies in Malaya, Singapore and Borneo together into the Federation of Malaysia in 1961. However, Singapore left the Federation after only three years and for some time the Federation was subjected to guerrilla attacks and a diplomatic campaign from Indonesia, its larger neighbour to the south. These were contained with the help of British troops and the confrontation came to an end with the fall of Sukarno in Indonesia. However, Malaysia is still subject to some internal strains and it has been involved in a dispute over territory with the Philippines.

Indonesia itself was for long controlled by the nationalist leader President Sukarno, through an uneasy alliance of nationalists and Communists. The country became deeply involved in anti-Western power politics and Sukarno's policies only aggravated Indonesia's enormous economic problems. In 1965 a Communist plot to seize power, in which Sukarno's part is still not clear, backfired and led to a military takeover and a bloody campaign against the Communists, and against Chinese influence in the republic. It also brought about Sukarno's replacement by an army-dominated government.

Throughout these years European influence in the area declined. The French, despite their original membership of SEATO withdrew from direct commitment in South East Asia after the débâcle in Indo-China (see page 423). In 1967 Britain announced that she too would withdraw her military presence in the area apart from token forces in Hong Kong. On the other hand American influence has remained strong especially in East Asia where the United States has built up a string of defence agreements from Japan through Taiwan, the Philippines, and Thailand to Australia and New Zealand. The Americans also came to take over French commitments in Indo-China after 1954 (see page 425).

The European powers maintained their economic interests in Asia, but perhaps the most important force for the future in economic development is Japan. After the Korean War the country enjoyed an unbroken boom, and by the late 1960s led the world in many productive activities, notably in shipbuilding. In 1978 Japan had the third largest Gross National Product in the non-Communist world after the United States and West Germany. This was a remarkable achievement for a nation of 100 million people living on a group of crowded islands with few natural resources, and not surprisingly the Japanese have sought to extend their economic influence throughout East Asia. They have, for instance, come to play an important part in the economic development of Indonesia since the fall of Sukarno.

**Communist China.** If Japan has emerged as the most successful industrial power in Asia, China is still its most potent political force. After its involvement in the Korean War the country was subjected to a drastic reshaping of its economy and society as Mao Tse-tung and his fellow Communist leaders sought to fashion a new sort of Communism which would transform their enormous but technically backward country. During the 1950s the Chinese were apparently prepared to foster friendship with any country which was not involved in the Western alliances and the able Prime Minister, Chou En-lai, forged links with Nassar, Nkrumah of Ghana, and other neutralist leaders. During the 1960s, however, the situation changed. China was now openly at odds with the Soviet Union and became involved in a conflict of arms with India. Within the country there was apparently a long fought and obscure power struggle going on, and in 1966–1968 it was brought to the brink of anarchy, as Mao mobilised his fanatical young supporters, the Red Guards, to defeat his enemies within the party leadership. Military aid was given to the Communists in Vietnam (see below page 423), but there was no direct involvement as there had been in Korea. By the late 1960s China was apparently equally at odds with both the Soviet Union and the United States and the bid to become the acknowledged leader of the underdeveloped world had suffered setbacks both in Africa and Indonesia. The disruption caused by the Red Guards' "Cultural Revolution" removed China almost entirely from international affairs except in Vietnam.

The Red Guard leaders of the Cultural Revolution were opposed by the more pragmatic and responsible leaders of Mao's government. Chou En-lai and others saw that the perpetual revolution was bringing work to a halt, leading to a fall in output and in living standards. They were supported by many workers who were tired of the constant haranguing they received from the Red Guards. There were many clashes, and in Shanghai and Wuhan what were described as "major battles", before the army moved in to bring the activities of the Red Guards to an end.

Chou En-lai emerged as the head of an alliance between the army and the bureaucracy. He reinstated the once-disgraced but very able Teng Hsiao-p'ing, although he also had to accept many of Mao's supporters in positions of power in the Communist Party and in the government.

Chou was responsible for breaking down the barriers between China and the West. In 1969 President Nixon relaxed the restrictions which the United States had imposed on trade with China. This gave China a chance to obtain some of the capital equipment she needed if she were going to begin modernisation of her economy. And although the United States opposed Communist China's entry into the United Nations in October 1971 (see page 455) relations between the two countries continued to improve. A visit in April 1971 by an American table tennis team was followed in July by one from Secretary of State Henry Kissinger, which was itself a prelude to the visit by President Nixon in February 1972.

The left wing under Mao's wife, Chiang Ch'ing, campaigned against this "revisionism". But Chou had the support of the army, the majority of the bureaucracy and of the people as a whole. However, on Chou's death in January 1976 Mme Mao was still influential and she prevented Teng Hsiao p'ing from succeeding to the leadership. But in September 1976 Mao died and Mme Mao lost her powerful protector. When next she demanded a resurgence of the Red Guards, the army moved quickly to put down the attempted risings. Millions of people were killed in fighting which went on through 1977. Mme Mao and her leading followers ("the Gang of Four") were arrested and Teng Hsiao p'ing was restored to the position of deputy Prime Minister.

Chou's successors in government have shown that they want to see China become an industrialised country. They welcome aid and investment by Western countries with whom they seem to wish to live at peace. They have allowed the development of an anti-Mao movement in China, whose history in the late 1970s has some resemblance to that of Kruschev's Russia in the 1950s (see pages 388–9).

**Vietnam, 1953–1978.**    The focus of great power conflict in Asia in the post-war years has been Indo-China and in particular the area called Vietnam. By 1954 the French were hard pressed in their struggle with the Viet Minh (see page 378) and on May 8 they suffered a major setback in the north with the loss of the key stronghold of Dien Bien Phu. It was an outright defeat of an imperial power by the people of a small and underdeveloped nation and, although the French might have continued the struggle in the south, they had already chosen to go to the conference table. The peace conference in Geneva was attended by Britain, France, the United States and the Soviet Union. Also represented were the two governments of Vietnam, the Communists and the anti-Communists, and the representatives of the other states of Indo-China, Cambodia and Laos.

Eventually it was decided to partition the country north and south of the 17th parallel at least for the time being. The north was

FIG. 64.—AMERICAN ARTILLERY POUNDS A VIETCONG STRONGHOLD.

controlled by Ho Chi Minh and the Communists, the south by a government led by Ngo Dinh Diem. National elections were to be held over the whole country within two years and a Control Commission was set up with Polish and Canadian members and an Indian Chairman.

However, the settlement was ill-defined even on the point of the border between north and south and never showed signs of working properly. The Viet Minh withdrew 100,000 of their men from the south, but left many others, to form the nucleus of a guerrilla opposition to the Diem government. As in Korea, the south was socially and politically unstable. Meanwhile Cambodia and Laos were established as independent and neutral states, but there too Communist forces remained powerful, and in the case of Laos controlled a large part of the country with their Pathet Lao troops. They held the north and east of the country and helped to supply Communist forces in South Vietnam.

The Diem government had not signed the Geneva settlement and refused to be bound by it. Diem soon established a semi-dictatorial position and made little progress with his promised social and economic reforms. This and the corruption of his government led to widespread unrest and several attempts on his life. Communist influence grew and as early as 1957 the guerrillas, or Vietcong, were taking control of the countryside. In 1961 the National Liberation Front was established as the political arm of the Vietcong with its headquarters in Hanoi. Communist forces began to enter the south via Cambodia and Laos.

These developments led the Americans, who had never entirely withdrawn from the south, to increase their military aid to Diem, but by 1963 a quarter of the population of the south was under Vietcong control. Even more direct American involvement followed the attack on an American warship in the gulf of Tonkin by torpedo boats in 1964. American aircraft retaliated by bombing North Vietnamese coastal installations and in 1965 the Americans began a policy of general bombardment of North Vietnam which was to continue with a few halts until 1968. In 1963 the hated Diem government was overthrown in a *coup d'état* but none of the military dominated administrations which followed showed any promise of winning the loyalty of the people of South Vietnam. By 1967 the Americans had 400,000 troops in the south in action with the South Vietnamese Army against the Vietcong. Yet these powerful and well-equipped forces scored no permanent victories and in January, 1968, the Vietcong were able to launch devastating attacks in the major South Vietnamese cities, including the capital Saigon.

By this time the war had become the centre of the international power struggle. The North was helped with military aid from both Russia and China, while in the South the Americans were joined by token forces from South Korea, Australia and New Zealand. However France openly denounced the American campaign and other American allies, such as the United Kingdom, refused to commit themselves to the war. In fact the American government was faced with mounting criticism both at home and abroad for their policies. In the meantime the Vietnamese, both northern and southern, suffered all the horrors of modern conventional warfare.

In the autumn of 1968 the outgoing president of the United States, L. B. Johnson, called a halt to the American bombing of the North and after some preliminary negotiations the representatives of North Vietnam, South Vietnam, the National Liberation

Front and the United States met in Paris. The negotiations dragged on with no satisfactory outcome. However, the American policy of gradually reducing their forces in Vietnam continued, and South Vietnam took on an increasing military responsibility. The year 1970 proved critical for the North Vietnamese. They lost ground to the South Vietnamese in the Mekong Delta, and several important supply routes through the Cambodian ports. Their main efforts were directed to building up new supply bases in Laos and Cambodia. During 1970 American forces were reduced to 350,000 men. President Nixon appeared confident that the war was moving to a conclusion in favour of South Vietnam and the U.S.A. But in March 1971, South Vietnamese forces which had invaded Laos were involved in a disastrous retreat.

By this time the Americans had been in Vietnam for twelve years; fatal casualties totalled 53,000 and aircraft losses were particularly high. President Nixon hoped that the South Vietnamese would soon be able to look after themselves and withdrew another 100,000 American troops in 1971. Great anti-war pressures were building up in the United States and growing opposition to American involvement in the war was evident in Congress itself. However, American air bombardment of North Vietnam was intensified as ground troops were withdrawn. But opposition to the American nominee, President Thieu, was developing within South Vietnam: after parliamentary elections in 1970 about two-fifths of the lower house of the parliament was opposed to Thieu's government. On March 30, 1972 the North Vietnamese began another offensive. The reply to this was intensified American bombing and the mining of North Vietnamese ports with the purpose of preventing military supplies, mainly from Russia, reaching North Vietnam by sea.

However, in January 1973 a ceasefire was signed between the U.S.A. and North Vietnam—a policy reluctantly accepted by President Thieu. The ceasefire left the communist areas in South Vietnam under the control of the communist Provisional Revolutionary Government, which controlled about a third of South Vietnam. The 17th parallel was accepted as the demarcation line for the ceasefire, but not necessarily permanently. More American troops were now withdrawn, but widespread fighting both in North and South Vietnam continued. The year 1974 saw no great offensive by the North Vietnamese, who seemed anxious to do nothing which would halt the continued American withdrawal of ground forces. American efforts were in any case weakening under the impact of the Watergate scandal, the resignation of President Nixon and the accession to the Presidency of Mr. Ford. The continued American withdrawal produced serious problems for South Vietnam—it created much unemployment in the towns, and at the same time American financial aid was reduced. The North Vietnamese continued successfully to consolidate their areas of control in South Vietnam and to build up their new supply bases.

In 1975 the war took a dramatic turn and by the early summer had been won by the North Vietnamese. An enormous offensive, spearheaded by powerful forces of tanks, aircraft and big guns, overran one South Vietnamese stronghold after another. The important coastal towns fell with astonishing rapidity and by May the communist forces were in control of Saigon. This was a shattering blow to the efforts which America had put into the struggle for fifteen years and closed a whole epoch in the history of Vietnam, from the time of the French defeat in 1954. It was a signal triumph for communism in South-East Asia which will have a profound influence on the future of that part of the world.

**Vietnam after the Americans.**   North Vietnam and the Vietcong had relied on Russian aid during their struggle with the French, Americans and South Vietnamese. After 1975 they provided Russia with a powerful ally in this region. China saw this as a threat. In 1978 she invaded Vietnam on the pretext that the Vietnamese had sent troops across the Chinese border. There was a short period of fierce fighting during which the Chinese forces were badly mauled by the Russian-armed Vietnamese. The Chinese were forced to withdraw across their border and for a time there was an uneasy peace in the region.

Cambodia had been at peace until 1970 when the country became involved, unwillingly, in the war. A small Communist party, the Khmer Rouge, grew as one of the groups most opposed to their country's involvement in the war and to the bombing of their cities by both United States and Vietcong planes.

After the victory of the North Vietnamese and the withdrawal of the United States, the Khmer Rouge defeated the American-supported government of Prince Sihanouk. Under the leadership of Pol Pot the Khmer Rouge formed a government which in 1978 merited the description of "the world's worst violators of human rights". In 1970 Cambodia had a population of about 7 million. By the end of 1979 this was estimated to have shrunk to about 2 million, the rest having been the victims of political persecution or of one of the many diseases which have ravaged the country in the aftermath of a famine brought on by government interference with the lives of the people. Anyone suspected of loyalty to the old regime has been killed—including doctors, engineers, lawyers, civil servants, teachers and their families. About 3 million are said to have died in this way.

In January 1979 the Vietnamese, once the allies of the Khmer Rouge, invaded the country to help a former Khmer Rouge officer, Heng Samrin, to take power. The Khmers took to the hills and waged a guerrilla war against the Vietnamese-supported government much as the Vietnamese themselves once did in their own country against the French and Americans.

In its turn Vietnam has been condemned by the way it has treated any suspected opponents, particularly those in the former South Vietnam. A mass exodus of these people has taken place during the non-monsoon periods of 1978 and 1979. Sailing in makeshift boats and primitive junks they have made their way into the China Sea. Some have been picked up by friendly ships (many of them British) and have been accepted as immigrants by Western countries. Others have been less fortunate, thousands have died; many others are still in camps in Hong Kong and Malaysia where they wait for some government to offer them a permanent home. Those who once protested against the American participation in the Vietnam War and who sloganised "Ho, Ho, Ho Chi-m'inh, The Vietcong are going to win" are remarkably silent in the face of the effects of the victory they wished for.

# chapter twenty-five

# FRANCE, 1940-1978

**The Capitulation of France.** From September, 1939, until May, 1940, the French forces waited behind the Maginot line. During this lull before the real fighting, known as the "phoney war", there were rumours that a peace might yet be negotiated with Hitler and hopes were raised that the worst might still not happen. Pro-Fascist elements in France were lying low, but they were able to damage morale while the strong French Communist Party following Stalin's new line after the Nazi-Soviet Pact, denounced the war as "imperialist" and called for peace. All this helped to reinforce the defensive "Maginot mentality" and to undermine the French will to take the offensive.

In the spring of 1940 however it was clear that Hitler would soon launch a blitzkrieg on the west, and in March Daladier, one of the negotiators of the Munich agreement, was at last replaced by Paul Reynaud as Prime Minister. On May 10 the Germans launched their attack on the Netherlands, Belgium and Luxembourg, penetrating with their armoured columns through the defence line on the Meuse and surrounding large French forces at Sedan. The Maginot line had been completely outflanked and scarcely a shot was fired from it. The French were not so weak in tanks and aircraft as some critics have supposed, but they were ineffectively deployed. The theory of concentrated mobile armies so successfully put into practice by the Germans had been advocated by General Charles de Gaulle, but his advice was not heeded and the French strength was dissipated over a four-hundred mile long front. The Germans, despite having only parity of arms with their enemy, were therefore able to penetrate and disorganise the allied front with results that led to the Dunkirk evacuation.

In the demoralisation that followed, the French will to resist collapsed. Reynaud was replaced by Marshal Pétain, the First World War hero, who was now convinced that France should capitulate. Under his guidance the surrender was signed in Compiègne in June. However not all Frenchmen agreed with this course of action. De Gaulle, now a general, had escaped to England and was soon busy with the creation of a Free French movement, a movement which won the allegiance of at least some French overseas territories such as Chad and the French Cameroons.

**France, 1940–1944.** The armistice gave direct control to the Germans of northern France including the whole of the Channel and Atlantic coast. The independent French government with Pétain as head of state and Laval as Prime Minister, was set up at Vichy and allowed to rule the mainly agricultural areas of southern France and the Mediterranean coast. The Vichy National Assembly accorded Pétain dictatorial power until a new constitution could be evolved. In fact he retained these powers throughout the war. Vichy was a semi-Fascist state, feebly imitating the corporate state of Mussolini. Pétain was a conservative, who seems sincerely to have believed that France could be reborn by abandoning the traditions of the Revolution of 1789. The Vichy escutcheon replaced the words "Liberty, Equality, Fraternity" with "Work, Family, Fatherland". The press was strictly controlled, trade unions abolished and Jews and Freemasons subjected to vicious persecution. A Vichy militia was created to carry out these policies and later to round up workers for forced labour in Germany. It was this latter activity that drove many Frenchmen to join the underground, the maquis who continued the internal resistance of the Germans and collaborators.

As a result of an internal power struggle, Laval was dismissed in December, 1940 and replaced by Admiral Darlan, a fanatical Anglophobe and an ardent admirer of the Nazi system. He placed French industry and manpower at the service of the Germans and at the critical time in the war in the Middle East ordered the authorities in Syria to co-operate with the Germans. Some of his supporters even advocated the handing over of control of France to the Germans. In April, 1942, Laval returned to power and seems to have done a little to check the outflow of French workers. However, 1942 brought the Anglo-American invasion of North Africa and the complete control of the whole of France by the Germans. The 100,000 strong Vichy Army was dissolved and outright Fascists such as Marcel Déat included in Laval's cabinet. The militia were used to round up even more young men for service in Germany and consequently the resistance efforts of the maquis increased. Arms were dropped from Britain and during the D-day landings the French resistance performed valuable service in sabotaging German road, rail and water transport. When the allies advanced towards Paris the Vichy state was officially declared at an end and Laval and some of his supporters fled to German protection at Sigmaringen. With the collapse of Germany he was brought back to Paris and shot as a traitor.

In the meantime Charles de Gaulle had succeeded after much difficulty in getting himself recognised as leader of the Free French in 1943. At first the allies had tried to negotiate with Darlan in North Africa but he was assassinated and it was clear that the resistance movement would only recognise de Gaulle. A provisional government was formed in Algiers and after D-Day it moved to France with de Gaulle at its head. Allied forces entered Paris on August 24, 1944, and the next day de Gaulle made a formal arrival at the head of Free French troops. To de Gaulle's fury, the Americans were still prepared to negotiate with the Vichy authorities, but it was clear that most Frenchmen wanted de Gaulle. Even so, it was not until October, 1944, that his Committee of National Liberation was finally recognised by Churchill and Roosevelt as the provisional government of France. As a result of these difficulties de Gaulle developed a deep suspicion of Anglo-American policies.

De Gaulle headed a coalition government which was able to lead France through the last stages of the war against Germany and which carried out a number of important social and economic reforms. However, de Gaulle was not happy at the head of a coalition administration. In the elections of October, 1945, the Communists, Socialists and the liberal Catholic Mouvement Republicain Populaire (MRP) were returned with about 30 per cent of the vote each. De Gaulle

FIG 65.—MEMBERS OF THE RESISTANCE ROUND UP GERMANS IN PARIS, AUGUST, 1945.

resigned in January, 1946, and was succeeded by a civilian Socialist politician, Félix Gouin.

**The Fourth Republic.** The French Assembly elected in the autumn of 1945 had the task of devising a new constitution to replace that of 1875 which had collapsed in 1940. Their first attempt was rejected and the second constitution was only narrowly accepted in a referendum—an inauspicious start to the Fourth Republic. In fact the new constitution was remarkably like the old one. One important difference was that women were given the vote for the first time. There was a system of proportional representation and the legislative bodies were to be the National Assembly and the Council of the Republic. The latter was a watered-down version of the old Senate with very little legislative power. However, the President was to be chosen by the combined Assembly and Council. Local government with some minor changes remained more or less the same as that of the Third Republic. A disturbing feature of the political situation was the indifference the French showed towards the new Constitution —nearly one-third abstained from voting in the referendum. Seven million voted against it and eight million for it. Amongst the large minority who opposed it was de Gaulle who disapproved especially of the circumscribed powers of the President.

In 1945 France was in need of drastic social and economic reform but this proved almost impossible under the political system of the Fourth Republic. The reorganisation of French industry in Jean Monnet's "Monnet Plan" was largely successful, but the inflationary spiral of rising wages and prices led to widespread discontent. In general wages lagged behind prices and a vast black market developed to defeat the rationing system. The wealthier classes enjoyed the benefit of the black market and this increased social unrest. Trade union agitation grew after 1947 when the Communists left the coalition and turned to industrial action. The Communists dominated the French General Confederation of Trade Unions and this led to a break-away by non-Communists under Léon Jouhaux in the "Force Ouvrière".

Yet economic and social problems could not be effectively tackled because of the weakness of the party system. Governments relied on three-party coalitions generally made up first of Socialists, MRP and Communists and later of Socialists, MRP and Radicals, and, as under the Third Republic, new elections were not necessarily held on a change of government. Under this new system the government was unable to introduce legislation which did not please all its diverse

FIG. 66.—DE GAULLE EXHORTS HIS FOLLOWERS SOON AFTER HIS RESIGNATION IN JANUARY, 1946.

members and was constantly threatened by the breaking away of splinter groups jockeying for power.

Moreover, there were powerful political groups opposed to the whole system. On the one hand there were the Communists, on the other the remnants of the old conservative-Vichy group. Another powerful critic was de Gaulle who formed his own national movement outside the Assembly—the Rally of the French People—in 1946 to attack the constitution and combat Communism. It claimed to be above party politics and to be only concerned with national welfare. However, it claimed 80 members in the National Assembly in 1946 and 120 in 1951. The existence of the RPF only increased the fragmentation of the Assembly and the instability of the many short-lived governments. The ludicrous weakness of the system was demonstrated in 1953, when it needed thirteen ballots in the Assembly and Council to secure the election of René Coty as President.

The outstanding Prime Minister of the Fourth Republic was Pierre

Mendès-France, and in his brief ministry of 1954–1955 he was able
to make a start in resolving the French colonial problems notably in
Indo-China and North Africa. But Mendès-France, like the lesser
premiers of this period, fell because he could not rely on a strong and
loyal majority in the Assembly.

Yet another complicating factor was introduced into French politics by the success of the followers of Pierre Poujade in the 1956
elections when they won 52 seats in the Assembly. Poujade won
the support of the discontented amongst the propertied classes; he
attacked the weak and corrupt political system, he denounced the
burden of taxation and demanded the maintenance of French imperial
power in North Africa. His popularity was not long-lived, but for a
while it did reduce de Gaulle's RPF membership in the Assembly to
22, winning away from it the vote of the frustrated middle class.

Mendès-France had been succeeded by Edgar Faure and then by
Guy Mollet who stayed in power for eighteen months but fell himself
in 1957 after the Suez débâcle and his inability to deal with the Algerian problem. There followed a still more unstable period in which
French politics were completely dominated by the problem of Algeria.

**The Nationalist Revolt in French North Africa.** The setbacks in
Indo-China (see pages 378 and 423) forced the French to reassess
their position in North Africa in the face of mounting nationalist
unrest there (see page 375). In this process the key figure was Pierre
Mendès-France who became Prime Minister in 1954 soon after the
fall of Dien Bien Phu. It was Mendès-France who steered through
the Geneva settlement in Indo-China and he also turned his powers of
conciliation to North Africa. He opened direct negotiations with
Habib Bourguiba, leader of the nationalist Neo-Destour party and
reached an agreement in 1955 on the country's progress to independence. Mendès-France fell from power in 1955, but his successors
continued his policies, and in 1956 Tunisia became an independent
state with control over her own foreign policy and armed forces. In
1958 the French withdrew all their troops from the country except
those in the leased naval base at Bizerta.

During the same period the independence of Morocco was also
recognised though the process was more troubled. For a time the
French tried to rule through puppet Sultans and from 1953 to 1955
French troops fought a harsh war against terrorists and guerrillas.
In 1955, however, the legitimate Sultan, Sidi Mohammed ben Yussef,
was released and the next year the independence of Morocco was
recognised. Spanish Morocco and the international zone of Tangier

were incorporated into the state of Morocco and in 1958 de Gaulle was to settle the outstanding problems between France and the new Moroccan monarchy.

The problem of Algeria, however, was to prove much more intractable than that of Tunisia or Morocco.

**The Algerian Crisis.** Tunisia and Morocco had been French protectorates with comparatively small French populations. Algeria was constitutionally part of metropolitan France with representatives in the National Assembly. About a million white French settlers, or colons, lived in Algeria and dominated the country's political life. Although they constituted nine-tenths of the population the indigenous Moslems had made slow progress to political or social equality—for instance they constituted less than one per cent of the higher civil service.

The French inhabitants were mostly townspeople engaged in busi-

FIG. 67.—FRENCH PARATROOPS PATROL THE EUROPEAN QUARTER OF ALGIERS

ness and determined to hold on to their privileges. In this they had the support of many army leaders in the country. By 1954 the French had some 500,000 troops stationed in Algeria and the cost of their maintenance was one of the fundamental causes of inflation in France and thus of the plague of social and industrial unrest.

Yet the French were unable to stifle Arab nationalism and after 1954 the nationalist campaign became increasingly violent. Its proclaimed aim was to complete independence and an end to the privileges of the colons. It set up a headquarters in exile and the National Liberation Front (FLN) was later able to operate from bases in Tunisia and Morocco. They attacked French military installations and committed acts of terror on French residents and Moslems who co-operated with them. The French immediately increased their military effort. In the next four years there were some 200,000 Algerian casualties and 13,000 French. Both sides were guilty of the most terrible atrocities. The bloodshed and the acts of torture committed by French troops provoked a reaction against the war in many Frenchmen, but the colons and the army were determined to crush the resistance and it became increasingly hard for the government in Paris to control them.

**The Fall of the Fourth Republic.** Many army leaders had lost faith in the civilian politicians after the withdrawal from Indo-China and the other North African territories. They were prepared to resist any government concessions to the Algerian rebels and in this they had the support of the right-wing "Algerian lobby" in the Assembly.

In May, 1958, Pierre Pflimlin, a man who was known to favour a settlement of the war, became Prime Minister. The result was a revolt by the Algerian generals led by Salan and Massu. Within a fortnight the government was in a state of collapse and the Algerian Army was threatening to invade France. At this moment many people turned to de Gaulle who had been out of active politics for many years. The army leaders trusted him and believed that they could use him to their own ends. The politicians in Paris believed that he alone could control the army. It was the moment for which de Gaulle had been waiting and he emerged from his retirement offering to assume the powers of the republic to deal with the crisis. On June 1 the National Assembly, by a vote of 329 to 224 gave de Gaulle personal powers for six months and the task of preparing a new constitution. He at once set about the business of restoring France to order with a government drawn from every shade of political opinion, except the Communists and Poujadists.

**The Constitution of the Fifth Republic.** The constitution of the Fifth Republic was radically different from that of the Third and Fourth. In the first place the powers of the National Assembly were considerably reduced. For instance the government had the power to tax by decree if the Assembly delayed a money bill by more than seventy days. The whole parliamentary timetable was in the hands of the government which was thus able to give priority to its own measures. Another notable feature was the power of the President. He was able to dissolve the Assembly and assume emergency powers in the face of internal disorder. Yet another new feature was the introduction of single-member constituencies in place of the old system of proportional representation. A two-tier system of elections was devised so that if no candidate emerged with a clear majority on the first round the weakest candidates would retire to give a straight choice on the second round. Members of the government did not sit in the Assembly although they were responsible for it. Moreover they and the Prime Minister were appointed by the President. A vote of censure on the government required a majority of the whole Assembly and in any case did not necessarily bring down the government. In fact France had moved decisively from a parliamentary to a presidential system and the extent to which the President really controlled power became increasingly apparent as time went by. At this time the President was elected by an indirect vote, but after 1962 by direct universal suffrage.

In September a referendum was held on the new Constitution and, in contrast to that on the Fourth Republic, 84 per cent of the electorate voted, 74 per cent in favour. In the general elections that followed the Socialists were reduced to 40 seats and the Communists to a mere 10. The new Gaullist Union pour la Nouvelle République won 188 seats and the government also had the support of the MRP and other right-wing groups. The left had suffered a heavy setback which was made worse by the electoral system of two votes. However they did recover to some extent in the mid-sixties, partly through ballot agreements between the Socialists and the Communists.

On January 8, 1959, de Gaulle was formally proclaimed President of the Fifth Republic and Michel Debré was appointed as Prime Minister, a post he was to hold until 1962. He was followed by M. Pompidou until 1968, who was replaced in his turn by M. Couve de Murville. But although these three were men of great political ability de Gaulle remained not only Head of State, but also the effective leader of the government.

**The Settlement of the Algerian Problem.** It was the Algerian crisis which brought de Gaulle to power and it was his most important task to settle it. The army leaders and the colons fully expected that he would support their policy of maintaining French control, but in this they were to be sadly disillusioned.

The President began by apportioning larger sums to the economic development of Algeria and increased the number of Moslems in positions of authority. At the same time he weeded out many unreliable officers in the army in Algeria. In 1959 he announced that four years after the fighting was brought to an end the Algerians would have the right of determining their own future—a promise which infuriated the colons, but did not satisfy the FLN who refused to call off their campaign. De Gaulle pressed on with the negotiations with the FLN, however, and removed General Massu from his command. There followed a military revolt in Algeria, but de Gaulle was not to be toppled as easily as his civilian predecessors and most of the army remained loyal. The Assembly voted him emergency powers and he continued to move towards meeting the nationalist demands. In November, 1960, he declared that independence for Algeria was inevitable and this led in April, 1961, to a major military revolt led by Salan. The President once again stood firm and appealed to the army and the people to stay loyal. The revolt collapsed and a number of leaders were arrested. Others escaped and set up the OAS (Secret Army Organisation) which fought against the government by terrorist methods and tried unsuccessfully to assassinate the President. Nothing, however, would deflect him from his course, and in July, 1962, Algeria became an independent nation.

De Gaulle had thus released France from one of its heaviest burdens and immensely increased his prestige. Even the Communists could hardly criticise him for carrying out a policy they had advocated since 1945. In the elections of 1962 his supporters won an outright majority in the Assembly, a situation without precedent in France under democratic conditions.

**The End of the French Empire.** The constitution of 1946 had provided for the representation of the colonies in the National Assembly and in the High Council, but this scheme had never really worked and de Gaulle was determined that the country should not be plagued by any further colonial wars. In 1958 he therefore offered the states in French Africa the choice of immediate independence or association with France in the French Community. The Community gave self-government, but some control by France in international affairs. The advantage of the Community was that it promised the former colonies a good deal of aid from France and all except Guinea opted for it. By 1960 however the old idea of the Community was destroyed for the member states all decided to have full independence. Most of them, however, retained strong cultural and economic links with France.

**Foreign Policy.** The liberation of the Empire was part of de Gaulle's general policy of winning the friendships of the peoples of Asia, Africa and Latin America and restoring France's reputation in the Third World after the Suez Affair and the wars in Indo-China and Algeria.

**De Gaulle's Foreign Policy.** A good deal has already been said about de Gaulle's foreign policy (see page 393). In general he sought to dissociate France from the policies of the United States and her ally Great Britain and to take France and her European associates into an independent position, committed neither tó East nor West. For this reason he opposed Britain's membership of the Common Market and withdrew France from NATO. He was bitterly critical of American actions in Vietnam and cultivated good relations not only with Russia and Eastern Europe but also with Communist China. He was at pains to develop French cultural influence often in competition with American influence—for instance in French-speaking Quebec and Latin America.

His independent line was also demonstrated in his defence policy. He scorned the Nassau agreement and successfully developed French nuclear weapons (the first explosion was in 1960) and French military aircraft. He also refused to sign the Limited Test Ban Treaty of 1963.

**De Gaulle's Internal Policy.** De Gaulle despised the old politicians and their methods. On a number of occasions he appealed direct to the people in referenda in which he was always assured of a comfortable majority. Even though the UNR suffered some electoral setbacks in the mid-1960s his personal position was for long un-threatened. The government controlled radio and television to their own advantage and a great many reforms were carried through by decree.

One of the President's first steps was to revalue the franc and the currency became increasingly healthy as the country was released from the crippling burden of the Algerian War. By 1963 France was already accumulating considerable gold reserves and the balance of

Fig. 68.—President de Gaulle Welcomes Chinese Communist Diplomats to the Elysee Palace.

payments problem was solved. Industrial production increased thanks not only to de Gaulle but to the work of men like Monnet and to the benefits of the Common Market. Wages and prices were controlled by government decree to prevent inflation. Subsidies were withdrawn in order to increase efficiency. For some years it seemed that de Gaulle was completely successful and comparatively few Frenchmen mourned the loss of full democratic rights.

However, there was discontent. The workers resented wage fixing and the government's policy of control over the information services came in for a good deal of criticism. Nor was France free from the wave of student unrest that was building up in many countries in the late 1960s. In the spring there were student demonstrations in Paris which the government unwisely tried to deal with heavy-handedly. The riots then became increasingly anti-Gaullist and although the traditional left-wing politicians were not too keen to ally with the students, the unions did push forward wage claims. Factories were taken over and there was a paralysing general strike.

De Gaulle, after an apparent period of uncertainty, remained firm. He had the support of the army in the last resort, but he was prepared to respond to popular demands. Elections were called and he offered a new plan for greater public participation in jobs and sanctioned large wage increases. In the elections he scored yet another overwhelming victory and his enemies were divided and demoralised.

However the wage increases, the loss of production and the shaking of confidence in the franc led to an adverse balance of trade in the autumn of 1968 and a run on the franc which threatened to destroy the carefully hoarded gold reserves. In the currency crisis which followed, the speculators exchanged their francs for the buoyant German mark. A meeting of world financiers was called at Bonn and international aid was given to France. However de Gaulle refused to take the obvious, though to him humiliating, course of devaluing the franc. Instead, in November, he imposed drastic economies on the government and the people. This in its turn once more created unrest in France though not on the scale of the June riots.

De Gaulle's policies were to suffer another blow in 1968 with the Russian invasion of Czechoslovakia which convinced many people that he was wrong in his claim that NATO no longer served a useful purpose. However, early in 1969 he announced that he had every intention of serving out his term as President into the 1970s.

However, despite his declaration, the pressure of events was telling against him. The economic difficulties of France increased rather than declined and devaluation appeared to be an inevitable need.

In a national referendum the President failed to secure the clear national majority for his policies which he had demanded, and he resigned, his place being taken by one of his most ardent admirers and followers, M. Pompidou. General de Gaulle died towards the end of 1970, and the outburst of national grief in France was a clear recognition by the French people of the great importance of his role in the revival of modern France.

**De Gaulle's Achievement.** De Gaulle followed a controversial course after his elevation as ruler of France. He was bitterly criticised abroad not only by British and American commentators, but by many of his Common Market partners. At home he awoke the wrath of both the left and the extreme right in French politics. He seemed to have an unshakeable confidence in his ability to judge what was right for the nation as a whole. He often incorporated aspects of his rivals' programmes into his own policies, creating a curious amalgam

Fig. 69.—Student Demonstrators in the Latin Quarter of Paris, May, 1968.

of revolutionary and conservative, dictatorial and democratic, radical and nationalistic elements. At critical points he made concessions to the popular will, as in the summer of 1968, but he fearlessly resisted opponents of his rule whether they were rioting students or the secret killers of the OAS. It is at least certain that he did the country immeasurable service in saving it from disaster in 1958 and reviving its sense of purpose which had been so badly undermined during the Third and Fourth Republics.

**France in the Years 1970 to 1978.** The general political trend in France during these years was towards a strengthening of the extremes at the expense of the moderate forces of the centre. This was especially shown in the local elections in 1971, when the extreme Gaullists and the Communists both made gains at the expense of the centre parties. The Gaullist grouping in the Chamber of Deputies, the UDR (Union des Democrates pour la République) came increasingly under challenge from the Left. This was especially the case in the general election of 1973, in which the Communists and Socialists formed a united front which put forward important social and economic demands—a monthly national minimum wage, retirements on full pension at age 60, the 40-hour week, the nationalisation of financial institutions and large industrial combines, the phasing-out of France's nuclear armaments. The Communists were now declaring themselves in favour of the democratic process and were becoming openly critical of certain aspects of Soviet Communist policy. The Gaullist UDR had been at the same time weakened by the scandals of corruption among some of their leading supporters. The election results saw a surge forward of the Communist–Socialist bloc and a decrease of the Gaullist vote, but the UDR was still the dominant force with the aid of allies among the lesser political parties. However, President Pompidou concluded that the French people, although still rejecting communism, were demanding certain progressive reforms. In the autumn a monthly minimum national wage was introduced, retirement at 60 made easier, special safeguards for workers' salaries when companies failed, more participation of workers in industrial concerns and more profit-sharing schemes. France's first mediator (ombudsman) was appointed to investigate complaints by individuals against injustices by government departments, etc.

President Pompidou, one of whose important actions had been to welcome Britain's entry into the Common Market, died in April, 1974. This led to one of the most narrowly contested presidential elections for many years. The candidate supported by the Gaullists (although he himself was not a Gaullist) was Giscard d'Estaing, the finance minister. His main opponent was M. Mitterand, the candidate of the united left of Socialists and Communists. M. d'Estaing secured a very narrow victory on the second ballot—50.8 per cent of the vote against Mitterand's 49.19—a serious shock for the old-school Gaullists. One result of this election was the reduction of the Gaullists in the French cabinet from 10 to 5. It had important social consequences, for a number of the old Gaullist dictatorial policies were repudiated by d'Estaing. For example, press censorship was ended, political censorship of films and illegal telephone tapping, which had been used by previous Gaullist governments, were now ended. The minimum monthly wage was also increased. Thus the pressures of the Left, a certain amount of disarray among the Gaullists and the fact that the new President was an Independent Republican, all contributed to a greater liberalisation in French life.

These years in France saw many of the same problems as elsewhere in Europe—inflation, unemployment and considerable social discontent. In general the French were more successful than, for example, Britain and Italy, in controlling these problems. Their industry was highly efficient and their balance of trade reasonably healthy. Nevertheless, discontent exhibited itself at times in very extreme forms. The terrorist type organisation known as the Proletarian Left (Gauche Prolétarienne) committed 82 acts of violence and sabotage and the government declared the organisation illegal. Discontent with their general conditions also led to a great unrest among the police force itself.

France continued on her independent course of building up her own nuclear armaments and by 1976 was the world's third nuclear power. Her atmospheric atomic tests in the Pacific led to widespread protests and considerable international unpopularity. France also boycotted international disarmament discussions on the grounds of the disproportionate power of the super-powers of Russia and the United States. Thus the Gaullist policies of independence of NATO and the creation of powerful national armaments was continued under the presidency of Giscard d'Estaing.

chapter twenty-six

# THE UNITED NATIONS, 1945–1978

**The Origins of the United Nations.** During the later stages of the Second World War, various ideas were put forward for an international organisation to replace the discredited League of Nations. Churchill proposed three regional groups which would be represented on a supreme world council with the victorious great powers standing over all. However, there were objections to such an idea: there were fears that it would encourage a new isolationism in the United States and that the regional groups would become close and exclusive trading areas. After a good deal of discussion, the general idea of the United Nations was formulated at the Dumbarton Oaks Conference in October, 1944, and the first draft of the Charter of the United Nations was signed by fifty-one nations on April 25, 1945, in San Francisco.

Article 1 of the Charter gave the purpose of the organisation as the maintenance of world peace and security. It also declared that all peoples should enjoy an equal right to self-determination and it extended the aims of the organisation to the development not only of political concord but cultural and economic co-operation as well. Article 2 stressed that the organisation would not interfere in the internal affairs of member states except to enforce measures already approved by the Security Council.

The principle of one member one vote was adopted from the start and decisions in the General Assembly, where all members were represented, required either a simple majority or a two-thirds majority according to the importance of the motion. The Assembly controlled and delegated power to a number of important councils and committees, for instance the Trusteeship Council and the Social and Economic Council. It also controlled the financing of the organisation and the administration arm of the United Nations—the Secretary General and his international civil servants. The Assembly meets once a year in September, but it may be convened to deal with crises at other times. Most of its committees and councils are in almost permanent session and of these the most important is the Security Council.

**The Security Council.** The Security Council is the permanent

Fig. 70.—The U.N. Comes of Age: the twenty-first meeting of the General Assembly in September, 1966.

decision-making organ of the United Nations and all members are bound to carry out its resolutions. In 1945 it was composed of eleven members of which six were elected for terms of two years and the other five (United States, Soviet Union, Great Britain, France and China) were permanent members. In 1963 the Security Council was increased to fifteen with the same five permanent members. This change was dictated by the fact that the membership of the organisation had doubled by that time. On most matters apart from procedural ones the decisions of the Council have to have the approval of all the permanent members. That is to say that the five powers all wield the right of veto. With the exception of the United States they have all used this power, Russia on many occasions.

In 1945 when the allies were still united against Hitler, unanimity was feasible and in any case all the great powers wished to protect themselves against the decisions of the others—though many smaller powers objected to the idea of the veto. One limitation however was that at Yalta it had been agreed that no great power could prevent the discussion of a dispute to which it was party—though of course the right to veto decisions remained intact. Included in the right of veto was the power to prevent the admission of any nation to which a permanent member objected.

**"Uniting for Peace", November, 1950.** During the intense period of the Cold War it was increasingly obvious that the Russians could paralyse the organisation by the use of the veto and that under other circumstances other great powers might also obstruct the organisation in its peace-keeping role. A motion was therefore passed in the Assembly by 50 votes to 5 which greatly increased the Assembly's powers.

Under the terms of the Uniting for Peace Resolution, the Assembly could recommend and take action in a crisis if the Security Council failed to exercise its authority. Any seven members of the Security Council or a simple majority of the Assembly could call for an emergency debate within twenty-four hours. At the same time a United Nations Observation Commission was established and the UN Observers could be sent at once to crisis areas. The Uniting for Peace Resolution turned out to be very important in practice and was used in connection with both Suez and Hungary in 1956 and the Congo crisis in 1960.

Another important safeguard against the effects of disagreement within the Security Council is Article 51 of the Charter, which allows local collective action to meet aggression in the period before the Security Council has had time to act. Thus the various regional security organisations—NATO, SEATO, CENTO and the Warsaw Pact could claim to act under the terms of this article in certain circumstances.

**The Secretariat.** The chief officer of the United Nations is the Secretary General who, with his staff, is responsible both for the running of the United Nations Headquarters in New York and for the implementation of many of the decisions of the Assembly and Council. The Secretary General is also responsible for bringing problems before the Council and for the drawing up of an annual report on the organisation's work. He is elected by the Assembly on the recommendation of the Council.

The post has been held in succession by Trygvie Lie of Norway, Dag Hammarskjold of Sweden, U Thant of Burma, and Kurt

Waldheim of Austria. The Secretary General is a figure of considerable influence in world affairs even though he has no forces or economic resources at his disposal. He is supposed to stand above national interests, but the Secretaries General have in fact been involved in international controversies on a number of occasions. Lie had to give up the post because the Russians objected to his supposed anti-Communist bias. Hammarskjold ran into a good deal of criticism from both East and West before his mysterious death in an air crash during the Congo crisis (see page 454). And at one stage the Russians sought to replace him not by his deputy U Thant but by a troika, three men representing the interests of the main power blocs.

**The Agencies of the United Nations.** Peace-keeping is the chief task of the United Nations but not its only one. Both through subcouncils and committees of the Assembly and through separate UN Agencies the organisation is also responsible for international cooperation and development in social, economic and cultural fields as well.

One of the most important bodies of the United Nations is the Economic and Social Council, which is elected by the Assembly for a three-year term. It is concerned with the world strategy to deal with refugees and the victims of natural calamities and to tackle the economic development problems of the poorer countries of the world, especially those which have only achieved independence since 1945. It has a number of regional commissions for various geographical areas such as Latin America, the Far East, and so on, and these are able to make special recommendations to the Economic and Social Council as a result of their investigations.

The economic and financial work of the organisation took a great step forward after 1961. In December of that year it was unanimously decided by the Assembly to designate the sixties as the "United Nations Development Decade" in which every effort should be made to expand the trade, industry and agriculture of the underdeveloped countries. It was calculated at that time that less than 25 per cent of the world's population received the diet of 2,200 calories a day reckoned to be necessary for a healthy life. During the decade member states were supposed to contribute on a rising scale to the development programme. There was in fact a steady growth in aid, although political considerations could not be held in check entirely. For instance, the great powers naturally favoured aid to those countries which were associated with them in the international power groupings.

In 1967 the Council for the United Nations Development Programme succeeded in getting a pledge from over a hundred governments for £80,000,000 for 1968 and U Thant declared that the target for 1970 would be twice as much. A permanent Trade and Industry Board was set up to co-ordinate a world trade policy with organisations such as EEC. In 1968 the Board established the International Trade Centre to aid the developing states in international trade. In the same way the United Nations Industrial Development Organisation was supposed to gain the help of wealthy nations in the expansion of industry in the underdeveloped world.

Almost from the first, the United Nations has also been able to carry on this sort of work through the other agencies. The International Labour Organisation (ILO) with its headquarters in Geneva, was the one part of the League of Nations which survived and was taken over by the United Nations. It is concerned with world labour conditions. The Food and Agricultural Organisation (FAO) in Rome is concerned with world food supplies and agricultural development in the more backward countries. The United Nations Educational, Scientific and Cultural Organisation (UNESCO) in Paris co-ordinates

FIG. 71 THE U.N. IN ACTION: a U.N. troop train with Norwegian soldiers arrives in Port Said in 1956.

educational research and promotes international scientific and cultural co-operation. From the immediate post-war period onwards it has been very successful. It gave enormous help to educational institutions disorganised by the war and it has continued to stage conferences of educationists, scientists and technologists.

Another important agency had been the United Nations Relief and Works Agency (UNRWA) which spent about £17,000,000 in 1967 on regular relief work. In that year it was suddenly faced with an extra 100,000 refugees in the Middle East as a result of the Arab–Israeli war. The International Refugee Organisation was directly responsible for refugee work until 1952, after that it was replaced by a High Commissioner for Refugees, who co-ordinates the efforts of all the agencies concerned with the needs of refugees.

The United Nations International Children's Fund (UNICEF) was set up in 1946 to look after the special problems of child care in countries affected by war or other calamities. The World Health Organisation (WHO) has given enormous sums to develop health services in various countries and to fight disease. By 1966 WHO had helped over twelve hundred projects in 152 different countries.

Amongst the key agencies have been the two financial bodies of the UN. The International Monetary Fund (IMF) has been concerned with short-term loans especially those needed to meet currency crises. The International Bank for Reconstruction and Development (The World Bank) has been the source of long-term loans for development projects. In the first twenty-one years of the Bank's existence, it advanced loans of £4 billion to developing countries.

**The Trusteeship Council.** Another very important body within the United Nations is the Trusteeship Council which, like the Economic and Social Council, is elected by the Assembly. The Council took over the ultimate responsibility for the old League of Nations Mandates and for territories taken from Italy and Japan in 1945. These numbered eleven in all and although none of them were directly administered by the United Nations, it was the responsibility of the administering power to answer to the Trusteeship Council. One improvement over the old Mandate system was that the peoples of the Trusteeship territories had the right of direct appeal to the Council. The ultimate aim was to lead all the territories involved either to independence or to union with other existing states. An example of the latter was the North Cameroons which became part of the state of Nigeria.

The most troubled trust territory has been South West Africa, administered by South Africa since after the First World War. The South Africans also refused to allow a UN investigating committee to visit the territory. The question of South West Africa has naturally attracted the attention of the independent African states but as yet it is unresolved.

The Trusteeship Council also has a general brief to look after the interests of all colonial peoples whether or not their territories came under the mandate or trusteeship systems.

**The Political Work of the United Nations.** Since 1945 the United Nations has been deeply involved in almost all the major international problems and there is only room here to pick out some examples of both its successes and its failures.

In the immediate post-war period the work of the United Nations was made very much more difficult by the conflict of the great powers in the Cold War. All too often it was unable to take any action at all in these years because of the Russian veto. In 1946 a complaint from Persia that Russian troops had not been removed from the north of the country by the agreed time resulted in a UN request to Russia with which the Soviet Union complied. On the other hand the Russians obstructed effective action when, in December, 1946, the Greek government complained that Albania, Bulgaria and Yugoslavia were giving assistance to Communist guerrillas in the Greek civil war. Although a special commission of inquiry upheld the Greek claim, Russia prevented Security Council action and the Communist states refused to co-operate with the United Nations Special Commission on the Balkans which was set up to secure the peaceful settlement of disputes in the area. The Security Council was also unable to help in the Berlin Blockade or indeed the German problem as a whole.

It had more sucess in dealing with colonial questions. For instance in 1946 British and Indian troops which had controlled Indonesia since after the defeat of Japan, withdrew from the country. The Dutch then decided to send in their own troops although the Indonesians had proclaimed an independent republican government. Hostilities soon broke out and the question was brought to the United Nations despite Dutch protests that it was entirely their affair. A truce was signed in 1948, but war broke out again in January, 1949. Again the United Nations called for an end to hostilities and the creation of an independent state of Indonesia. A commission was set up to help deal with the problem and in December the state was established with Dutch recognition. The Dutch did retain control of Western Irian (New Guinea) which the Indonesians claimed.

Eventually the United Nations were able to supervise the hand-over of the territory in 1962.

Less successful has been the role of the United Nations in the Arab–Israeli conflict. The United Nations inherited the problem from the British in 1948, but the partition of the state of Palestine which they proposed (see page 375) was unacceptable and their mediator, Count Bernadotte, was assassinated by Jewish terrorists. His successor Dr Ralph Bunche was eventually able to bring about the truce in 1949. After 1956 the UN maintained a peace-keeping force along the Egyptian border with Israel, but in early 1967 this was withdrawn at Nasser's request. U Thant was much criticised for thus abdicating the peace-keeping responsibility, but it seems likely that in any case India and other nations supplying troops for the force would have withdrawn their own contingents. In fact one of the great weaknesses of the organisation is that it lacks any permanent peace-keeping force of its own.

The part of the United Nations in the Korean War has already been described. Officially the South Koreans were supported by a United Nations army, but in fact the force was a predominantly American one with British and some other support. Control of strategy was effectively in the hands of the Americans. After the 1953 truce, the United Nations committee for the reunification of Korea remained in being, but achieved no success in the following fifteen years.

On the other hand the UN had some success at about the same time in settling the fate of the former Italian empire in Africa. Libya was established as an independent state and Somaliland became the Republic of Somalia. Eritrea was unified with Ethiopia. Clearly the moral was that the UN could function very much better when it was involved in problems which were not a direct concern of the big powers. Another example of positive peace-keeping has been Cyprus. When violent inter-communal strife broke out between Greeks and Turks in the country in 1963–1964 a UN force was sent in and it has remained there ever since. The United Nations were able to help in keeping the two sides apart and prevent intervention from Turkey.

The only example of the United Nations applying sanctions has been against the rebellious state of Rhodesia. The sanctions involved an embargo on trade with the Rhodesians and all UN members were pledged to enforce it, but in fact it was ignored by both South Africa and Portugal quite openly and by other countries less overtly. This exemplifies another of the problems of the organisation. Its resolutions have been ignored by the Republic of South Africa on apartheid, South West Africa and Rhodesia, but there was very little that could be done to compel obedience.

**The Congo Crisis.** An outstanding example of the United Nations in action was the Congo crisis; it showed that the UN could raise and maintain an international army, but it revealed the weaknesses of the organisation. It also created a precedent because it did clearly involve intervention in the internal affairs of a country.

The origins of the crisis can be found in the failure of Belgium to prepare its colony for independence. In the face of the mounting tide of African nationalism the Belgian government decided to grant the Congo independence in 1960, but at that time this enormous territory lacked any national political parties or experienced politicians, any African higher civil servants or army officers, and indeed almost any graduates or doctors.

Almost immediately there was conflict between the government of President Kasavubu and Prime Minister Lumumba on the one hand and other politicians such as Moise Tshombe from the mineral-rich province of Katanga who wanted the Congo to become a loose federation. At the same time there was a mutiny in the army and violent attacks on Europeans still in the country. The Belgian government sent in paratroops to rescue Europeans, while the Congolese government called for UN assistance to help hold the country together.

A United Nations army was created by Hammarskjold, drawing on the troops of neutralist states as far apart as Eire and Indonesia. They took over from the Belgians and helped to restore some sort of order in which the other UN agencies could get to work to repair some of the damage that had been done to the economy and social structure of the Congo. In September, 1961, the UN force moved against the rebellious forces of Katanga and forced them to sign an armistice. After a further rebellion in Katanga the local army was suppressed by the UN in 1961. The United Nations force eventually withdrew in 1964.

The United Nations had not been able to prevent the murder of Lumumba or a great deal of the inter-tribal violence. It tried not to get involved in the confused internal politics of the country which eventually led to General Mobutu, the commander-in-chief, declaring himself head of state in 1966. On the other hand, it did prevent the country from disintegrating and it did bring some medical and economic relief. Its intervention was criticised in many quarters. The Russians claimed it was an American attempt to reimpose colonial rule in another guise, while certain European business interests bitterly opposed the action against Katanga, in which they had a vast financial stake. The Congo intervention was enormously expensive and almost brought the United Nations into bankruptcy, because the Russians and some other states refused to pay their share towards it. It also led to the death of Hammarskjold on a flight to Northern Rhodesia during the Katanga crisis. On the other hand it seems certain that the people of the Congo would have suffered even more terribly had the UN not taken some initiative.

**Disarmament.** Obviously one of the most important steps towards securing world peace would be the agreement upon world disarmament. Sadly, the United Nations cannot be said to have made any progress in the years 1945–1978 in getting an actual reduction in either conventional or nuclear weapons. But it has helped to control the proliferation of the most destructive weapons and it has kept the discussion open through all these years.

The Atomic Energy Commission, set up in 1946, hoped to arrange for the international control of the production of atomic energy, but the Soviet Union refused to agree to international control and inspection till existing stockpiles had been destroyed. America, the only state with atomic weapons at this time, refused to give up her weapons during this difficult period of the Cold War, unless the system of control and inspection was established first.

In 1952 the Disarmament Commission was set up to replace two existing bodies and it was given the job of negotiating disarmament by stages. In 1957 the Assembly gave the Commission the task of arranging the cessation of nuclear testing and setting up an effective system of international inspection to guard against the secret development of nuclear arms. The partial Test Ban Treaty was the first fruits of this work, but the United Nations itself was unable to get any further than this. This was recognised by the two superpowers, Russia and the United States—they undertook bilateral talks outside the aegis of the United Nations Organisation. The agreement known as SALT 1 (see page 407) and the still-to-be-ratified agreement known as SALT 2 shows that these two powers are able to reach agreements—but they have done so outside the framework of the United Nations. One important development came in 1967. By that time it was clear that both Russia and America were capable of landing men on the moon in a matter of years and it was therefore most urgent that an agreement should be made on international relations in space. The Treaty of Principle

Governing the Activities of States in the Exploration and Use of Outer Space was therefore signed in Moscow, Washington and London. It involved arrangements for mutual aid in space and for the banning of the use of space for military purposes.

In some sense the United Nations performance has been disappointing. The jealousies of the big powers and the existence of the veto prevented the development of an international peace-keeping force and all too often United Nations resolutions have been ignored. The clash of rival ideologies has obstructed the work of peace-keeping and the enforcement of international law. Germany, Vietnam, and Korea remain divided. All powers still spend vast sums which are desperately needed for economic development, on armaments. Even when there has been progress in international relations it has often been the result of bilateral negotiations between Russia and America rather than through the United Nations.

**Admission of Communist China to the United Nations.** On the brighter side, important changes occurred during 1971 and 1972 in the policy of the United States towards Communist China. In July, 1971, President Nixon announced his acceptance of an invitation to visit China in the following year. This had been preceded by the relaxation in April of American trade and travel restrictions against China, including the release of dollars for use by the Chinese. In June the 20-year-old embargo on direct trade with China was ended. To confirm and consolidate this new phase in the relations of China and the United States, President Nixon visited Peking in 1972 and was warmly received by the Chinese leadership.

Associated with these developments was a change of American policy on the question of the admission of Communist China to the United Nations. While now supporting the admission of China, the United States at the same time proposed that Nationalist China (Formosa) should also remain a member. This two-China policy, however, ran into unexpected difficulties in the United Nations, where in fact the General Assembly voted for the exclusion of Nationalist China. In 1972 the Communist Chinese delegates accordingly took their place in the United Nations and the delegates of Nationalist China retired under protest.

In another sphere, Korea, moves began to be made in 1972 between the governments of North and South Korea for investigations into the possibility of the future re-unification of the two states.

The year 1972 also witnessed the signing of important treaties between the United States and Russia for the limitation of nuclear inter-continental missiles (see page 454) and between West Germany and East Germany for important relaxation of restrictions on access to Berlin and on personal travel through the Berlin Wall between East and West Germany. There was also mutual renunciation of any attempt to alter the Oder-Neisse frontier by force.

The organisation has achieved most impressive successes in its economic and social work; it has existed as a forum for almost all the nations of the world (127 were members in 1970) and by this very existence has averted many potential crises. Certainly its record surpasses that of the League. Twenty years after the Versailles agreement the League perished in the holocaust of the Second World War: the United Nations still exists as a real force in international affairs a generation after its creation.

**The United Nations in the Period 1970–1978.** The year 1970 was the twenty-fifth anniversary of the foundation of the United Nations. Politically, it was a year of re-appraisal and of disappointment that the United Nations had not been able to make a greater contribution to world affairs and that diplomacy between the Great Powers was still the dominant world factor. However, the organisation made preparations for the second United Nations Development Decade, beginning on January 1, 1971. In 1970 itself a number of significant developments occurred. The United Nations was able for the first time to call together a World Youth Assembly with 758 delegates to discuss contemporary political and social problems. In the same year the Treaty on the non-proliferation of Nuclear Weapons came into force among the great nuclear powers. In the main this treaty, signed under the aegis of the United Nations, was of the utmost importance, for it effectively prevented the possibility of the general spread of atomic weapons beyond the Great Powers.

During this period the United Nations acted as a centre of world opinion on all outstanding questions, although its practical achievements were limited. The strong representation of the newly-created African states ensured, of course, that the South African policies of apartheid would be constantly challenged, and in 1970 ten African states attempted to secure the expulsion of South Africa from the United Nations. Although this effort failed, the United Nations Assembly registered a very strong condemnation of apartheid on several occasions during this period. Similar condemnations of the Smith régime in Rhodesia were made and sanctions were applied, with, unfortunately for the policy, a number of deliberate evasions—

especially by the old régime in Portugal and by South Africa. Nevertheless, all these expressions of majority opinion in the United Nations, whatever the attitudes of some of the Great Powers, proved extremely important in creating a climate of world opinion. On the other hand, the failure of United Nations efforts to get some constructive negotiations between Israel and the Arab states in the Middle East was a great disappointment. United Nations discussions on the Middle East in this period took on an increasing anti-Israeli character, especially on account of Israel's refusal to carry out the United Nations resolution of 1967 and withdraw from territories she had overrun. At the same time majority votes in the United Nations condemned Israel's attacks across the frontier of Lebanon against guerrilla centres in that country. This attitude was coupled with a condemnation of all use of violence. After the Israeli–Arab war of 1973 the United Nations Emergency Force supervised each stage of the military disengagement which had been agreed upon at the Geneva Conference, and a United Nations Force occupied the buffer zone established between the Israeli and Egyptian forces. In June, 1974, United Nations troops were similarly deployed between the Syrian and Israeli forces on the Golan heights. This was a service of great importance. In 1975 the anti-Israeli trend in the United Nations was strengthened by the adoption by the Assembly of a resolution which equated the idea of the Jewish homeland (Zionism) with racism and established a special committee to help the movement for the creation of a Palestinian state in the Middle East.

Under the aegis of the United Nations considerable progress was made in this period in dealing with other urgent matters. Among these was the serious increase in the hijacking of aircraft by supporters of the Palestinian Liberation movement. In 1970 a resolution of the General Assembly condemned all hijacking by a vote of 105 to 0, and this led on to the improvement of security arrangements by international airlines and their governments. Special committees were also set up to ensure the peaceful uses of the sea-bed and ocean floor and for the peaceful uses of outer space. In 1972, a convention was agreed by United Nations members prohibiting biological warfare. Resolutions condemning the use of napalm and incendiary bombs as inhuman were also passed by large majorities. However, a resolution condemning nuclear weapons and declaring the need to ban them permanently was supported by the Soviet Union but opposed by China. The abstentions from this resolution numbered 46 and included the United Kingdom, the United States and France. This highlighted the prevailing distrust among the Great Powers when it came to matters relating to the "balance of terror" which the possession of nuclear weapons had established between the Soviet Union and the western powers. The United Nations could only give its blessing to direct negotiations between the Soviet Union and the United States on the limitation of nuclear arms, and, while these negotiations were hopefully undertaken, no final agreements had been reached at the end of this period.

On the social and economic front the United Nations continued its enormous work of previous years. For example, in 1970 the United Nations Development Programme gave assistance to 93 developing countries amounting to 95.5 million dollars. Since 1959 the total aid thus given amounted to over 1,300 million dollars. The World Food Programme involved the distribution of very extensive relief to flood victims in Ceylon, Ecuador and Hungary and to victims of serious drought in parts of Africa and the Middle East. Especially valuable aid was given to the victims of the terrible Peruvian earthquake of 1970. This important humanitarian work continued throughout this period.

Thus the United Nations was struggling in this period to prevent warfare between states, but, although it did valuable policing work in Cyprus and the Middle East and relief work in Bangladesh, the principle of the settlement of disputes by peaceful means was still not generally accepted, as the Turkish invasion of Cyprus, the war between India and Pakistan and between Israel and the Arab states clearly showed. Far more important on the international scene were the relations between the two super-powers of the United States and the Soviet Union and the emergence of China on to the world's stage.

# BOOKS FOR FURTHER READING

The following are a number of the more important works on the period 1789–1968.

## A. General

Grant, A. J., and Temperley, H., *Europe in the Nineteenth and Twentieth Centuries.*

Lipson, E., *Europe in the Nineteenth and Twentieth Centuries.*

Thomson, D., *Europe since Napoleon.*

Ergang, R., *Europe since Waterloo.*

Morgan, M. C., *Freedom and Compulsion.*

Knowles, L. C. A., *Economic Development in the Nineteenth Century.*

Gathorne-Hardy, G. M., *A Short History of International Affairs.*

Taylor, A. J. P., *The Struggle for Mastery in Europe, 1848–1918.*

## B. The Principal Countries, mainly to 1914

FRANCE

Young, A., *Travels in France during the Years 1787–1789* (edited by C. Maxwell).

Thompson, J. M., *The French Revolution.*

Goodwin, A., *The French Revolution.*

Elton, G., *The Revolutionary Idea in France.*

Salvemini, G., *The French Revolution* (trans. by I. M. Rawson).

Cobban, A., *A History of Modern France*, Vol. I.

Woodward, E. L., *French Revolutions, 1789–1871.*

Butterfield, H., *Napoleon.*

Fisher, H. A. L., *Napoleon.*

Rose, J. Holland, *The Revolutionary and Napoleonic Era, 1789–1815.*

Thompson, J. M., *Louis Napoleon and the Second Empire.*

Bury, J. P. T., *France, 1815–1941.*

Dickinson, G. Lowes, *Revolution and Reaction in Modern France.*

Dubreton, F. Lucas, *Restoration and the July Monarchy.*

Plamenatz, J., *The Revolutionary Movement in France, 1815–1871.*

Clapham, J. H., *The Economic Development of France and Germany, 1815–1914.*

Cooper, A. Duff, *Talleyrand.*

Guedalla, P., *The Second Empire.*

Arnaud, R., *The Second Republic and Napoleon III.*

Simpson, F. A., *The Rise of Louis Napoleon.*
  *Louis Napoleon and the Recovery of France.*
Brogan, D., *The Development of Modern France.*
Thomson, D., *Democracy in France.*
Jellinek, *The Paris Commune, 1871.*
Bodley, J. E. C., *France.*
Daudet, Leon, *Clemenceau.*

### GERMANY

Pinson, K. S., *Modern Germany, its History and Civilization.*
Pascal, Roy, *The Growth of Modern Germany.*
Marriott, J. A. R., *The Evolution of Prussia.*
Gooch, G. P., *Studies in German History.*
Valentin, V., *1848—Chapter of German History.*
Eyck, E., *Bismarck.*
Taylor, A. J. P., *Bismarck.*
Ponteil, F., *1848.*
Robertson, Sir Charles Grant, *Bismarck.*
Ward, A. W., *Germany.*
Berlin, I., *Karl Marx.*

### ITALY

*The Works of G. M. Trevelyan.*
Berkely, G. F. H. and J., *Italy in the Making.*
King, Bolton, *Life of Mazzini.*
  *A History of Italian Unity.*
Marriott, J. A. R., *The Makers of Modern Italy.*
Trevelyan, J. P., *A Short History of the Italian People.*
Thayer, W. R., *The Life and Times of Cavour.*
Whyte, A. J., *Evolution of Modern Italy, 1715–1920.*
  *Political Life and Letters of Cavour.*
Croce, B., *History of Italy, 1871–1915.*

### AUSTRIA

Taylor, A. J. P., *The Hapsburg Monarchy.*
Steed, H. W., *The Hapsburg Monarchy.*
Pribram, A. F., *Austrian Foreign Policy, 1908–1918.*
Herman, A., *Metternich.*
Cecil, A., *Metternich.*
Nicolson, H., *The Congress of Vienna.*

### RUSSIA

Maynard, Sir J., *The Russian Peasant.*

Pares, Sir B., *A History of Russia*.
Vernadsky, G., *A History of Russia*.
Sumner, B. H., *Survey of Russian History*.


## C. The Years 1914-1939

Mansergh, N., *The Coming of the First World War*.
Fay, S. B., *The Origin of the World War*.
Dickinson, G. Lowes, *The International Anarchy*.
Churchill, W. S., *The World Crisis*.
Cruttwell, C. R. M. F., *A History of the Great War*.
Nicolson, H., *Peacemaking, 1919*.
Jackson, J. H., *Clemenceau and the Third Republic*.
Hart, H. B. L., *The Real War, 1914–1918*.
Carr, E. H., *International Relations between the World Wars*.
Moon, P. J., *Imperialism*.
Wiskemann, E., *Italy*.
Salvemini, G., *Under the Axe of Fascism*.
Bullock, Alan, *Hitler*.
Wheeler-Bennett, *The Nemesis of Power* (*German Army after 1918*).
Churchill, W. S., *The Gathering Storm*.
Hill, C., *Lenin and the Russian Revolution*.
Deutscher, I., *Stalin*.
    *The Prophet Armed* (*Trotsky*).
Seton-Watson, R. W., *Britain and the Dictators*.
Morley, F., *The Society of Nations*.
Chambers, F. P., *This Age of Conflict*.


## D.

THE EASTERN QUESTION

Seton-Watson, R. W., *The Rise of Nationality in the Balkans*.
Marriott, J. A. R., *The Eastern Question*.
Hudson, G. F., *The Far East in World Politics*.
Temperley, H., *England and the Near East*.
Mowat, R. B., *History of European Diplomacy, 1815–1914*.

OTHERS

Woodward, E. L., *Three Studies in European Conservatism* (*Metternich, Guizot, the Papacy*).
Taylor, F. S., *The Century of Science, 1840–1940*.

## E. The Years 1939–1978

Lord Montgomery of Alamein, *A History of Warfare.*

Churchill, W. S., *The Second World War.*

Young, Peter, *World War, 1939–1945.*

Macintyre, D., *The Battle of the Pacific.*

Behr, E., *The Algerian Problem.*

Boyd, A., *The United Nations: Piety, Myth and Truth.*

Buchan, A., *China and the Peace of Asia.*

Hoskyns, C., *The Congo since Independence.*

Luard, E., *The Cold War: A Reappraisal.*

Rees, D., *Korea—the Limited War.*

Seton-Watson, H., *The East European Revolution.*

Werth, A., *De Gaulle.*

Beloff, M., *The United States and the Unity of Europe.*

Mowatt, R. C., *Ruin and Resurgence, 1939–1965.*

Taylor, A. J. P., *From Sarajevo to Potsdam.*

Postan, M. M., *An Economic History of Europe, 1945–1964.*

Knapp, W., *A History of War and Peace, 1913–1965.*

# QUESTIONS

## CHAPTER 1. THE FRENCH REVOLUTION, 1789

(1) What were the burdens of taxation on the peasantry before the Revolution?

(2) Why was there such a large "bourgeois" element in the leadership of the Revolution?

(3) Describe the state of the Nobility in France before the Revolution.

(4) Why was the Church the object of attack and criticism during the eighteenth century?

(5) Describe the system of administration in France before 1789. What were its weaknesses?

(6) What foreign influences affected the development of educated opinion in France before 1789?

(7) What were the similarities and differences in the views of Voltaire, Montesquieu and Rousseau?

(8) Why was it that the attempts to reform the financial system of France before 1789 failed?

(9) Summarise the reasons for the calling of the States General in 1789.


## CHAPTER 2. EVENTS OF THE REVOLUTION

(1) What were the main demands of the "cahiers"?

(2) What was the importance of the action of the Third Estate in declaring itself the National Assembly, June 12, 1789?

(3) What was the importance of the capture of the Bastille, July 14, 1789, and what were its immediate results?

(4) Outline the work of the Constituent Assembly from July 14, 1789, to the time of its dissolution in September, 1791.

(5) Give an account of the part played by Louis XVI in the events between the calling of the States General in 1789 to the end of the Constituent Assembly in September, 1791.

(6) What were the main parties of the Legislative Assembly?

(7) What circumstances led to the outbreak of war between France and Austria in April, 1792?

(8) How did Prussia and Britain become involved in war with France?

(9) Make a table of important developments between the opening of the Legislative Assembly in September, 1791, and the opening of the Convention in September, 1792.

(10) What were the reasons for conflict between (a) the Jacobins and Girondists, (b) Robespierre and the Hébertists, (c) Danton and Robespierre?

(11) What were the causes of the downfall of Robespierre?

(12) Summarise the part played by the Commune and the Committee of Public Safety in the Revolution.

(13) How do you account for the ultimate success of the French on land against Austria, Prussia and Britain?

(14) Make a table showing in what ways the France of 1795 differed from the France of 1788.

## CHAPTER 3. THE REVOLUTIONARY AND NAPOLEONIC WARS

(1) What was the Constitution of the Directory?

(2) What was the importance of the First Italian campaign of Bonaparte?

(3) What circumstances enabled Bonaparte to become First Consul?

(4) What reorganisation of France was undertaken by Bonaparte as First Consul?

(5) How do you account for the failure of Bonaparte to defeat Great Britain?

(6) Why is the year 1807 often regarded as the peak of Napoleon's achievements and power?

(7) For what reasons did Britain open the Peninsular Campaign?

(8) Why did Napoleon experience increased *nationalist* resistance in Europe between 1808 and 1812?

(9) For what reasons did Alexander I break away from the Treaty of Tilsit with Napoleon?

(10) What was the importance of Napoleon's Moscow Campaign?

(11) Why was Napoleon able to rally the French to his support once again after his escape from Elba?

(12) Summarise the reasons for the downfall of Napoleon.

## CHAPTER 4. THE CONGRESSES, 1815–1824

(1) To what extent was the settlement of the Congress of Vienna dictated by the idea of defence against future French aggression?

(2) What disputes occurred between the Allies over Poland and Saxony and how was agreement finally brought about?

(3) To what extent was the principle of Nationality ignored by the Congress?

(4) How did the principle of the Balance of Power enter into the settlement?

(5) In what parts of the settlement was the principle of Legitimacy most in evidence?

(6) Examine the work of each of the Congresses from 1818 to 1822 and show (a) their positive achievements, (b) the reasons for diplomatic conflict between the Great Powers.

(7) Why did the Congress System come to an end?

(8) Would it be correct to say that the Congress System failed?

CHAPTER 5. FRANCE, 1815–1848

(1) Give the main details of the Charter of 1814.

(2) Who were the Ultra-Royalists and what were their aims?

(3) Describe the activities of the Ultra-Royalists in the years 1815–1816?

(4) Why were Louis XVIII and Richelieu able to restrain the Ultra-Royalists in the years 1816–1819?

(5) Why were the Ultra-Royalists able to gain increasing influence in the years 1819–1824?

(6) Explain the importance of Villèle and Chateaubriand in the years 1821–1827.

(7) What policy was pursued by Charles X at home and abroad?

(8) What were the reasons for the revolution against Charles X in 1830?

(9) What were the difficulties facing Louis Philippe in the first five years of his reign?

(10) Despite the difficulties of the Orleanist Monarchy, Louis Philippe was able to reign for eighteen years. How is this to be explained?

(11) What part did (a) domestic affairs, (b) foreign policy, play in the decline of Louis Philippe's power?

(12) Was Louis Philippe altogether unsuccessful in his foreign policy?

CHAPTER 6. THE SECOND REPUBLIC AND THE SECOND EMPIRE, 1848–1870

(1) How did the Socialists attempt to increase their influence in the Second Republic? Why did they fail?

(2) What were the main reasons for the election of Louis Napoleon Bonaparte as President in December, 1848?

(3) How did Louis Napoleon Bonaparte strengthen his position in the years 1848–1852 and eventually succeed in establishing the Second Empire?

(4) Describe the system of government established by Napoleon III.

(5) Why was there little opposition to Napoleon III in France during the first ten years of the Empire?

(6) Why did more opposition develop in France in the years 1866–1870?

(7) Give an account of the foreign policy of Napoleon III and show how it affected his position in France.

(8) Why did war break out between France and Germany in 1870?

(9) What were the causes of France's defeat in 1870–1871?

## CHAPTER 7. AUSTRIA, 1815–1850

(1) What were the political principles of Metternich?

(2) Describe the government of the Austrian Empire before 1848 and explain how grievances and discontent arose.

(3) In what way was Kossuth's policy an advance upon Magyar nationalism?

(4) How did the March Laws of 1848 change the situation in Hungary?

(5) What were the causes of conflict between the Croats and Slovenes on the one hand and Hungary on the other?

(6) What were the reasons for the failure of the Hungarian Revolution of 1848–1849?

(7) What were the reasons for the failure of the revolutions of 1848 in those parts of the Empire other than Hungary?

## CHAPTER 8. GERMANY, 1815–1850

(1) Why did the German Confederation of 1815 satisfy neither the Nationalists nor the Liberals?

(2) Why was Metternich especially anxious to suppress freedom in the German universities?

(3) Why was Metternich able to gain the acceptance of the Carsbad Decrees by the German states?

(4) Explain the importance and activities of the student movements in Germany in these years.

(5) Why was there very little revolutionary activity in Prussia before 1848?

(6) Why did the revolution in Berlin fail?

(7) Why was it possible to call together the Frankfurt Parliament?

(8) Give the reasons for the failure of the Frankfurt Parliament.

(9) Write brief notes on (a) the Zollverein, (b) the Prussian Constitution of 1850, (c) Frederick William IV, (d) the Treaty of Olmütz.

CHAPTER 9. THE UNIFICATION OF GERMANY, 1850–1870

(1) What was the nature of the crisis which occurred in Prussia upon the accession to the throne of William I, 1861?

(2) What were the main political ideas of Bismarck?

(3) Why was Bismarck interested in the Schleswig-Holstein controversy?

(4) By what diplomatic stages did Bismarck prepare for war against Austria?

(5) How do you account for Prussian victory in the Seven Weeks' War?

(6) How do you account for Bismarck's leniency in the Treaty of Prague with Austria, 1866?

(7) What were the reasons for the defeat of France by Prussia in 1870? (Consider both the preliminary diplomacy of Bismarck and the military aspect.)

(8) Make out a table which summarises the main achievements of Bismarck in the period 1861–1871.

CHAPTER 10. THE UNIFICATION OF ITALY, 1815–1870

(1) What were the main reasons for the settlement of Italy made in 1815?

(2) How was the influence of Austria exerted in the affairs of Italy between 1815 and 1848?

(3) How did the Young Italy movement differ from that of the Carbonari?

(4) What was the importance of the accession to the Papacy of Pius IX in 1846?

(5) What were the reasons for the failure of the Italian risings of 1848–1849?

(6) Trace the careers of Mazzini and Garibaldi up to and including 1849.

(7) How do you account for the policy of Victor Emmanuel II towards the Catholic Church in Piedmont?

(8) How did Cavour (*a*) strengthen the internal position of Piedmont, (*b*) gain the alliance of Napoleon III?

(9) How do you account for Napoleon III's agreement with the Austrians at Villafranca, 1859?

(10) How far had the unification of Italy been advanced by 1861?

(11) What was Cavour's attitude to Garibaldi's expedition of 1860 and how do you account for it?

(12) Why are the following years important in the history of Italian Unification: 1849; 1852; 1854–1856; 1858; 1859; 1860; 1861; 1863; 1866; 1867 and 1870?

## CHAPTER 11. BISMARCK AND GERMANY, 1870–1890

(1) Describe the main points of the constitution of the German Empire, 1871.

(2) For what reasons did Bismarck oppose the Roman Catholic Church and the Social Democratic Party? How far was he successful in his aims?

(3) How did Bismarck's policy on the question of tariffs and colonies change and why?

(4) What were the general aims of Bismarck's foreign policy in these years?

(5) Describe Bismarck's policy towards Russia in these years and explain the difficulties that arose.

(6) Describe the *circumstances* that led to the formation of the alliances with which Bismarck was directly concerned.

(7) How do you account for Bismarck's success in keeping Russia and France apart during this period?

(8) Make a table which shows the advantages to Germany of each of the alliances formed by Bismarck in this period.

## CHAPTER 12. FRANCE, 1870–1914

(1) What were the causes of the Paris Commune?

(2) Why was it possible to establish a Republican form of government in France by 1875?

(3) Describe the policy of Jules Ferry.

(4) Why was General Boulanger able to gain so much support in France, and why did his movement fail?

(5) What were the *effects* on French politics of the Panama Scandal and the Dreyfus case?

(6) What were the main political and social developments in France during the years 1899–1914?

(7) What reasons can you give for the instability of French governments in the years 1870–1914?

CHAPTER 13. THE EASTERN QUESTION, 1815–1878

(1) What were the causes of the Greek War of Independence?

(2) How is the success of the Greeks to be accounted for?

(3) What was the importance of the Treaty of Unkiar-Skelessi, 1833?

(4) Examine the foreign policy of Lord Palmerston in relation to the Mehemet Ali affair, 1839–1841.

(5) What were the long-term and immediate causes of the Crimean War?

(6) Did the Crimean War serve any useful purpose to the Allies?

(7) What circumstances led up to the Congress of Berlin, 1878?

(8) How did the Treaty of Berlin modify the Treaty of San Stefano?

(9) How would you account for the Russian acceptance of the Congress of Berlin and of the final treaty?

(10) Was the integrity of the Turkish Empire worth maintaining during the nineteenth century?

CHAPTER 14. RUSSIA, to 1914

(1) Why can Peter the Great be regarded as one of the "Enlightened Despots" of the eighteenth century?

(2) Give an account of the "liberal phase" of the reign of Alexander I.

(3) Why did Alexander I abandon his "liberal" policies?

(4) Describe the policy and achievements of Nicholas I, 1825–1855.

(5) What were the terms and the results of Alexander II's Edict of Emancipation, 1861?

(6) Give an account of the reforms of Alexander II. How can his later "reactionary" policy be explained?

(7) How do you account for the growth of terrorism in Russia? Why did it fail in its objects?

(8) Compare the policies of Nicholas I and Alexander III.

(9) What were the reasons for the development of the Russian Social Democratic Party up to 1914?

(10) What was the importance of the career of Sergei Witte?

(11) What was the difference in policy between the Russian Social Democrats and the Social Revolutionary Party?

(12) What were the causes of the Russo-Japanese War, 1904–1905, and what were its effects on the internal affairs of Russia?

(13) Why did the efforts to introduce a liberal parliamentary system in Russia before 1914 fail?

(14) Describe the activities of the Russian Social Democratic Party in the years 1898–1914.

(15) Write notes on (a) Nihilism, (b) the Bolsheviks and Mensheviks, (c) Red Sunday, (d) the Treaty of Portsmouth, (e) the Second Duma.

(16) What was the importance of the career of Stolypin?

## CHAPTER 15. THE BACKGROUND TO THE FIRST WORLD WAR, 1914–1918

(1) What was the importance of Africa to the Great Powers after 1870?

(2) What important developments affecting the relationships of the European Powers occurred in the Far East after 1870?

(3) State the reasons for the following:

(a) The Dual Alliance of France and Russia, 1893

(b) The Anglo-French Entente, 1904

(c) The Anglo-Japanese Treaty, 1902

(d) The Triple Entente, 1907.

(4) Explain the influence of events in Africa on the relationship of the Great Powers between 1880 and 1914.

(5) Why did the World War of 1914–1918 begin in the Balkan Peninsula?

(6) What attempts were made to prevent war and improve international relations before 1914?

(7) Make a list of the possible causes of the First World War.

## CHAPTER 16. THE GREAT WAR, 1914–1918, AND THE POST-WAR SETTLEMENT

(1) What was the Schlieffen Plan?

(2) What was the importance of British naval power in the first year of the war?

(3) Why was the allied Dardanelles Campaign embarked upon, and what were the results of its failure?

(4) What was the importance of the Siege of Verdun and the Battle of the Somme, 1916?

(5) Why was the year 1917 one of great difficulties for the Allies?

(6) What were the main reasons for the entry of the United States into the war?

(7) What were the main causes of the German defeat in the Great War?

(8) What were the effects of the war upon Europe?

(9) Make a table showing to what extent the Fourteen Points of President Wilson were applied in the Peace Treaties.

## CHAPTER 17. RUSSIA, 1914–1939

(1) What were the causes of the first Russian Revolution of February, 1917?

(2) What were the main causes of the October Revolution, 1917? Why was the term "proletarian revolution" applied to it?

(3) What were the external and internal problems facing the Bolsheviks in the years 1917–1924?

(4) What reasons could you give for the maintenance of Bolshevik power in Russia in the years 1917–1924?

(5) What were the effects on the internal condition of Russia of the death of Lenin, 1924?

(6) What were the differences of political outlook between Stalin and Trotsky?

(7) What were the aims and achievements of the Five Year Plans?

(8) What possible explanations can be given of Stalin's policy of the "purge" in Russia before 1939?

## CHAPTER 18. ITALY AND GERMANY, 1918–1939

(1) What were the economic and political effects of the Great War on Italy?

(2) How do you account for the rise of fascism in Italy?

(3) How was the Italian Corporate State organised?

(4) What important political disturbances occurred in Germany in 1919?

(5) Describe the constitution of the Weimar Republic. How did it differ from the Imperial Constitution of 1871?

(6) Explain the rise of the Nazi Party in Germany, 1921–1933.

(7) What is the importance of Mustapha Kemal in the history of modern Turkey?

CHAPTER 19. INTERNATIONAL AFFAIRS, 1919–1939

(1) What difficulties arose over the Reparations question in the years 1919–1925?

(2) What were some of the difficulties facing the League of Nations in the years 1919–1929 and to what extent did it succeed in promoting the cause of peace?

(3) In what directions did aggression succeed in the years 1929–1939?

(4) What were the economic and political results of the Economic Depression of 1929–1931?

(5) How would you explain the success of (a) Japan against China, (b) Mussolini against Abyssinia, (c) General Franco in Spain, (d) Hitler against Austria and Czechoslovakia?

CHAPTER 20. THE SECOND WORLD WAR, 1939–1945

(1) What factors led to the Nazi successes of 1939–1941?

(2) What were the basic reasons for Hitler's attack on Russia?

(3) Why did Hitler indefinitely postpone Operation Sealion?

(4) What changes occurred in the Allies' favour in 1942?

(5) Examine the part played by the United States in the Pacific area.

(6) Why was "unconditional surrender" of Germany and Japan insisted upon by the Allies?

(7) What were the main reasons for the victory of the Allies?

CHAPTER 21. EUROPE AND THE COLD WAR, 1945–1953

(1) What were the main decisions of the wartime allied conferences?

(2) What was meant by the "Stalinist line"? Give examples of its operation in the east European states.

(3) What were the main stages in the development of the Cold War?

(4) Explain the origins of NATO.

(5) Why did the Berlin Blockade occur?

CHAPTER 22. NATIONALISM, COMMUNISM AND THE DECLINE OF THE ASIAN EMPIRES

(1) What were the origins of the Arab–Israeli conflict and what were its results in this period? (See also Ch. 26 on UN.)

(2) How would you account for the French defeat in Indochina?

(3) What was the importance of the rise of Chinese communism?

(4) What were the origins of the Korean war and what were the results? (See also Ch. 26 on UN.)

CHAPTER 23. UNITY AND CONFLICT IN EUROPE, 1953–1978

(1) What changes occurred in the east European states in 1953–1956?

(2) What were the origins and results of the Hungarian rising of 1956?

(3) Write notes on (a) the Common Market, (b) EFTA.

(4) What were the main difficulties facing NATO in the period up to 1968?

(5) What was the nature of the Berlin problem in this period and what efforts were made to solve it?

(6) Why did the reunification of Germany prove impossible in this period?

(7) Give a brief account of (a) the Summit Conference of 1960, (b) the Cuba crisis, (c) the 1963 Test-ban Treaty.

(8) Describe the stages leading to the Czechoslovak crisis of 1968 and attempt to assess the motives of the Soviet Union.

CHAPTER 24. EUROPE AND THE THIRD WORLD, 1953–1978

(1) What were the main causes of the Suez affair, 1956? What was the significance of the whole episode?

(2) Write notes on (a) the Baghdad Pact, (b) SEATO.

(3) What were the main stages in the development of the Vietnam problem after 1953?

CHAPTER 25. FRANCE, 1940–1978

(1) What explanations can be given for the fall of France in 1940?

(2) What were the nature and policies of the Vichy regime?

(3) What were the main political problems facing France in the period 1945 to 1958?

(4) What were the main reasons for General de Gaulle's return to political power in 1958?

(5) Explain the nature of the Algerian problem both before and after the end of the Fourth Republic.

(6) Attempt some assessment of both the external and internal policies of General de Gaulle up to 1968.

(7) What were the general political trends in France during the period 1970–1976?

## CHAPTER 26. THE UNITED NATIONS, 1945–1978

(1) Explain the functions of the Security Council and its composition.

(2) For what reasons was the veto procedure introduced?

(3) Through what agencies is the economic and social work of the United Nations carried out?

(4) What was the importance of the "Uniting for Peace" resolution of 1950?

(5) Show the part played by the United Nations in the following (*a*) the Greek civil war, (*b*) Korea, (*c*) Palestine, (*d*) Suez, 1956, (*e*) the Congo.

(6) Why had atomic and conventional disarmament not been brought about by 1970?

(7) Explain the importance of the work of the Trusteeship Council.

(8) Mention some of the world problems with which the United Nations was concerned in the years 1970–1976.

# INDEX

*Major events are indexed in their own right and the reader should consult the index in the ordinary way for them. If the subject is not found, he should refer to the entry for the country affected and search there. The headings used for these multiple entries are those set out in the table of contents on pp v and vi. In many cases countries have had two names, such as Prussia and Germany or South West Africa and Namibia and both may need to be looked at.*

*Wherever possible dates have been included to assist the reader, who will find the abbreviations WWI and WWII used for the 1914 and 1939 wars respectively. The index is compiled on the letter-by-letter system.*